CLOSETED WRITING AND LESBIAN AND GAY LITERATURE

to Gary

- with apologies
- that this book
- isn't written
- in bullet points

Closeted Writing and Lesbian and Gay Literature
Classical, Early Modern, Eighteenth-Century

DAVID M. ROBINSON
The University of Arizona, USA

ASHGATE

© David M. Robinson 2006

All rights reserved. No part of this publication may be reproduced, stored in a retrieval system or transmitted in any form or by any means, electronic, mechanical, photocopying, recording or otherwise without the prior permission of the publisher.

David M. Robinson has asserted his moral right under the Copyright, Designs and Patents Act, 1988, to be identified as the author of this work.

Published by
Ashgate Publishing Limited
Gower House
Croft Road
Aldershot
Hampshire GU11 3HR
England

Ashgate Publishing Company
Suite 420
101 Cherry Street
Burlington, VT 05401-4405
USA

Ashgate website: http://www.ashgate.com

British Library Cataloguing in Publication Data
Robinson, David M., 1965 Jan. 22-
Closeted writing and lesbian and gay literature : classical, early modern, eighteenth-century
  1.Homosexuality in literature 2.Homosexuality and literature 3.Gays' writings – History and criticism 4.European literature – History and criticism
  I.Title
  809.9'3353

Library of Congress Cataloging-in-Publication Data
Robinson, David M., 1965 Jan. 22-
  Closeted writing and lesbian and gay literature : classical, early modern, eighteenth-century / by David M. Robinson.
    p. cm.
  Includes bibliographical references and index.
  ISBN 0-7546-5550-4 (alk. paper)
  1. Homosexuality in literature. 2. Homosexuality and literature. 3. Gays' writings—History and criticism. 4. European literature—History and criticism. I. Title.

PN56.H57R63 2006
809'.93353--dc22

2005032865

ISBN-10: 0-7546-5550-4
978-0-7546-5550-3

Printed and bound in Great Britain by Antony Rowe Ltd, Chippenham, Wiltshire.

Contents

Preface   *vii*
Acknowledgements   *xv*
Note: On Terminology   *xvii*

Part One. Intentionality: Closeted Homosexual Writing   1

1 Closeted Writing before "The Closet"   3

2 "Philips-Lover" and the Abominable Madame de Murat   19

3 The Closeting of Closeting:
Cleland, Smollett, Sodomy, and the Critics   37

Part Two. Intentionality: Closeted Homophobic Writing   85

4 Pornographic Homophobia:
L'Academie des dames and the Deconstructing Lesbian   87

5 "For How Can They Be Guilty?":
The Sophisticated Homophobia of Manley's *New Atalantis*   117

Part Three. Continuity   161

6 Metamorphosis and Homosexuality I:
Ovid's "Iphis and Ianthe" and Related Tales   163

7 Metamorphosis and Homosexuality II:
Iphis, Ianthe, and Others on the Early Modern Stage   199

Postscript   251

Bibliography   *259*
Index   *285*

Preface

In this book, I explore literary depictions of same-sex lust and love. In addition to providing what I hope are entertaining and illuminating interpretations of a wide variety of texts—poetry, drama, and both fictional and nonfictional prose, some well known and some little known, written in English, French, and Latin, and published in Britain and France, between the late sixteenth and mid-eighteenth centuries (as well as one profoundly influential classical work, Ovid's *Metamorphoses*)—the book is intended to rehabilitate several concepts and methodologies typically held in disrepute by historians of sexuality over the past two decades. Recent demonstrations of greater theoretical openness by leaders in the field make this a particularly good time to revisit both the historical knowledge and historiographic practices that have held sway since LGBT Studies and queer theory came into their own in the late 1980s and early 1990s.

The most old-fashioned of the concepts I would like to resurrect is closeted writing. Constructionist historians and critics—or, more precisely, *differentist* historians and critics, who treat historical difference as virtually absolute—have charted the rise to dominance in the nineteenth and twentieth centuries of conceptions of sex, gender, and sexuality often taken for granted in the West today. Such conceptions include, among others, the idea of fixed, lifelong sexual orientation (homo, hetero, or sometimes bi); the notion that sexual orientation springs from and reveals fundamental aspects of the self; the formation of identity around sexual orientation; and the idea of closeting one's sexual orientation. While inspired particularly by the first volume of Michel Foucault's *History of Sexuality* (1976/1978), differentist scholars have largely shed the overemphasis, in that early stage of Foucault's project, on medical and juridical discourses in the development of modern sexuality. Instead, they increasingly chart the wide range of people, groups, events, practices, discourses, ideas, and ideologies that have led to current understandings and experiences of things gendered and sexual. Unfortunately, the success of Foucault's work, at least as most commonly understood by historians of sexuality, has led to widespread dismissal of pre- or early modern closeted same-sex writing, in theory and practice. To ask whether a given piece of writing from the less-than-recent past might be accurately or meaningfully described as closeted has come to be regarded as naively anachronistic, as well as uninteresting.[1]

---

[1] What I term 'differentist,' Fradenburg and Freccero call 'alteritist' (xv), crediting Sara

Of course, any concept of closeted writing depends on the notion of authorial intention—on reading for authorial intention in order to determine textual meaning. And historiographic dismissal of pre- and early modern textual closeting is bolstered by the disfavor into which reading for authorial intention has long since fallen among literary critics, ever since Wimsatt and Beardsley debunked the "intentional fallacy," Barthes announced "the death of the author," and Derrida deconstructed language, writing, meaning, and virtually everything else.

In opposition to these entrenched perspectives in both historical and literary study of pre- and early modern sex, gender, and sexuality, I argue in part one of this book for the value of speculation—of "wild surmise," as James Creech (echoing Keats) put it in his brilliant, neglected book *Closet Writing/Gay Reading* (50–51)—about authors' textual and even sexual desires and intentions, in full recognition that they can rarely be proven conclusively, and, if proven, could never exhaust textual meaning. I begin by arguing, in chapters one through three, that "the closet" or "closeting"—in the sense of deliberate concealment of same-sex erotic sympathies, desires, and activities from some observers, and coded communication of them to others—is anything but a recent invention. I thus attempt to revive the supposedly retrograde practice of seeking out closeted homosexual writing. To do so, I investigate primarily three texts—a pseudonymously authored commendatory verse prefacing Katherine Philips's *Poems* (1667); a scandal novel by Henriette de Castelnau, comtesse de Murat, *Les Memoires De Madame La Comtesse De M**** (1697); and John Cleland's pornographic *Memoirs of a Woman of Pleasure*, popularly known as *Fanny Hill* (1748–49)—each of which is enriched when read as closeted writing.[2]

Like differentist scholars, I rely upon historical contextualization in my interpretation of these several-hundred-year-old works. But I complement that approach, as well as my old-fashioned goal of looking for closeted writing, with two old-fashioned methodologies: close reading and biographical criticism. Depending on one's perspective, my project is either modest or ambitious. Whereas much of the work on pre- and early modern sex, gender, and sexuality written in the past fifteen to twenty years has been devoted, at least in part, to ruling out certain interpretations and methodologies as anachronistic, my explorations are offered in support of greater historiographic and critical pluralism. Rather than assert, a priori, what will or will not, can or cannot be found in a

---

Suleri with the coinage (*The Rhetoric of English India* [1992] 12). Fradenburg and Freccero's vital essay presaged, and surely contributed to, the recent evolution in constructionist theory (e.g., Halperin [2002b] makes several of the key points—regarding identification, alterity, and theoretical and methodological variety—they advocated).

[2] See also Robinson (2004), in which I argue for reading Margaret Cavendish's utopian science-fiction romance, *The Blazing World* (1666), as closeted lesbian writing, and which, but for the economics of academic publishing today, I would have included in Part I of this book.

particular pre- or early modern text, my primary aim is to demonstrate that some of the concepts, arrangements, and strategies we have been taught to view as recently invented can actually be found in earlier periods. And crucial to such a demonstration is the sort of "unhurried, undefensive, theoretically galvanized practice of close reading" (23) that Eve Sedgwick (1997) advocated almost a decade ago, in a trenchant and moving call for less prescriptive, less dogmatic queer criticism. Of Sedgwick's three modifiers—'unhurried,' 'undefensive,' 'theoretically galvanized'—the one I attempt most to emulate, within the space permitted, is the first. Through contextualization both historical and biographical, I divulge homosexual content others have missed, or reveal as homophobic what others have thought homophilic. Above all, by taking enough time to trace, and where possible to untangle, some of these texts' complexities, I hope to show how much richer they are, and often how much more familiar, than our current theories would lead us to believe.[3]

As for, specifically, pursuing closeted writing, focusing on authorial intention, and using biographical criticism, my aim is to demonstrate that something crucial is lost to LGBT Studies and queer theory when, conditioned to anthropomorphize texts, discourses, and ideologies, we ignore that they were written, spoken, and thought by *people*, some of whom loved and lusted after members of their own sex, under conditions that prevented them from communicating their thoughts and feelings openly.

While part one is concerned with closeted *homosexual* or *homoerotic* writing, part two continues my argument for the pursuit of authorial intention from a different direction, focusing on what might be called closeted *homophobic* texts. Exploring one example each of pornography and satiric scandal-writing (Nicolas Chorier and Jean Nicolas's *L'Academie des dames* [1680], Delarivier Manley's *New Atalantis* [1709]), in chapters four and five I spotlight rhetorical and representational strategies conventionally employed by writers hostile to homosexuality who nonetheless wish to appear sophisticated—discursive conventions too often misunderstood, or missed entirely, by critics and historians reluctant to speculate about authorial intention. In this case, intentionalist reading highlights important strands in the history of homophobia.

In part three, I let authorial intention take a back seat, while emphasizing an argument earlier chapters imply but don't, until chapter five, explicitly make: that the history of sexuality *must* pay serious attention to continuities and similarities between the treatment of same-sex lust and love in various times and places. Over the past twenty or so years, a consensus has developed within LGBT Studies and

---

[3] For critics alert to the contradiction between close reading and biographical criticism: I use the former phrase in a general rather than New Critical sense, to mean a sustained, attentive, detailed engagement with a particular text, the goal of which is first and foremost to understand the text itself, and only secondarily to make a larger theoretical or historical argument (see Lentricchia and DuBois).

queer theory that past sexual systems in the West were predominantly, even fundamentally, different from present ones, a perspective epitomized in routine references to contemporary categories and phenomena as recent "inventions"— often by scholars whose knowledge of the periods preceding their own seems somewhat dubious (cf. Aers, Salih). Without denying that conceptions and experiences of love, lust, gender, and sex vary enormously across time and place, in chapters six and seven I offer a detailed exploration of Ovid's "Iphis and Ianthe" and related tales from the *Metamorphoses*, and their reinterpretation on the early modern stage. I intend these two chapters, and my book as a whole, as an addition to the small but growing body of work aimed at turning the field's most influential theory back into hypothesis. For while differentist scholars have succeeded quite stunningly in highlighting the radical strangeness of past rhetorics, representations, conceptions, and systems of sex, gender, and sexuality, they've done so too often by obscuring the equally radical familiarity of the past, the continuities and similarities between one time, one place, and another.[4]

Now, at this promising moment in the field's history, when antagonism and conformity may be giving way to greater tolerance for differing opinions and approaches, it is important to do more than pay lip service to what might be called 'continuist' approaches to the history of sexuality. Rather than merely acknowledge transhistorical and transcultural continuities and similarities, I'd like to see our field enthusiastically explore them, as part of our shared attempt to understand the past, ourselves, and the multiple, complex relationships between the two.[5]

But let me state unequivocally that I do *not* long for an earlier era of scholarship untroubled by the theories of Derrida, Foucault, Butler, et al. As I wrote above, I'm fully aware that the meanings of every text (certainly every literary text) inevitably exceed, and often thwart, the intentions of the author (although, as Hammond [2002] convincingly demonstrates, and as I sometimes argue in the following chapters, textual ambiguity may often be an *intentional* strategy for conveying homoerotic meaning to receptive readers). Moreover, authorial intentions are always, to a greater or lesser degree, unknowable to readers, especially ones far removed from the author's time and place. This is as much an historical as literary critical dilemma. Historical knowledge—like all knowledge, to some degree—is always partial (in both senses of the word). Accordingly, my interpretations center repeatedly on gaps and silences, disappearances and absences, the evidence of things unsaid and unknown—the latter term used as Sedgwick (1988) employs it, to signify not just "simple" ignorance, but a range of constructed ignorances—conscious, unconscious, and

---

[4] Ironically, while asserting difference and discontinuity between modern sexuality and everything preceding it, differentists have too often obscured differences and discontinuities *within* given periods (on which, see Gaca, 4–6; Sedgwick [1990] 44–48]).

[5] For the term 'continuist,' I'm indebted, again, to Fradenburg and Freccero (xvii).

semi-conscious—achieved through suppression and repression; avoidance, denial, disavowal; open secrets; taboos; censorship and self-censorship; and more. My work, in other words, would be impossible without the benefit of the last half-century of critical theory. I don't pretend otherwise.

And yet I'd like to question some of the absences in our own texts, some of the gaps in our own historical accounts, some of the contradictions in our own critical and historiographic practice and theory. I want to shake up our sense of what we know about the history of sexuality, by revealing some of what we don't know, have forgotten, ignore, or unknow.

* * * * * *

Some final points.

1. In my book's title, I've had to choose concision over precision: the phrase "lesbian and gay literature" should ideally be "the literature of male and female homosexuality." Aside from the anachronism of using 'lesbian' and 'gay' (see "Note: On Terminology" below), I realize that many of the texts I discuss, especially those that treat homosexuality unsympathetically, would not normally be considered examples of lesbian or gay literature. I might, of course, have referred simply to "the literature of homosexuality," but at the risk of obscuring one of the fundamental aims of the book.

2. Namely: to consider closely both female and male homosexuality, and especially their interrelation in particular texts, as a sign of their interrelation in the cultural imagination of particular times and places. While not denying their very real historical differences, I feel that in this respect, as in others, differentist scholars have overstated the contrast between past and present. While by no means inevitable, an association between male and female homoeroticism—indeed the existence of an umbrella category at least partially analogous to the modern concept 'homosexuality'—is found in much pre- and early modern writing, if it hasn't been dismissed in advance as anachronistic. In much of what follows, I point out this frequent male-female linkage. Moreover, I investigate the motivations and effects of particular convergences and divergences of male and female homoeroticism, and of homo- and lesbophobia.

3. Just as I recognize legitimate political reasons for sometimes treating male and female homosexuality separately (and for sometimes treating them together), I also recognize the legitimate political aims motivating much of the best differentist, anti-identitarian, and otherwise queer work with which I often disagree. On the one hand, I value academic intellectuals' commitment to rigorous questioning of popular, commonsense understandings of the world, even when such understandings seem reassuring, and especially when they seem "natural." On the other hand, I take issue with the routine ascription, in LGBT and queer academic circles, of political radicalism to certain theoretical or methodological positions (constructionist, universalizing, deconstructive, anti-identitarian,

performative, queer) and political conservativism to others ("essentialist," minoritizing, humanist, identitarian, gay or lesbian). I especially object to many academic theorists' treatment of lesbian and gay agency, particularly lesbian and gay activism, past and present. One extremely influential example will have to suffice: Foucault's account (1976/1978) of the nineteenth-century invention of "the homosexual" by sexologists and other doctors and scientists erased the role of Karl Heinrich Ulrichs and other homosexual activists in formulating the notion of a female soul in a male body (and vice versa), in suggesting that sexologists study the phenomenon, and in resisting the pathologizing pseudo-science sexologists produced. Notwithstanding explicitly anti-homophobic intentions, scholarship and politics premised on this historically inaccurate component of Foucault's work— scholarship and politics that too often treat labels such as 'homosexual' and 'gay' primarily as traps set by hegemonic power—replicate the erasure of lesbian and gay lives that LGBT Studies and queer theory are dedicated to contesting.[6]

4. I have deliberately chosen *not* to offer an overarching theory of early modern and eighteenth-century homosexuality, nor to rely upon other scholars' accounts of long-term diachronic change. Obviously, many things change over time, among them conceptions of sex, gender, and sexuality. But with all due respect to my colleagues' valuable work, contemporary LGBT theory, history, and criticism often seem to proceed from an *assumption* of diachronic change, and to overgeneralize, extensively and fundamentally, about the past, the present, or both. It's my firm belief we have a great many more primary texts to discover, and a great deal more complexity and nuance to appreciate in the texts we think we know, before our grand narratives of diachronic development can be sufficiently grounded.[7]

---

[6] Foucault's historical inaccuracy about the invention of the notion 'homosexuality' continues to affect LGBT and queer scholarship (e.g., Andreadis, 183, n.45). For much more reliable, and interesting, accounts of the late nineteenth- and early twentieth-century popularization of medical, scientific, and *political* notions of homosexuality and lesbianism, see Kennedy's biography of Ulrichs (1988); Stanley on Edward Carpenter's letters from appreciative lesbians, including the writer Edith Ellis, wife of sexologist Havelock Ellis; and Eribon's indispensable essay (2001) placing Foucault's work on sexuality in the context of late nineteenth- and early twentieth-century literary and philosophical discourse on male homosexuality, especially his exploration of the contrast between Foucault's brief, previously untranslated remarks on male homosexual history in *Histoire de la folie* (1961) and the famous claims in the first volume of *The History of Sexuality*. See also Halperin's extremely thoughtful defense (1995) of Foucault's work for gay scholarship and politics, particularly valuable for his recognition of actual and potential anti-gay effects of queer politics.

[7] Cf. Hammond (2002), who repeatedly foregrounds an overarching model of diachronic change in English textual representations of male homoeroticism over the course of the seventeenth century, yet implicitly (at numerous points) and explicitly (in the book's conclusion) reveals his heart to be elsewhere, in uncommonly sensitive close reading of

Preface

5. Given that belief, I've chosen to examine, both at length and in detail, a larger number of primary texts than is customary (even after omitting Cavendish's *Blazing World*). It is my contention that, for many of my primary texts, scholars have misconstrued their meanings—and, yes, their authors' *intentions*—due to hurried reading or overly selective excerpting. In addition, as the notion of closeted writing before the modern period has been so thoroughly discredited, I've tried to offer more examples (space permitting) than can easily be dismissed as "mere" exceptions, and to examine writings from a variety of genres.[8]

6. In an effort to make this book maximally accessible to scholars working in any subfield of LGBT Studies, those exploring other intellectual terrain, and even (dare I hope?) interested nonscholars, I do my best not to assume prior knowledge of the texts and issues discussed. Part of that effort means, when necessary, quoting hefty excerpts from the material under consideration. I must therefore beg the indulgence of specialists for whom some of my texts are familiar.

7. I have kept in-text citations to the minimum necessary information: page number alone, if possible; preceded by author's last name, if not clear from context, and year of publication, if the bibliography includes multiple works by the author.

8. Because of length restrictions, I've had to relegate the original-language versions of many translated quotations to an online appendix (see www.davidmrobinson.net). All translations are mine unless otherwise noted. Except for introducing the i/j and u/v distinction where lacking, converting long ʃ to *s,* and using circumflexes for macrons in Greek and Arabic, I retain texts' original spelling.

9. Regarding my choice of texts: while I consider them all *significant*, I do not claim they form a homosexual canon. For instance, my focus on the *Metamorphoses* in part three is not meant to imply that other classical material reworked by early moderns mightn't yield equally compelling evidence of long-term continuity in the history of homosexuality. On the contrary, by demonstrating the applicability of the concepts and approaches I aim to rehabilitate to texts drawn from a variety of genres, written in a variety of modes, with varying degrees of canonicity or obscurity, I hope to suggest that such methods ought to be integrated into the study of other work as well, and into the history of sexuality in general.

10. I ought perhaps to explain my combined English-French focus. For those who study English rather than Comparative Literature, it's worth remembering that the English Channel is and was anything but an impermeable barrier, particularly during the seventeenth and eighteenth centuries. People crossing the narrow strip of water carried texts and ideas back and forth so frequently that it is useful, and largely

---

"micro-discourses" generated by and around particular authors and texts—close reading, moreover, that skillfully integrates, into the process of historical contextualization, both intentionalist and biographical research and interpretation (although Hammond never names the former as such, and acknowledges the latter only to disclaim it [186]).

[8] On the crucial importance of genre, see Salih; on the tendency to generalize from a single genre, see Elfenbein (1).

accurate, despite the language difference, to consider the two countries a single cultural field in many respects, at least when making claims about the conceivability or inconceivability of particular ideas in either place. In particular, given the wide circulation in England of French texts (particularly scandalous, libertine, and pornographic ones) both in the original French and in English translation, French discussion of male and female homosexuality is not only valid but crucial for understanding the nature and extent of early modern and eighteenth-century British thinking on the subject. Indeed, had I the time and expertise, I would follow the lead of Borris (2004), Castle (2003), Gerard and Hekma, Turner (2003), and a few others in addressing notions of same-sex love in early modern Europe as a whole.

11. What we would call closeting has been expressed by means of a variety of metaphors—such as veiling, cloaking, masking—among which a future study might profitably distinguish, tracing patterns and implications in their uses. There have also been various closeting strategies, including, among others:

> *Dropping Hairpins*: in which, ostensibly, homosexuality isn't discussed, but listeners who pick up on the speaker's discreetly coded references perceive homo-specific meaning.
> *Platonizing*: in which the speaker repeatedly stresses the innocence or spirituality of the bonds in question, implicitly defending against a carnal interpretation.
> *Posing as the Enemy*: in which the speaker explicitly raises the issue of homosexuality, but to condemn it, all the while pointing alert, homo-sympathetic readers toward a homo-positive reading.

In future chapters, we'll see examples of the second two strategies especially. Nevertheless, I want to avoid the temptation to taxonomize early modern and eighteenth-century closeting, much less to define its dominant strategy or mode.

I especially wish to emphasize that I am *not* trying to historicize "the early modern closet" or "the eighteenth-century closet." While I value work that teases out the homosexually relevant meanings of the various spaces referred to as 'closets' in early modern and eighteenth-century England—private or semi-private spaces reserved for prayer, writing, and intimate conversation (cf. Rambuss, Stewart [1997])—I also feel our attempts to historicize "the closet" have suffered from the same nominalist tendencies that mar theories about the recent invention of homosexuality, theories often preoccupied with the coinage and circulation of particular terms ('homosexual,' 'heterosexual,' etc.). Just as a concept functionally equivalent to 'homosexual' was widely available prior to the late nineteenth-century invention of the term and its European cognates, so too the core meaning of 'closeting'—concealing one's same-sex desires from those who would respond unfavorably, and revealing them, usually in coded form, to those who might condone or even share them—was, I hope to show, part of the conceptual storehouse of many classical, early modern, and eighteenth-century minds.

Acknowledgements

I am indebted to many people for sundry sorts of support, as I've toiled away at this project year after year. Of course, blame for any and all lapses of logic, instances of ignorance, slipshoddities of style, or failures of fact or form, trivial or tremendous, should be laid squarely at my door. Blessings alone should attend upon:

Marc Schachter, Amy Richlin, and Maxine Wolfe, who read all of the book in manuscript form, and George Haggerty, who read a hefty portion—their comments, both encouraging and critical, were invaluable;

Chris Mounsey, Rick Incorvati, and Jeff Merrick, who enabled me to publish, after helping me to polish, early versions of some of the chapters;

James Turner, Elizabeth Wahl, Carol Barash, Valerie Traub, and Carolyn Dinshaw, who generously shared their work with me prior to publication;

James Turner and Randolph Trumbach, who bestowed upon me, thanks to the miracle of photocopying, otherwise inaccessible texts;

James Turner and Catherine Gallagher, who provided instruction, expertise, and support before, during, and after the writing of my dissertation;

Janet Adelman, Margaret Doody, and Maxine Wolfe, who, at painful junctures, recommended rhetorical strategies toward which I did not naturally gravitate, but that have subsequently proven indispensable;

the librarians of the Huntington Library, the University of Arizona, the William Andrews Clark Memorial Library, the British Library, the Bibliothèque Nationale, UCLA, UC Berkeley, USC, the New York Public Library, the Los Angeles Public Library, NYU, and the CUNY Graduate Center, who provided expert and expeditious assistance on innumerable occasions;

the William Andrews Clark Memorial Library, for scanning the print reproduced on my book's cover and generously permitting me to use it;

librarian extraordinaire Scott Jacobs, who obtained the cover image, even though the Clark was closed for repairs;

administrators at the University of Arizona and the Huntington Library, who generously funded portions of my research;

David Orvis, who with speed and efficiency formatted my sprawling manuscript and compiled the index, while gently drawing my attention to errors and inconsistencies in the text;

Erika Gaffney, Ann Newell, Meredith Coeyman, and Melissa Riley-Jones, who in their various editorial capacities shepherded my manuscript into print;

the Lesbian and Gay Caucus of the American Society for Eighteenth Century Studies—especially George Haggerty, Sally O'Driscoll, Hans Turley, Katherine Binhammer, Jody Greene, John Beynon, and Sue Lanser—who, year in and year out, have instantiated my ideal of a scholarly community, undertaking a collective intellectual endeavor with enthusiasm, creativity, humility, and humor, and who, particularly in Sue's case, have proven that affection, respect, and scholarly disagreement can happily commingle;

the University of Arizona's Department of English—above all, Susan Aiken, Chris Carroll, Greg Jackson, and my erstwhile office-mate, Naomi Miller—who showered me with support from the moment I arrived in Tucson, dazed and dubious and homesick for New York;

John Morrow, Jim Allender, and Scott Singer, who helped me thread my way through the labyrinth, to reach, if not an exit, at least a better-lit and more commodious passageway where I could get some writing done;

Robert Kaplan, who delights me with his conversation, and reminds me with his excitement and courage that our work can be both pleasure and solace;

Margaret Doody, who has been my mentor and friend for twenty (gasp) years, and whose example never ceases both to humble and inspire me;

Maxine Wolfe, who continues to share with me her incomparable gift for friendship, and (as I said once before) to make me marvel that so much political astuteness, intellectual sophistication, practical know-how, unimpeachable integrity, and loving-kindness can fit into such a small body;

Marc Schachter, who deserves a far better friend than I've been these past few years, yet who still put his time, intelligence, extraordinary thoughtfulness, and love at my disposal;

my parents, grandmother, brother, and sister, who have probably been placing bets on *when*, but never *if*, I'd finish this book, and who have demonstrated their love for me in countless ways throughout the years;

and my partner, Gary, who linked arms and hearts with me as I lay pinned beneath writer's block; helped free me from its weight, with both love and a project-management, time-tracking, multicolor Excel document; then watched, yet accepted, as a never-ending series of deadlines came and went; and is now happier than anyone to see these words finally in print. (.ydwmx Ktw) bhw) yn))

To all these people, and to the many more I ought to single out for mention but have not, I offer my heartfelt gratitude.

Note: On Terminology

For convenience's sake, I refer to the academic field in which I toil as, most broadly, LGBT Studies, or more narrowly, Lesbian and Gay Studies. Reflecting different habits and purposes, other scholars draw the boundaries still more narrowly (Lesbian Studies, Gay Studies, Bisexual Studies, Transgender Studies) or more broadly (The History of Sexuality, Sexuality Studies, Gender Studies, Gender and Sexuality Studies). As for queer theory, like many of its practitioners (among whom, however, I do not number myself) I consider it more a tool or method set than a field unto itself. Moreover, I hope to demonstrate that reapplying older methods and implements to the field can cultivate fruit queer theory fails to harvest.

Despite the risk of anachronism, I use terms such as 'lesbian,' 'homosexual,' 'bisexual,' 'transgender,' and occasionally even 'gay' when discussing pre- and early modern texts. As I've already begun to argue, I believe LGBT Studies of the past two decades has overprivileged discontinuity and difference and obscured continuity and similarity. I intend to highlight the latter by using modern terms. I *don't* mean to imply that early modern and eighteenth-century conceptions of same-sex acts and desires, or same-sex-oriented individuals, are *identical* to early twenty-first-century ones, much less to imply a transhistorical or transcultural lesbian, gay, or homosexual *identity*. But the recognition of historical and cultural difference in the meanings attached to love, sex, and sexual desire between women and between men is *not* an insurmountable barrier to transhistorical or transcultural use of modern Western terms. Readers accustomed to a stricter, more defamiliarizing diet may, of course, substitute 'female same-sex eroticism,' 'male same-sex eroticism,' or similarly flavorless ingredients for 'lesbianism,' 'homosexuality,' and the like—or season liberally with scare quotes.[1]

I employ the term 'homophobia' to refer to opposition or antipathy toward homosexual desires, acts, images, individuals, etc. Where necessary, I distinguish between 'homophobia' and 'lesbophobia.' For the sake of euphony, I occasionally pair 'homophobic' with 'homophilic' rather than 'homosexual' or 'homoerotic.' As discussed in chapter four, I sometimes speak of particular homophobia*s*, homosexualitie*s*, lesbophobia*s*, etc.

---

[1] For positions on this issue with which I substantially agree, see Brooten, 18; Cady (1992); Castle (1993) 1–20; Donoghue, 7; Fradenburg and Freccero, xiii–xxiv; Young, "Introduction" and "Conclusion"; and especially Summers (1992).

I use the terms 'pro-lesbian' and 'pro-gay' as synonyms for 'lesbian-affirmative' and 'gay-affirmative' or 'lesbian-sympathetic' and 'gay-sympathetic.' All such terms are meant to signal, among other things, that individuals so designated needn't have been same-sex-oriented themselves.

I use the terms 'erotic' and 'sexual' interchangeably. I don't mean to imply that no useful distinction can be made between the two. Harriette Andreadis, for instance, discriminates productively between them, as when she writes of Katherine Philips:

> [She] used the conventions of her time to express in her own poetry a desexualized—though passionate and eroticized—version of platonic love in the love of same-sex friendship. I wish to draw here the fine distinction between a generalized erotic and emotional passion... and the narrowly focused genital, particularly male genital, definition of sexuality that was pervasive in early modern England. (58)

A distinction between the erotic and the sexual, even when expressed as carefully as Andreadis's, might seem to imply that since "the sexual" was and still often is conflated with "the genital," the erotic therefore equals "the nongenital." I don't think that's what Andreadis means; rather than *ex*clude the genitals, she wants to *in*clude the rest of the body, privileging no particular site, act, or sensation as definitive. And yet, at least to my ears, to say that Philips's poetry is "desexualized" still risks repeating a costly mistake against which Terry Castle warns: "obscur[ing] the specificity, one might almost say melodrama, of lesbian desire—its incorrigibly *lascivious* surge toward the body of another woman" ([1993] 11).

When I use the term 'sexuality,' I mean, roughly, 'things sexual.' I don't mean to imply the more clearly modern, medical/psychological concept to which Foucault referred by the French word 'sexualité,' and that Halperin and some other historians reserve for modern usage (cf. Gaca).

In addition to 'differentist' and 'similarist,' 'discontinuist' and 'continuist,' I sometimes use the contrasting terms 'universalizing' and 'minoritizing,' borrowed from Sedgwick (1990), where she defines minoritizing work as that which "see[s] homo/heterosexual definition... as an issue of active importance primarily for a small, distinct, relatively fixed homosexual minority," in contrast to universalizing work, which sees homo/heterosexual definition "as an issue of continuing, determinative importance in the lives of people across the spectrum of sexualities" (1). Thus, when I refer, as in chapter four, to a "universalizing model" of lesbianism, I mean the idea that any woman might experience and even act on sexual desires for other women, as opposed to a minoritizing model, in which such desires and acts are confined to certain (types of) women, who are therefore considered "lesbians," "tribades," "sapphists," etc. As Sedgwick later explains, she "specifically offer[s] minoritizing/universalizing as an *alternative* (though not an equivalent) to essentialist/constructivist, in the sense that... it can do some of the same analytic work as the latter binarism, and rather more tellingly" (40; but see Halperin [2002b] on the costs of sidestepping the essentialist-constructionist debate).

To refer to interpretations that seem to contest or disregard the author's intended meaning, I use either the term 'resistant' or 'dissident' reading, the latter taken from Sinfield (1992; esp. 49), from whom I also borrow the notion of an 'ideological faultline.'

I use the term 'pornography' to designate works, whenever written, that explicitly represent sexual activity, with a primary aim of arousing the reader. Thus, while I recognize the value of exploring historical changes in salacious representations of sex, I also wish to resist the dominance of the differentist account of a seventeenth- or eighteenth-century "invention" of pornography, contemporary with other supposed eighteenth-century inventions (homosexuality, the two-sex model of sex, companionate marriage, the novel, etc.).[2]

I occasionally use the term 'feminist,' by which I mean "promoting, or intended to promote, the interests of women." Some critics prefer the term 'protofeminist.'

As for the existence of early modern terms roughly equivalent to 'lesbian,' 'homosexual,' etc., my own views, especially on the homo-relevance of the term 'sodomy,' accord with Randy Conner's:

> [W]hile it may be difficult in terms of premodern French language or culture to discover a single term, such as *sodomite*, to cover all persons engaging in same-sex eroticism, this is not to say that no such terms, or persons designated by them, existed[,] or that... such terms as *sodomy* (in French, *sodomie*) represent 'utterly confused categor[ies]' (Goldberg, 18; quoting Foucault [1976/78] 101)].... [P]ersons engaging in same-sex eroticism and transgendered behavior inhabited a world in which, despite the relative absence of verbalized self-identification, they were identified and categorized by others in terms with which many of them must have been familiar. (129)[3]

Indeed, like Joseph Cady ([1996] 133–36), I've found that in most cases the precise meaning of 'sodomy' (e.g., nonprocreative sex, buggery, homosexual buggery, male homosex in general, male and female homosex in general) can be determined from context (cf. Stewart [2002] 143). As for 'tribade,' I agree with Kenneth Borris that although "[Valerie] Traub sharply distinguishes nonpenetrative erotic relations of apparently 'chaste' feminine friends ('femme-femme' in her terms) from definitively 'unnatural' tribadism (231),... these

---

[2] See Hunt, and Hunt (ed.), for the most influential positing of the modern "invention" of pornography. For thoughtful discussion of alternative terminological choices, see Moulton, 11, and Turner (2003) 5.

[3] On early modern naming and terminology, see also—in addition to the rest of Conner's essay, which includes a list of homo-relevant terms from early modern France (142–43)—Cady (all) and Dall'Orto (1989).

categories interpenetrated" (19). I also occasionally employ the terms 'platonic,' 'socratic,' and 'sapphic' to refer to male or female same-sex love when conceived of as deriving in some way from Plato, Socrates, and Sappho.

Above all, my terminological preferences reflect an anti-nominalist perspective. While recognizing the profound and extensive power of discourse, of *words*, to shape consciousness, I nonetheless do not equate the conceivable with the nameable. One can conceptualize things for which one's linguistic community has no ready terms.

Consider, for example, two snippets of early modern commentary on Ovid's story of Salmacis and Hermaphroditus: translator George Sandys's (1632) reference to "*Hermaphrodites:* not in that of both sexes but for defiling themselves with either" (209), and commentator Andrew Ross's (1589) assertion, "They that are given to that abominable sin of *Sodomy*, and are both active and passive in it, may be truly termed *Hermaphrodites*" (173; both from Silberman, 651, n.26). Sandys both registers more than one possible meaning for 'hermaphrodite' — ambiguous anatomical sex; bisexual behavior—and signals that he means the latter. Ross utilizes two available terms, 'sodomy' and 'hermaphrodite,' to denote a concept for which his culture provides no ready label, but which is evidently thinkable: the nonhierarchical, non–gender-differentiated, same-sex desire, behavior, or orientation that, as I argue in chapter six, the *Metamorphoses* tries to render invisible.

While agreeing, therefore, that we must attend to the terms used in particular times and places to discuss sex, gender, and sexuality—as well as the absence of such terms—terminology is only one of many clues to meaning and experience, and not necessarily the most important.

PART 1

Intentionality: Closeted Homosexual Writing

Chapter 1

Closeted Writing before "The Closet"

Narcissism, Naiveté, and Other Grounds for Dismissal

Discussing closeted gay writing, at least in academic forums, is a perilous undertaking. Nongay critics typically reject the notion as reading too much into texts. For them it constitutes a willful and perverse misreading, an inversion, even negation, of proper reading, a sort of anti-reading or un-writing.[1]

But such charges are only one subset of a more comprehensive prohibition against reading for less-than-explicit gay content, the full range of which Eve Sedgwick enumerated, with characteristic brilliance, in a memorable list she might have entitled, "How to Suppress Gay Criticism in Eight Easy Steps" ([1990] 52–53). Her summation of these often contradictory but nonetheless popular rhetorical moves (e.g., "Passionate language of same-sex attraction was extremely common during whatever period is under discussion—and therefore must have been completely meaningless"; "Same-sex genital relations may have been perfectly common during the period under discussion—but since there was no language about them, *they* must have been completely meaningless") is that, while they "reflect... some real questions of sexual definition and historicity[,]... they only reflect them and don't reflect *on* them: the family resemblance among this group of extremely common responses comes from their closeness to the core grammar of *Don't ask; You shouldn't know*" (53). Such arguments, when successful, cordon off virtually the entire corpus of world literature from pro-gay analysis. As for unequivocally gay texts—most of them written in the last half-century or less—they are typically ignored, or dismissed as insufficiently universal to merit critical attention, by virtue of their explicitly gay focus.

Most of us working in LGBT Studies have grown adept at countering such dismissal and prohibition from without (thanks, in no small measure, to work such as Sedgwick's and Sinfield's). Yet we are, on the whole, much less skilled, and much less interested, in opposing such arguments when proffered from within our own ranks. Not that any of us intends to foreclose pro-gay or anti-homophobic textual inquiry. Quite the opposite. Yet for much of the past two decades, many among us have seemed intent on foreclosing *certain varieties* of such inquiry.

---

[1] Alan Sinfield garnered precisely that response to his interpretation of Auden's 1955 poem "The Truest Poetry is the Most Feigning," which, according to Sinfield, elaborates "a closeted gay aesthetic" ([1994] 60–64).

Using arguments disconcertingly similar to those Sedgwick targets, historians and critics studying pre- and early modern sex, gender, and sexuality have often proven themselves as quick to dismiss their colleagues' work as have homophobic scholars to dismiss our collective intellectual endeavor. And by far the most common form such intra-group dismissal has taken has been the charge of anachronism, of failure to accept the supposed epistemic divide in Western history separating B.H. from A.H., "Before Homosexuality" from "After Homosexuality." Our fields' rise to prominence in the late 1980s and early 1990s was accompanied, and perhaps enabled, not only by an in-your-face, ACT UP–like defiance of scholarly and critical homophobia, but also by a down-your-nose disavowal of insufficiently "sophisticated," insufficiently "rigorous" lesbian and gay work. The litmus test was acceptance of the modern "invention" of homosexuality.

But more damaging even than dismissing continuist work has been *ignoring* it. Continuists critiqued the dominant, Foucauldian paradigm (or pseudo-Foucauldian paradigm, as Halperin argues [1998/2002]) on a variety of grounds: contesting interpretations of particular texts; presenting overlooked evidence; disputing the conclusions of authoritative theorists and scholars (Foucault, Bray, Stone, Laqueur, Trumbach, Halperin, Butler). Yet in differentist scholarship of the late '80s through late '90s, citation of continuist work (let alone serious engagement with it) is rare. With the exception of differentists' favorite foil, the supposedly essentialist, indisputably A-List John Boswell, as well as a B-List of hard-to-ignore but not-particularly-sought-after invitees (such as Bruce Smith, Amy Richlin, Bernadette Brooten, and Terry Castle), continuists taking issue with the discontinuist paradigm were relegated to a C-List or D-List of disciplinary nobodies. Until the recent crisis in academic publishing, and with the exception of female scholars conversant with lesbian-feminist debates on the history of sexuality (who tended to exhibit a less ideologically restricted pattern of citation), scholars published by Routledge, Duke, Zone, or (to a lesser extent) *GLQ* rarely cited those published by Haworth/Harrington Park, Cassell, or *Journal of the History of Sexuality*.[2]

As mentioned in my preface, leading differentist scholars have begun, at long last, to call for greater historiographic and critical pluralism, echoing (although

---

[2] My own work is deeply indebted to Boswell, Smith, Brooten, Castle, and especially Richlin, as well as a great many other continuist scholars. Of those routinely ignored by differentists, I'm most indebted to Cady, Creech, Donoghue, Schleiner, and Summers. Other continuist work I particularly admire includes Patricia Parker (1993a), Adelman, Hutson, and Park and Nye on Laqueur and the supposed dominance of "the one-sex model" prior to the eighteenth century; Cressy on Stone; Aers on the alleged early modern "invention" of subjectivity; Eribon, Stanley, and Kennedy on the supposedly medical rather than gay subcultural invention of "inversion" and "homosexuality" in the late nineteenth and early twentieth century; and the contributions to Gerard and Hekma. Of course, I've also learned from constructionist scholars (usually on the continuist end of the constructionist spectrum), especially Dinshaw, Fradenburg and Freccero, Sedgwick, and Sinfield.

often without acknowledgment) continuist writing of the past decade and more.[3] Yet old disciplinary habits die a slow, lingering death, as a field's classic texts continue to influence newcomers' work, even while the *eminences grises* have moved on to newer perspectives. Take, for instance, Harriette Andreadis's treatment, in *Sappho in Early Modern England* (2001), of Elizabeth Wahl's *Invisible Relations* (1999). The two projects are remarkably congruent: both document an increasing, anxious cultural awareness of female homosexuality over the course of the seventeenth century (in England, for Andreadis; in England and France, for Wahl), paying particular attention to the ways in which female friendship writing enabled women to both express and conceal erotic desire for one another. Yet the extent of Andreadis's engagement with Wahl is to (inaccurately) criticize her for "situat[ing Katherine] Philips in a historical context that assumes the binaries of hetero-/homo-sexuality, which were not culturally stable until much later," and with "attribut[ing] to Philips a quite modern, twentieth-century subjectivity and self-consciousness about normative sexualities" (192, n.9).

Or consider Paula Loscocco's even more recent treatment (2003) of virtually everyone else who's written on the homoerotics of Philips's verse. Contrasting her own discursively focused explication of the poems to predecessors' supposedly biographical and ideological explications, Loscocco obscures the degree to which her work accords with, and grows out of, criticism that takes what she considers a less theoretically sophisticated approach. Inadvertently, she reveals precisely what Fradenburg and Freccero highlight in differentist writing: the unacknowledged pleasure its authors take in renouncing pleasure (figured in Loscocco's case as resistance to "temptation" [83]), as well as its stance of dispassionate objectivity. In contrast, Fradenburg and Freccero urge us "to recognize and confront the pleasure we take in renouncing pleasure for the stern alterities of history," arguing that "[t]he opposition between transhistoricist perspectives which seek, in the past, the allure of the mirror image, and historicist perspectives that 'accept' the difference of past from present, is itself highly ideological" (xix).

Perhaps most disturbing is Valerie Traub's treatment—in her ambitious, exhilarating book, *The Renaissance of Lesbianism in Early Modern England* (2002)—of precisely this aspect of the continuist/differentist debate, and of Fradenburg and Freccero's essay in particular. For while Traub's book displays a truly rare intellectual generosity, that generosity fails when she dramatically misrepresents Fradenburg and Freccero's argument. Asking "how to postulate a continuism that is not naive" and "what... a *sophisticated* continuism [would] look like," she faults Fradenburg and Freccero for erecting a binary opposition that, in fact, *differentists* insist upon, and that Fradenburg and Freccero explicitly critique. After quoting their assertion that "[t]he opposition between transhistoricist

---

[3] Compare, for instance, Halperin's remarks (2002b) regarding continuity and discontinuity, similarity and difference, with Boswell (1990) 149; Summers (1992) 19; and Richlin (1993b) 529–30, 571.

perspectives which seek, in the past, the allure of the mirror image, and historicist perspectives that 'accept' the difference of past from present, is itself highly ideological," Traub sums up their argument as follows: "Correlating identification across time with pleasure, and resistance to identification with ascesis or a foreclosure of pleasure, they celebrate as *particularly queer* the pleasures of the mirror" (333). She then launches into a series of questions culminating in a declaration of her critical intent:

> But is this pleasure genuinely queer, that is, resistant? Or is the pleasure of identification yet another emanation of the similitude that, since the Renaissance at least, has been a primary means of representing female homoeroticism? Why is it that identification is associated with pleasure, while forgoing identification in the name of historical alterity is correlated with an austere asceticism? Does opposition to collapsing the past into the present necessarily evacuate pleasure from the historical enterprise? Why is pleasure conceived only as the singular, ego-confirming gratification of the mirror? And what is it that would make the "allure of the mirror image" acceptable as a form of historicist practice? As these questions imply, I want to trouble Fradenburg and Freccero's opposition between identification as pleasure, on the one hand, and alterity as ascesis, on the other. (334)

Fradenburg and Freccero's point, however, was that *differentists* have erected this opposition, charging continuists with seeking mirror images in the past in a naive quest for the comforting pleasures of identification, while themselves claiming to have renounced pleasure in order to better apprehend historical truth, found solely in historical difference (the stance exemplified by Loscocco, above, and Masten, below). Fradenburg and Freccero urged differentists to abandon this opposition, to admit the pleasures they derive from their own approach and to value the different pleasures, and different insights, that continuist and discontinuist work can offer. For while it's true that, as Traub argues, identificatory perspectives "can obscure the ways that historical difference can provide us with critical resources and understandings otherwise unavailable" (334), the reverse is also true: anti-identificatory perspectives can obscure the ways that historical similitude can provide us with critical resources and understandings otherwise unavailable. Fradenburg and Freccero thus advocated a both/and approach.

Among the many effects of differentism such as Traub's has been the general abandonment, as irredeemably anachronistic, of the notions of the closet and closeted writing when discussing the pre- and early modern world. Thus Traub asks, "[W]as there, in fact, an early modern closet?" (344), and concludes by characterizing the early modern period as a time "prior to the regime of the closet" (345). And thus, in *Textual Intercourse* (1997), Jeffrey Masten characterizes his approach as "eschewing a historical methodology that finds only versions or expressions of itself in the past" and instead accepting "the impossibility of sleeping with the dead[,]... the impossibility, even as it figures as an intractable curiosity or desire, of searching the annals of the past for erotic subjects motivated by our desires and living our practices with the cultural and political meanings we associate with these desires and practices.... The point," he concludes, "is not to bring the Renaissance out of the closet, but to bring the closet out of the Renaissance—to account for the abiding differences in the ways this period represented sexuality and its connections with modes of textual production" (6–7). Masten's often brilliantly argued book is thus launched (as Traub's is concluded) through caricature and repudiation of continuist work ("find[ing] only versions or expressions of itself in the past"), and through a display of supposedly mature self-denial and objectivity (resisting a seemingly "intractable curiosity or desire" and instead accepting "the impossibility of sleeping with the dead").

Compare this approach to that taken in a work to which Masten acknowledges himself indebted (168, n.30), Sedgwick's *Epistemology of the Closet*:

> Over and over I have felt in writing the book that, however my own identifications, intuitions, circumstances, limitations, and talents may have led its interpretations to privilege constructivist over essentialist, universalizing over minoritizing, and gender-transitive over gender-separatist understandings of sexual choice, nevertheless the space of permission for this work and the depth of the intellectual landscape in which it might have a contribution to make owe everything to the wealth of essentializing, minoritizing, and separatist gay thought and struggle also in progress. (13)

Sedgwick's work has had an incalculable impact on subsequent gay and queer scholarship. Yet her respect for other approaches has too rarely been emulated.

With her example in mind, let me be clear: my aim is not to dismiss Masten, Traub, Loscocco, Andreadis, or others for having themselves dismissed continuist scholarship. While I sometimes disagree with their work, I also find it, like much differentist work, genuinely illuminating. My aim, instead, is to highlight and contest the persistent strain in differentist writing that "others" and dismisses so-called essentialist, minoritizing, separatist gay and lesbian scholarship; that ignores it; or that appropriates its insights without acknowledgment.

Moreover, such "othering" and dismissal repeatedly focuses on historians' and critics' employment of the central metaphor of contemporary Western gay experience: the closet. And in this respect, notwithstanding its appeal to nuance (historical, linguistic, discursive, conceptual), differentist critique is remarkably heavy-handed and reductive. Again, Masten's "eschew[al of] a historical methodology that finds only versions or expressions of itself in the past" and Traub's "opposition to collapsing the past into the present" are typical, suggesting that continuists posit complete *identity* between past and present. The result, differentists imply, is not historicism, but narcissism (e.g. Traub, 348).[4]

---

[4] Traub goes a step further, diagnosing among lesbians a "collective melancholic response to the culturally disavowed trauma of historical elision" (350). While this may

Identity

Identity, in fact, has been doubly targeted by differentists, who portray similarists as not only seeking *identical* versions of themselves in the past, but also ascribing to these past selves fully fledged gay and lesbian *identities* (e.g., Greenberg, 308–309; Trumbach [1987b] 116; Rocke, 191; cf. Borris, ed., 375, n.32). I would submit, however, that identity is the wrong, or at least an insufficient issue to raise in proving the differentist case.

Of course, if by "homosexual identity" one means that a person's homosexual desires and behaviors provide, or are perceived to provide, a key to that person's entire being; that a person self-identifies on the basis of those desires and behaviors over and above any other potential bases for identification; that a homosexual identity must be stable, wholly coherent, and non–self-contradictory; that an individual's sexual activities must be exclusively homosexual, as must those of his or her same-sex-desiring associates; or that, in order to have any identity at all, a person must necessarily conceive of him- or herself above all as an individual, rather than primarily as a member of a larger social grouping, then "homosexual identity" probably *is* a modern Western development.

In contrast, I assume something far less grand when I posit the existence of pre- or early modern homosexual writers and readers, who conceive of themselves as characterized at least in part by an enduring sexual or romantic attraction to members of their own sex:

1. Their "identity" *might* include a sense of being different to some degree from other men or women, even from most of society, on the basis of same-sex attraction.
2. It *might* include awareness of having to hide that difference in order to avoid persecution or punishment.
3. It *might* include valuing that difference as a source of pleasure, affection, friendship, or love.
4. It *need not* be the most important element of an individual's self-concept.
5. It *need not* involve association with a whole subculture, network, or even small circle of other same-sex–oriented individuals; sex with even one other person might easily suffice.
6. It *need not* be connected to any particular theory about the causation of same-sex desire (Nature, the stars, disease, the Devil…).

---

indeed accurately characterize some forms of continuism, my point is that Traub, in typical differentist fashion, reduces all continuist work to a naive search for reassuring forebears in the past, while appropriating the insights of continuist scholars such as Fradenburg and Freccero, especially their valuing of both similarity and difference (e.g., Traub's assertion that she has "attempted to privilege neither continuism nor alterity" [353]).

7. It *need not* entail the assumption that all men who desire men or all women who desire women are identical, or fit one or two clearly recognizable types.

In other words, while not claiming that a pre- or early modern individual who qualifies under my definition of "homosexual writer or reader" would have had as relatively stable, fundamental, or highly elaborated a same-sex identity as do many lesbians and gay men today, I see no reason why some women who loved and desired women and some men who loved and desired men could not have had the sort of less-developed identities or self-concepts I've just described.[5]

One should not, of course, *assume* such self-awareness, nor a desire to communicate it textually, in any particular time, place, group, or individual. But neither should one rule them out in advance on the grounds of anachronism. Creech made this point eloquently when he refused to allow the Foucauldian account of the nineteenth-century "invention" of homosexuality to close off whole avenues of speculation. As he wrote:

> I do not want to suggest… that at this juncture we should avoid speculating about anachronistic concepts such as coming out… before the invention of homosexuality and the panoply of concepts—like the closet—which develop from it. For such speculation may eventually reveal that our current problem with these terms has been that our conceptual arsenal contains instruments still too unrefined to catch the nuances of attitude and behavior in the mid-nineteenth century which, mutatis mutandis, might be profitably considered the functional equivalents of that complex of self-knowledge or behavior which we call "coming out." (69)

It's most likely true that, as Foucault argued, only in the modern period is sex commonly taken for the locus of subjectivity, the locus of truth. It's also likely true that, as Sedgwick argued, only in the modern period are same-sex sexuality and the

---

[5] For much of this critique of differentist requirements for lesbian or gay "identity," I'm indebted to environmental psychologist and longtime lesbian activist Maxine Wolfe; see also Salih and Borris (e.g., 260). The latter's "General Introduction" provides an excellent critique of entrenched anti-identitarian assumptions regarding the "recent construction" of homosexuality (some differentists, most notably Halperin, have come round to this view of identity as well). Noteworthy, too, is Patterson's discussion of identity (22–28), particularly his emphasis upon pleasure, relation, and recognition, rather than shame, as spurs for homosexual identity-formation. And see especially Bly, who, in studying plays performed by the Whitefriars theater (1607–1608), "suggest[s] that there is a space for identification as a sodomite in early modern culture,… glimpsed in the bonds of shared laughter," and "propos[es] a theatre in which one erotic minority which consistently served *as* the object of humour in other theatres reveals its own homoerotic, humorous pleasure" (20–21). Significantly, focusing on homoerotic puns, Bly emphasizes "motivation"—in other words, *intention*—arguing that the Whitefriars syndicate deliberately wrote homoerotic material that would appeal to homosympathetic members of its audience.

closet commonly taken for the truth of sex. Yet if we remain open to similarity, to approximate or functional equivalence, instead of only identity or difference, we can more productively explore the longstanding Western awareness that people often selectively conceal and disclose same-sex love and desire.

Homosexuality and Secrecy

Given the universality, or near-universality, of linking sexuality to gender, and making them both intelligible at least in part through mockery, shame, stricture, punishment, taboo, and the like, sexual secrecy may also be universal. Indeed, given the connection of sex to reproduction and reproduction to religion and spirituality, even approved forms of sex are often shrouded in secrecy, as feelings and behavior that are, or ought to be, sacred and mysterious. Be that as it may, closeting at least some forms of sex is clearly not restricted to the modern West. As Karma Lochrie (1996) writes, "The closet as the primary figural representation of homosexuality is very recent, but the attachment of secrecy to sexuality and to groups of people is not" (147).

Lochrie demonstrates the degree to which the sexuality of women in particular has been entwined with secrecy, arguing that in the Middle Ages women themselves came to be defined as secrets, secrets they could only *be* but not *know*, secrets to be exchanged among men (9). And if we narrow our focus further, to female chastity, we find an even closer analogue to the notion of closeted homosexuality. For as Simon Goldhill argues, discussing Greek literature of the early Christian era, "within patriarchal concerns for female chastity lurks the problem of how to *know* for sure about the integrity of the female body—and the related problem of the *knowingness* of the female" (121).

Such masculine fears about women's ability to *appear* yet not *be* chaste have at times included fears they might secretly have sex with one another. The locus classicus for such anxieties is Martial's epigram "Ad Bassam tribadem" (Martial 1.90), translated here by Robert Fletcher (1656):

> Cause amongst males thou nere was seen to be
> Nor as unchast no fable feigned thee,
> But all thy offices discharged were
> By thy own sex, no man intruding there,
> I grant thou seem'dst *Lucretia* to our eye,
> But (o mistake!) *Bassa* th'art out ont, fie.
> Two Twatts commit the fact, and dare it can,
> Whiles a prodigious lust supplies the man,
> Th'hast made a riddle worth the *Thebane* guile,
> Where no man is, adultery bred the while. (41–42)

Martial foregrounds the crisis of knowledge female chastity produces for men: how can they be certain a woman is chaste if the usual signs of chastity can be deceiving? Men's knowledge turns out to be inadequate; women's, dangerously excessive: Bassa (and presumably her female sexual partners) possesses illicit sexual knowledge, both of tribadism and of how to conceal it from men.

Not that men necessarily respond to such concealment with anxiety. Martial's epigram, in fact, can be read—perhaps *should* be read—primarily as witty paradox (after all, the speaker isn't sure Bassa's activities even count as adultery). At least one subsequent poet, in an attempt to surpass Martial, seems to have done so. In reply to a homoerotic poem of praise from John Donne (aged twenty or so at the time), eighteen-year-old Thomas Woodward composed an even more fascinating poem of his own:

> Have mercy on me and my sinfull Muse
>> Which rub'd and tickled with thyne could not chuse
> But spend some of her pithe and yeild to bee
>> One in that chaste and mistique tribadree
> Bassaes adultery no fruit did leave
>> Nor theirs which their swolne thighs did nimbly weave
> And with new armes and mouthes embrace and kis
>> Though they had issue was not like to this
> Thy Muse, Oh strange and holy Lecheree
>> Beeing a Mayd still, gott this Song on mee.

Martial played up the paradox, from a phallocentric point of view, of sex between women: adultery existing (or "bred," in Fletcher's additionally paradoxical translation) without a man. Woodward goes further, likening Bassa's "fruitless" adultery with the oxymoronic "mistique tribadree" and "strange and holy Lecheree" in which his and Donne's muses engage. More paradoxically, and more ingeniously, still, Donne's muse, although a virgin ("a Mayd") impregnates Woodward. Bassa's male-less adultery pales in comparison.[6]

Such witty paradoxes, however, are beside the point: female chastity has in the past been viewed, at least at times, as potential cover for lesbianism. Nor are male-focused analogues difficult to find, most obviously the widespread, longstanding disbelief in clerical celibacy. Granted, churchmen were usually accused of secret *heterosexual* activity—fornicating with nuns, corrupting female confessees, and the like—yet accusations of homosexual vice have also been common. In addition, a specifically homosexual stock figure appears throughout much of Western history: the pederastic philosopher or schoolmaster. As Thomas Hubbard points

---

[6] The poem, signed "T.W.," is most extensively discussed by Klawitter; see also Andreadis, Halley, Orgel (1996a), Traub (2002), and Wahl. Of related interest is Pebworth and Summers (1984).

out, "Texts... show that even in Plato's own day, some were skeptical whether... a chaste pederasty could exist in reality; later satirical texts... take it for granted that these philosophical pretensions were fraudulent covers" (9). Or as Goldhill writes, discussing a dialogue from Achilles Tatius's novel *Leucippe and Cleitophon*, "Philosophy is construed... merely as a shameful veil for unnatural desires, where young men and not virtue is the pursuit" (106).[7]

One of Hubbard's examples, Juvenal's *Satire 2*, is particularly noteworthy. The satirist charges his supposedly wise and virtuous targets with secret vice—but since he's excoriating effeminacy, the vice in question is receptive anal intercourse, rather than pederasty. Moreover, Juvenal contrasts what we would call closeted men with those who flaunt their deviance, reserving his outraged invective for those who conceal unmanly desire and activity under an outward appearance of masculine virtue.

Or consider yet another strand in the history of closeting: the recognition that custom rather than desire often motivates behavior, especially where sex is concerned. Such awareness can be found as far back as Plato's *Symposium*, in which Aristophanes declares that there are men who "are lovers of boys and by nature are not interested in marriage and having children, though they are forced into it by custom [νομου]. They would be satisfied to live all the time with one another without marrying" (192b). Differentists would do well to recall this remark, at least those who argue that male-male sexuality in ancient Greece bears little if any relation to modern homosexuality since even the most ardent of Greek boy-lovers, as well as their male partners, also married and fathered children. The mere facts of marriage and procreation tell us nothing about sexual desire or orientation. And the recognition of marriage's irrelevance to the question of desire—as well as the recognition, more broadly, of a contrast between public adherence to custom and private sexual transgression—is nothing new.[8]

Perhaps echoing this moment from Plato, Montaigne confesses, in "*Upon some verses of* Virgill," to a bias against marriage, writing, "Of mine owne disposition, would wisedoom itselfe have had me, I should have refused to wed her. But we may say our pleasure; the custome and use of common life overbeareth us. Most of my actions are guided by example, and not by election" (tr. Florio [1613] 477). In fact, in "*Of custome, and how a received law should not easily be changed*," Montaigne goes even further, asserting not only that custom commonly *does* determine public behavior, but also that it *should*. Restricting deviance from the norm ("the fashions and forme customarily received") to the private realm, and explicitly sanctioning only *mental* deviance, he nonetheless encourages a closeted

---

[7] See Goldhill, 99–100, and the "Boy of Pergamum" episode in Petronius's *Satyricon*. For the persistence of this stereotype into the mid-seventeenth century, see Hammond (2002) 17–18 (regarding Hobbes on Plato's *Symposium*) and Rocco.

[8] I thank Marc Schachter for this example and for the next two, from Montaigne.

inner life, at least for "a man of understanding" (52).[9]

Early modern pornography, arising in part from such philosophical, religious, and political freethinking, also encourages private *behavioral* deviance. In Nicolas Chorier and Jean Nicolas's *L'Academie des dames* (1680), for example, in the course of instructing her friend Octavie in erotic philosophy and practice (including sex between women, as we shall see in chapter four), the worldly wise Tullie advises:

> Learn thus at present that all that you can do conveniently, without offending the eyes of your Domestics & your Husband, is permitted to you; & on the contrary that which you cannot execute without peril is forbidden.... Far from despising the Laws, & the Customs that are established by long usage, [a woman] must venerate them, & observe them with so exact a regularity, that on the exterior her life differs in nothing from the honorable, while underneath this veil she searches out her entertainments.... This conduct surprises you perhaps but you must know that it is less prejudicial to Civic life.... [Y]ou must follow the opinions of the wise, & the customs of the people, & in reserving for yourself your most secret thoughts & actions[,] you must sacrifice to it the outside, & all exterior appearances. (123; 126–27)

It is unclear whether this advice is meant to apply to both sexes or only to women (in which case it intensifies the patriarchal dichotomizing of public and private, advocating female independence only within a greatly restricted private realm, consisting exclusively of spaces where a woman's actions will be unobserved by any potentially disapproving eye). Either way, though, the passage accurately conveys the often-unacknowledged reality of private sexual life. Laws and religious decrees are public; sex acts are mostly private. Outward conformity to laws and decrees, and to the norms they are intended to uphold, communicates little or nothing about private thought and conduct. On the contrary, there's usually an enormous difference between what people do privately and what they admit publicly—especially where sex is concerned.[10]

Of course, a great many sexual acts and desires might require veiling from public scrutiny. Yet it has long been recognized that homosexual ones particularly necessitate concealment. Boccaccio's *Decameron* (1351) provides a fictional example in the tale of Pietro di Vinciolo of Perugia (story ten, day five), in which a lover of young men marries "more to beguile others and to abate the general suspect [*la generale oppinion*] in which he was held by all the Perugians, than for

---

[9] For an exemplary reading of Montaigne's famous essay on friendship as simultaneously concealing and revealing a sexual dimension to his relationship with La Boétie, unnameable because egalitarian (unlike pederasty), see Schachter (2001).

[10] In Chorier's original Latin version, the *Satyra sotadica* (1660), such moments read more clearly as satirical, portraying learned women as debauched and hypocritical. See also Barrin's 1683 pornographic dialogue *Vénus dans le clôitre* (25–33).

any desire [*vaghezza*] of his own" (Halperin [2002a] 39). As for an example from real life, consider the remarks of Gallimard, a lawyer in the Parlement de Paris, who testified to police interrogators in 1724 not only that a man he'd encountered on the street "wanted very much to get to know me, and that we would live together, and he would pay for half of the room, that we would live together like two brothers, that we would drink and eat together," a proposition the lawyer found quite attractive, but also "that he [Gallimard] had a wife but hardly ever made use of her [they were separated], that his marriage was a stratagem, cover-up, and that he had not taste for women, that he preferred ass to cunt" (Rey, 185).

An even more pertinent example can be found in *Vies des dames galantes* [ms. late 16th/early 17th c.; pub. 1665–66], Brantôme's well-known account of sexual shenanigans among the late sixteenth-century French aristocracy. Among the scandalous doings he chronicles, Brantôme prominently features sex between women. In the process, he provides clear evidence for a sophisticated early modern awareness of homosexual closeting.

Not unlike recent scholars, Brantôme first approaches the subject of same-sex sexuality via the question of terminology, as he attempts to explain the phenomenon of lesbianism:

> [S]uch women, who love this practice and will not suffer men, but devote themselves to women, as men themselves do, are called [or "call themselves" (*s'appellent*)] *tribades*, a Greek word derived, as I have learned from Greeks, from τριβω τριβειν which is the same as saying *fricare,* to rub [*freyer*] or friquer, or to rub each other; and tribades are called *fricatrices*, in French fricatrices, or those who perform the friquarelle in the art of *donna con donna*, as it has still been found today. (121)[11]

Far from treating "this practice" as an archaic topic of purely antiquarian interest, Brantôme asserts its continuance down through the centuries, reporting, "It is said that Sappho of Lesbos was a very good mistress in this art, indeed, they say, that she invented it, and that the lesbian ladies have imitated her in it since, and continued down to this day; as Lucian says: that such women are the women of Lesbos, who will not suffer men, but approach other women as men themselves do" (121).

Of course, Lesbos is not France. Nor, for that matter, is Turkey, which according to Brantôme is another hotbed, or hot bath, of dame-on-dame desire. Yet rather than rendering lesbianism safe, because distantly "other," Brantôme maximizes the play of exotic distance and titillating proximity:

---

[11] In translating Brantôme, I've consulted (but also departed from) Merrick and Ragan (2001). On *fricarelle* and *frayer*, see Guiraud, 351–52. Note the relationship to English *frig, friggin', frickin'*, etc., as in John Florio's definition, in *World of Wordes* (1598), of *Fricciare*: "... to frig, to wriggle, to tickle" (139).

Closeted Writing before "The Closet" 15

Now, from what I've heard said, in many localities and regions there are many such women and lesbians, in France, in Italy and in Spain, Turkey, Greece and other places. And where the women are secluded, and do not have their complete freedom, the practice continues strongly: for, such women burning in their bodies, surely must, so the women [*elles*] say, make use of this remedy, to cool off a bit, or else they burn all over [*du tout qu'elles bruslent*].

The Turkish women go to the baths more for this lechery than for anything else and are greatly given over to it. Even the courtesans, who have men at their disposal and at all hours, still make use of these fricarelles, seek each other out and love each other, as I've heard it said by [or *of (à)*] some in Italy and in Spain. In our France, such women are common enough; and yet it is said it is not long that they have dabbled in it, indeed that the fashion for it was brought from Italy by a lady of quality whom I will not name. (122)

Brantôme then proceeds to recount two stories of Frenchwomen who follow this fashion, including "a woman of society who was quite superlative in it, and who loved many ladies, honoured them and served them more than men do and made love to them as a man to his mistress" (123) and "two ladies of the court who loved each other so strongly, and were so ardent about their business, that wherever they were, could neither keep nor refrain from at least making some sign of love play or from kissing, which made them a great scandal and gave men much to think about" (126). In Brantôme's account, lesbianism is *both* foreign *and* French, old *and* new, ancient *and* modern.

And it includes the concept of closeting, raised here as climax to a fascinating anecdote that draws together many of the central concerns of my argument. Unlike the passage on lesbian terminology, a learned authorial lecture, imparting seemingly scientific, if arcane, knowledge to an implicitly passive audience, this later anecdote is intensely conversational, in tone, form, and content. For Brantôme relates a verbal exchange between himself and a friend (Louis-Bérenger du Guast), about a text written in dialogue form (Firenzuola's *On the Beauty of Women*), itself in conversation with an earlier textual dialogue (Plato's *Symposium*):

M. du Gua and I were reading a little book in Italian one day that is entitled *On Beauty*, written in dialogue form by Signor Angelo Firenzuola, a Florentine, and came across a passage where he says that some women who were created by Jupiter in the beginning were made of this nature, that some started to love men and the others the beauty of each other; but, some purely and in sanctity, as of this type there is found in our time, as the author says, the very illustrious Marguerite of Austria, who loved the beautiful Laodomie Forteguerre; the others wantonly and lasciviously like Sappho, the Lesbian, and in our time in Rome the great courtesan Cecile, the Venetian; and these by nature hate to marry, and flee the conversation of men as much as they can. (127)[12]

---

[12] The relevant portions of Firenzuola's dialogue, as well as Laodomia Forteguerri's

Brantôme is referring here to Aristophanes' speech in the *Symposium*, one of the best-known stories in all Plato's dialogues, which Firenzuola summarizes in a *Dialogue on the Beauty of Women* (1541). According to this explanation of love's origin, human beings were originally spherical, equipped with two of everything of which we sport only one today—two faces, two pair of arms, two pair of legs, two sets of genitals. These original humans came in three varieties—all-male, all-female, and half-male/half-female. For attempting to attack the gods, Zeus sliced them in two, inadvertently creating love, the longing of post-slice humans for their missing halves.

As in the original Platonic story, Firenzuola's somewhat shortened account (16–17) posits three corresponding human types, characterized by innate and inherited sexual/affectional orientations: men attracted to men (in Plato, men attracted to boys), women attracted to women, and men and women attracted to each other. Brantôme omits most of the story, and discusses only women, but retains a tripartite organizing structure, dividing women into those who love men, those who love each other's beauty, and those who love each other purely and in sanctity. In the process, he appears to establish a much firmer divide between lesbianism and "pure" female-female love than Firenzuola.[13]

But Brantôme isn't finished with his anecdote:

> About that, Monsieur Du Guast criticized the author, saying that it was false that this fair Marguerite loved that fair lady with a pure and holy love: because, since she had attached herself to her rather than to others who might have been as beautiful and virtuous as she, it was to be presumed that it was in order to make use of her for her sensual pleasures, no more or less than others; and, to cover up her lasciviousness, she said and proclaimed that she loved her in a holy way, as we see several like her do, who veil their loves with such words.
>
> That is what Monsieur Du Guast said about it; and whoever wants to discuss it further, can do as he pleases. (127)

---

sonnets to Margaret of Austria and one other woman, are reprinted, in English translation with commentary, in Borris, 274–84. On Forteguerri's sonnets to Margaret, rumors about Margaret's lesbianism, and both Firenzuola and Brantôme's remarks on the two women, see Eisenbichler.

[13] Halperin (1990) argues that Aristophanes' speech does *not* posit something like our notion of sexual orientation; nor an umbrella category of homosexuality, including both males and females; nor even male homosexuality alone (he points out the "boys/men" detail). Even if he were correct (but I think he's not [see Barkan, 125, n.41]; yet see Carnes for an interesting, radically constructionist view), what matters is that early moderns like Brantôme read the story as discussing sexual orientation. See below, ch.5, for more on Aristophanes' speech; see Brisson for a mythographic and psychological interpretation of the story.

There are several points I wish to make about this passage. First, it provides not just an unambiguous example of female friendship suspected of lesbianism, but one that predates by half a century the growth of anxious anti-lesbian awareness in Western Europe that some scholars (e.g., Andreadis) now date to the mid- to late seventeenth century.[14] Second, the person voicing suspicion is a reader, depicted as resisting, indeed reversing, conclusions drawn by a written text. Of course, he isn't engaged in resistant lesbian reading, but rather in libertine, anti-lesbian reading. Nevertheless, Brantôme implicitly rejects the firm divide he seems to establish between sexual and nonsexual female friendship, by suggesting the latter may be the former in disguise. Which leads to my third point: the person under suspicion is accused not only of engaging in lesbian sex, but of purposely attempting to conceal this activity by strenuously "proclaiming" (*elle disoit et publioit*) that her love is "saintly," spiritual, nonsexual. She is accused of covering up (*couvrir*), of veiling (*ombrager*), her lesbian desires and activities—accused, in other words, of closeting them.[15]

I wish especially to emphasize these passages from Brantôme and Firenzuola because they include so many elements central to the continuist view of the history of homosexuality: the importance of classical discourse on love and friendship; the imaginability of *types of people* with enduring sexual and affectional orientations, rather than only *categories of acts* in which anyone might potentially, if sinfully, engage; the conceivability of male and female homosexuality as similar or analogous; the focus on dissident reading, on contesting authors' obvious intentions and meanings; and, of course, the accusation of deliberate closeting. None of these "inventions," it would seem, are quite as recent, quite as modern, as we've been led to believe.[16]

---

[14] While Traub used to espouse this position ([1996] 33, citing Cavalli's 1651 opera *La Calisto* as the first text in which female friendship is suspected of lesbianism), her recent work (2002) recognizes earlier examples. On problems with treating 1650 as a water-shed, see Borris (2004) 12.

[15] For *ombrager* as, figuratively, 'to veil' (*voiler*), see Dubois et al., 354.

[16] Again, see Borris's critique of "the acts paradigm" and "recent constructionism" (2004).

Chapter 2

"Philips-Lover" and the Abominable Madame de Murat

The first half of this chapter examines an anonymous mid-seventeenth-century English poem, included among the commendatory verses prefacing Katherine Philips's posthumously published collection, *Poems* (1667). The second explores a late seventeenth-century, semi-scandalous French novel by Madame de Murat, *Les Memoires De Madame La Comtesse De M**** (1697). In contrast to subsequent chapters, here I'm concerned with mere snippets from my central texts—two lines from the poem, a few paragraphs from the novel—that are easily overlooked. Yet by placing these snippets in the context not only of the works in which they occur, but also of contemporary texts that discuss or represent lesbianism, I make the case for reading each one as an example of covert lesbian writing.

Philo-Philippa, Female Writing, and Love Between Women

It's well known that in the seventeenth century, writing for a public audience was charged with dangerous sexual significance—at least for women, who risked accusations of immodesty, unchastity, even prostitution. It's less well known that in a cultural milieu in which Poet and Muse were traditionally imagined as romantic, even sexual, partners, female writing itself, regardless of context or content, sometimes gave rise to lesbian associations. For instance, as several critics have noted, Ben Jonson attacked female poet Cecilia Bulstrode's versifying by figuring it as lesbian rape, charging her in "Epigram on the Court Pucell" with "forc[ing] a Muse" "with Tribade lust."[1]

In chapter one, we briefly examined another linkage of tribadism with poetic production, Thomas Woodward's verse to Donne, "Have mercy on me and my

---

[1] "Epigram on the Court Pucell" (wr. before 1609), from *Underwood* (1640), rpt. Jonson (1982) 195–96; see poem 10 in *The Forrest* (1616), rpt. Jonson (1963; see 96–97 on the poem's earlier, differently titled appearance). On these poems' relation to seventeenth-century literary conceptions of lesbianism, see Andreadis (2001), Mueller, Teague, Traub (2002), and Wahl. For a good example of the heterosexual conception of Poet-Muse relations, see the second of Donne's sonnets "To Mr. B.B.," beginning, "If thou unto thy Muse be married" (Donne [1967] 68; see also Halley).

sinfull Muse." Although Woodward's treatment of lesbianism is a far cry from Jonson's unabashed hostility, both poets treat the subject explicitly, using variants of the same word, 'tribade,' which despite its ambiguities clearly denoted at least two things: sex between women, and female masculinity, both culturally stigmatized at the time.[2]

Although, not surprisingly, women writers seem not to have invoked an explicitly tribadic muse, some managed subtly to suggest sex and love between women when alluding to Calliope & Company. One such example can be found among the commendatory verses prefacing Katherine Philips's posthumously published collection *Poems* (1667). As Elaine Hobby argues, "Philo-Philippa" ("Philips-Lover"), the anonymous author of "To the Excellent *Orinda*" (Philips's *nom de plume*), responds "in an equally coded manner" to the coded female homoeroticism of Philips's own poetry ([1991] 196).[3]

"To the Excellent *Orinda*" opens:

Let the male poets their male Phoebus choose,
Thee, I invoke, Orinda, for my muse;
He could but force a branch, Daphne her tree
Most freely offers to her sex and thee,
And says to verse so unconstrained as yours,
Her laurel freely comes, your fame secures:
And men no longer shall with ravished bays
Crown their forced poems by as forced a praise.

As Hobby insightfully argues, Philo-Philippa gives a lesbian twist to the tale of Apollo and Daphne from Ovid's *Metamorphoses* (Book I, *ll*.452–567). In the latter, Apollo, struck by Cupid's arrow, is inflamed with "love" for the nymph Daphne. But she's a marriage-resister:

---

[2] According to Brooten, *tribade* ultimately derives from Greek τριβας (*tribas* [with macron over α), "which probably derives from the verb *tribô*, 'to rub'..., but may also derive from *tribakos,* 'experienced'" (5). Introduced from Latin into French by Henri Estienne in *Apologie pour Hérodote* (1566), it quickly became the most common French word to refer to women who have sex with women, particularly in anatomical writing. It often (but by no means always) included the idea that such women had enlarged clitorises, with which they would penetrate other women (or, as Turner [2003] points out, young men [*xii*]). See Bonnet, as well as Andreadis (2001), Braunschneider, Lanser (2003b), Park, Traub (2002), Wahl, and especially Borris (2004) 19–20.

[3] On the homoeroticism of Philips's friendship poetry, see Wahl and Lange first, particularly on contemporaries' and followers' response to this aspect of the poems. Among other relevant discussions, most important are Andreadis, Barash, Easton, Hobby, Lilley, Loscocco, Price, and Traub (2002). Another lesbian-suggestive muse moment occurs in Cavendish's *The Lady Contemplation* (Robinson [2004]).

> Her, many sought: but she, averse to all,
> Unknowne to Man, nor brooking such a thrall
> Frequents the pathlesse Woods; and hates to prove,
> Nor cares to heare, what *Hymen*... is, or Love.
> Oft said her Father; Daughter, thou do'st owe
> A Son-in-law, who Nephews may bestowe.
> But she, who Marriage as a Crime eschew'd
> (Her Face with blushing shamefac'tnes imbew'd)
> Hung on his necke with fawning armes, and said,
> Deare Father, give me leave to live a Maid:
> This boone *Diana's* sire... did her afford. (Sandys, 38–39)

Like other tales about Diana and her nymphs, this one too, while stressing chastity, hints at female homoeroticism, a hint that comes through in Sandys's commentary on the poem (accompanying his 1632 translation), when he writes: "*Daphne affects Diana*, which is chastity: preserved by solitarinesse, labour, and neglect of Curiosity: Apollo *Daphne*; drawne on with a barren hope" (73). To *affect* meant to "aim at, aspire to,... seek to obtain or attain," but also to "be fond of,... fancy, like, or love." Apollo *affects* Daphne in both senses, seeking to obtain her precisely because he loves (i.e., *lusts after*) her. But "a Lover's name shee flyes:/ And emulating un-wed *Phoebe* [Diana],... joyes/ In spoyles of salvage Beasts, and sylvan Lares;/ A fillet binding her neglected haires" (38). Sandys's elaboration of his phrase "Daphne affects Diana" is thus accurate: imitating the huntress Diana, the nymph pursues a life of chastity. And yet the syntactic parallelism—Daphne affects Diana; Apollo, Daphne—suggests female homoeroticism, too.[4]

Such mismatching results in tragedy, at least for the huntress become the hunted. Pursued to exhaustion by a god who won't take 'no' for an answer, Daphne appeals to her river-god father for help: "May Earth, for too well pleasing; me devour:/ Or, by transforming, O destroy this shape,/ That thus betrayes me to undoing rape" (40). Instantly, the nymph is changed into a laurel tree, although retaining enough of her personality to shrink from Apollo's kisses. But when he declares, "Although thou canst not bee/ The wife I wisht, yet shalt thou be my Tree,/ Our Quiver, Harp, our Tresses never shorne,/ My Laurell,... thou shalt ever more adorne," she "all allowes:/ In signe whereof her gratefull head shee bowes" (41). Ever since, a metaphorical laurel wreath ("the bays") has crowned the brow of poets, presumptively male, who credit females with inspiring creative endeavor.

In Philo-Philippa's version of the story, as in Ovid's, love-making and poetry-making blur. But as Hobby argues, not only does Philo-Philippa's Daphne flee a man's sexual advances, she also, once transformed, "[m]ost freely offers" herself

---

[4] On homoerotic visual representation of Diana and her nymphs, see Simons's excellent article.

to other women, particularly Orinda. Philo-Philippa thus subjects Ovid's myth to a dissident reading, treating male poetic creation as rape, and female poetic creation as both natural and consensually erotic. And as Hobby notes, Philo-Philippa hints that just as Daphne freely offers herself to Orinda, Orinda, as befits a muse, offers herself, through her poetry, to Philo-Philippa, enabling the latter to bring forth "To the Excellent *Orinda*."[5]

Later in the poem, Philo-Philippa responds to yet another tale from the *Metamorphoses* in order to subtly suggest lesbian eroticism. The tale, "Iphis and Ianthe" (examined at length in chapters six and seven), involves a girl raised as a boy (Iphis), who falls in love with another girl (Ianthe), who believes herself in love with a boy. The night before their marriage, Iphis and her mother pray to Isis for help, and the goddess transforms Iphis's sex. The next morning the now opposite-sex couple is married.

Philo-Philippa mentions the tale while arguing that Orinda's literary achievements disprove women's inferiority (*ll.*23–38). After listing time-honored, misogynist teachings about women (they're incapable of rationality; they have no souls; they think of nothing but appearance and amusement), she charges men with purposefully fostering female inferiority. As she pithily puts it, "To keep their greatness, was to make us less" (*l.*38). Nurture rather than nature is to blame:

> Shall it be our reproach, that we are weak,
> And cannot fight, nor as the School-men speak?
> Even men themselves are neither strong nor wise,
> If Limbs and Parts they do not exercise.
>   Train'd up to Arms, we *Amazons* have been,
> And *Spartan* Virgins strong as *Spartan* Men:
> Breed Women but as Men, and they are these;
> Whilst *Sybarit* Men are Women by their ease.
> Why should not brave *Semiramis* break a Lance,
> And why should not soft *Ninyas* curle and dance?
> *Ovid* in vain Bodies with change did vex,
> Changing her form of life, *Iphis* chang'd Sex.
> Nature to Females freely doth impart
> That, which the Males usurp, a stout, bold heart.
> Thus Hunters female Beasts fear to assail:
> And female Hawks more metall'd than the male:
> Men ought not then Courage and Wit ingross,
> Whilst the Fox lives, the Lyon, or the Horse.
> Much less ought men both to themselves confine,
> Whilst Women, such as you, *Orinda*, shine. (*ll.*59–78)

---

[5] Lange (103–104) argues this point, too. For an interesting comparison, see Barash, Mermin, Straub (1987), and Teague on Anne Killigrew's "Upon the saying that my Verses were made by another" (1686).

Philo-Philippa asserts women and men's intellectual and even physical equality. "Breed Women but as Men," and women will excel as scholars and soldiers. Conversely, raise men like women, and you'll have "soft," "Sybarit" men, men who love sensuality and luxury, men who "curle and dance." A little later, Philo-Philippa even argues for female superiority: "'Tis true, *Apollo* sits as Judge of Wit,/ But the nine Female learned Troop are it:/ Those Laws, for which *Numa* did wise appear,/ Wiser *Ægeria* whisper'd in his ear" (*ll*.95–98).

Equally unconventional is her "argument from nature" (citing animal behavior as model or foil for humans), used since antiquity in discussions of eros, particularly when opposing homosexuality (Goldhill, 49–67). Ovid uses this very approach when Iphis bemoans her "unnatural" desire. But Philo-Philippa appeals to natural history to argue from the other side of the political spectrum. And although she's making a point about gender rather than homosexuality, the passage occurs in close proximity to the "Iphis and Ianthe" lines—lines that, as I'm about to argue, defend female homosexuality. Her feminist argument from nature thus refutes, albeit obliquely, Ovid's anti-lesbian one.

Philo-Philippa's Semiramis reference is likewise noteworthy. Whereas the warrior Queen of Babylon was famous among men more for lustfulness and cruelty than for battle prowess (reputedly spending the night with male soldiers and then having them killed), Philo-Philippa mentions only the martial aspect of her legend, presenting Semiramis as Amazon or Spartan virgin, rather than pitiless, and decidedly heterosexual, nymphomaniac.[6]

Then there's Ninyas, Semiramis's son and successor, who ignored his kingly duties in order to live a life of uninterrupted sensual indulgence. Philo-Philippa omits all suggestion of selfishness and irresponsibility, merely describing him as curling and dancing—not inherently objectionable activities. Indeed, the line's phrasing, "And why should not soft *Ninyas* curle and dance?"—following as it does the identically phrased, approving reference to Semiramis, "Why should not brave *Semiramis* break a Lance"—suggests the poet may not mind male effeminacy. She seems to feel that, what with the energy men spend enforcing unnatural differences between the sexes in order to keep women down, soft men who prefer to curl and dance might be a welcome change.

However, the reference to Iphis and Ianthe is the poem's most interesting moment, and certainly its most daring:

Ovid in vain Bodies with change did vex,
Changing her form of life, *Iphis* chang'd Sex.

Objecting to Ovid's solution to the "problem" of Iphis and Ianthe's love, Philo-Philippa makes a radical feminist distinction between sex and gender. Ovid was wrong to obsess over physical, anatomical change, she claims. What's really at

---

[6] See Holderness on Semiramis as "a focal point for early feminist debate" (97).

issue—what Ovid's unrealistic, authorially imposed, anatomical change obscures—is gender, what Philo-Philippa calls Iphis's "form of life."

Interestingly, Philo-Philippa makes Iphis the agent of transformation: she changed her form of life and thereby changed sex. But in Ovid's story, Iphis is acted upon rather than acts. Her mother raises her as a boy, changing her gender; Isis transforms her body, changing her sex. Philo-Philippa's revision thus exemplifies the poem's primary message: women can be subjects rather than objects, they can act rather than be acted upon, and if in doing so they follow Orinda's example, they can accomplish wonders.

In other words, Philo-Philippa engages in resistant reading. She recognizes that Ovid's intentions, as expressed through "Iphis and Ianthe," are antipathetic to her own. So she appropriates the story and rewrites it. There's no need for a physical sex-change. Ovid missed, and obscured, the important issue: because Iphis was taught to act like a boy, she was, for all intents and purposes, male. The most important part is not the miraculous, physical sex-change; on the contrary, by "vex[ing]" Iphis with this implausible metamorphosis, Ovid spoiled the story. Instead, what matters is the transformation of Iphis's allotted-at-birth gender. Despite all the propaganda about natural, immutable sex differences, all it took to make Iphis manly was raising her as a boy.

Like Philo-Philippa, Philips herself emphasizes the essential sameness and equality of the sexes: the essence of a person is the soul, which is neither male nor female, but human (e.g., "A Friend" [95, *ll*.19–24]). But Philo-Philippa is more daring, at least in her approving allusion to a story about clearly *sexual* love between females. She implicitly condones Iphis's lesbianism. Placing Ovid's character in a context that celebrates women who surpass their supposedly natural inferiority (Semiramis leading armies, Orinda writing top-notch poetry), Philo-Philippa endorses the real change Iphis underwent: the gender-change, rather than sex-change, from girl to boy. Of course, "To the Excellent *Orinda*" advocates a multifaceted gender-change for women, involving the use rather than suppression of their physical and intellectual talents. But in Ovid's story, prior to metamorphosis, the only "masculine" attribute Iphis evinces is sexual attraction to another girl. At worst, Philo-Philippa treats this specifically lesbian result of Iphis's upbringing as unobjectionable, and at best, as desirable.

Moreover, her "Iphis and Ianthe" reference seems implicitly to acknowledge that lesbianism is likely to come to mind for readers both of "To the Excellent *Orinda*" and of Philips's own poetry, the subject and occasion of Philo-Philippa's. And if some readers, in response to the argument that (im)properly raised women can do anything men can, are likely to think of one masculine activity only the latter can perform—having sex with women—Philo-Philippa's text says even *that* particular "form of life" is possible, and should be permissible.

Or rather *whispers*, not *says*, would be more accurate. The explicit subject of "To the Excellent *Orinda*" is Philips's poetic accomplishment as representative of women's potential to excel at conventionally masculine endeavors. Like Philips herself, Philo-Philippa maintains deniability. More precisely, while Philo-Philippa drops hairpins, and Philips platonizes (see above, x), both women rely upon their contemporaries' tendency to unknow the possibility of lesbianism among chaste, virtuous women. Thus the author of "To the Excellent *Orinda*" can call herself a "Philips-Lover" and count on *philo* being read, by most readers, as an innocent declaration of friendly love—of *amity*—rather than romantic or carnal *amour*. Aside from self-consciously naughty gossips like Brantôme and du Guast, only readers sensitive to pro-lesbian meanings would be likely to register the ones Philo-Philippa discreetly offers.[7]

* * * * * *

As I suggested in my preface, the reluctance on the part of LGBT historians and critics to investigate or even acknowledge pre- and early modern closeting is surely related to the less-than-sterling reputation that reading for authorial intention acquired in the wake of Wimsatt and Beardsley's unmasking of "the intentional fallacy," Barthes's announcement of "the death of the author," and Derrida's deconstruction of language, writing, meaning, and virtually everything else. Countless critics have benefited from the challenges offered by these and other theorists to longstanding assumptions about textual meaning—its creation, location, transmission. So have countless teachers: any instructor who has successfully disabused students of the notion that literature means whatever you want it to mean soon finds herself battling the reduction of all textual interpretation to a search for authorial intention, reassuringly singular and knowable. Faced with such interpretive naiveté, and the intellectual inflexibility that often undergirds it, even those of us disenchanted with Theory begin to sound like fellow travelers, arguing that textual meaning often proves contradictory, ambiguous, or slippery, and that, for understanding a literary work's potential meanings, extratextual fields and contexts (historical, cultural, linguistic, psychological, anthropological, philosophical...) can prove equally revealing as, even *more* revealing than, the author's biography.

Yet one extreme has replaced another. Before New Criticism championed the text, the whole text, and nothing but the text, literary interpretation devolved too often into biography; ever since, biography has been largely banished from legitimate criticism and theory. Or rather, it's been relegated to the margins, interesting in its way but inferior to serious theory and criticism, or hidden in the shadows, where many of us bolster textual interpretation with biographical evidence, yet avoid acknowledging, let alone theorizing, what we're doing. For LGBT Studies and the History of Sexuality, one of the consequences of thus

---

[7] On amity and amour, see Wahl. On the nuances of Ovid's "Iphis and Ianthe," see below, ch.6.

devaluing authorial biography is obliviousness—sometimes genuine, sometimes willful—to the possibility of closeted writing.

Since we don't know Philo-Philippa's identity, biographical information is irrelevant to reading "To the Excellent *Orinda*" as coded lesbian writing. It's even possible she wasn't really a woman, a possibility Philips herself registered, writing to a friend that "[Philo-Philippa] pretends to be a woman, writes very well, but I cannot imagine who the Author is, nor by any Inquiry I can make, have hitherto been able to discover" (Philips [1990], Letter 26, II:78; quoted in Andreadis, 199, n.59). What we know for certain is the poem is written in the voice of a woman; takes issue with two well-known Ovidian tales; and generates, in the process, counter-stories that might be read as affirming erotic love between women—counter-stories that, in the context of the poem as a whole, might encourage, and serve as evidence for, a lesbian-affirmative reading of Philips's own poetry.

While I still prefer to speculate about Philo-Philippa's intentions, I would thus not go to the mat with anti-intentionalist, anti-biographical colleagues over "To the Excellent *Orinda*." I would, however, over *Les Memoires De Madame La Comtesse De M* (1697), by Henriette de Castelnau, comtesse de Murat. In her case, authorial biography all but compels a verdict of closeted writing.

The Abominable Madame de Murat

Several of the turn-of-the-eighteenth-century reports of Parisian lieutenant-general of police René d'Argenson recount the scandalous behavior of a noblewoman who flaunted, among other shocking practices and beliefs, her lesbianism. Under the heading "Disorders of Madame de Murat," d'Argenson writes:

> *6 December 1699.* — I have the honor to send you the memoir that it pleased you to ask of me, concerning madame de Murat; it is not easy to express in detail all the disorders of her conduct, without wounding the rules of decency [*l'honnesteté*], and the public is pained to see a lady of this birth in such shameful and such flaunted [*déclaré*] dissoluteness.

> *24 February 1700.* — …The crimes that are imputed to madame de Murat are not of a kind that can be easily proven by means of information, since it has to do with domestic impieties and a monstrous attachment to persons of her sex. However, I would like very much to know what she would respond to the following facts:
> A portrait pierced with several knife cuts, by the jealousy of a woman whom she loved and whom she left, several months ago, to attach herself to madame de Nantiat, another woman of the utmost dissoluteness, less known for the fines levied against her because of gaming, than for the disorder of her morals [*mœurs*]. This woman, lodged at her home, is the object of her continuous adoration, in the presence even of valets and some pawnbrokers.
> The execrable oaths proffered while gaming and the infamous discussions over the

dining table, to which M. the comte de Roussilon, now on bad terms with [*brouillé avec*] madame de Murat, was witness.

Dissolute songs sung during the night and at all hours.

The insolence to piss out the window, after a long debauch.

Her impudent [*audacieuse*] conversation with M. the vicar of Saint-Cosme, equally removed from both *modesty* [*pudeur*] *and religion.*

1 December 1701. — ...I will add, in regard to madame de Murat of whom this memoir makes mention, that she has returned to Paris after an absence of eight days, that she has reconciled with madame de Nantiat, and that the horrors and abominations of their reciprocal friendship justly horrify all their neighbors.

4 December 1701. — I take the liberty of sending you a letter that I received, this morning, concerning the abominable conduct of mesdames de Murat and de Nantiat, who create new public scenes every day: the writing of this letter appears constrained, and one can easily suspect that the reconciliation of these two women has excited sentiments of jealousy or vengeance in the heart of a third, who reigned previously over that of madame de Murat; but the blasphemies, the obscenities and the drunkenness with which they are reproached are not less true for that. Thus, I hope that the King will very much want to use his authority to expel them from Paris or even to imprison them, if one cannot do otherwise.[8]

By the time these reports were written, the author was able to draw upon a longstanding anti-lesbian rhetorical tradition, one that offered a variety of tones, motifs, structures, and strategies for confronting the troubling notion that women might not only love but also have sex with other women, and that some even *preferred* such relationships (Robinson [1998] ch.1). Here, the chief anti-lesbian rhetorical strategy is demonization. D'Argenson depicts lesbianism as something that, as Claude Courouve puts it (in discussing the term *abominable*), "inspires terror and repulsion" (35), referring to lesbianism as "a monstrous attachment for persons of her sex," and speaking of "the horrors and abominations of their reciprocal friendship [which] justly horrify all their neighbors," and of "the abominable conduct of mesdames de Murat and de Nantiat." D'Argenson combines the tried-and-true idea of lesbian monstrosity with traditional religious condemnation of homosexuality.[9]

---

[8] Under the gracious auspices of the editors, this half of the chapter originally appeared, in different form, in Merrick and Sibalis (2001). Merrick kindly helped me fine-tune the translations. He and Ragan translate the passages in their documentary collection (2001). For more on d'Argenson's reports and Murat's life and work, see Wahl, as well as Bonnet ([1995] 80–81), whom I regret having failed to cite in my original article. I also regret having inadvertently metamorphosed *Micheline* Cuénin into *Michel.*

[9] Note that *abominable* was frequently used, including by d'Argenson himself, to characterize *male* sodomites and their activities in the seventeenth and eighteenth centuries

******

Most early twenty-first-century readers wouldn't be surprised at d'Argenson's horrified moralizing. While very much current today, it's what one expects to encounter in a text (particularly a police report) written three hundred years ago. Of course, anyone familiar with gossip and scandal novels of the period, such as Delarivier Manley's *The New Atalantis* (1709) or Anthony Hamilton's *Mémoires de la Vie du Comte de Grammont* (1713), has encountered a markedly different anti-lesbian tone: the amused condescension of the man or woman of the world (an amusement that, as I argue in chapter five, masks a good deal of anxiety; see also Sedgwick [1988] and D.A. Miller [1989]). Indeed, both *The New Atalantis* and *Grammont* provide masterful examples of a tongue-in-cheek rhetorical strategy I call 'mock ignorance.' When a character such as Manley's Lady Intelligence exclaims, "Two beautiful ladies joined in an excess of amity... innocently embrace! For how can they be guilty? They vow eternal tenderness, they exclude the men, and condition that they will always do so. What irregularity can there be in this?" (154), her pose of innocence and ignorance merely underscores the *knowingness* of everyone involved—author, characters, and readers. Simultaneously mocking lesbians on the one hand, and moralistic, prudish lesbophobes on the other, author and readers of such texts congratulate themselves and one another on their sophisticated superiority.

The period saw other approaches to discussing and representing lesbianism, however. In contrast to d'Argenson's horrified moralism and Manley's arch-but-anxious worldliness, Madame de Villedieu, in her best-selling *Mémoires de la vie de Henriette-Sylvie de Molière* (1672), evinces an untroubled neutrality. In this extremely popular novel (English tr. 1672 [pts. 1–2], 1677 [pts. 1–6]), the countess d'Englesac, enemy of Henriette-Sylvie, attempts to turn the queen mother and the entire court against her. But Henriette-Sylvie receives protection from an interesting quarter:

> [T]he good & virtuous Madame _____ was still on my side. She loved passionately, said she, beautiful women, & the desire [for] the vermilion of my lips had made her come to be one of my friends, in order to be able to kiss me to her heart's content sometimes; (what will your Highness say about this effect of my beauty?) this desire, I say, having attached to my interests a person like that; it was impossible for the Comtesse d'Englesac to succeed further in her initial designs.... (147–48)

As recent editor Micheline Cuénin points out, the lady portrayed here as having lesbian tendencies is associated with *les dévotes*, a pious crowd at court

---

(Courouve, 35–38; Merrick [1997]). Small as it is, this detail suggests that a bigendered category encompassing both tribadism and male sodomy may have been conceivable long before the mid-nineteenth-century "invention" of modern homosexuality.

overlapping with, although not identical to, the learned, literary women disparagingly dubbed *les précieuses*. Yet whereas most ascriptions of lesbianism to *les précieuses* occur in satirical, anti-*précieuse* contexts (see Wahl), this passage is neutral. Although there is *some* amusement in the narrator's voice ("what will Your Highness say about this effect of my beauty?"), or at least an implicit suggestion that Madame _____'s desire is unusual, neither the text nor any of its characters denigrate the lesbian. At worst, this "good & virtuous" woman might seem shallow, motivated by Henriette-Sylvie's beauty. But so are several of her male protectors. And unlike them, Madame _____ never tries to take sexual advantage of Henriette-Sylvie's vulnerability. What's more, other characters' *bad* opinion of the heroine, as opposed to Madame _____'s *good* one, is at least equally ill-founded. And since Madame _____ successfully protects Henriette-Sylvie, for whom readerly sympathies have been engaged, it's likely at least some readers would have responded positively to this female character who voices same-sex desire.

But if, for some readers, such slightly amused tolerance refutes the common assumption that past societies have been uniformly anti-gay and anti-lesbian, for others it risks confirming the competing belief, particularly prevalent until recently among differentist scholars, that lesbianism simply didn't signify, didn't matter, in times past, because it doesn't include a penis (unlike male homosexuality) and can't result in pregnancy (unlike heterosexual fornication and adultery).[10]

* * * * * *

Yet if moralistic condemnation, libertine mockery, and amused tolerance all seem believable late seventeenth-century responses to lesbianism, what most readers today would *not* expect to find in a turn-of-the-eighteenth-century text is a pro-lesbian rejoinder to anti-lesbian thinking. At least one such text has been identified: Aphra Behn's poem "To The Fair Clarinda Who Made Love To Me, Imagin'd More Than Woman" (1688). So far as I know, it's the closest thing to a clearly sexual, lesbian-affirmative text written by a woman for public circulation in early modern or eighteenth-century England or France. As other critics have noted, Behn seems playfully to exploit phallocentric definitions of sex as necessarily involving a penis, definitions according to which sex between women is a contradiction in terms, "innocent" because insignificant, in both senses of the latter ('unimportant' and 'meaningless'). Behn's speaker thus declares,

---

[10] The most nuanced version of this perspective (distinguishing "femme-femme" love from the figure of the tribade) is Traub's early influential article (1992b). Her recent book, like Wahl's and Andreadis's, documents mounting anxiety over the course of the seventeenth century, particularly the latter half, regarding sex and love between women.

In pity to our Sex sure thou wert sent,
That we might Love, and yet be Innocent:
For sure no Crime with thee we can commit;
Or if we shou'd—thy Form excuses it. (*ll.*12–15)

Here and throughout, "To the Fair Clarinda" exemplifies dissident pro-lesbian writing, lightheartedly hijacking anti-lesbian rhetoric and turning it against itself, so that strategies intended to erase or contain lesbianism encourage it instead.[11]

In addition to anti-lesbian writing of both the earnest and arch varieties, as well as tolerant if amused texts such as *Henriette-Sylvie,* Behn's poem responds to and exploits the graphic depiction of sex between women in late seventeenth-century writing, such as Chorier's *Satyra Sotadica* (1660); its French translation/adaptation, *L'Academie des dames* (1680); the anonymous *L'Escole Des Filles* (1655; 1668); and Barrin's *Vénus dans le cloître* (1683).[12] Behn could count on much of her libertine audience having read scenes like the following—perhaps this scene itself, from Barrin's *Vénus*—in which, as two young nuns share both verbal and physical intimacy, the languages of ideal friendship and female same-sex sexuality become indistinguishable:

> *Angélique.* — ...Let me embrace you so that our hearts speak to one another in the midst of our kisses.
> *Agnès.* — Oh God! how you squeeze me in your arms! Are you dreaming that I'm naked but for my nightshirt? Oh! you set me all afire!
> *Angélique.* — Ah! how the ruby redness with which you are enlivened at present augments the brightness of your beauty! Ah how this fire that now shines in your eyes makes you pleasing!...
> There's no doubt my most dear one, and you'll remark in what follows that there's nothing sweeter in the world than to have a true friend, who can be the depository of our secrets, of our thoughts, and of our afflictions also. Ah! how soothing it is to open the heart in such occasions! So speak, my darling, I'm going to sit on your bed close to you. It's not necessary for you to get dressed, the season will let you stay as you are; it seems to me that you're more pleasing this way and that, the closer you approach to the state in which nature gave birth to you, the more charm and beauty you have. Embrace me, my dear Agnès, before beginning, and confirm by your kisses the mutual protestations we

---

[11] For a fuller reading, see Robinson (2001a); cf. Faderman, Stiebel, and especially Andreadis, Traub (2002), and Wahl, whose readings overlap with mine at many points. For a very different interpretation, see Ballaster (1992), Lange, and Martin, all of whom argue for the duality, fluidity, or indeterminacy of Clarinda's sex. I find their readings interesting but unconvincing, mostly because the poem's title signals that Clarinda is indeed a woman, and that her gender-shifting and gender-blending is a flight of fancy.

[12] On the publication dates and various versions of *Vénus dans le cloître,* see Turner (2003) and Foxon. Barrin's authorship is uncertain.

made to love one another eternally. Ah! how pure and innocent these kisses are! Ah! how they're filled with tenderness and sweetness! Ah! how they fill me up with pleasure! A little respite, my little heart, I'm all on fire, you make me desperate [*tu me mets aux abois*] with your caresses. Oh God! love is powerful! and what will become of me if simple kisses transport and stimulate me so sharply?

Agnès. — Ah! how difficult it is to keep within the limits of one's duty when we give free rein so many times to this passion! Would you believe it, Angélique? These triflings (*badineries*), which, at bottom, are nothing, have acted marvelously on me. Ah! ah! ah! let me breathe a bit, I feel like my heart is too tight right now! Ah! how these sighs relieve me! I'm beginning to feel a new affection for you, stronger and more tender than before. I don't know where it's coming from; can simple kisses cause such disorder in a soul? (20, 24–26)

If Philips purports or is supposed to use erotic language metaphorically, to express spiritual feelings, Angélique uses spiritual language to express erotic feelings ("there's nothing sweeter in the world than to have a true friend"; "Ah! how pure and innocent these kisses are!"). This nun, however, is no innocent. Skeptical about religion, critical of patriarchy, and pragmatic to the point of cynicism about life in a repressive environment, Angélique is thoroughly capable of employing the exalted, supposedly nonsexual language of friendship to cover lesbian desire and activity, which would otherwise lead to trouble with convent authorities. "Mrs. B.," wooing Clarinda, takes a page from Angélique's instruction manual, although for more clearly pro-lesbian purposes.[13]

* * * * * *

To return, at last, to the abominable, or admirable, Madame de Murat: it's my contention she authors another pro-lesbian text of the period—or rather, a pro-lesbian textual moment, a brief swipe at anti-lesbian crusaders that culminates in a subtle, closeted, but nonetheless amusing lesbian joke. Her novel *Les Memoires De Madame La Comtesse De M* (1697), which Joan DeJean describes as an "allegedly autobiographical work by a notorious woman" ([1991] 258, n.26), purports to be the first-person heroine's attempt to restore her reputation, sullied by accusations of sexual misconduct. While virtually all her suspected misdeeds are heterosexual, at one point the heroine and her female domestic partner are accused of maintaining a lesbian relationship:

---

[13] On the form of lesbophobia exemplified by such pornographic (pseudo)lesbian *badinerie*, see ch.4. On the intertwining of male and female homoerotic/platonic/friendship discourse, as well as homophobic and lesbophobic discourse that mimics it, see ch.5.

The absence of Saint-Albe left his wife at full liberty to exercise her hatred against me;... finally she resolved to work to ruin me entirely, & to succeed in that she took it into her head to compose some Letters herself, in which she said horrible things of Mademoiselle Laval and me; these Letters were put into the hands of the [Spiritual] Director of whom I have already spoken, who imagining that the glory of God demanded that he revenge himself for the little store I set by his counsels, with a hypocritical circumspection had them shown to Mademoiselle Laval's Husband, then to my Mother & Husband; he didn't rest there, he found means to have the Queen informed of my bad conduct, & to beg her to interpose her authority, to remedy the disorders about which he groaned & of which it would have taken him nothing to see the falsity, if he had wanted to take the trouble to examine by whom these Letters had been given to him, but Prudence & Charity are virtues that false zeal does not know....

When reputation is torn apart by the indiscreet zeal of the falsely devout, it is an evil without remedy. The Letters of which I have spoken caused a great stir; Madame de Châtillon warned me that even the Queen had heard tell of them, & that an order was solicited from that Princess to imprison us, Mademoiselle Laval and me. All that was done, as I have already said, through the pious efforts of the Director of whom I have spoken. I do not doubt at all that our enemies would have obtained what they wished, if Madame de Châtillon, had not had the goodness to disabuse the Queen, but she justified me, in such a manner that the Director could not harm us.

Nevertheless Madame de Châtillon counseled us to go live in a Community, until my husband and Mademoiselle Laval's had been obliged to render us justice[;] we followed this counsel, & I can say that we followed it without repugnance. (v.2; 88–94)[14]

As in much indisputably homophobic writing, which treats homosexuality as a sin, indeed *the* sin, not to be named among Christians, lesbianism is referred to here in vague yet effective terms: "horrible things" (*des choses horribles*), the strongest words so far used to describe any of the accusations leveled at the narrator, and a phrase that will be echoed in d'Argenson's reference to "the horrors" of Murat's relationship with Nantiat. And yet the passage's antipathy is directed squarely at those who try to ruin women by accusing them of such things in the hopes of inciting royal punishment, as in real life d'Argenson would do a few years later, with success (Murat and Nantiat were placed under house arrest in separate chateaux).

This approach (skewering anti-lesbian crusaders while barely pausing to condemn lesbianism itself), combined with what we know of Murat's subsequent reported behavior, might lead us to question whether she really endorses her heroine's characterization of such acts as "horrible things." So might the fact that heroine and friend are advised to move into an all-female community in order to *prevent* further suspicion. As Christopher Rivers explains, in ancien régime France the convent was a paradoxical place, "both part of... society and removed from it, a commonplace and an enigma, simultaneously quotidian and exotic to those outside its walls" (387). The

---

[14] DeJean's book (258, n.28) alerted me to Murat's representation of anti-lesbian accusation.

convent offered both freedom and imprisonment. Some women sought refuge there from abusive husbands; others were confined by husbands wanting wayward spouses kept under surveillance. In both cases, the desirability of a convent was predicated upon the assumption that it guaranteed its inhabitants' "virtue": by excluding men it excluded sexuality. And yet, it was precisely in its relationship to sexuality that the paradoxical nature of the convent was most evident. In his study of libertine convent novels, Rivers makes this point particularly well: "The convent novels often articulate the notions that interdiction serves to heighten, not diminish, sexual desire and that the true secret of the cloister is the fact that it shuts sexuality in as well as out" (388). In other words, while Murat's readers knew that having recourse to a convent in order to safeguard a woman's reputation was a routine practice, they also knew "what goes on in convents": that they were sites of license, especially lesbian license.[15]

Might not, then, Madame de Châtillon's counsel, and the two women's following it "without repugnance," be a surreptitious joke aimed at lesbian or pro-lesbian readers? Another d'Argenson entry about the abominable Murat strengthens this suspicion. The policeman writes:

> *11 February 1702.* — ...Madame de Murat continues to distinguish herself by her ardors [*emportemens*] and by the disorder of her morals [*mœurs*]. She knows that the King is informed of them; but she counts on there not being found a single religious community bold enough to receive her. I do not think, actually, that there is one, and I could not have a good opinion of those that would want to run the risks: thus, what other course could one take, in regard to a woman of this character, than to lock her up in a distant château, where [a sum of] 100 écus will suffice for her subsistence and for that of the oldest female servant one could choose? (94)

I can't help but have the same doubts about the community that accepts Murat's heroine and her friend. Or, to be more precise: noticing that Murat's text unknows the by then well-known association (both real and imagined) between nunneries and lesbianism, and seeing that several years later Murat is reportedly well able to conceive of the suspicions aroused by a female religious community taking in a woman accused of lesbianism, I consider it quite probable she's having some

---

[15] I thank Merrick for that last formulation. On the association between nunneries and lesbianism, see, e.g., Marvell's "Upon Appleton House," Cavendish's *The Convent of Pleasure* (about a nonreligious convent), and *Vénus dans le cloître*. Other types of female communities and community spaces, such as boarding schools, brothels, harems, and public baths, were regularly associated with sex between women, sometimes as permanent arrangement, sometimes as initiation preparatory to the "real thing" (e.g., *EROTOPOLIS. The Present State of Betty-Land* [London, 1684] 148–49). See Traub (2002) on seventeenth-century lesbian-relevant representations of convents, harems, bathhouses, and Diana & nymphs; Turner (2003) on *Vénus dans le cloître*; below, ch.5, on the "new Cabal" in Manley's *New Atalantis*; Wahl on the *précieuses*; Donoghue on some of these texts, as well as later ones; Weigert and Simons on earlier material.

covert pro-lesbian fun, treating her allegedly autobiographical heroine and that heroine's female friend to a sojourn in an all-female community, as if rewarding them for weathering a bout of anti-lesbian persecution.

* * * * * *

Like the plays I examine in chapter seven, "To the Excellent *Orinda*" attests to the usefulness of Ovid's *Metamorphoses* for early modern writers interested in addressing sexual love between women. It attests as well to the longstanding interrelation of feminist and lesbian thought. And if for nothing else, the subtle pro-lesbian suggestiveness of Philo-Philippa's poem is significant for what it says about how Philips's own poetry may have been read by at least some of her readers. After all, Philips is once again a canonical seventeenth-century poet. But what does Murat's joke—a fleeting moment in an obscure, otherwise heterosexually focused text—really matter?

As with so many questions, the answer depends on one's perspective. In "Paranoid Reading and Reparative Reading" (1997), Sedgwick borrows the concept of strong versus weak theory from psychologist Silvan Tomkins, who himself borrows it from systems theory. Strong theories strive for universal validity, weak theories for local validity. As Tomkins explains in *Affect, Imagery, Consciousness* (1963):

> Any theory of wide generality is capable of accounting for a wide spectrum of phenomena which appear to be very remote, one from the other, and from a common source. This is a commonly accepted criterion by which the explanatory power of any scientific theory can be evaluated. To the extent to which the theory can account only for "near" phenomena, it is a weak theory, little better than a description of the phenomena which it purports to explain. As it orders more and more remote phenomena to a single formulation, its power grows. (v.2, 433–44; in Sedgwick, 13)

As a field, the History of Sexuality has been enamored of strong theory ever since the first volume of Foucault's paradigm-altering trilogy first appeared. And if one is more or less satisfied with revising Foucault's claims; if one is convinced by formulations that posit the "invention" of homosexuality in the late nineteenth (or early eighteenth or late seventeenth) century, or the "insignificance" of lesbianism prior to the mid-seventeenth (or mid-eighteenth or early twentieth) century, one can simply dismiss Murat's little joke as a curiosity or exception.

But if one is dissatisfied with our field's strong theories; if one believes their acceptance is premature; if one regards them as hypotheses not borne out by the available evidence, too often dismissed as mere exception because it contradicts the reigning theoretical paradigm, then this fleeting fictional moment might seem quite significant, quite suggestive, indeed. It might suggest, for instance, that a great deal more primary research remains to be done before we can make broad generalizations about the history of homosexuality that are adequately grounded historically. One might be struck, as I am, by the potential for isolated moments in little-known texts otherwise unconcerned with same-sex eroticism to trouble the grand historical narratives ascendant in our field, narratives based on material with which many of us are by now quite familiar (cf. Borris [2004]).

Not that entire works, even familiar ones, can't surprise us as well. In a recent article (Robinson [2004]), I demonstrate as much by examining Margaret Cavendish's fantastical prose fiction *The Blazing World*. In that essay (omitted from this book with infinite regret, for considerations of length), I argue for reading *The Blazing World* as closeted lesbian writing, in which the author takes platonic love between women to an incoherent and comic extreme, where its definition (spiritual, innocent, nonsexual) can no longer be taken for granted. Other interpretations of course are possible. Given Cavendish's strategies of both daring self-assertion and deliberate self-protection, even mystification (not unlike Philips, Behn, and Manley's), it's no accident one can read *The Blazing World* as knowingly, albeit covertly, pro-lesbian; or unconsciously if suggestively homoerotic; or even read it and never think of lesbianism at all. Portions of Cavendish's audience would have read the work in each of these ways. But the pro-lesbian interpretation has, until recently, eluded even attentive Cavendish scholars. What I therefore try to demonstrate is how much more available it was to some of Cavendish's seventeenth-century readers—those inclined to laugh at platonic love, and smile at lesbian love—than later critics have tended to assume.[16]

But such understanding requires a kind of reading most of us have been trained to avoid, one that ("Intentional Fallacy" and "Death of the Author" be damned!) speculates about what an actual human being meant to say, and searches for contradictions not only to reveal an author's slip-ups, but also, perhaps, her only partial cover-ups, her winks and signals to those in the know. In this chapter, I've offered such a reading of moments from little-known texts, Philo-Philippa's poem and Madame de Murat's novel. In the next chapter, I offer such a reading of a seminal (and priapic) achievement of eighteenth-century fiction.

---

[16] Cf. Velasco; also Hammond (2002), for similar treatment of platonic love by seventeenth-century English writers wishing to create textual space for *male* homoeroticism, "writers [who] deploy various kinds of indefinition, using a language which permitted multiple interpretations and allowed scope for denying dangerous constructions," "writers [who] engage in the pleasures of teasing their readers with homoerotic possibilities,... for readers [who] enjoy the pleasures of teasing out half-secret meanings" (6–7). As for Robinson (2004), it requires the following correction: near the bottom of page 147, the numbered items should *not* be numbered, but rather set apart from the rest of the paragraph like the items at the top of the next page. The erroneously numbered sentences constitute a single item (namely, the first of "three ways to understand the Duchess's reasoning").

Chapter 3

The Closeting of Closeting: Cleland, Smollett, Sodomy, and the Critics

Cleland's "Putative Homosexuality": Gay and Feminist Criticism on *Memoirs of a Woman of Pleasure*

My major example of closeted writing—John Cleland's pornographic classic, *Memoirs of a Woman of Pleasure* (1748–49), popularly known as *Fanny Hill*—has received a great deal of gay, lesbian, queer, feminist, and otherwise anti-homophobic critical attention. As Peter Sabor demonstrates in an outstanding review essay (2000), during the latter half of the twentieth century critics gradually went from seeing *Memoirs* as homophobic to seeing it as "an innovative text that recognizes the polymorphous nature of sexuality" (569). I largely agree with his account of this critical evolution. But I wish to emphasize something at which he only obliquely hints, in his concluding prediction:

> I believe that the present decade might see a fruitful combination of gender and queer theory approaches to *Memoirs of a Woman of Pleasure* with further historical research. While readings of the novel have become increasingly reluctant to take a notoriously elusive text at face-value, and ever more adept at exploring its subtextual ramifications, they have not taken full advantage of research that has added much to our knowledge of its author, his milieu, and his oeuvre. (573)

In contrast, or as supplement, to Sabor's account of the rise of gay, queer, and feminist interpretations of *Memoirs*, I want to foreground a different trend over the course of the 1990s: as critics boldly eyed the text's homoerotic and queer meanings, they pointedly overlooked its author. Few critics have ventured to suggest, and only in passing, that Cleland purposely wrote a homoerotic text. Yet the case for reading *Memoirs* as, at least in part, closeted homosexual writing is remarkably strong. Close reading of both the novel itself and the context provided by other mid-century depictions of sodomitical men (such as Smollett's *Roderick Random* and *Peregrine Pickle*, Charke's *Henry Dumont*, Garrick's *Miss in Her Teens*, and the anonymous *Satan's Harvest Home*) argues persuasively for a veiled pro-sodomitical message.

As Sabor details, until the mid-to-late 1980s critics routinely generalized the homophobia expressed by some of *Memoirs*' characters to the novel as a whole. Two factors prompted reassessment. Most important was the publication in 1985 of new critical editions (one by Sabor, one by Peter Wagner) that reinstated the text's bowdlerized sodomitical episode. The other was a pioneering 1981 essay in which Nancy K. Miller interpreted Cleland as a textual female impersonator, narcissistically bonding with other men through his novel's protagonist. Following Miller's lead, and supplied with irresistible new material by Sabor and Wagner, scholars in Gay Studies, Gender Studies, and the History of Sexuality turned their attention to sexuality and gender in *Memoirs*, producing dramatically different readings from their predecessors. Yet the possibility that Cleland's novel might be a closeted text received little consideration.

Considering the influence of Sabor's edition, this neglect is rather surprising. For in his introduction Sabor explicitly raised the possibility of Cleland's same-sex orientation, reporting some of the supporting biographical evidence:

> [Cleland's] isolation and bitterness [late in life] must have had social, as well as literary origins. In 1781 Josiah Beckwith found it understandable 'that he should pass under the Censure of being a Sodomite, as he now does, and in Consequence thereof Persons of Character decline visiting him, or cultivating his Acquaintance'.... The rumour might have had a factual basis (Cleland seems never to have married) or have evolved because of the homosexual episode in the *Memoirs*.... In either case, the elderly Cleland, with his quirky views, captious personality and shabby-genteel surroundings, is a figure on the margins of society. (xiii; quoting Merritt, 306)

Tellingly, not even Sabor's own reading of the novel integrated this information. Thus, in a note on the "due vengeance" one character predicts will overtake the novel's sodomites, Sabor wrote:

> Two pamphlets published in 1749 took opposite stands on the question: the anonymous *Satan's Harvest Home* denounced homosexuality, but Thomas Cannon's *Ancient and Modern Pederasty investigated and exemplified* was written, according to Cleland himself, 'evidently in defence of *Sodomy*'.... Since Cleland's alleged debt of £820 that produced his year-long imprisonment was to Cannon, the anti-homosexual diatribe in the *Memoirs* might have had a personal motivation. Ironically, Cleland was subsequently accused of homosexuality himself.... ("Explanatory Notes," 201)

Although Sabor apparently believed the character's "anti-homosexual diatribe" to be endorsed by Cleland, his evidence easily supports the opposite conclusion. Cleland wrote a novel with a long, explicit, male-male sex scene; "seems never to have married"; in later life "pass[ed] under the Censure of being a Sodomite"; and knew—well enough to borrow a large sum of money from—a man who published a pamphlet defending sodomy, at a time no respectable member of society publicly questioned that sodomy was, to use Fanny's term, "odious" (156). Wouldn't it make more sense to speculate, *at least as a working hypothesis*, that the accusations of sodomy were true, and that, whatever the nature of Cleland's conflict with Cannon, his characters' condemnations of sodomy were meant to appease dominant morality?[1]

Much to Sabor's credit, in his review essay he does consider that possibility, revising his earlier assumption that Cleland endorses his characters' homophobia (564). Yet forty years after J.H. Plumb "hint[ed] at Cleland's putative homosexuality" in the introduction to a 1965 edition of *Memoirs* (Sabor [2003] 563), seriously considering the possibility *Memoirs* is a closeted text is almost unheard of. Only a handful of critics have done so.

The earliest was Julia Epstein (1989). Whereas Miller had read *Memoirs* as "female impersonation" promoting narcissistic male bonding (e.g., 50), what Miller pathologized as "narcissism" Epstein called "homoeroticism." The difference in perspective was significant, leading Epstein to assert, for instance, "Cleland creates a female voice that thinly disguises a masquerading homoerotic male voice" (140). Epstein also posited a radical rather than retrograde use of disguise: instead of seeking merely to bond with other men at the expense of women, Cleland attempts "to get away... with a complex critique of the politics of sexual ambiguity in the eighteenth century" (149).

Nevertheless, like Miller, Epstein ultimately conflated the homosocial and homosexual. Indeed, acknowledging the heated terminological debates among historians of sexuality, she admitted she "ha[d] not resolved the lexical difficulties, but rather ha[d] variously used the terms 'homosexual,' 'homoerotic,' and 'homosocial' in [her] essay" (152, n.17). Yet such "various" use of the terms rendered *homophobia* invisible. *Memoirs* may indeed exhibit "a homoerotic phallocentrism" (148), in which homosociality and homosexuality merge. Yet the novel explicitly foregrounds a major obstacle: homophobia. In contrast, Epstein's terminological looseness (e.g., 147) erased the novel's own concern with homophobia, and the possibility Cleland meant to write, in part, for other men aware of homophobia's contradictions and sodomy's attractions. Conflating sexual and nonsexual male bonding obscured the explicitly sexual desire some men felt for others, the sex acts some of them engaged in, and the anti-sodomitical condemnation of their desire and activity.

The only critic to make a sustained case for reading *Memoirs* as a closeted text is Donald Mengay (1992). Like Epstein, he saw the homoerotic potential of Miller's sexist, narcissistic, "transsexual" Fanny (e.g., 188). Yet he also noticed Miller's brief, concluding acknowledgment of homophobia (57), in which, as Mengay put it, "[s]he suggests that social constraints—in essence, homophobia—and not necessarily narcissism forced Cleland to use a female persona to avoid a too blatant picture of inversion" (188). In his short but daring piece, Mengay

---

[1] On Cannon and his pamphlet (no copy of which has survived), see Foxon (who reprints Cleland's letter) and William Epstein.

argued for reading *Memoirs* as not merely "homoerotic" but specifically "homosexual" (or "bisexual"), and written with a full awareness of the constraints imposed by homophobia.

Over the next eleven years, only one other published work, Lisa Moore's *Dangerous Intimacies* (1997), seriously suggested such an interpretation (although in somewhat different terms). Moore "consider[ed] the construction in *Memoirs*... of a 'phallocentric' male homosexuality and... trace[d] its relation to female homosexuality and female sexual agency in the novel" (57–58). In the course of her argument, she raised the possibility of Cleland's homosexuality (58–59), concluding that "Whether the spur is textual, biographical, or both, it seems clear that part of the scandal surrounding *Memoirs of a Woman of Pleasure* is the scandal of homosexuality" (59). And part of the reason for Cleland's scandalous treatment of both male and female homosexuality, she argued, is his writing for a variety of intended readers, including homosexual ones.[2]

Not that other readings are necessarily wrong, much less uninteresting. Precisely because of homophobia's contradictions, critics who assume a homophobic authorial presence behind *Memoirs* can still produce insights that converge with Mengay's and Moore's. Three studies from the 1990s (Edelman [1991/1994], Kopelson [1992], McFarlane [1997]) exemplify this convergence.[3]

Although drawing upon different theorists and critics (respectively, Derrida; Barthes and Stallybrass & White; Dollimore), each study portrayed *Memoirs* as a paradigmatically homophobic text, in which the dominant, heterosexist order undoes itself. Subjecting the novel's representation of homosex to careful scrutiny, these critics variously revealed contradiction, incoherence, homoeroticism, and queerness lurking beneath its seemingly straightforward repudiation of sodomy and effeminacy. The marginal turned out to be central, the supposedly repellent, fascinating. Perhaps most interestingly, in both Kopelson and McFarlane's accounts, Cleland's unspeakable male sodomites threatened to speak back through the very words and images meant to define and dismiss them.[4]

McFarlane's analysis of *Memoirs* (in his important book, *The Sodomite in Fiction and Satire 1660–1750*) made the most of this near-reversal, this convergence of homosexuality and homophobia, with the former potentially displacing the latter. Borrowing the concept of "transgressive reinscription" from

---

[2] For an unpublished 1990s reading of *Memoirs* as closeted writing, see Robinson (1993). Only very recently, in Fowler and Jackson's anthology (2003), do two more critics (Fowler and Kubek) briefly consider such possibilities. Two other contributors—Beynon and Krouse—follow Moore in questioning the novel's ostensible anti-lesbianism, and in connecting it to the treatment of sodomitical male sex. On the novel's female homoerotics, see also Todd (1980), Donoghue, Lanser (2003b), and Jad Smith.

[3] I thank Halperin for bringing Edelman's essay to my attention.

[4] See especially the delicious conclusion of Kopelson's essay (181–82). For two recent pieces explicitly building on these three readings, see Haggerty (2003) and Jad Smith. (For Haggerty's nod to the possibility of Cleland's homosexuality, see below, 81, n.36.)

Jonathan Dollimore, McFarlane argued that "*Memoirs* transform[s] sodomitical practices even as [it] mimic[s] them, reproducing sodomitical fantasy in the same terms that would reject it, and, in the process, offer[s] to [its] readers a position from which to indulge in the erotics of the sodomitical spectacle" (146). Not that *Memoirs* offers what Foucault would call a "reverse discourse." As McFarlane explains, that would require "an open appropriation of sodomitical practices by the self-proclaimed sodomite" (146). Instead, "through its sodomitical... fantasy[,]... [*Memoirs*] exercises (and then exorcises) the reader's sodomitical gaze" (146). Most valuably, McFarlane combined this theoretically informed perspective with a focus on Restoration and eighteenth-century understandings of sodomy pioneered by historians such as G.S. Rousseau, Randolph Trumbach, and Rictor Norton. The result remains the most careful historical contextualization of Cleland's treatment of sodomy to date.[5]

Nevertheless, McFarlane's exploration of *Memoirs* was limited from the outset by his failure to imagine a rhetorical possibility other than simple homophobic condemnation, transgressive reinscription, or reverse discourse. For just as, in transgressive reinscription, homophobic discourse might mimic its target (and inadvertently liberate or license homosexual transgression), so too might homosexual discourse mimic its antagonist. That possibility is precisely what McFarlane, Edelman, and even Kopelson overlooked: the possibility that *Memoirs* constitutes an example of closeted homosexual writing, one in which sodomitic discourse mimics, and critiques, homophobia.[6]

Considering the theoretical tenor of the times, it's not surprising these three critics—all of whom offer valuable analyses of *Memoirs*—failed even to mention closeted homosexuality. By the 1990s, it had become virtually unspeakable in most academic circles when considering texts predating the late-nineteenth-century "invention" of homosexuality, except as a foil for theoretically sophisticated approaches. Not surprisingly, therefore, although Mengay's essay appeared in the same issue of the same collection as Kopelson's, it was almost universally ignored, or misrepresented.[7]

---

[5] See Rousseau (1987/1991) and Trumbach (1987a & 1993) for their discussions of *Memoirs*.

[6] For a text in which we probably do find reverse discourse (sodomites enthusiastically appropriating the terms and concepts used to condemn them), see the alleged molly-house bawdy song quoted in *A Genuine Narrative of All the Street Robberies Committed since October last, by James Dalton, And his Accomplices* (London, 1728); rpt. Norton, ed. (2002) 295–354; the song can be found online as well, with helpful commentary, at Norton, ed. (2000–2004).

[7] Aside from Moore, only McFarlane discusses Mengay's essay (misleadingly grouping it with Edelman and Kopelson's pieces); Todd Parker cites it. No other critic, including the fifteen contributors to *Launching Fanny Hill* (2003), even mentions it, let alone seriously engages with it.

Critics have accorded similar treatment to the biographical evidence suggesting Cleland's possible homosexuality. During the 1990s, only two, other than Mengay and Moore, broached the subject: Philip Simmons (1990) and Felicity Nussbaum (1995). Both raised the issue only in passing; neither took it seriously. Yet the slight difference in their approaches underscores how the critical climate changed between 1990 and 1995.

Simmons's explanation of *Memoirs'* sodomitical episode closely resembled those offered by Edelman, Kopelson, and McFarlane, apart from his choice of theorist (Bataille). As for Cleland's sexuality and its potential effect on the novel, Simmons took up the subject only to drop it like mildly interesting trivia. Discussing the "seemingly gratuitous violence against Fanny" that enables the sodomites to escape unpunished, Simmons remarked, "[it] raises the possibility that Cleland's sympathies actually lie with the two men, though in its ambiguity the scene also preserves the conventional sanction against homosexuality" (61). He even cited, in a footnote, the biographical evidence from Epstein and Merritt. Yet Simmons stressed that "Cleland's own putative homosexuality retains the status of an unconfirmed rumour" and that "[w]ithout stronger evidence, there remains the possibility that the homosexual scene in the *Memoirs*, rather than any behaviour of his own, was the origin of the rumour about Cleland" (61, n.33). With that appeal to one of Sedgwick's Eight Easy Steps (see above, ch.1, p.3), Simmons dismissed Cleland's "putative homosexuality" and how it might have shaped *Memoirs*. In the process, he safeguarded his own argument, which depended upon positing a uniform, heterosexual-male (or heterosexual male–identified) readership whose subjectivity *Memoirs* (like other novels) helps construct.

Even more than Simmons, however, Nussbaum exemplifies the predominant attitude in 1990s Gender Studies, LGBT Studies, queer theory, and the History of Sexuality toward the notion of pre- and early modern closeted writing. Notwithstanding the originality and importance of her work on *Memoirs*, it demonstrates the way anti-identitarian, differentist scholarship proved as dismissive of certain types of gay inquiry as the homophobic scholarship Sedgwick skewered in *Epistemology of the Closet*. Most revealing of all, Nussbaum effected this dismissal offhandedly, as if stating something on which we all agree.

The subject first arose in connection with one of the central questions in Cleland criticism: whether *Memoirs'* sexual politics are ultimately liberatory or oppressive. Nussbaum argued that the novel employs sexual liberation as an oppressive ruse:

> The *Memoirs* makes available to its heroine, author, and readers heterosexual, homosexual, bisexual, autosexual, and omnisexual erotic responses from which the shopper for erotic novelty may choose.... [But it] liberates female sexual desire in order to channel it away from autoeroticism and homoeroticism toward bourgeois heterosexual pleasure.... Women entice women; sexual desire for the same sex is necessary but must be rechanneled toward men in order to be fully satisfying. (27–28)

While Nussbaum went on to make a persuasive case (to which Moore subsequently offered a persuasive rejoinder [168, n.16]), it's how she began this passage that disturbs me: "While the narrative voice in the novel lends itself to assuming that the 'real' author is homosexual, the text presents a tangle of sexual practices rather than a prior original and fixed identity" (27). Earlier, she'd taken a somewhat different approach to the "real" author, commenting that "[t]hough the colonizing impulse has not before been connected to the first pornographic novel in English, *Memoirs of a Woman of Pleasure,* it is curious that at least part of the novel was probably written during John Cleland's stint in Bombay" (24), and then briefly discussing the possible influence of this fact on the novel (24–25). Granted, the biographical tidbit served merely as a "curious" introduction to Nussbaum's close reading of the text. Yet at that point she treated Cleland and his Bombay sojourn as unproblematically real. Only when considering the notion that "the novel lends itself to assuming that the 'real' author is homosexual" did the scare-quotes appear. Notice, too, the word-choice: reading *Memoirs* as homosexually authored would have been *assuming*—always an intellectual failing—rather than, say, *positing* or even *deducing.*

This dematerialization of the author is even more disturbing given Nussbaum's ultimate, and welcome, concern for the way both *Memoirs* itself, and critics who celebrate its treatment of gender and sexuality, can obscure material reality:

> The undecidability of mixing genders ambiguously in the *Memoirs* nevertheless has decided material effects. In this case, as I have argued, these effects may contribute to the construction of the heterosexual/homosexual binary, the oppression of women and the alienation of women from each other, and the colonization of the sexualized Other.... In the *Memoirs* the pleasuring body obliterates the laboring body and the material conditions of the sex worker. Having relinquished her property, Fanny moves from the entrapment of prostitution to the prison of domesticity in which her pen is silenced, her earnings appropriated, and her body parts remapped. Gender fluidity may be enlisted in the cause of oppression as well as liberation. (34–35)

That final point, too often forgotten by fans of gender trouble and sexual transgression, is well taken. But so too is one Nussbaum gave no indication of having considered: that *sexual* fluidity—fluidity in terms of sexual desire and activity, resistance to the heterosexual/homosexual binary—may also be enlisted in the cause of oppression.

At the risk of seeming to manhandle Nussbaum, I want to finish, for the moment, this account of gay, queer, and feminist Cleland criticism, by singling out one other sentence from her essay, because it epitomizes, in both language and content, precisely the theoretical mindset I wish to contest:

> My point here is not, of course, to debate whether Fanny's inscribed body is actually male or female, or whether Cleland is gay, straight, or bisexual. Resisting discovery,

> Fanny's body contests the norms that determine its intelligibility; Cleland's sexual proclivities can only be the subject of speculation. (33)

Intentionally or not, with that casual "of course" Nussbaum put critics who *are* interested in Cleland's "sexual proclivities" firmly in their place—namely, nowhere, nowhere that *matters*. And leaving aside the accuracy of her assertion about Cleland's proclivities—an assertion masquerading as observation (isn't it possible his proclivities might be revealed by further historical research?)—I want to challenge Nussbaum's disparaging use of the term 'speculation.' It recalls the phrase 'mental masturbation,' with which Sedgwick (1991) takes issue:

> What seems likel[y]... is that the literal-minded and censorious metaphor that labels any criticism one doesn't like, or doesn't understand, with the would-be damning epithet "mental masturbation," actually refers to a much vaster, indeed foundational open secret about how hard it is to circumscribe the vibrations of the highly relational but, in practical terms, solitary pleasure and adventure of writing itself. (110)

Something similar underwrites critical dismissal of certain topics as "mere," "pure," or "only" speculation. The same something, I suspect, that leads critics quick to scare-quote "reality," "knowledge," "objectivity," and the like to turn round and dismiss others' work because it involves speculating on what, most likely, cannot be definitively proven. Such critics seem to be defending against the foundational open secret of literary criticism: that all our interpretations are more or less plausible speculation, rather than historical, much less scientific, fact.

And for Lesbian & Gay Studies and the History of Sexuality specifically, dismissal of the potential significance of an author's sexual desires and activities for interpreting her work is, to a much larger degree than most scholars will admit, a defensive move. It distances the sort of work we do from history and criticism written outside academia, work that often asks, and tries to answer, questions of the "Is She or Isn't She?" variety: "Was Emily Dickinson a lesbian?" "Was Abraham Lincoln gay?" I, too, want to encourage speculation about authors' sexual desires, activities, associations, concepts, and self-concepts, in full recognition of the hazards of such an approach, and of the value of continuing to develop other questions, methodologies, and interpretive frameworks. Call me old-fashioned, but I *am* interested in whether particular individuals in the past (from high-born to low-, famous to unknown, vicious to virtuous) were what most of us today would consider lesbian, gay, bisexual, or transgender. An LGBT or Queer Studies that finds such questions uninteresting is, at least to me, an LGBT or Queer Studies that has gotten above itself, wandered too far from its unpretentious, embarrassing, gossipy roots.

Accordingly, in the rest of this chapter, as in the previous one, I mean to demonstrate how mere speculation, even rash speculation, about authors' sexual desires, literary intentions, and the interplay between the two, can sharpen and enrich our understanding of literary texts—which, after all, make up a crucial part of the history of homosexuality.[8]

Two Young Sparks, a Long-Breath'd Kiss, and a Most Significant Erection: *Memoirs* vs. *The History of Dom B****

Critics and historians seem not quite to have realized, or at least not to have articulated, how extraordinary Cleland's treatment of male-male sex actually is. For *Memoirs* contains, in the once-expurgated, now-famous sodomitical scene, one of the most positive treatments of male homosexuality in seventeenth- and eighteenth-century British and French literature.

The episode begins with Fanny at an inn waiting for a stagecoach, looking out an upstairs window, watching as "a single horse-chaise stopt at the door, out of which lightly leap'd two young gentlemen, for so they seem'd" (156).[9] Fanny believes they've stopped at the house only briefly, because "they gave their horse to be held in readiness against they came out" (156), a precaution taken, as we subsequently learn, to enable a quick get-away. She hears them enter the next room (divided from hers by only a thin partition), and, after being served, lock the door from the inside.

Curious "to see who they were, and examine their persons and behaviour," but "without any particular suspicion, or other drift, or view," Fanny examines the partition for a hole to peep through (157), finally noticing a "paper-patch" near the ceiling. She climbs on a chair, pierces the paper with a needle, and "appl[ies her] eye" to the hole, with the following results:

> I commanded the room perfectly, and could see my two young sparks romping, and pulling one another about, entirely to my imagination, in frolic, and innocent play.
>
> The eldest might be, on my nearest guess, towards nineteen, a tall comely young man, in a white fustian frock, with a green velvet cape, and a cut bob-wig.
>
> The youngest could not be above seventeen, fair, ruddy, compleatly well made, and to say the truth, a sweet pretty stripling: He was, I fancy too, a country lad, by his dress, which was a green plush frock, and breeches of the same, white waistcoat and stockings, a jockey cap, with his yellowish hair long, and loose, in natural curls.
>
> But after a look of circumspection which I saw the eldest cast every way round the room... he said something to his companion that presently chang'd the face of things.
>
> For now the elder began to embrace, to press, to kiss the younger, to put his hands in his bosom, and give such manifest signs of an amorous intention, as made me conclude the other to be a girl in disguise, a mistake that nature kept me in countenance in, for she had certainly made one, when she gave him the male stamp.

---

[8] Again, see Robinson (2004) for the application of this approach to Margaret Cavendish's *Blazing World* (1666).

[9] Quotations from *Memoirs* are from Sabor's edition.

In the rashness then of their age, and bent as they were to accomplish their project of preposterous pleasure, at the risque of the very worst consequences, where a discovery was nothing less than improbable, they now proceeded to such lengths as soon satisfied me, what they were.

For presently the eldest unbutton'd the other's breeches, and removing the linnen barrier, brought out to view a white shaft, middle-siz'd, and scarce fledg'd, when after handling, playing with it a little, with other dalliance, all receiv'd by the boy without other opposition, than certain wayward coynesses, ten times more alluring than repulsive, he got him to turn round with his face from him, to a chair that stood hard by, when knowing, I suppose, his office, the Ganymede now obsequiously lean'd his head against the back of it, and projecting his body, made a fair mark, still cover'd with his shirt, as he thus stood in a side-view to meet but fronting his companion, who presently unmasking his battery, produc'd an engine, that certainly deserv'd to be put to a better use, and very fit to confirm me in my disbelief of the possibility of things being push'd to odious extremities, which I had built on the disproportion of parts; but this disbelief I was now to be cur'd of, as by my consent all young men should likewise be, that their innocence may not be betray'd into such snares, for want of knowing the extent of their danger, for nothing is more certain than, that ignorance of a vice, is by no means a guard against it.

Slipping then aside the young lad's shirt, and tucking it up under his cloaths behind, he shew'd to the open air, those globular, fleshy eminences that compose the mount-pleasants of *Rome,* and which now, with all the narrow vale that intersects them, stood display'd, and expos'd to his attack: nor could I, without a shudder, behold the dispositions he made for it. First then, moistening well with spittle his instrument, obviously to render it glib, he pointed, he introduc'd it, as I could plainly discern, not only from its direction, and my losing sight of it; but by the writhing, twisting, and soft murmur'd complaints of the young sufferer; but, at length, the first streights of entrance being pretty well got through, every thing seem'd to move, and go pretty currently on, as in a carpet-road, without much rub, or resistance: and now passing one hand round his minion's hips, he got hold of his red-topt ivory toy, that stood perfectly stiff, and shewed, that if he was like his mother behind, he was like his father before; this he diverted himself with, whilst with the other, he wanton'd with his hair, and leaning forward over his back, drew his face, from which the boy shook loose curls that fell over it, in the posture he stood him in, and brought him towards his, so as to receive a long-breath'd kiss, after which, renewing his driving, and thus continuing to harass his rear, the height of the fit came on with its usual symptoms, and dismiss'd the action. (157–59)

Although a great deal can be and has been said about this passage, I want to focus primarily upon the most startling detail: the "Ganymede's" erection.[10]

---

[10] For critics' discussion of this scene, and the novel's treatment of sodomy more generally, see Sabor (2000), as well as Fowler, Haggerty (2003), Hammond (1996), Krouse, Kubek, Todd Parker, and Jad Smith. Citing the *OED*, Sabor glosses "carpet-road" as "smooth, sheltered water 'near the shore, where vessels may lie at anchor in safety'" (*Memoirs,* "Explanatory Notes," 201).

Clearly, the youth derives sexual pleasure from being penetrated, pleasure one would expect to confirm his already suggested effeminacy. Yet it doesn't. On the contrary, Fanny remarks that his penis "stood perfectly stiff, and shewed that if he was like his mother behind, he was like his father before...." Astoundingly, Western culture's most supremely effeminizing act—receptive anal intercourse with another man—reveals, in Cleland's representation, a masculinizing potential. And whereas recent gay history leads us to expect, in accounts of eighteenth-century male-male sex, *either* masculine libertines *or* effeminate mollies, Cleland presents a youth *both* masculine *and* effeminate, on the basis of his anatomical and erotic capacity both to penetrate and to be penetrated. Such a depiction is unheard of in the eighteenth century.[11]

The closest example I've found occurs in the French pornographic novel attributed to Jacques Charles (or Jean Charles or Jean-Charles) Gervaise de Latouche, *L'histoire de Dom B***, Portier Des Chartreux* (*The History of Dom B[ougre], Porter for the Carthusians* [c.1741/1742]), a work that, according to Julie Peakman, "had a huge impact in Britain, the translation being available as early as 1743" (21; see also Wagner [1988]). At a midnight orgy, the protagonist and narrator, Saturnin, allows the "Antiphysical" monk Père Casimir (referred to as "le Bougre" [217]) to penetrate him anally in exchange for permission to penetrate Marianne, Casimir's niece, vaginally. Accordingly, Saturnin mounts Marianne, Casimir mounts Saturnin, and the following ensues:

> [W]hatever pain I felt, and although Casimir tore me up, the pleasure of doing as much to the Niece, whose Cunt suffered more from the largeness of my Dick, than my Ass suffered from that of her uncle's Dick, consoled me for my pain. When the difficulties of entry were past on both sides[,] it was smooth sailing; sometimes the pleasure stopped me in the midst of the work, but soon Casimir reawaking my valor, impelled me to do as well as he. Thus pushed and pushing, the blows I received from the Uncle, went as in an echo, to ring and to lose themselves in the Cunt of the Niece.... (225)

For a moment—when Saturnin says, "the pleasure stopped [him] in the midst of the work" and Casimir was doing "well"—he perhaps hints at receptive pleasure. But the next sentence shifts focus from Saturnin's posterior—where he receives thrusts or blows [*coups*] from the Uncle—through his penis, into Marianne's

---

[11] I therefore disagree with Haggerty ([2003] 177), McFarlane (171), Moore (72), Jad Smith (198), and especially Weed, all of whom stress either the youth's metaphorical hermaphrodism or his effeminacy. (Haggerty, however, makes the most interesting use of this moment.) The ganymede's erection, and its explicit linkage to masculine potency ("like his father before"), makes this detail powerfully unconventional. For a reading of *Memoirs* as celebrating androgyny, see Roussel, ch.2 (written before Sabor and Wagner restored the novel's sodomitical episode). As for the dichotomy between masculine libertines and effeminate mollies, Trumbach insists upon it most famously and influentially (e.g., [1998] 3–5). For a critique of his work, see Haggerty (2000).

vagina. And there the focus remains, at the site of heterosexual intercourse, as Saturnin and Marianne engage in a contest of staying power (Saturnin wins, five orgasms to four).

Still, the text treats sex between men with tolerance. Casimir delivers a defense of buggery (paraphrased by Saturnin, who considers it quite skillful [227]). When a now-pregnant Marianne absents herself from the midnight orgies, Saturnin samples antiphysical pleasure, at least as a temporary substitute: "I tried Casimir's remedy, & in his tracks, I soon made myself formidable in the Ass of all the Novices." And although, as he explains, "a little while later I fell back into my old errors, & the pleasures of the Cunt removed me from those of the Ass," as narrator he vigorously defends his experimentation (229). In fact, except for social rank (commoner rather than aristocrat), Saturnin perfectly illustrates Trumbach's libertine model of sexuality (albeit half a century too late): primarily desirous of women, but bisexual enough to enjoy penetrating beautiful boys.[12]

Yet far more surprising than tolerating a form of sodomy that, if usually illicit, had long been considered manly, is Saturnin's matter-of-factly allowing Casimir to anally penetrate him, notwithstanding the opprobrium directed at anal-receptive adult males throughout Western history. Saturnin, however, has an extravagantly heterosexual excuse for this otherwise outrageous act: he hasn't had sex with a woman in eight years; he's extremely aroused by Marianne; and she's holding his erect penis while allowing him to finger her vagina, when Casimir halts the action and announces the requirements for further access. Saturnin's unmanly act is entirely in the service of heteromale desire. Indeed, Latouche has merely elaborated upon a commonplace narrative: a man crossdressing to gain admittance to a woman's abode, bed, and body. As in that familiar scenario, Saturnin engages in an action that would normally effeminize and humiliate, but that here reinforces his identity as a properly penetrative, properly heterosexual man.[13]

Had Latouche depicted Saturnin enjoying being penetrated, the scene would have been daring indeed. But no male in *Dom B**** takes pleasure in receptive anal sex. At best, the existence of such willingly penetrable men is implied: when a group composed of seven or eight men and one woman are "fuck[ing] as much in the Ass as in the Cunt" (228), presumably some men must provide the former without getting any of the latter. Nevertheless, *Dom B**** does not *depict* a man enjoying such activity. While quite celebratory of, and imaginative regarding, sexual experimentation, the author is unable or unwilling to extend the bounds of acceptable masculinity to encompass homoerotic anal receptivity.

---

[12] Responding to criticism, Trumbach added the caveat that "every predominant system produces its variant," and thus the replacement of one model of sexuality by another was not total ([1989] 139). Yet that slightly more complex formulation still fails to account for *Dom B**** (cf. Robinson [1993]).

[13] For a mid-eighteenth-century example, see Smollett's *Peregrine Pickle*, ch.66.

Pornography as Prophylaxis and Other Projects of Preposterous Pleasure[14]

In contrast, Cleland's daring is startling. It would be startling even today, in a work aimed primarily at heterosexual readers, since a straight male might have difficulty dismissing the penetrated youth as simply a "passive homosexual," a would-be woman, an Other. He might find himself reminded that, just as virtually all men have penises, and thus (presumably) can fuck, virtually all men have anuses, and thus (presumably) can be fucked—and enjoy it. It's no wonder homosexuals have typically been portrayed as *either* masculine *or* effeminate, and *either* insertive *or* receptive. A figure such as Cleland's ganymede, "like his mother behind... [but] like his father before," threatens to collapse the distinction between male and female, masculine and feminine, and perhaps even reveal gender as a fiction.[15]

It's also no wonder the two paragraphs in which the simultaneously feminine and masculine, penetrated yet erect youth appears are absent from most editions of *Memoirs*, even pirated ones, and explained away in others as an "interpolation" by someone else, as if, like the character it portrays, the novel had been sodomized. Of course, given its duration and explicitness, the scene would most likely have been bowdlerized even without the ganymede's extraordinary erection. Cleland violates too thoroughly the period's conventions for representing male homosexuality.[16]

Indeed, compared with other seventeenth- and eighteenth-century depictions of male-male sex, as well as most other sex scenes in *Memoirs*, the young sparks' encounter is not only unconventional, but also (dare I say it?) *realistic*. For instance, while Fanny implies the elder boy has a large penis, she describes his partner's appendage as "middle-siz'd." Of course, this detail reinforces the youth's mild effeminization, and his immaturity. But in Cleland's outlandishly priapic novel, in which most every pair of breeches harbors an "engine" of colossal proportions, the mention of a "middle-siz'd" member strikes a more probable, less fantastic, note. As does the mid-intercourse kiss: both the fact of its inclusion and the accurately imagined details of its execution. Add to these the ganymede's unprecedented erection—unimaginable, even today, to many men who've never been penetrated (as well as to many who have)—and the resulting passage is uniquely realistic for its time and place.

---

[14] On the homophobic connotations of 'preposterous,' see Patricia Parker (1993b).

[15] Both D.A. Miller (1991) and Edelman make this point particularly well.

[16] See Sabor (2000) 571, correcting his earlier reference to the supposed interpolator, "Drybutter, the bookseller," as "an apparently non-existent figure" ([1985] xxvii). Subsequent evidence (Norton [1992] 176–77) has shown that, notwithstanding his multiply suggestive name, and although there's no evidence he wrote the sodomitical passages, "Samuel Drybutter was the bookseller... pilloried in 1757 for selling copies of *Fanny Hill*." He was satirized as a sodomite in the 1770s.

Moreover, the sodomy Fanny describes is clearly meant to excite at least *some* readers, however much she, and Cleland, may profess otherwise. And profess they soon do—indeed, have already done so: when Fanny realizes the youths are about to have anal intercourse, an act that, "based on the disproportion of parts," she'd previously considered impossible, Cleland defends the explicitness of the depiction she (and thus he) is about to offer. "This disbelief," she declares, "I was now to be cur'd of, as by my consent all young men should likewise be, that their innocence may not be betray'd into such snares, for want of knowing the extent of their danger, for nothing is more certain than, that ignorance of a vice, is by no means a guard against it." In order to prevent young men being misled into receptive anal intercourse, they should be cured of their ignorance and disbelief. Where vice is concerned, well warned is well armed.

Yet the cure hadn't worked for Fanny: both her madam (Mrs. Cole) and another prostitute had already informed her of the practice. Only witnessing it has the desired effect. Fanny would therefore seem to recommend that young men be cured of their ignorance and disbelief in the same way as she: by witnessing the act. Cleland thus justifies his explicit representation of same-sex anal intercourse as a form of prophylaxis, exposing all those impressionable, imperiled young men to the sight of two men committing sodomy, to prevent their being "betray'd into such snares."

Such reasoning had long been a stock, mock excuse for pornography, the tongue-in-cheek moral justification adding to the illicit fun. In satire, such justifications had served a more complex purpose, enabling readers to avoid feeling guilty about lingering over depictions of wickedness. Cleland, though, plays a double game, purporting to offer satire to his homophobic audience, while supplying homosexual readers with porn. He addresses the sodomitically intolerant through his narrator-heroine, with whom all readers have been encouraged to identify. Yet he manipulates her words to provide sexual excitement, and an anti-homophobic laugh, for the sodomitically inclined.

Speculation? Undeniably. But reinforced by the episode's conclusion:

> All this, so criminal a scene, I had the patience to see to an end, purely that I might gather more facts, and certainty against them in my full design to do their deserts instant justice, and accordingly, when they had readjusted themselves, and were preparing to go out, burning as I was with rage, and indignation, I jumped down from my chair, in order to rouse the house upon them, with such an unlucky impetuosity, that some nail or ruggedness in the floor caught my foot, and flung me on my face with such violence, that I fell senseless on the ground, and must have lain there some time e'er any one came to my relief, so that they, alarm'd, I suppose, by the noise of my fall, had more than the necessary time to make a safe retreat, which they affected [sic], as I learnt, with a precipitation no body could account for, till, when come to my self, and compos'd enough to speak, I acquainted those of the house with the transaction I had been evidence to. (159)

Fanny's assertion that she "had the patience to see to an end" "so criminal a scene" "purely that [she] might gather more facts, and certainty against [the sodomites]" is patently ridiculous (unless, notwithstanding her disbelief in the practice, she's a legal expert on buggery, sometimes defined as anal penetration, sometimes anal penetration resulting in seminal emission). After she'd seen a young man kiss, embrace, and caress another; seen him fondle his partner's erect penis; seen him pull down the youth's pants and turn him round; seen him take out and lubricate his own penis; seen him insert it in the ganymede's anus—surely by then Fanny had no need to "gather more facts," no need to see one or both criminals reach orgasm, in order to gain sufficient "certainty" to have them punished. Had that been her only aim, she would have alerted the household to their activities *in medias res,* rather than wait till they were preparing to leave. But "burning as she was with rage, and indignation"—or with, as Cleland would have at least some of us conclude, sexual excitement—she could not look away from the peepshow until the sex act was complete.[17]

Gay Bashing Eighteenth-Century–Style: *Peregrine Pickle* and *Henry Dumont*

Another clue to Cleland's intentions is his choice, in a moment of quite unexpected narrative violence, to slam Fanny's face against the floor, knocking her unconscious and preventing her alerting the household until the youths have escaped. And once again, other texts of the time, factual and fictional, prove instructive.

Take, for instance, the trial proceedings for Richard Manning and John Davis, accused of attempted sodomy at an inn on New Year's Eve, 1744. Compared with *Memoirs'* sodomitical episode, the account of their activity, and of the behavior of hostile witnesses, reveals both startling similarities and significant differences:

> **Richard Manning,** was indicted for a misdemeanour, in unlawfully, and wickedly laying hands on John Davis, with an intent to commit the detestable sin of sodomy; And **John Davis,** for unlawfully, and wickedly permitting, and suffering the said Richard Manning to lay hands on him, with an intent to commit the said sin of sodomy, December 31 [1744].

> *Sarah Holland.* My husband keeps the Mermaid Inn in Great Carter Lane. On the 31st of December, between 9 and 10 at night the prisoners came in together and asked for a pot of beer. I did not know but they might be country gentlemen, so I run into the room and asked them if they would have a fire, they said no, they should not stay. I went into the next room where my husband was in bed. There is a wainscot partition between the 2 rooms, about 5 feet high, and the rest is glass, and a curtain to part of it. I looked

---

[17] Julia Epstein makes a similar argument (145). On the legal definition of sodomy in mid-eighteenth-century Britain, see both Goldsmith and Gilbert.

through the glass, and saw them sitting facing one another with their knees jammed in together. I said to my husband, I believed they were sodomites. Then I looked through a thin curtain and saw them kissing one another. A little after I looked in again, and saw Manning's hand in Davis's breeches. After that Manning put his tongue into Davis's mouth: they seeing a candle in my room, got up and came to the window to look if they could see the shade of any body; then they set down again, and Davis shewed what he had [i.e., exposed his penis] to Manning; they kissed one another for some time, and then Davis opened his breeches: I had not patience any longer, and called Robert Wright, and said, I have heard talk of sodomites, and I believe these are some; Wright said he had not patience; I looked again, and saw them acting as man and woman...; I saw them act as such. Then I lifted up my sash, thinking they would go away. *What do you mean*, said I, *by 2 men acting as man and woman*.

Q. [Question from the Court] Was Manning's back or his face to Davis?

Holland. I believe his face.

Q. When you saw the first fact, why did not you discover it?

Holland. I don't know. When they found I had discovered them, Davis run into the yard with his breeches down, thinking he was going into the street, and some gentlemen stopped them both.

...Edward Morey. I happened to be at Mr. Holland's and saw the prisoners in a back parlour that looks into the yard. Mrs. Holland called me into the little room, where she lies in, where Mr. Holland was then in bed, and desired me to stay. There is a partition wainscot 4 or 5 foot high, the rest is glass. She took hold of the corner of one of the curtains and desired me to look. According to her desire I did look, and saw the prisoners knees close to one another, and their faces as close together as ever mine and my wife's were—they were sitting face to face. Mr. Manning got out of his chair and looked to the glass to see if anybody was looking. I went into the back yard with a design to look through the window, and presently Mrs. Holland cried out, *nasty rogues, vile fellows*. I met Davis at the entry door going into the yard with the lower part of his breeches unbuttoned, and his shirt out. He said, *for God's sake let me go, or I am ruined to all intents and purposes*. He said, it was the first crime that ever he committed of that kind before.—Manning denied it to all intents and purposes, was in a great rage, and asked me whether I would accuse him of being guilty of any such thing—they were sober to my thoughts.

Robert Wright. I lodge at Mr. Holland's. On the 31st of December, a little after 9, I was going to bed; Mrs. Holland met me at the foot of the stairs, and said, *Wright, come here*. I went into the little room, the candle was out. Said she, *I have heard talk of sodomites, I believe there are some here*. Says I, *I don't like the thoughts of them*. I looked through the glass and saw them close together: says she, *look now, they are bussing* [kissing]. At last Davis got up, he had got his shirt hanging out of his breeches: he went between Manning's legs, and here he went — — Mrs. Holland had not patience any longer, but threw up the sash, and said, *you damned dogs, what are you doing of?*

Both the setting and overall plot of the two episodes—one ostensibly factual, one fictional—are quite similar. And what appears most conventional in Cleland's scene—Fanny spying on the perpetrators from a hidden vantage point—turns out to be realistic. So, too, it would seem, is Fanny's hostile fascination. For all Mrs. Holland's protestations that she "had not patience," she watched what she strongly suspected was sodomy for quite a while. When asked by the Court why she didn't intervene earlier, she replies only, "I don't know." Yet when matters progressed beyond kissing and fondling to intercourse, but *before* Manning and Davis had achieved satisfaction, Mrs. Holland, unlike Fanny, did interrupt the encounter. And unlike Cleland's sodomites, Manning and Davis were arrested, then sentenced to pillory, prison, and probation.[18]

Similarly, in Tobias Smollett's *The Adventures of Peregrine Pickle* (1751), in a scene Smollett eliminated when cleaning up the novel for its 1757 reissue, a pair of sodomitical characters only narrowly escapes violent, life-threatening punishment—the sort of "very worst consequences" risked by Fanny's young sparks. In Smollett's novel, after a ludicrous, drunken dinner hosted by a pedantic Doctor for an English painter, Italian Count, German baron, French Marquis, and the novel's protagonist, Peregrine, the host is "seized with such a qualm, that he begged Peregrine to lead him to his chamber" (242). In their absence, "the count, tired with the eternal babble of the painter, reeled towards the sleeping baron, whom he viewed with rapture, repeating from the *Il Pastor Fido* of Guarini" lines (given in Italian by Smollett) that translate, "Like the thirsty sick man, who long desired the forbidden liquor, such am I, a long-time ill, burning and consumed with amorous thirst." But the count is not content merely to rhapsodize:

> Then [he] boldly ravished a kiss, and began to tickle him under the ribs, with such expressions of tenderness, as scandalized the virtuous painter, who, conscious of his own attractions, was alarmed for his person, and staggered in great hurry and discomposure into the next room, where he put himself under the protection of our hero, to whom he imparted his suspicion of the count's morals, by describing the indecency of his deportment.

---

[18] For the trial proceedings, see Norton (2000–2004; <http://www.infopt.demon.co.uk/1745mann.htm>), who cites *The Proceedings on the King's Commissions of the Peace...* (London, 1744 [1745 New Style]) 75–76, 80. See Haggerty (2003) for an important discussion of other sodomy trials (from *Select Trials...* [1742]) in relation to *Memoirs*. Haggerty investigates the way they "codify a particular understanding of sodomy as unnatural, as victimizing, and as a violation of the terms of human intercourse," focusing on the way "sodomy emerges as a site of voyeuristic pleasure." While he emphasizes he "can make no claims about the authenticity of these accounts as historical fact" (169), I hesitate to dispense entirely with their factual value, although I recognize the impossibility of verifying most of their details. Nonetheless it matters, I would argue, that trial records are more likely to be factual, or more likely to be *more* factual, than Cleland's novel. For an excellent comparative use of both literary and criminal documents, see Merrick (1999).

> Peregrine, who entertained a just detestation for all such abominable practices, was incensed at this information; and stepping to the door of the dining-room where the two strangers were left together, saw with his own eyes enough to convince him, that [the painter's] complaint was not without foundation, and that the baron was not averse to the addresses of the count. Our young gentleman's indignation had well nigh prompted him to rush in, and take immediate vengeance on the offenders; but, considering that such a precipitate step might be attended with troublesome consequences to himself, he resisted the impulse of his wrath, and tasked his invention with some method of inflicting upon them a disgrace suited to the grossness of their ideas. (242)[19]

Peregrine, though, is unable to decide on a satisfactory punishment. Although his servant Pipes, a sailor, suggests "sew[ing] them up in bags, with a reasonable quantity of ballast in each, and throw[ing] them over the Pont Neuf into the river" (242–23), Peregrine is "at a loss how to behave" until the landlady passes by. Without telling her what to expect, he sends her to the count and baron with a message.

> The lady very graciously undertook the office, and entering the apartment, was so much offended and enraged at the mutual endearments of the two lovers, that instead of delivering the message with which she had been entrusted, she set the trumpet of reproach to her mouth, and seizing the baron's cane, which she found upon the sidetable, belaboured them both with such eagerness of animosity, that they found themselves obliged to make a very disorderly retreat, and were actually driven down stairs, in a most disgraceful condition, by this exasperated virago, who loaded them with just invectives all the way, publishing their shame, not only to those of her own family, but likewise to the populace, who began to crowd about the door, and in all probability would have espoused her revenge, had not their lacqueys, who were in waiting, conveyed the delinquents into the Remise, and carried them off with great expedition.
> Peregrine was so delighted with the manner of the chastisement they had undergone, that he embraced the mistress of the hotel with transport, for the spirit she had exerted.... (243)

This is exactly the sort of outcome Cleland could have depicted, but didn't: the homosexual men are discovered having sex; their discoverers contemplate murder; the homosexuals are "lucky" to get off with a beating and expulsion (partially unclothed) into the street; they narrowly escape mob violence; their persecutors make merry.[20]

---

[19] On the 1757 excision of this scene, see n.1 to p.242. Omitted from the middle of the lines from *Il Pastor Fido*, according to editor James Clifford, is 'If you ever reach the liquor, poor one, drink rather of death, extinguish your life rather than your thirst'" (n.2 to p.242). On the poet Mark Akenside as the pedantic and probably sodomitical doctor, see Rowland.

[20] On the way Peregrine then celebrates, and its consequences—scenes involving crossdressing, fisticuffs, and a threat of castration—see Edelman, Haggerty (1999 & 2003),

Charlotte Charke's *The History of Henry Dumont, Esq., and Miss Charlotte Evelyn* (1756) provides an even starker contrast to *Memoirs*. Its incidental sodomitical character, Billy Loveman, suffers the full fury of both author and protagonist. The day after Henry and Charlotte make a "magnificent appearance" at a Tunbridge ball, Henry receives a letter from Loveman that, in abominably spelled English (suggestive of foreign, perhaps French, pronunciation), confesses the writer's "ardunt pishon" and "bondless luf," and requests a meeting with the "lufly objeckt... this evening at the fish-ponds, vher [he] may be happy in paeing [his] rispex to the divine charmur of [his] soul" (58–59). Henry, "being intirely innocent of such unnatural proceedings" (59), assumes the letter is intended for Miss Evelyn. She, however, immediately comprehends its import:

> Miss Evelyn read the amorous epistle, laughing inwardly to a violent degree during the perusal; then returning the paper, Mr. Dumont, said she, I don't suppose the person who wrote it, would cast his eyes upon an odious Female; and I am positive the letter was meant as directed.
>
> Dear Madam, replied Dumont, 'tis impossible; 'tis true I have heard there are a set of unnatural wretches, who are shamefully addicted to a vice, not proper to be mentioned to so delicate an ear as yours; but my behaviour could not in any degree give the smallest hope to the unnatural passion of such a detestable brute. I therefore think it highly incumbent on me, to make an example of the villain.
>
> Miss Evelyn would fain have dissuaded him from his purpose, but in vain; for young Dumont was apprehensive, that the bare mention of his name from the mouth of such a wretch, might throw an imputation on his character, which he had rather suffer death than deserve.
>
> Mrs. Evelyn (the heroine's mother) was of the young gentleman's mind, and urged him to put his revenge in immediate execution; advising him, to consult with Lord Worthland and Sir John Generous, and entreat them to be witnesses; as an affair of this nature must be necessary to prevent any calumny the monster might possibly raise on account of the deserved treatment and disappointment he should meet from Mr. Dumont. (60–61)

Dumont takes Mrs. Evelyn's advice, informing Loveman's ridiculously effeminate "vale de chamber," Mr. Turtle, to expect him "at the time and place appointed" (63, 64). What ensues is all too familiar today (for which reason—continuity between past and present—as well as the stark contrast with Cleland's novel, I offer the following, lengthy quotation):

> The pretty creature had not been gone above a quarter of an hour, before Lord Worthland and Sir John Generous came to pay a visit; who were immediately informed of the affair, and resolved to join with Mr. Dumont in his revenge on the unnatural

---

McFarlane, and Robinson (1993). On all or most of Smollett's treatments of sodomy, see Day, McFarlane, and Robinson (1993).

scoundrel, for daring to make such an attempt upon a very honourable and worthy young gentleman.

About the hour of five after dinner, they went to the fish-ponds, which was the place proposed. Lord Worthland and Sir John went in a little before, and called for a bottle of champaign by themselves in a different room. Mr. Dumont came in a few minutes after, and was conducted by Mr. Loveman's footman, up one pair of stairs, to the enamoured swain, who had been waiting impatiently for his arrival above an hour.

When he came in he saw an elegant cold collation set forth, the window curtains close drawn and pinn'd; but found no body in the room; when asking for the gentleman, the servant sneered, and told him, his Lady would wait upon him directly; when immediately there appeared from the inner-chamber, this odious creature in a female rich dishabille; who running to Mr. Dumont, cried out, 'I come, I fly, to my adored Castalio's arms! my wishes [sic] lord!'—stopping here, with a languishing air, said, Do my angel, call me your Monimia! then with a beastly transport, kissed him with that ardour, which might be expected from a drunken fellow to a common prostitute. Mr. Dumont being now fully convinced of his horrid design, without farther ceremony knocked him down, and disciplined him with his cane; till the monster was almost immoveable.

The noise of his falling brought up Lord Worthland, Sir John, and the landlord, who were surprised to see Mr. Loveman's odd transformation; but he recollected his footman carried up a large bundle, little conceiving what it contained, or to what end it was brought.

Lord Worthland and Sir John would have bestowed their favours on him; but Mr. Dumont desired they would not rob him of the least part of his revenge, nor indeed was there any need; for Dumont who never suffered passion, without just grounds to influence his mind, thought he had so justifiable an excuse for it on this occasion, he gave it full scope, and left the wretch just life enough to confess his crime, and publickly beg pardon.

The history of this affair in a few minutes got wind, sufficient to blow a whole mob together. And when the male-madam was permitted to decamp as he was, leading between two to his chariot, they snatched him from his supporters, and very handsomely ducked him in the fish-pond; nor had he a friend on his side, for even his own coachman and footman, tho' they were not assistant in his punishment, were heartily glad to see him undergo it. Mr. Dumont having had sufficient revenge, his anger began to subside, and as the wretch wore a human form (tho' in principle below a beast) his pity and good nature resumed their throne, and by dint of a handful of silver thrown to the populace, they suffered the shameful object of their contempt to be hurried as fast as possible to his lodgings, where the news had got before him; and as a farther addition to his misfortune, poor Mr. Turtle, who was sent with the letter, (not knowing the contents of it,) as injured wives are apt to shew violent resentment, when they find their husbands are engaged in intrigues, flew about the house, raving like a distracted thing, menacing bitterest revenge on him and his filty creter; adding, corse me, if I forgive this willingy [sic]; this is the second time you have wronged me; if I bear it a third, the fault shall be mine; I desire we may saprate, ungrateful man; I have ever been true to you, and this is my reward.

Mr. Loveman, who was in too miserable a condition to expostulate with his offended fair; begged madam for that time to set aside its anger, and give what assistance he cou'd towards his relief. Surgeons were sent for, under whose hands he remained for above a month, before he could be moved. At the expiration of which time, he was forced to go privately away from Tunbridge, for fear of a second encounter; and the frac[as] between him and his lady was made up, (as one of the servants informed us, who overheard their discourse) with a faithful promise to retire from the world, and live *shepherdesses together in some remote country*.

Mr. Dumont satisfied the poor landlord, for the preparations made for him by the love-sick squire, and some damages done in the fray. Then the three friends returned home, and gave the history of their adventure to Miss Evelyn and her mama. Mrs. Evelyn tho' she allowed the justice of the thing, could not help pittying the unhappy creature; but Miss said, she could not entertain the least grain of compassion, for that in her opinion, no punishment was sufficiently severe for such unnatural monsters. (64–69)

As in *Peregrine Pickle*, where Smollett explicitly endorses his hero's homophobia (informing us, "Peregrine... entertained a just detestation for all such abominable practices"), Charke makes her anti-sodomitical antipathy unmistakable. Blending author and characters' perspectives, Charke's prose—in references to Loveman as a "wretch," "the pretty creature," "the unnatural scoundrel," "this odious creature," "the male-madam," and "the shameful object of [the mob's] contempt"— hovers between omniscient (but not impartial) third-person narration and free indirect discourse, yet without the latter's typical irony. She explicitly defends her protagonist's near-murderous rage (on the grounds that "Dumont... never suffered passion, without just grounds to influence his mind"); praises the "pity and good nature" that prompts him at last to relent, bribing the mob not to murder Loveman; yet informs us that Loveman does not deserve mercy, since, although "the wretch wore a human form," he was "in principle below a beast." Like Charlotte Evelyn, her heroine and fictional namesake, Charlotte Charke believes, or wants readers to believe she believes, "she could not entertain the least grain of compassion [for Loveman], for that in her opinion, no punishment was sufficiently severe for such unnatural monsters."

Such sentiments might seem strange coming from Charke, who in *A Narrative of the Life of Mrs. Charlotte Charke, Written By Herself* (1755) had related her own adventures as a frequent crossdresser, on- and offstage, including several years spent passing as a man and living with a woman ("Mrs. Brown") as husband and wife. Yet at best the *Narrative* flirts, obliquely, with the possibility of lesbian eroticism. And its presentation of Charke's crossdressing, while deliberately sensational (Charke hoped the book's sales would alleviate her poverty), is nonetheless ambiguous, even contradictory, in its attitude toward gender transgression. In fact, the gay-bashing episode in *Henry Dumont* seems to function, at least in part, as authorial self-defense, as Erin Mackie argues:

[I]n her fiction [Charke] violently separates herself from those very violations on which her own life bordered so closely. The violence of this condemnation is itself eloquently overcompensatory; the vitality of the threat Loveman presents is exposed in the brutality required to crush it. By bashing Loveman, Charke defends not only Henry Dumont, but also herself against the imputation of homosexuality.... By drawing moral and gender boundaries very sharply here Charke seems to be revising and correcting the blurriness and ambivalence of her position in the *Narrative*. Perhaps it became apparent that her naively matter-of-fact allusion to her "marriage" would not succeed in guarding her from damaging accusation. (854)

As we shall see, Smollett's textual homophobia also seems intended, at least partially, to deflect suspicion from what might otherwise have seemed homoerotic in his semi-autobiographical work. For the moment, though, it's enough to note the glaring contrast between Cleland's treatment of his sodomitical characters and Smollett and Charke's treatment of theirs.[21]

Kindler, Gentler Gay Bashing: *Miss in Her Teens*

In the spate of mid-century homophobic representations that constitutes such a crucial, under-explored context for *Memoirs of a Woman of Pleasure*, the bashing of Billy Loveman in Charke's *Henry Dumont* occupies the harshest, most violent extreme. In comparison, the scene from *Peregrine Pickle*, while still unwaveringly homophobic, is less sadistic. Still less cruel, and less violent, is David Garrick's short play *Miss in Her Teens; or, The Medley of Lovers* (1747), a text that, as John Franceschina points out (201), Charke echoes in *Henry Dumont*.

The play features an effeminate male character (originally played by Garrick) named Mr. Fribble, a word that meant "[a] trifling, frivolous person." Fribble's homosexuality, unlike that of Charke's Loveman and Smollett's count and baron, is only intimated. Yet that indirection is itself part of the homophobic fun, as when Fribble goes a'courting:

> [Miss] Biddy. But pray, Mr. *Fribble*, do you make use of a Huswife? [*OED*: "a pocket-case for needles, pins, thread, scissors, etc."]
> Frib. I can't do without it, Maam; there is a Club of us, all young Batchelors, the sweetest Society in the World; and we meet three times a Week at each other's Lodgings, where we drink Tea, hear the Chat of the Day, invent Fashions for the

---

[21] On the contexts for, effects of, and possible motivations behind Charke's complex gender presentations, see, in addition to Mackie's important essay, those contained in Baruth, ed. (1998), as well as Donoghue. On the gay-bashing scene from *Henry Dumont*, see also Straub (1992) and Felicity Nussbaum (1998). Fielding's *Amelia* (1752) contains a brief reference to near-fatal gay-bashing, in which a prostitute named "Blear-Eyed Moll" and "several of her companions [in jail], having got Possession of a Man who was committed for certain odious unmanlike Practices, not fit to be named, were giving him various Kinds of Discipline, and would probably have put an End to him, had he not been rescued out of their Hands by Authority" (33). On this scene, see Stephen Shapiro.

Ladies, make Models of 'em, and cut out Patterns in Paper. We were the first Inventors of Knotting, and this Fringe is the original Produce and joint Labour of our little Community.

Biddy. And who are your pretty Set, pray?

Frib. There's *Phil Whiffle, Jacky Wagtail*, my Lord *Trip*, *Billy Dimple*, Sir *Dilbery Diddle*, and your humble—

Biddy. What a sweet Collection of happy Creatures!... [Yet] I think all our Sex have great reason to be angry; for if you are so happy now you are Batchelors, the Ladies may wish and sigh to very little purpose.

Frib. You are mistaken, I assure you; I am prodigiously rallied about my Passion for you, I can tell you that, and am look'd upon as lost to our Society already; He, he, he!

Biddy. Pray, Mr. *Fribble*, now you have gone so far, don't think me impudent if I long to know how you intend to use the Lady who shall be honour'd with your Affections?

Frib. **Not as most other Wives are us'd, I assure you**; all the domestic Business will be taken off her Hands; I shall make the Tea, comb the Dogs, and dress the Children myself, ***if I should be bless'd with any***; so that, tho' I'm a Commoner, Mrs. *Fribble* will lead the Life of a Woman of Quality; for she will have nothing to do, but lie in Bed, play at Cards, and scold the Servants. (II.i., 20–22; boldface emphasis mine)

Fribble's assurance he won't use his wife as other men use theirs communicates more than he intends, reinforcing Miss Biddy's insinuations (pitched just over her suitor's head) about the happy bachelors' sexual self-sufficiency. The love poem Fribble then recites, far from counteracting this impression, makes the sodomitical subtext all but explicit:

No Ice so hard, so cold as I,
'Till warm'd and soften'd by your Eye;
And now my Heart dissolves away
In Dreams by Night, and Sighs by Day;
No brutal Passion fires my Breast,
Which loaths the Object when possess'd;
But one of harmless, gentle Kind,
Whose Joys are center'd—in the Mind:
Then take with me, Love's better Part,
His downy Wing, but not his Dart. (23)

Chaste moralists might applaud such virtuous, platonic sentiments, but the play's audience can be counted on to know what real women want, what real men have, what Fribbles lack: love's all-important "dart."

Fribble's inadvertently comic wooing is soon interrupted by the entrance of a rival, a braggart and beau named Flash. A ludicrous duel ensues, interrupted in turn by the entrance of Captain Loveit, the play's hero, exemplar of correct, "natural" masculinity, in contrast to the fribblish and flashy extremes. After physically ejecting Flash, Loveit frightens off Fribble with mere words. Yet they reveal the actual violence underlying the text's ostensibly lighthearted, good-natured homophobia. "Thou art of a Species too despicable for Correction," Loveit declares. "[T]herefore be gone, and if I see you here again, your Insignificancy shan't protect you" (32). Not having transgressed as egregiously as Charke or Smollett's sodomites, Fribble has not transgressed as egregiously as Charke or Smollett's sodomites, and so is let off with a warning. Yet clearly, like the texts for which Loveit, Dumont, Evelyn, Peregrine, and Pipes speak, their attitudes toward male homosexuality differ in degree, not kind.

Garrick, in fact, evokes homophobic violence earlier in the scene, although briefly. In response to Miss Biddy's characterization of Fribble's "little community" as "a sweet collection of happy creatures," the comical suitor replies:

> Indeed and so we are, Miss.—But a prodigious *Fracas* disconcerted us a little on our Visiting-Day at *Billy Dimple's*—three drunken naughty Women of the Town burst into our Club-room, curst us all, threw down the China, broke six Looking-glasses, scalded us with the Slop-Bason, and *scrat* poor *Phil Whiffle's* Cheek in such a manner, that he has kept his Bed these three Weeks. (21)

As in *Peregrine Pickle*, Garrick delegates homophobic violence to insufficiently feminine females (a "virago" in *Peregrine*, "drunken naughty Women of the Town" here), who preserve the hero from contact with sodomitical effeminacy. Yet as in Smollett's text, authorial desire to cause sodomites both physical and psychological pain is unmistakable, along with the expectation that readers will wish to share in the fun.[22]

---

[22] On the effeminophobia of *Miss in Her Teens*, including Garrick's violence toward Fribble, see Senelick. I disagree, however, with his assertion that "For the sake of politeness and plot, Garrick did not impute sexual deviancy to his character" (54–55), an assertion Fahrner repeats (9). On the implied homosexuality of Garrick's next effeminate character, Daffodil in *The Male-Coquette; or, Seventeen-Hundred Fifty-Seven* (1757), which Garrick wrote but did not play onstage, see Fahrner, although I'd describe this homophobic portrayal as euphemistic, rather than "veiled" or "encoded." It's worth mentioning that Fribble & his "pretty Set" in *Miss in Her Teens* echo Maiden and his "prettiest Company" in Thomas Baker's *Tunbridge-Walks, or the Yeoman of Kent* (1703), which, as Senelick points out (52), "was revived in 1738 (and would be again in 1748 in the wake of Garrick's successful refurbishing of the effeminate role)."

Sex: *Roderick Random*'s Sodomites

In contrast, as mentioned above, it is Fanny, *Memoirs*' woman of the town, whom Cleland subjects to physical pain; the sodomites she attempts to punish escape unharmed. True, some other fictional sodomites of the time go unpunished, but unlike Cleland's, they suffer meta-textually, held up for ridicule by their mocking authors.

In chapter five, we'll examine groups of authorially ridiculed sodomites from the anonymous *La France devenue italienne* and Nathaniel Lancaster's *The Pretty Gentleman*. I'd like, however, to conclude this contextualization of *Memoirs* by considering the two most famous homosexual characters in eighteenth-century English fiction, Captain Whiffle and Earl Strutwell, both of whom grace Smollett's first novel, *The Adventures of Roderick Random* (1748).

Roderick, the narrator-protagonist, encounters his first sodomite when Whiffle replaces Oakham, the tyrannical naval commander under whom the young man has been pressed into service. Whiffle's name meant, among other things, "[s]omething light or insignificant; a trifle," "to vacillate," "to flicker or flutter as if stirred by the wind," "[t]o talk idly; to trifle." It recalls Fribble's friend Phil Whiffle in *Miss in Her Teens* as well as Lord Whiffler in *The Intriguing Courtiers; or, The Modish Gallants* (1732; see Franceschina, 182). Capt. Whiffle's private surgeon, meanwhile, shares the same name—Simper—as one of Maiden's "pretty company" in *Tunbridge-Walks* (III, 30–31; see Senelick, 48). Yet Garrick and Baker's effeminates literally pale in comparison to Smollett's creation, whose entrance is especially unforgettable, both dazzling and unexpected:

> [O]ur new commander came on board, in a ten-oar'd barge, overshadowed with a vast umbrella, and appeared in everything quite the reverse of Oakhum, being a tall, thin, young man, dressed in this manner; a white hat garnished with a red feather, adorned his head, from whence his hair flowed down upon his shoulders, in ringlets tied behind with a ribbon.—His coat, consisting of pink-coloured silk, lined with white, by the elegance of the cut retired backward, as it were, to discover a white sattin waistcoat embroidered with gold, unbuttoned at the upper part, to display a broch set with garnets, that glittered in the breast of his shirt, which was of the finest cambrick, edged with right mechlin. The knees of his crimson velvet breeches scarce descended so low as to meet his silk stockings, which rose without spot or wrinkle on his meagre legs, from shoes of blue Meroquin, studded with diamond buckles, that flamed forth rivals to the sun! A steel-hilted sword, inlaid with figures of gold, and decked with a knot of ribbon which fell down in a rich tossle, equipped his side; and an amber-headed cane hung dangling from his wrist:—But the most remarkable parts of his furniture were, a mask on his face, and white gloves on his hands, which did not seem to be put on with an intention to be pulled off occasionally, but were fixed with a ring set with a ruby on the little finger of one hand, and by one set with a topaz on that of the other.—In this garb, captain Whiffle, for that was his name, took possession of the ship, surrounded with a crowd of

attendants, all of whom, in their different degrees, seemed to be of their patron's disposition; and the air was so impregnated with perfumes, that one may venture to affirm the clime of Arabie Fœlix was not half so sweet-scented. (195)

Roderick's friend Morgan, the ship's surgeon, "observing no surgeon among [Whiffle's] train," immediately sets out to ingratiate himself with the new captain. But his unsolicited approach has the opposite effect, for Whiffle's "nostrils were no sooner saluted with the aromatick flavour that exhaled from [Morgan]," than with cries of "Heaven preserve me! I am suffocated!" and "Will you not carry that monster away? or must I be stifled with the stench of him? oh! oh!" the captain "sunk down upon his settee in a fit" (196).

Revived by his servants (including *valet de chambre* Vergette, "French for a brush or clothes whisk, but also a sly pun on the sexual meaning of 'verge': a small penis" [Boucé, endnote, 460]), Whiffle sends for Roderick. But while the altogether cleaner and more pleasantly scented hero is allowed to approach, his attempts at medical examination produce equally alarming results, as when Whiffle cries, as Roderick tries to take his pulse, "What the devil art thou about?... dost thou intend to twist off my hand? Gad's curse! my arm is benumbed up to the very shoulder! Heaven have mercy upon me! must I perish under the hands of savages? What an unfortunate dog was I to come on board without my own surgeon, Mr. Simper" (198). Only the latter's arrival satisfies Whiffle, even as it incites gossip about their relationship:

> While I prepared [to bleed Captain Whiffle], there came into the cabbin, a young man, gayly dressed, of a very delicate complexion, with a kind of languid smile on his face, which seemed to have been rendered habitual, by a long course of affectation.—The captain no sooner perceived him, than rising hastily, he flew into his arms, crying, 'O! my dear Simper! I am excessively disordered! I have been betrayed, frighted, murdered by the negligence of my servants, who suffered a beast, a mule, a bear to surprize me, and stink me into convulsions with the fumes of tobacco.'—Simper, who by this time, I found, was obliged to art for the clearness of his complexion, assumed an air of softness and sympathy, and lamented with many tender expressions of sorrow, the sad accident that had thrown him into that condition; then feeling his patient's pulse on the outside of his glove, gave it as his opinion, that his disorder was entirely nervous, and that some drops of tincture of castor and liquid laudanum, would be of more service to him than bleeding, by bridling the inordinate sallies of his spirits, and composing the fermentation of his bile proceeding therefrom.—I was therefore sent to prepare this prescription, which was administered in a glass of sack-posset, after the captain had been put to bed, and orders sent to the officers on the quarter-deck, to let no body walk on that side under which he lay.
>
> While the captain enjoyed his repose, the doctor watched over him, and indeed became so necessary, that a cabin was made for him contiguous to the state-room, where Whiffle slept; that he might be at hand in case of accidents in the night.—Next day, our commander being happily recovered, gave orders, that none of the lieutenants should appear upon deck, without a wig, sword, and ruffles; nor any midshipman, or other petty

officer, be seen with a check shirt or dirty linen.—He also prohibited any person whatever, except Simper and his own servants, from coming into the great cabbin, without first sending in to obtain leave.—These singular regulations did not prepossess the ship's company in his favour; but on the contrary, gave scandal an opportunity to be very busy with his character, and accuse him of maintaining a correspondence with his surgeon, not fit to be named. (198–99)

That correspondence, of course, is sodomy, denoted here by the quintessential homophobic euphemism—"not fit to be named"—by means of which homosexuality is simultaneously exposed and evaded, by a speaker who, like Peregrine, can thus punish the sodomite without risking contamination. Homophobic mission accomplished, Roderick and his narrative have nothing more to say about Whiffle.

They do, however, have more to say about sodomy. Later, while attempting to advance his interests at court, Roderick takes up with two lords, Straddle and Swillpot, who advise him to solicit the patronage of a certain Earl Strutwell (based, according to Jeremy Bentham's private writings on pederasty, on Earl Tylney, whose emigration from England to Italy, where he died unmarried in 1784, was rumored to have been sodomitically motivated[23]). The Earl's ready promise of assistance elicits tears of gratitude from the young petitioner, which then prompt reciprocal signs of affection from the nobleman:

[H]e caught me in his arms, hugged and kissed me with a seemingly paternal affection.—Confounded at this uncommon instance of fondness for a stranger, I remained a few moments silent and ashamed, then got up and took my leave, after he had assured me he would speak to the Minister in my favour, that very day.... (309)

At the next visit, while "the *valet de chamber*... cast some furious looks at [Roderick], the meaning of which [he] could not comprehend," Strutwell greets the young man "with a tender embrace," and announces he has found him a position as an ambassador's secretary (309). Once again, Roderick's display of emotion prompts an even greater in return, as the Earl "pressed [Roderick] to his breast with surprizing emotion" (309).

Under pretext of "making light of the favour," Strutwell then "shift[s] the conversation to another subject," leading up to a discourse as dazzling and unexpected as Whiffle's grand entrance:

Among other topicks of discourse, that of the *Belle Lettre* was introduced, upon which his lordship held forth with great taste and erudition, and discovered an intimate knowledge of the authors of antiquity.—'Here's a book (said he, taking one from his bosom) written with great elegance and spirit, and though the subject may give offence

---

[23] Crompton, 43, n.93; "Sodom and Onan, A Satire" (1776), rpt. <http://www.infopt.demon.co.uk/1772sodo.htm> with Norton's annotation.

to some narrow-minded people, the author will always be held in esteem by every person of sense and learning.' So saying, he put into my hand Petronius Arbiter [i.e., his book, the *Satyricon*], and asked my opinion of his wit and manner.—I told him, that in my opinion, he wrote with great ease and vivacity, but was withal so lewd and indecent, that he ought to find no quarter or protection among people of morals and taste.—'I own (replied the Earl) that his taste in love is generally decried, and indeed condemned by our laws; but perhaps that may be more owing to prejudice and misapprehension, than to true reason and deliberation.—The best man among the ancients is said to have entertained that passion; one of the wisest of their legislators has permitted the indulgence of it in his commonwealth; the most celebrated poets have not scrupled to avow it at this day; it prevails not only over all the east, but in most parts of Europe; in our own country it gains ground apace, and in all probability will become in a short time a more fashionable vice than simple fornication.—Indeed there is something to be said in vindication of it, for notwithstanding the severity of the law against offenders in this way, it must be confessed that the practice of this passion is unattended with that curse and burthen upon society, which proceeds from a race of miserable deserted bastards, who are either murdered by their parents, deserted to the utmost want and wretchedness, or bred up to prey upon the commonwealth: And it likewise prevents the debauchery of many a young maiden, and the prostitution of honest men's wives; not to mention the consideration of health, which is much less liable to be impaired in the gratification of this appetite, than in the exercise of common venery, which by ruining the constitutions of our young men, has produced a puny progeny that degenerates from generation to generation: Nay, I have been told, that there is another motive perhaps more powerful than all these, that induces people to cultivate this inclination; namely, the exquisite pleasure attending its success.' (309–10)

Strutwell's defense of this "taste in love," this "passion," this "fashionable vice," "this appetite," "this inclination"—of sodomy, in other words—makes Roderick predictably "apprehensive." The reason, though, is surprising:

From this discourse, I began to be apprehensive that his lordship finding I had travelled, was afraid I might have been infected with this spurious and sordid desire abroad, and took this method of sounding my sentiments on the subject.—Fired at this supposed suspicion, I argued against it with great warmth, as an appetite unnatural, absurd, and of pernicious consequence; and declared my utter detestation and abhorrence of it in these lines of the satyrist:

'Eternal infamy the wretch confound
Who planted first, this vice on British ground!
A vice! that 'spite of sense and nature reigns,
And poisons genial love, and manhood stains!'

The Earl smiled at my indignation, told me he was glad to find my opinion of the matter so conformable to his own, and that what he had advanced was only to provoke me to an answer, with which he professed himself perfectly well pleased. (310–11)

At the end of the conversation, overjoyed at the seeming success of his application for favor, Roderick gives his watch to Strutwell as a present, then "fl[ies] to the lodgings of Lord Straddle," who had directed him to the Earl, and "force[s]" his diamond ring upon him "as an acknowledgment for [his] great service" (311–12).

Only when Roderick relates his good fortune to another acquaintance does he learn the truth:

> that Straddle was a poor contemptible wretch, who lived by borrowing and pimping to his fellow peers; that in consequence of this last capacity, he had, doubtless, introduced [Roderick] to Strutwell, who was... notorious for a passion for his own sex...; and that so far from being able to obtain for [Roderick] the post he had promised, his interest at court was so low, that he could scarce provide for a superannuated footman once a year, in Chelsea-hospital; ...and that the whole of his conduct towards [Roderick] was so glaring, that no body who knew any thing of mankind could have been imposed upon by his insinuations. (312–13)

Enlightened at last, Roderick remarks that Strutwell's "hugs, embraces, squeezes and eager looks, were now no longer a mystery; no more than his defence of Petronius, and the jealous frown of his *valet de chambre*, who, it seems, was at present the favourite pathic of his lord" (313). Next day Roderick attempts unsuccessfully to recover his watch and ring, but is never again able to obtain a private audience with the Earl. Like Whiffle, Strutwell exits the narrative unpunished.

Unpunished, that is, within the text itself. For both Whiffle and Strutwell are ridiculed by their author. On this point—Smollett's intent to satirize male homosexuality—all critics agree. As Paul Hammond says, Smollett's depiction of Whiffle, Strutwell, and their attendants provides readers a "lesson in how to recognize the signs of [this] deviant sexuality" (112).[24]

As others have observed (Beynon [2001], Fone, McFarlane), a similar lesson is provided by *Plain Reasons for the Growth of Sodomy, in England* (c.1728), reprinted in *Satan's Harvest Home: or the Present State of Whorecraft, Adultery, Fornication, Procuring, Pimping, Sodomy, And the Game at Flatts* (1749), which appeared the year after *Roderick Random*. In the first chapter, the enraged author condemns "the modern Modish way of bringing up young Gentleman" (47) for producing *Petits Maitres*, *Milksops*, and *Clouts*, who themselves engender "a Race effeminate as [themselves]; who, unable to please the Women, chuse rather to run into unnatural Vices one with another, than to attempt what they are but too sensible they cannot perform" (49, 50). In the second chapter ("The Effeminacy of

---

[24] See Beynon (2001), Bruhm (1993), Day, Fone (1995 & 2000), Goode, Haggerty (1999), Hammond (1996), McFarlane, Robinson (1993), and Rousseau (1987). Prior to Day's essay, critics commented only in passing on Smollett's sodomites, but noted his anti-sodomitical intent (e.g., Bruce, 77; Boucé, 113).

our Men's Dress and Manners, particularly their Kissing each other"), the author ridicules the dress and manners of "Master *Molly*" and his ilk (51):

> I AM confident no Age can produce any Thing so preposterous as the present Dress of those Gentlemen who call themselves pretty Fellows: their Head-Dress especially, which wants nothing but a Suit of Pinners to make them down-right Women. But this may be easily accounted for, as they would appear as soft as possible to each other, any Thing of *Manliness* being diametrically opposite to such unnatural Practices, so they cannot too much invade the Dress of the Sex they would represent....
>
> But of all the Customs *Effeminacy* has produc'd, none more hateful, predominant, and pernicious, than that of the Mens *Kissing* each other. This *Fashion* was brought over from *Italy*, (the *Mother* and *Nurse* of *Sodomy*); where the *Master* is oftner *Intriguing* with his *Page*, than a *fair Lady*. And not only in the *Country*, but in *France*, which copies from them, the *Contagion* is diversify'd, and the Ladies (in the *Nunneries*) are criminally *amorous* of each other, in a *Method* too gross for Expression. I must be so partial to my own *Country Women*, to affirm, or, at least, hope they claim no Share of this *Charge*; but must confess, when I see two Ladies *Kissing* and *Slopping* each other, in a *lascivious Manner*, and *frequently* repeating it, I am shock'd to the last Degree; but not so much, as when I see two *fulsome* Fellows *Slavering* every Time they meet, *Squeezing* each other's Hand, and other like *indecent Symptoms*. And tho' many Gentlemen of Worth, are oftentimes, out of pure good *Manners*, obliged to give into it; yet the Land will never be purged of its *Abominations*, till this *Unmanly*, *Unnatural* Usage be totally abolish'd: For it is the first *Inlet* to the detestable Sin of *Sodomy*. (50–52)

Smollett's depiction of Whiffle and Strutwell unmistakably shares the same targets.[25]

Each author, moreover, recognizes that appearances can be deceiving. In the above passage, the anonymous satirist admits that "many Gentlemen of Worth, are oftentimes, out of pure good *Manners*, obliged to give into" practices that encourage, and even signal, sodomy. He thus strongly recommends, "With this [*Man-Kissing*], all other *Effeminacies* should be abolished; and each Sex should maintain its peculiar Character" (54). As several critics have observed, Smollett subtly suggests, and mocks, a similar blurring of boundaries between hero and homo. For as Steven Bruhm (1993) points out, "only sixty pages after the Whiffle scene" Roderick himself engages in an "ostentatious dandiacal performance," wearing French fashions and "becom[ing] more affected, stylized, and artificial" (410); likewise, "[it] is in [this] manifestation as a 'pretty fellow,'" notes McFarlane, "that Roderick encounters Earl Strutwell" (138). And as Beynon (2001) argues, "Random's incessant embraces and kisses [bestowed] on his closest male friends also beg to be understood in light of his subsequent discovery that

---

[25] On *Plain Reasons* and *Satan's Harvest Home*, see Edelman (1990/1994), Haggerty (1999), McFarlane, and Moore. For earlier homophobic reaction to men kissing, see Franceschina (115) on Richard Head's popular novel *The English Rogue* (1665).

such activities are the favored mode of a sodomitical seducer like Earl Strutwell, and his proclamations of affection toward his male friends often sound little less than infatuated outbursts" (140; see also Bruhm, 407–408). Yet while Smollett clearly satirizes Roderick's sartorial metamorphosis, suggesting that masculine and effeminate apparel are easily distinguishable, he employs the similarity between Strutwell's physical displays of affection and those of Roderick and friends far less straightforwardly.

Of course, such fuzziness (as Bruhm terms it [407]) is to be expected in a modern homophobic scene—and most critics recognize, in Whiffle, a modern homophobic stereotype. As Sedgwick demonstrated so memorably in *Between Men* (e.g., 89), modern homophobia derives much of its power from obscuring the line that separates homosexual from homosocial, all the while insisting not only that such a line exists, but that its precise location is obvious. *Roderick Random* exemplifies this dynamic especially well. Consequently, as McFarlane explains, not only does Roderick fail to "'read' Strutwell in the same way that he 'read' Whiffle," but he also "cannot be certain that he does not appear as 'other' himself.... Roderick, who should, presumably, be identifying the 'other' in the person of Strutwell, instead fears that it has been identified in him..." (139–40). Yet while McFarlane, Bruhm, Beynon, and others insightfully demonstrate how Smollett's homophobic portrayals typify the homophobia of the period, and perhaps modern homophobia more generally, they nonetheless miss much of what's specific to Smollett himself, what differentiates his treatment of male-male desire from his contemporaries'.[26]

Interestingly, Robert Adams Day, the first critic to seriously consider the subject of Smollett and sodomy (1982), best appreciated the author's singularity in this regard, not only in *Roderick* and *Peregrine*, but also in *The History and Adventures of an Atom* (1769) and *Advice* (1746). Although I'm unconvinced by Day's ultimate claim—that Smollett's concern with homosexuality and homophobia are mere epiphenomena, symptoms of a more essential, anal-obsessive pattern—his essay remains valuable, not least for its willingness to consider Smollett's own consciousness, as revealed through his texts and through biographical information. For with the exception of the other early piece to consider Smollett's sodomitical characters (Rousseau's pioneering 1985 essay), subsequent criticism followed the field's dominant practices of historicizing but not biographizing.

And yet the details of Smollett's life illuminate the choices he makes in *Roderick Random*. For instance, faced with his direct, extended, frequent treatments of sodomy, some scholars have emphasized Smollett's realism, in

---

[26] For more on the resemblance between Roderick and Strutwell, and its illustration of Sedgwick's ideas on homosexuality, homosociality, and homophobia, see Bruhm (1993), 407–408. Unfortunately, this otherwise excellent piece is marred by uncritical differentism, particularly regarding "the birth of the closet" (405–407).

contrast to, as Tom Scott puts it (with unfortunate overgeneralization), the "genteel censorship of life as it is" characteristic of most other writers of the time (111). Rousseau, likewise, remarks that "Smollett was such a keen observer of the customs and mores of 'the town' that it is not surprising to find him dwelling on the matter at such length" (151). And indeed, Whiffle's pinky ring (which Rousseau calls "a telling detail, as revealing today as it was in the eighteenth century" [148]) suggests at least some observation of actual sodomites, or access to at least partially accurate sources of information.[27]

Judged from the standpoint of realistic observation, however, *Roderick*'s depiction of sodomites is remarkable for what it leaves out. Smollett draws extensively upon his experience as a surgeon in the British Navy to portray his hero's shipboard experience. He even makes overtly realistic claims for this section of the story, by having Roderick take part in an actual naval expedition, the ill-fated British siege of Cartagena, Columbia (1741), in which the twenty-year-old Smollett himself participated. As court-martial records show, the British Navy of the time was rife—or resplendent—with sodomy. Even if Smollett himself did not partake, he would have known such activity was taking place around him. And he would have known those engaged in it were not effeminate mollies, not Captain Whiffles, men who could never have survived as sailors, much less commanders, but rather were "normal" men and youths like himself. If Smollett had portrayed naval sodomy realistically, he would have depicted the "vice" among Roderick's rank-and-file shipmates (perhaps by having a sailor make a pass at Roderick). Instead, in both the Whiffle and Strutwell episodes, Smollett confines sodomy to an elite coterie.[28]

But setting aside biography for the moment, what most subsequent critics fail to appreciate in Day's essay, and to build upon, is his demonstration of a pattern pervading Smollett's oeuvre. Removing the Whiffle and Strutwell scenes from the context of Smollett's other writing, most critics miss the most powerful and poignant reason for their arresting presence in *Roderick Random*.

Take, for example, Bruhm's astute observation that Roderick, as a heterosexual male, inhabits a closet of his own, intimately connected to but subtly contrasting with Strutwell's homosexual closet:

> The gay closet in this novel functions as a self-protecting yet self-disclosing means of letting men in; the straight closet functions as a self-enclosing means of keeping men out. [¶] This isolation goes further than merely protecting the self from being duped by a

---

[27] On pinky rings as a traditional gay sign, see Grahn.

[28] On Smollett and the Cartagena expedition, see Boucé's notes to *Roderick*, 455–56. Beynon (2001) also objects to the supposed realism of Smollett's sodomitical portrayals, but on different grounds, implying that Smollett's characters are, by virtue of their stereotypicality, necessarily unrealistic (162). Yet some mid-eighteenth-century English sodomites might, for any number of reasons, have flaunted their violation of the dominant model of masculinity in ways that accorded with stereotype.

court full of queens. Roderick also deploys his closet to keep out his straight friends....
[For example, by] maintaining secrets, or by being selective in their telling, Roderick continually avoids honest and vulnerable admission to [his closest friend,] Strap. ([1993] 409-10)

Bruhm's analysis is correct. But it tells only half the story. It leaves out how much this novel—and how much Smollett in all his novels—resists this form of masculinity, how he yearns for loving, mutually vulnerable connection among men, yet repeatedly fails to create it, opting instead for the self-protective, self-sufficient masculinity Bruhm describes. What's missing from Bruhm's analysis of Smollett and sodomy, in other words, is an analysis of Smollett and love—love between men.[29]

Love: *Roderick*'s Masculine Friends

Significantly, the one critic who, like Day, explores a large portion of Smollett's body of work, is the one who comes closest to perceiving the significance of male love in *Roderick Random*. At the end of his chapter "Sodomitical Smollett," McFarlane examines Roderick's encounter, near the end of the novel, with "Don Rodriguez[,] [who] turns out to be Roderick's long-lost father" (142). Their interaction, McFarlane reveals, closely resembles that between Roderick and Strutwell. But with a crucial difference:

> The language of romantic infatuation which characterizes this episode can be indulged because of, and is cleansed by, the discovery of consanguinity. Whereas Earl Strutwell caught Roderick in his arms and kissed him with only a *"seemingly* paternal affection"—offering a perversion of this most sacred of homosocial relationships—Don Rodriguez can offer the real thing, clasping Roderick in his arms and crying "my son! my son!"
>
> This conclusion—meant... to be read in opposition to the Strutwell episode—represents the achievement of the homosocial ideal, a pure bond between men, cleansed of the "sordid and vicious disposition" that characterized other relationships in the novel.... But... [t]he thinly veiled erotic nature of this reunion, and the language of

---

[29] The following argument is drawn from my earliest extended foray into literary criticism and the history of sexuality (Robinson [1986]), in which I considered male friendship in Smollett's five novels, Richardson's *Sir Charles Grandison*, and Fielding's *Amelia*, arguing that mutual vulnerability proves virtually unattainable for the men depicted. In spite of the culture's idealization of egalitarian male friendship, in which the partners express equal affection and receive as well as give assistance, most male friendship in these novels remains trapped in a master/servant or patron/protégé model, with one partner resolutely maintaining superiority, holding back from deeper intimacy. As for the rare instances in which male characters bond in shared vulnerability, anti-sodomitical alarms quickly sound.

infatuation that preceded it, demonstrate again how in Smollett's sodomitical practices a disturbing sameness inheres within difference and the reviled "other" turns out to be "proximate." (142–43)

McFarlane's analysis of the Roderick/Rodriguez relationship is excellent. Yet he, too, overlooks Roderick's friendships that *weren't* "sordid and vicious," and that offered an intimacy even greater than between father and son. It is these tender, demonstrative, egalitarian friendships that, along with the portrayal of male sodomites, make *Roderick Random* such an unusual, important document in the history of sexuality, gender, and love.

Not coincidentally, these exceptional male friendships arise at sea, among the suspiciously nonsodomitical sailors aboard the *Thunder*, subjected to the whims of sadistic Captain Oakhum. These interconnected bonds are the most fully realized and successful male friendships not only in *Roderick Random*, but in most eighteenth-century British fiction.

Persecuted by both captain and surgeon, four men—sailor Jack Rattlin, and surgeon's first mate Morgan, second mate Thomson, and third mate Roderick, the center of the group—nurture one another through often horrific trials, including the most harrowing episode in all Smollett's work, in which Roderick is chained to the deck in the midst of battle as sailors are blown up around him (167–68). Thomson, however, is often separated from his friends and forced to bear the brunt of the surgeon's malice alone. Unable to stand the strain, he throws himself overboard.

When Roderick and Morgan learn of their friend's suicide, "The news of this event affected my fellow-prisoner and me extremely," writes Roderick, "as our unfortunate companion had justly acquired by his amiable disposition, the love and esteem of us both" (170). Thomson's suicide note only deepens Roderick's grief:

DEAR FRIEND,

I am so much oppressed with the fatigue I daily and nightly undergo, and the barbarous usage of doctor Mackshane, who is bent on your destruction, as well as mine, that I am resolved to free myself from this miserable life, and before you receive this, shall be no more. I could have wished to die in your good opinion, which I am afraid I shall forfeit by the last act of my life; but if you cannot acquit me, I know you will at least preserve some regard for the memory of an unfortunate young man who loved you.—I recommend it to you, to beware of Mackshane, whose revenge is implacable.—I wish all prosperity to you and Mr. Morgan, to whom pray offer my last respects, and beg to be remembered as your unhappy friend and countryman.

WILLIAM THOMSON (174)

The letter is remarkable for its believable depth of feeling. In most novels of the period, declarations of love from one man to another sound stilted and unconvincing, part of what Mark Kinkead-Weekes dubbed the "language of ought" in contrast to the "language of is." Here, however, when Thomson calls himself "an unfortunate young man who loved you," we believe him. His previous behavior has demonstrated the strength of his attachment, and the note's simple, tragic words convey his feelings powerfully. Likewise, we believe Roderick when he writes that he and Morgan "repair[ed]… to the cockpit, which I no sooner entered, than the idea of my departed friend presented itself to my remembrance, and filled my eyes with tears" (177). The rather conventional language ("my departed friend," "my remembrance," "filled my eyes with tears") is still moving in its simplicity, its ordinariness, describing a believable response to the sudden end of an equally believable friendship.[30]

The strongest, most emotional depiction of male friendship is yet to come. Transferred to a new ship after Whiffle replaces Oakhum, Roderick, on shore leave, accidentally encounters his "lamented friend" Thomson, whom he'd believed dead, but who had actually been rescued by a passing vessel. Describing their reunion, Roderick writes:

> Perceiving my confusion, which was extreme, he clasped me in his arms and bedewed my face with tears.—It was some time ere I recovered the use of my reason, overpowered with this event, and longer still before I could speak. So that all I was capable of, was to return his embraces, and to mingle the overflowings of my joy with his; while [my new commander], affected with the scene, wept as fast as either of us, and signified his participation of our happiness, by hugging us both, and capering about the room like a mad-man.—At length I retrieved the use of my tongue, and cried, "Is it possible, can you be my friend Thomson? No certainly, alas! he was drowned! and I am under the deception of a dream!"—Then I relapsed into tears. (202)

The tears, the embraces, the *credible* (at least on Roderick and Thomson's part) excess of emotion all convey the strength of the two men's love. As for the capering captain, introducing a bit of comic relief, he reaffirms the novel's ideal of *communal* male affection, while offering a utopian contrast to the infernal Oakhum. Roderick's description of the rest of his visit makes such utopianism explicit:

> Never were two friends more happy in conversation of one another than we, for the time it lasted.… In short, while [the ship] staid here, we saw one another every day, and generally eat at the same table, which was plentifully supplied by him…; *so that this small interval of ten days, was by far the most agreeable period of my life.* (204–205; my italics)

Unlike most of their fictional contemporaries, Roderick and Thomson are able to build an intensely loving relationship, climaxing in this brief, tender idyll. And as

---

[30] On the two types of language see Kinkead-Weekes, pt.3, as well as Robinson (1989) on male friendship in Richardson's fiction.

in Roderick's larger network of shipboard friendships, which forms the book's true emotional center, in this relationship Roderick appears at his best: giving and given to, supporting and supported, trusting and trusted, loving and loved. Of the many male friendships in eighteenth-century British fiction, these perhaps come closest to their authors' oft-professed, rarely realized ideal.

Love? *Roderick*'s Masculine Friends

In his paradigm-shifting book *Men in Love: Masculinity and Sexuality in the Eighteenth Century*, Haggerty offers a brief, intentionally perverse reading of *Roderick Random*'s sodomitical characters. Regarding Whiffle and his private physician, Simper, Haggerty writes:

> the "long course of affectation" in which these men are involved can also be read as a long course of affection.... The affectation that links these two characters, although histrionic and at times ridiculous, is an intimacy that is rendered almost sympathetic just in the care with which Smollett describes it. For whatever these two men do in private, what we see is their affectional relation. In spite of dress, manners, speech, affectation, I would claim, we are looking at men in love. (74)

Similarly, discussing the Strutwell episode, he argues:

> What becomes more and more obvious... is that Strutwell is describing more than a simple issue of behavior. The "passion" he describes and that Whiffle exhibits is much more than simple sexual behavior; for it involves an affectional and circumstantial system of relations that renders it an entity in its own right. We are not talking about sexual identity here, we are talking about an affectional system that creates a space out of which the concept of sexuality itself may emerge. (74–75)

In contrast, regarding Strutwell's apologia for sodomy, Hammond asserts that "the voluptuary's culminating argument, that 'the gratification of this appetite' produces 'the most exquisite pleasure,'" demonstrates that "[we] have here simply the language of vice and appetite, not of desire for the male body, let alone love" (113). Indeed, other characters inform us precisely how to view Whiffle and Strutwell, their behavior and desires: Whiffle, according to Morgan, "is disguised and transfigured, and transmographied with affectation and whimsies; and... he is more like a [baboon] than one of the human race" (196); the "passion" Strutwell defends is, according to Roderick (quoting Smollett's own anti-sodomitical satire *Advice* [*Roderick*, n.4 to p.310]), "A vice... that... poisons genial love, and manhood stains!" Haggerty's resistant reading of these episodes, however, helps us see what's at issue for Smollett: not just male bonding or homosociality, but male-male love. *That*'s what Smollett idealizes, what he portrays in the relationships between Roderick and his naval friends (especially Thomson), and what he fears must be distinguished from sodomy.

Such fears aren't groundless. As noted above, to a reader on the lookout for signs of sodomy Roderick's friendships provide ample grounds for suspicion. For instance, the author of *Plain Reasons for the Growth of Sodomy* would surely object to the sailors' embraces, and probably their tears. Even between family members, physical demonstrativeness disturbs this moralist: "For my Part, I hold it so ridiculous foolish Custom for a Man to *Kiss* even his own Brother, it favours too much of *Effeminacy*, to say the best of it" (53). Even without hugs, tears, and declarations of love, Roderick's male friendships are open to sodomitical interpretation. Consider his first meeting with Thomson. Looking at the "crowds of young fellows" in London's Naval Office, Roderick writes, "I consulted the physiognomy of each, and at last made up to one whose countenance I lik'd" (78). Roderick asks for help with the procedures of the office, which the attractive young man willingly gives. Soon, Roderick tells us, "I conceived a mighty liking for this young fellow, which (I believe) proceeded from the similitude of our fortunes: We spent the whole day together; and as he lived at Wapping, I desir'd him to take a share of my bed" (79). Even Roderick seems unsure why he's instantly drawn to Thomson, interjecting a parenthetical "I believe" that only serves to cast doubt on the explanation he proposes.

Hence the lessons in sodomitical appearance and behavior Smollett subsequently provides. To protect his characters from anti-sodomitical suspicion—and to protect himself, given the semi-autobiographical source of the *Thunder* material—Smollett presents identifiably homosexual characters as foils, as if to say, "*Those* are sodomites. Roderick and his friends are nothing like *them*." And thus, although Smollett might know sodomy to be common among sailors, he can on no account acknowledge the fact; such masculine sodomites would bear too close a resemblance to the protagonist and his friends, arousing rather than allaying suspicion. Instead, he employs two scapegoating stereotypes—the corrupt, debauched nobleman and the effeminate molly—fleshed out for maximum contrast with Roderick and friends. Whiffle and Strutwell are upper-class; Whiffle is extremely effeminate (far more so than Roderick in his "pretty fellow" guise); and both are associated, in a variety of ways, with foreignness, reinforcing the notion of homosexuality as a foreign (especially French and Italian) vice.[31]

---

[31] On homosexuality and foreignness, see especially McFarlane, and Beynon (2001). However, it's important not to *assume* (as do most critics) that such associations are wholly or even predominantly ideological rather than factual. As Norton (private communication [2004]) argues, "the English associated homosexuality with France and Italy not simply because they wanted to construct homosexuality as something 'foreign,' but because they observed that homosexual relations were much more openly practised in France and Italy than in any other European country. As Rocke's book has established, in some Italian cities, notably Florence, homosexuality really was very widely practised—Italy's reputation as 'the

Even with conventionally masculine men such as Roderick and his fellow sailors, such defensive maneuvers are inherently problematic, asserting black-and-white distinctions (sexual/nonsexual; masculine/feminine) where shades of gray predominate. But they're doomed to failure when confronted with the longest-lasting and most complex relationship in the novel, Roderick's friendship with Strap, his schoolmate, companion, servant, and sometime friend. Earlier critics dismiss the relationship as patently unimportant; recent ones conflate it with Roderick's other friendships, as yet one more locus of suspiciously demonstrative male affection. Yet the relationship is unlike any other in the novel.[32]

On one side is "[t]he attachment of Strap, [which] flow[s] from a voluntary, disinterested inclination" (16) and results in unwavering, unstinting devotion and service. On the other is Roderick's behavior, which ranges from grateful, even tearful appreciation (73), to matter-of-fact entitlement (62), to angry rejection (283), physical abuse (356–57), and abandonment (108). Like Roderick's other close friendships, this one includes physical demonstrativeness, but flagged by Roderick as one-sided and excessive (e.g., "such was his transport at finding me safe and sound, that he had almost stifled and stunk me to death with his embraces" [94]; "he leaped upon me in a transport of joy, hung about my neck, kissed me from ear to ear, and blubbered like a great school-boy who has been whipt" [252]).

Sexual issues aside, Roderick's situation is inherently uncomfortable: he's never cared for Strap as much as Strap cares for him. But there's more to his, and Smollett's, treatment of this particular friend. Strap is a weakling (94) and coward (408), and often behaves more like a stereotypical wife or mistress than a friend or servant (283–84; 358). In other words, unlike Thomson, Morgan, and Rattlin, Strap is effeminate. Consequently, far more than the sailors' embraces, Strap's threat to recall the "hugs, embraces, [and] squeezes" of the odious Strutwell, or the "correspondence... not fit to be named" of Whiffle and Simper. Indeed, it's hardly accidental that while Thomson, Morgan, and Strap all embrace Roderick, only Strap kisses him. No other man does so, except Strutwell.

Not surprisingly, until Roderick and Strap are safely married to women at novel's end, their friendship remains conflicted. So does Smollett's own relationship to Strap, whom he presents as invariably generous, loving, and faithful, yet ridicules more than any other positive character. This ridicule defuses

---

mother and nurse of sodomy' was well-earned.... It seems to me that this is a matter of observation first and ideology second, rather than the other way around. A stereotype portraying homosexuality as an exotic import obviously arises, and is probably strengthened by the universal psychological tension between Self and Other. Such stereotypes obviously take hold because they fit an ideological presupposition, but nevertheless they arise in the first instance, I think, from an observed kernel of truth." See also N.S. Davidson.

[32] See, e.g., Boucé (1976) 107; Grant, 129–30; Bruhm (1993) 407–408; and Beynon (2001) 140.

any tension caused by Strap's relationship with Roderick, signaling the reader not to take the bond seriously.[33]

And yet, ultimately, Smollett undermines even Roderick's relationship with Thomson. Describing their last visit, near the end of the novel, Roderick writes, "I should much wrong the delicacy of Mr. Thomson's sentiments, to say barely he was glad to see me: He felt all that the most sensible and disinterested friendship could feel on this occasion" (418). Suddenly, Roderick and Smollett have adopted the "language of ought": telling, rather than showing, the characters' feelings.

This retreat into formula reflects Smollett's attempt to bring the novel to a close, which for him means sacrificing the believability of almost all events and relationships, to achieve a neat, conventional, happy ending. And as is so often the case, the imperatives of narrative closure are relentlessly heterosexual. Thomson is now married; Roderick will be soon (to the suggestively named Narcissa, who, like her successors in *Peregrine Pickle, Ferdinand Count Fathom*, and *Sir Launcelot Greaves*, is more a functional placeholder—The Heroine—than an actual character). Male-male intimacy survives only in the relationship between Roderick and his newly discovered father, Don Rodriguez. There, to repeat McFarlane's observation, it may be safely couched in "the language of romantic infatuation," since its nature as "a father-son bond only emphasizes its utter purity" (143). At last, depicting a relationship that is, by definition, above suspicion, Smollett is free to indulge in homoerotic fantasy.

But what of that earlier, brief, utopian idyll, following Roderick and Thomson's unlooked-for reunion?

> Never were two friends more happy in conversation of one another than we, for the time it lasted.... In short, while [the ship] staid here, we saw one another every day, and generally eat at the same table, which was plentifully supplied by him...; so that this small interval of ten days, was by far the most agreeable period of my life. (204–205)

Although Smollett avoids obviously romantic or erotic diction, and omits the embraces found elsewhere, doesn't he leave the scene open to homoerotic interpretation (by using the word "conversation," for instance, with its alternate, sexual meaning)? And eroticism aside, doesn't he, with this powerfully understated passage, offer a rare and moving picture of male-male love?

Yes, he does. Yet the expressions of this love have been very carefully chosen. Even at the moment of miraculous reunion, Roderick and Thomson do not kiss, but only embrace; on their later visit they no longer even embrace. The physical tokens of their love are now money and food:

> Next day he accompanied me to the ship, where Mr. Brayl [the capering captain] entertained him at dinner, and having spent the afternoon together, [Thomson] took his

---

[33] For a more detailed analysis of the relationship, see Robinson (1986).

76   *Closeted Writing and Lesbian and Gay Literature*

> leave of us in the evening, after he had forced upon me ten pistoles [coins], as a small token of his affection.—In short, while we staid here, we saw one another every day, and generally eat at the same table, which was plentifully supplied by him, with all kinds of poultry, butcher's meat, oranges, limes, lemons, pine-aples, Madeira-wine, and excellent rum; so that this small interval of ten days, was by far the most agreeable period of my life. (204–205)

Even this substitution, or sublimation, doesn't suffice. To protect Roderick and Thomson from any suspicion of sodomy, a crucial, heretofore missing element must be added, the precise timing and phrasing of which epitomizes the novel's presentation of love between men:

> Never were two friends more happy in the conversation of one another than we, for the time it lasted: I related to him the particulars of our attempt upon Carthagena, of which he had heard but an imperfect account; and he gratified me with a narration of every little incident in his life since we parted.—He assured me, it was with the utmost reluctance, he could resist his inclination of coming down to Port-Royal to see Morgan and me, of whom he had heard no tidings since the day of our separation; but that he was restrained by the fear of being detained as a deserter.—He told me, that when he heard my voice in the dark, he was almost as much surprized as I was at seeing him afterwards; and in the confidence of friendship, disclosed a passion—

Can it be? Does Thomson, "in the confidence of friendship, disclose a passion" for Roderick? Is the "inclination" he has difficulty resisting the same "inclination" Strutwell will later defend?

Of course not. It *cannot* be:

> He told me, that when he heard my voice in the dark, he was almost as much surprized as I was at seeing him afterwards; and in the confidence of friendship, disclosed a passion he entertained for the only daughter of the gentleman with whom he lived, who, by his description, was a very amiable young lady, and did not disdain his addresses; that he was very much favoured by his parents, and did not despair of obtaining their consent to the match, which would at once render him independent of the world.—I congratulated him on his good fortune, which he protested should never make him forget his friend; and towards morning we betook ourselves to rest. (204)

Only with all doubts about Thomson's *passion* removed, can he and Roderick display their *affection*.

The Contradictory Mrs. Cole

Over and over, explicitly and implicitly, Smollett distinguishes what Roderick and his friends feel and do from the feelings and behavior of sodomites. He condemns *sex* between men, in order to present what matters most to him: *love* between men. As for Cleland, there is, perhaps, a momentary hint of sodomitical love in that "long-breath'd kiss" exchanged while the young sparks pursue their "project of preposterous pleasure." But love or no love, Cleland leaves no doubt that he depicts sodomitical *sex*. What, though, are readers meant to think and feel about it, and about these sodomites who, unlike Strutwell, swindle no one; unlike Whiffle, insult no one; unlike Strutwell and Loveman, attempt no man's virtue; unlike Whiffle and Fribble, usurp no man's rightful place (as captain, as suitor)? How ought readers to respond to these lads whose only offense is sodomitical sex?

And does it matter that the sex occurs in a text that, at least at one point, preaches toleration of "arbitrary," aberrant sexual tastes? For while discussing flagellation, Mrs. Cole, Fanny's madam and teacher, declares:

> [F]or her part, she consider'd pleasure of one sort or other, as the universal port of destination, and every wind that blew thither a good one, provided it blew nobody any harm: that she rather compassionated, than blam'd those unhappy persons, who are under a subjection they cannot shake off, to those arbitrary tastes that rule their appetites of pleasure with an unaccountable controul: tastes, too, as infinitely diversify'd, as superior to, and independent of all reasoning, as the different relishes or palates of mankind in their viands; some delicate stomachs nauseating plain meats, and finding no savour but in high season'd, luxurious dishes; whilst others again pique themselves upon detesting them. (144)

Such toleration of the vagaries of sexual desire would seem to encourage toleration of sodomy, as evidenced by the remarks of William Brown, tried and convicted for attempted sodomy in 1726, according to *Select Trials…From the year 1720, to this Time* (1742). Asked, in the words of one of the arresting constables, "why he took such indecent liberties with [Thomas] Newton," a male prostitute turned police agent who entrapped Brown in a well-known London cruising area nicknamed "The Sodomites' Walk," Brown was not ashamed to answer, "I did it because I thought I knew him, and I think there is no crime in making what use I please of my own body." If arrested for prostitution, Mrs. Cole might easily defend her own activities on the same grounds.[34]

---

[34] For Brown's trial, see *Select Trials…* (1742), 2nd edn., v.3, 39–40; rpt. McCormick, ed., 71. See also Norton (1992 & 2000–2004), which includes a satirical poem occasioned by Brown's standing in the pillory. On *Memoirs* in relation to the interplay between aesthetic philosophy, taste, and sexual norms in the eighteenth century, see Jody Greene. On Mrs. Cole's "sexual relativism" (or almost), see Jad Smith.

It comes as something of a surprise, then, after Fanny describes the sodomitical activity at the inn, when Mrs. Cole vehemently condemns male homosexuality:

> When I came home again, and told Mrs. *Cole* this adventure, she very sensibly observ'd to me, that there was no doubt of due vengeance one time or other overtaking these miscreants, however they might escape for the present; and that, had I been the temporal instrument of it, I should have been, at least, put to a great deal more trouble and confusion than I imagine: that as to the thing itself, the less said of it was the better; but that though she might be suspected of partiality, from its being the common cause of woman-kind, out of whose *mouths* this practice tended to take something more precious than bread, yet she protested against any mixture of passion, with a declaration extorted from her by pure regard to truth, which was, "*that* whatever effect this infamous passion had in other ages, and other countries, it seemed a peculiar blessing on our air and climate, that there was a plague-spot visibly imprinted on all that are tainted with it, in this nation at least; for that among numbers of that stamp whom she had known, or at least were universally under the scandalous suspicion of it, she could not name an exception hardly of one of them, whose character was not in all other respects the most worthless and despicable that could be, stript of all the manly virtues of their own sex, and fill'd up with only the very worst vices and follies of ours: that, in fine, they were scarce less execrable than ridiculous in their monstrous inconsistency, of loathing and contemning women, and all at the same time, apeing their manners, airs, lisp, skuttle, and, in general, all their little modes of affectation, which became them at least better, than they do these unsex'd male-misses." (159–60)

Surely this impassioned speech by Fanny's mentor proves that the novel, in Jad Smith's words, "constructs sex acts between men, especially those involving the anus, as a universal opprobrium" (200)?

Actually, it proves no such thing. Mrs. Cole's opinions should not be taken at face value, as sentiments endorsed by the author and expected to be shared by all readers. After all, neither Cleland nor Mrs. Cole follows her recommended approach: "the less said of [the subject]... the better." And then there's Mrs. Cole's unmistakable "partiality": as a woman, and especially a prostitute and madam, she sees sodomites as competition. Hearing her "protest against any mixture of passion" (claiming to be cool, calm, unemotional) and "declare [that her comments are] extorted from her" not merely by "regard to truth" but "pure regard to truth," one knows the Madam doth protest too much—beware the bawd who proclaims her purity. Competitiveness and greed belie the disinterested stance.[35]

The repetition of 'passion' further undercuts Mrs. Cole's portrayal of the sodomites as self-evidently Other. Falsely claiming her condemnation of "this infamous passion" is itself motivated by reason not passion, she unconsciously proves the point she made not long before, when professing toleration. There she argued that one's "tastes" are "superior to, and independent of all reasoning"; here,

---

[35] On Mrs. Cole's economic motivation for hating sodomites, see Todd (1980).

as in quick succession she uses "passion" in both its broadly emotional and narrowly sexual sense, she unwittingly demonstrates that many sorts of "passion" can subordinate reason, for her no less than for the sodomites she reviles.

But the most significant factor undermining Mrs. Cole's remarks, at least for alert, pro-sodomitical readers, is her characterization of "all who are tainted" with "this infamous passion" as stereotypical mollies—as Whiffles, Fribbles, Lovemans—when in fact the youths described do *not* fit the stereotype. She claims such men are immediately recognizable, "visibly imprinted" with "a plague-spot." But the sodomites first appear to Fanny as "two young gentlemen," and then, upon closer inspection, "two young sparks romping, and pulling one another about, entirely to [her] imagination, in frolic, and innocent play." Only when they begin to have sex can Fanny tell "what they were." Yet neither she nor Mrs. Cole notices that her experience disproves the madam's authoritative pronouncements.

Add to all this the sodomitical scene's reception—it seems to have figured in Cleland's prosecution for writing the novel (Foxon, 61), and was expurgated, as mentioned above, from subsequent editions, including pirated ones—and I can't help but feel that if Cleland had wanted to write an unambiguously homophobic episode, he would *not* have made it so congenial to homosexual readers. True, he tells homophobes what many of them expect and want to hear: sodomites are "odious," their "character[s]... the most worthless and despicable that could be"; they are "male-misses," "ridiculous" monsters who "loath and contemn women," yet "ape" the worst of them—in short, stereotypically effeminate mollies. Yet Cleland merely poses as the enemy. All the while, he attempts (too successfully for his own good) to arouse readers, and to encourage those able to admit their arousal to laugh: to laugh at Fanny, supposedly disgusted by the very idea of sex between men, yet so turned on she can't look away; and at Mrs. Cole, posing as the voice of wisdom and experience, yet revealing herself a greedy, hypocritical, stereotypical madam, precisely by stereotyping the young sodomites.

The Closeting of Closeting

In the first section of this chapter, I wrote that McFarlane, like Edelman and Kopelson, overlooked the possibility that *Memoirs* constitutes an example of closeted homosexual writing. In truth, though, I strongly suspect McFarlane didn't overlook the issue, but rather skirted it, as one would circumvent dangerous ground. Consider a sentence such as the following: "Reading this 'classic' of hetero-eroticism back through its sodomitical scene, I show how the novel offers its reader a position from which to engage in homoerotic fantasy by eliciting from the reader what we might call the sodomitical 'gaze'" (24). McFarlane's portrayal of an anthropomorphized text—actively offering its readers a homoerotic position, eliciting from them a sodomitical gaze—seems designed to sidestep, even as it obliquely acknowledges, what Cleland himself wished to offer and elicit.

One of the shortest yet one of the best examinations of *Memoirs*' sodomitical episode suggests even more strongly such evasive intentions. Paul Hammond's trenchantly argued discussion of *Memoirs* in *Love between Men in English Literature* (1996) is clear-sighted and illuminating from start to finish, especially on the text's typically unnoticed contradictions, and how its meaning is radically transformed if one imagines a dissident homosexual reader. In fact, Hammond all but calls *Memoirs* a closeted gay text—*yet doesn't quite say so.*

Writing in 1996, he described a "text which ostensibly denounces sodomy [but] also provides an alternative perspective, and gives the reader an opportunity for homoerotic pleasure even as the act is being condemned" (113). He called the episode in question a "complex" one that "invites contradictory modes of reading" (114), and added, "the episode provides much more than Smollett's kind of cautionary knowledge: those innocent young men about whom Fanny is so concerned could actually learn some useful hints on sexual technique from her detailed description" (115). He even posited the existence of a sodomitically inclined male reader to whom the book would appear to address itself, teaching him to recognize himself and his desires (116). In other words, Hammond posited a double-voiced text actively inviting homo-affirmative interpretation and providing homoerotic pleasure, matched with a homosexual audience seeking out textual material congenial to its desires and experiences. The only thing missing from the scenario? An *author*, writing such a text for such an audience.

The omission of any speculation about Cleland's intentions, much less sexuality, was no oversight. Hammond's work was itself a closeted text, in which he covertly unmasked Cleland as a closeted writer. Readers willing to entertain the critically unfashionable concept, willing to brave offhand dismissal by scholars such as Nussbaum, Simmons, et al., could decode the hidden message. At the same time, theoretically mainstream readers could enjoy Hammond's text- and reader-centered argument, blissfully unaware of, or choosing to ignore, the pleasure he secretly offered to unsophisticated, intentionalist readers (like me).

Of course, the obvious rejoinder to such speculation is "So what?" So what if Hammond didn't come out and say "Cleland was homosexual" and "*Memoirs of a Woman of Pleasure* is a closeted homosexual text"? What if Cleland *were* homosexual? Would that biographical information really enhance our reading of his novel? If Hammond, McFarlane, and others can make compelling, intelligent arguments about textual homoeroticism while avoiding the notorious pitfalls of authorial intention and literary biography, what's the problem?

There are several. One involves critical theorists' tendency to anthropomorphize 'society,' 'culture,' 'ideology,' 'power,' 'discourse,' and other abstractions. One needn't subscribe to models of human agency that assume autonomous individuals, in order to consider it worth remembering that particular people and groups of people within social systems, rather than the systems themselves, produce, reproduce, consume, and contest accounts of the world and its workings. Notwithstanding the valuable insights of Barthes, Foucault, and others, texts do not speak themselves; neither do discourses and ideologies. They're spoken by people. Such a perspective doesn't preclude recognizing and exploiting the fact that textual meaning exceeds and may even subvert authorial intention, but it does relegitimize intentionalist speculation.

Indeed, outlawing such speculation from textual analysis is absurd, if only because it's such an integral part of most people's reading experience. Even if they're employing a working fiction, most people now and in the past seem to have operated on the assumption that communication is possible, that writers and speakers intend to formulate and transmit certain messages, and that these intentions and messages can be understood if writer and reader, speaker and hearer, have a competent grasp of the same language. Of course, as this chapter itself demonstrates, the ability to reveal texts' contradictions, gaps, and slippages, and to analyze the larger cultural narratives, codes, discourses, and ideologies embedded in them, or in which they are embedded, is indispensable. But it's also crucial for academics to remember that most people don't read as we do. If authorial intention is a fallacy, it is nonetheless one that has had enormous impact upon how a great many readers have read texts, and thus upon what those texts have meant to those readers. A text that seems incoherent, self-contradictory, or ambiguous to a Derridean, Lacanian, or New Critic (and what text wouldn't?) may still have seemed to say, and have been consciously intended to say, something specific to various audiences.

Such a perspective, important for literary and cultural studies in general, is essential for LGBT Studies and queer theory. Take, for instance, the historically gay cultural practice known as camp. As Sedgwick demonstrates in *Epistemology of the Closet,* when she contrasts it to kitsch, speculation about authorial intention is integral to camp:

> Camp... seems to involve a gayer and more spacious angle of view. I think it may be true that, as Robert Dawidoff suggests, the typifying gesture of camp is really something amazingly simple: the moment at which a consumer of culture makes the wild surmise, "What if whoever made this was gay too?"... Unlike kitsch-attribution, then, camp-recognition doesn't ask, "What kind of debased creature could possibly be the right audience for this spectacle?" Instead, it says *what if:* What if the right audience for this were exactly *me?* What if, for instance, the resistant, oblique, tangential investments of attention and attraction that I am able to bring to this spectacle are actually uncannily responsive to the resistant, oblique, tangential investments of the person, or of some of the people, who created it? And what if, furthermore, others whom I don't know or recognize can see it from the same "perverse" angle? Unlike kitsch-*attribution*, camp-*recognition* always sees that it is dealing in reader relations and in projective fantasy (projective though not infrequently true) about the spaces and practices of cultural production. Generous because it acknowledges (unlike kitsch) that its perceptions are necessarily also creations.... (156)

Since Sedgwick's primary approach to lesbian and gay studies was a universalizing rather than minoritizing one (again: "seeing homo/heterosexual definition... as an issue of continuing, determinative importance in the lives of people across the spectrum of sexualities" rather than "as an issue of active importance primarily for a small, distinct, relatively fixed homosexual minority" [1]), she didn't primarily carry out the kind of "what if," projective readings theorized here (although her reading of James's "The Beast in the Jungle" might qualify). James Creech, however, set out to theorize and model precisely such speculative criticism, recognizing (as in the passage quoted in chapter one) that if there are closeted texts out there, the only way to receive the partially concealed messages they were meant to convey to certain readers is to engage in "wild surmise" about their authors' sexual desires or identities, to commit oneself to rash speculation about their intentions, even though one's speculation may turn out to be mistaken. Indeed, in many cases such questions will prove irresolvable. Nonetheless, the asking, the speculation, is fruitful, even necessary, for greater appreciation of dissident LGBT and queer authorial, readerly, and textual possibilities (cf. Hutcheson [2001a] 266).

Another, related problem with avoiding the issue of authorial intention, and thus of closeted homosexual writing, is that it deforms lesbian and gay criticism. Granted, such avoidance is, in part, a reasoned intellectual choice supported by diverse forms of anti-intentionalist theory. But it's *also* a defensive reaction to homophobic hostility, falsifying and diminishing LGBT and queer history and culture. Our abandonment of speculation about authorial intention has *not* been freely chosen. After all, Barthes and Foucault, while undeniably brilliant, were also gay men who remained closeted for most of their lives and in most of their writings, and their theories and methods are partially constrained by that closeting, as they are partially enabled by it. Not that their forms of semiotic and discursive analysis are not valuable for LGBT intellectual inquiry, as are numerous other language-, idea-, and structure-focused approaches to the study of history and culture. But history and culture are also—are indeed preeminently—about people.

Critics such as Hammond implicitly incorporate this humanist perspective into their work by stressing the competing meanings different readers might derive from the same text. They recognize that if a text falls behind the sofa and nobody reads it, it doesn't communicate, it doesn't signify, it doesn't mean. And they recognize that different readers may derive different meanings from the same text.

Yet still missing from this (obviously rudimentary) account of the creation of textual meaning is the author—in this case a potentially lesbian, gay, bi, trans, or otherwise queer author. Given the relentlessness with which homophobic people have enforced invisibility on LGBT and queer people; have misrepresented, dismissed, silenced, and even exterminated us; and have often labored to erase the traces of this misrepresentation, dismissal, silencing, and extermination, I refuse to accept, much less to celebrate, "the death of the Author." Some authors should not go gentle into that good night.

I therefore do *not* agree with Nussbaum and so many others that (terminology aside) the question "Was John Cleland gay?" is irrelevant or uninteresting, and thus unworthy of being asked. Again, such a question may be *irresolvable*. Yet 'irresolvable' does not mean 'false,' nor 'unimportant.' We may not be able to *prove* that Cleland (or Shakespeare, Bacon, Thomson, Philips, Cavendish, Scott) were same-sex oriented. But the perspective that stresses irresolvability is the one to which we should be saying, "So what?" Instead, LGBT and queer scholars have allowed the automatic homophobic rejoinders to such speculation—Sedgwick's Eight Easy Steps—to constrain, even dictate, our critical practice.[36]

Rather than capitulate, I suggest we go on the offensive. And once again, Sedgwick's work points the way. We need to get campier. We need to engage in "projective fantasy (projective though not infrequently true)." We need to say, "John Cleland was one crafty bugger, and a size queen to boot!" both because of its possible truth-value, and because such identification and projection is the necessary perspective, the rash speculation and wild surmise, that enables us to see how willingly, how *exceptionally* his text offers itself to readers like us, enables us to see that we're neither tendentiously unwriting nor masterfully deconstructing *Memoirs* if we identify with the young sparks instead of Fanny or Mrs. Cole. Cleland has courted such a reading. He has cruised and seduced us into it.

Finally, despite homophobia's devastating effects on the historical record, I am firmly convinced we have abandoned the hunt for traces of closeted lesbian and gay lives and writing prematurely. Considering the material I've presented in this and the previous chapters (and in Robinson [2004]), I think Creech's hopeful, tentative prediction—that "such speculation may eventually reveal that our current problem... has been that our conceptual arsenal contains instruments still too unrefined to catch the nuances of attitude and behavior... which, mutatis mutandis, might be profitably considered the functional equivalents of that complex of self-knowledge or behavior which we call 'coming out'" (69)—is likely to turn out to have been correct: the present paucity of our findings has more to do with the inadequacy of our critical lenses than with a lack of material upon which to focus.

---

[36] The traces of such constraint are evident even in Haggerty's otherwise excellent piece on Cleland's novel and mid-eighteenth-century homophobia (2003), when, in his sole reference to Cleland's possible homosexuality, Haggerty writes, "It is not necessary to posit a sodomitical author... to understand how a scene like [the sodomitical episode in *Memoirs*] functions in eighteenth-century culture" (175). One would think, from this phrasing, Cleland criticism had been overly focused on proving the author gay.

PART 2

Intentionality: Closeted Homophobic Writing

Chapter 4

Pornographic Homophobia: *L'Academie des dames* and the Deconstructing Lesbian

Thus far, I've been arguing for the legitimacy, even necessity, of keeping alert for signs of closeted homosexual writing, even before the "invention" of homosexuality. Above all, this requires a renewed focus on authorial intention. Not as the sole determinant of textual meaning, nor as something unitary and unconflicted or easily and conclusively knowable. The past half-century of literary criticism and critical theory has amply demonstrated the limitations and fallacies of such seemingly common-sense notions. But the naiveté of intentionalist reading has been overstated. Speculation about authorial intention—using all available clues (intra-, inter-, and extratextual), including, when available, authorial biography—can illuminate aspects of a text that non- or anti-intentionalist practices obscure.

In these next two chapters, I want to continue my brief for authorial intention from a different angle, by focusing upon what might be called "closeted homophobic texts." Like the term 'homosexual'—indeed, like any abstraction—the term 'homophobia' renders some aspects of the world more perceptible and some less so, in the process not only reflecting social and psychological reality but also helping create it. Of course, careless use of here-and-now terms to describe there-and-then things guarantees anachronism. Nevertheless, the absence of a name for a particular concept or phenomenon at a given place and time by no means proves that concept or phenomenon went unperceived. One may productively analyze a particular society using terms and concepts foreign to it. The solution for anachronism is not nominalism.[1]

One important approach to both the opportunities afforded and problems created by the unavoidable use of abstractions has been, as Sedgwick recommends, "to pluralize and specify [them]" ([1988/1993] 25). In an effort to highlight complexity and diversity, critics increasingly speak of 'knowledges' and 'ignorances,' 'homosexualities' and 'heterosexualities,' 'masculinities' and 'femininities.' So too with 'homophobias.'

---

[1] On nominalism and related issues in differentist work, see Boswell's articles, and Koertge.

Not that I'll be dispensing with the singular form. In its most general sense—hostility toward same-sex sexuality and romantic love—'homophobia' is a useful umbrella term, especially when distinguished from and paired with 'heteronormativity.' Nevertheless, I intend in what follows to explore different homophobia*s*.

In this chapter, in which I examine the late seventeenth-century pornographic fiction *L'Academie des dames*, I argue that the text's seemingly "anything goes" approach to sex conceals distinct yet complementary homophobias: a libertine homophobia directed at sodomitical sex between men, concealed or disavowed precisely because it belies the text's libertine ethos, and an even more thoroughly disavowed lesbophobia. The latter is especially easy to miss, as the authors' careful erasure of lesbians (*n.*) is concealed by an exuberant foregrounding of lesbian (*adj.*) sex. Yet once this particular lesbophobia is recognized, the heterosexual masculinity it produces and that produces it is quite familiar from mainstream heteropornography today.[2]

In chapter five, where I explore the depiction of lesbian and bisexual women in the early eighteenth-century scandal novel *The New Atalantis*, I contend that the author, Delarivier Manley, relies upon a characteristically gossipy rhetorical device I call 'mock ignorance.' In one sense, such urbane homophobia is not in fact closeted: although critics today, unfamiliar with its rhetorical conventions, often mistake the author's intentions, readers of the time would have recognized them as satirical. And yet, mock ignorance is a strategy that disavows authorial anxiety, projecting a worldly playfulness that, particularly in this case, conceals the author's reliance upon homophobia to do some serious ideological work.

Both texts, sometimes implicitly and sometimes explicitly, register awareness of the sort of blatant, vituperative homophobia we've already examined—voiced by Cleland's Fanny and Mrs. Cole, the author of *Satan's Harvest Home*, Madame de Murat's Spiritual Director, and others. In both cases, *L'Academie des dames* and *The New Atalantis*, the authors take pains to distance themselves from such overt censoriousness. Yet without minimizing the texts' susceptibility to pro-lesbian or pro-gay interpretations, I hope to demonstrate that such interpretations are *dissident* readings. When it comes to same-sex sexuality—or at least certain forms of it—both authors instruct their readers in how the texts are *intended* to be read.

Nonprocreative Sex: Heterosexual

L'Academie des dames (1680), the first French translation, adaptation, and abridgement of Nicolas Chorier's *Satyra sotadica* (1660)—possibly carried out, as James Grantham Turner notes, by "Jean Nicolas junior, son of the Grenoble publisher who sold Chorier's *Satyra* to local notables" ([2003] 319)—consists of

---

[2] For my choice of the term 'pornography,' see "Note: On Terminology" above.

seven dialogues (*entretiens*) between nineteen-year-old Tullie and her fifteen-year-old, soon-to-be-married cousin Octavie. Already married, Tullie offers to instruct Octavie in the sexual knowledge needed as woman and wife. The lessons are as much practical as theoretical—"hands on," if you will—particularly in the second dialogue, called the "Tribadicon" in the Latin original (evoking the *Satyricon*, but centered on female rather than male homosexuality.) Far more than in Cavendish's *Blazing World* (Robinson [2004]), the interaction depicted demonstrates why 'conversation' in the seventeenth century could signify physical as well as verbal intimacy. In the first four dialogues, the talk flows primarily in one direction, as Tullie regales Octavie with accounts of heterosexual escapades. By the fifth dialogue, the now-married Octavie recounts adventures of her own, undertaken with her husband Pamphile.[3]

Starting with dialogue five, the kinkiness of the sex increases steadily. As Foxon puts it, "The plot continually provides new shocks as apparently stable background figures like mothers and husbands are disclosed as having highly irregular relationships; it is as though a series of gauzes were lifted showing each time more complex groupings" (38). This increasingly daring content includes (listed here in no particular order) cunnilingus, fellatio, anal intercourse, role-playing, "normal" sadism (heterosexual "defloration"), "abnormal" sadism (whipping), and group sex. In addition to these innovations in content, the author introduces one innovation in form: Tullie and Octavie's dialogue becomes a quatrologue for part of *entretien* six, when they're joined by two men, Cleante and Medor, for further conversation, both verbal and physical.

As Turner demonstrates, both *Satyra* and *L'Academie*'s attitude toward male and female homosexuality—practices and desires typically considered "unnatural"—is complex and contradictory. Insofar as these are libertine texts, such contradictions should come as no surprise. For as Turner explains:

---

[3] This chapter revises Robinson (1998), ch.4. I've used the first edition of *L'Academie Des Dames* (A Ville-Franche, Chez Michel Blanchet, 1680), the only known copy of which resides in the British Library; James Turner generously lent me his photocopy. Quotations are from volume one, unless otherwise indicated. Quotations from Turner are from *Schooling Sex* (2003), unless otherwise indicated. For *Satyra*, I've used the 1910 edition of Liseux's French translation, which includes the seventh dialogue (added in 1678); I was unable to consult Liseux's 1882 Latin/French edition. On *Satyra*'s deliberate mystifications regarding authorship and translation, see Turner and Foxon. Turner refers to the author of *L'Academie* as "Chorier" and of *Satyra* as "Nicolas." In slight contrast, when referring to the former, I shall speak of "Chorier-Nicolas," since most of the work is still Chorier's. Turner provides by far the best analysis to date of both texts, analyzing them, with exemplary erudition and insight, within the context of sixteenth- and seventeenth-century European sexual writing. See also Jacob, Toulalan, and especially Leibacher-Ouvrard (1992a, 1992b, 1995).

> Nature in libertine doctrine signifies both the supreme sanction of desire, the Enlightenment goddess of pleasure, and the abject, the bestial, the excretory 'mud' from which women must fashion themselves by 'a fervid *conatus* [exertion, effort] of the mind'. Like the openly homosexual [Antonio] Rocco, [author of *L'Alcibiade fanciullo a scola*,] Chorier conceives sexuality both as a 'natural' physical inclination and as a play of cerebral and discursive *figurae*, to be cultivated and recombined in the spirit of aristocratic connoisseurship. This dichotomy can never wholly be resolved, since libertine discourse must reintroduce *some* explicit physicality to distinguish itself from the respectable text; nevertheless, the preference in Chorier is increasingly given to élite voluptuarism, to whatever opinions and pleasure are furthest removed from 'the grovelling malignity and stupidity of the vulgar herd' (VII.220). Consequently the dialogue is riven with conflict whenever *ingeniosa libido* takes a recherché and 'unnatural' form, and particularly when that form is homoerotic. (191)[4]

While not downplaying conservative, heteronormative currents in these texts, particularly *Satyra,* Turner is especially concerned with exploring their perverse crosscurrents, in keeping with his overall thesis:

> '[Q]ueer' eroticism underlies the (mainly) heterosexual tradition [following *L'Alcibiade.*]... *L'Escole des filles* and its successors [including *Satyra* and *L'Academie*] pursue the same goal as *L'Alcibiade*: an aestheticized, voluntary, Epicurean sexuality, an *amour philosophique* removed as far as possible from animal 'necessity'. (xii)

I agree with most of Turner's sensitive, illuminating reading of *L'Academie*, as well as his overall thesis. Nonetheless, I wish to trace the contours of the text's homophobias more closely.

A good place to start, for comparison's sake, is Chorier-Nicolas's handling of nonprocreative *heterosexual* sex, often referred to in *L'Academie* as *bagatelles* (frivolities) or *badineries* (silly or foolish things; trifles). As Turner notes, "this chic but insubstantial category includes lesbianism, sodomy, fellatio, adolescent masturbation" and more (328). But its heterosexual, male homosexual, and lesbian manifestations receive significantly different treatment.[5]

For instance, in discussions of anal intercourse, with which Tullie has had some experience, repressive moral views and relativistic, libertine ones mix and collide, as in the following exchange:

> *Octav.* Would that Venus would destroy Fabrice & Marius, for having violated in your place the laws of nature.
> *Tull.* Those who pride themselves on their wit [*esprit*], say that there is nothing one should condemn in this pleasure, that the ass of a woman is not of another nature than the other parts of her body, & that it is not worse to put dick in her Backside than to have it masturbated in her [*ses*] hands. However it may be, Octavie, the thing appears

---

[4] On Rocco and *L'Alcibiade*, see Turner, and below, ch.5.
[5] For the seventeenth-century meaning of *bagatelle* and *badinerie*, see Dubois et al.

ridiculous to me, if it isn't wicked in itself.

Octav. It appears both ridiculous & vile to me, & I cannot comprehend the pleasure one finds in such extravagant mad acts; nor conceive how this dissoluteness took hold of the greater part of souls to corrupt their innocence. (261)

Octavie even declares, "I would die rather than abandon myself thus to vile pleasures" (262). But Tullie challenges these virtuous sentiments—"O the beautiful words!... O! the chaste girl?" (262, 263)—and gets Octavie to admit she's let Pamphile try to penetrate her anally.

Chorier-Nicolas thus presents a spectrum of opinion ranging from Octavie's complete condemnation at one extreme, to Tullie's taste- rather than morality-based dislike (anal sex appears "ridiculous" to her) in the center, to the libertine, subversive tolerance voiced by those who pride themselves on their *esprit* (and who reject the idea of the *contra natura*) at the other extreme. Upon first consideration, the spectrum appears more heavily weighted to the negative: its central term is Tullie's distaste, and it omits the true opposite of Octavie's opinion, namely, advocacy of heteroanal intercourse and condemnation of vaginal intercourse. However, Octavie's stance is undercut by her defensive hypocrisy, leaving Tullie's arbitrary, taste-based dislike squaring off against the reasoned argument for toleration put forth by those priding themselves on their *esprit*. We may thus detect implicit textual endorsement of heteroanal intercourse—but let's defer that conclusion for a moment.

After condemning anal intercourse, Octavie asks Tullie to explain its origin:

[O]blige me, Tullie, by teaching me how this vice was born, how it was received by men, & authorized by custom, & Finally for what reason there are peoples who are infected with it and others who are not. As for me, I believe this fire came from Hell to sully the innocent flames of Love. (265)

Both the content of her questions—particularly the desire to explain the origin of anal sex—and the terms used—especially 'vice' and 'infect'—more commonly occur in discussions of homosexuality, the male version of which is so often conflated with anal sex. Not surprisingly, then, the discussion quickly becomes a debate on male homosexuality, without any attempt to explain the transition, indeed as if the transition were completely "natural," or no transition at all.

The segue occurs while Tullie and Octavie discuss procreation. In order to explain why some men enjoy penetrating their wives anally, Tullie turns to biology (after a brief, possibly facetious appeal to astrology). She asserts that "prudent" nature gives men an inborn penchant for loving women more than men, and attracts them more to women's distinguishing part, the vagina, than to other parts of the female body. She further claims that the "natural instinct" pushing men toward this part is the desire for immortality through procreation (267). But she then cites the arguments of "the most Wise" (*les plus Sages*), particularly

"Socrates... & Plato" (267), who argue that men and women possess a superfluity of "seed" (*semence*), of which Nature has provided more than procreation requires. Since Tullie has also just said sexual desire (at least in men) arises from, or is closely linked to, the desire to ejaculate (in which "men find true Bliss" [266]), these arguments amount to a defense of nonprocreative sex: although procreation may be the main purpose of sexual desire—Nature's way of enticing women into enduring the pains of childbirth, and men into assuming paternal responsibilities (277)—there's a superabundance of sexual desire, more than can be used up making babies. "And that," we're informed, "is what led men to search amongst their own Sex & amongst ours for the means by which to satisfy their Lust" (269).[6]

Further on (277-78), Tullie proceeds to refute the Sages' arguments. Yet her refutation is unconvincing, either on its own, or in the context of a pornographic fiction whose *raison d'être* seems to be the celebration of sexual pleasure divorced from procreation.

Most tellingly, like fellatio, another nonprocreative hetero act characterized as strange, perhaps even wrong (II.18–19, 31, 34), heteroanal intercourse is depicted in lengthy detail, on more than one occasion. The choice not merely to discuss such acts, but to represent them in detail, strongly suggests that, as far as nonprocreative heterosex is concerned, Chorier-Nicolas shares what Turner calls the "urbane and ironic counter-ideology" *Satyra*'s central female characters espouse, "a strategy of dissimulation and subversion that turns a world bound by the rules of sexual politics into a world of free play, where the political exists only as a trace that increases the piquancy of pleasure: 'imagine that everything is permitted and prohibited at the same time' (210; quoting *Satyra*, V.111). Chorier-Nicolas, in other words, condemns nonprocreative heterosex in order to increase readers' thrill, deliberately constructing heteroanal intercourse and fellatio, and *reading* about them, as forbidden pleasures.

Nonprocreative Sex: Male Homosexual

The text's treatment of male homosex (nonprocreative by definition) seems to resemble its treatment of nonprocreative heterosex. As with the latter, Tullie and Octavie explicitly condemn male-male sex, using terms such as 'madness,' 'evil,' 'plague,' 'crime,' 'vice,' 'stain,' and 'disgraceful' or 'infamous' (*folie, mal, peste,*

---

[6] Turner (178, 194) sees such origin stories as implicitly condoning the practices thus explained. Yet while that may be the case, to some extent, in *Satyra* and *L'Academie*, origin stories for male homosexuality and lesbianism are typically part of a homophobic discourse of mastery—scholarly, scientific, religious, medical, or otherwise. See, for instance, Brantôme's explanation of the "invention" of lesbianism, quoted earlier (13–16). For other examples, see below (175–77), on Orpheus in Ovid's *Metamorphoses,* and Robinson (1998) 12–18.

crime, vice, tache, infame [II.270, 272, 273, 276, 277, 280]). And yet, insofar as the arguments against nonprocreative heterosex double as arguments against homosex, they prove equally unconvincing, as in Tullie's unacknowledged change of topic when explaining the origin of heteroanal intercourse. Concluding her explanation, she asserts, "& that is what led men to search among their own Sex & among ours for the means by which to satisfy their Lust; so much so that what in the beginning was only the intemperance of some Aesthetes [*Delicats*] finally became in certain Provinces the Vice of a whole People" (269). *Intemperance* and *Delicats* (the latter means someone of "an excessive sensitivity in matters of taste, of pleasure" [Dubois et al., 136]) lay the blame on excess in sensation, desire, and behavior. But for readers of *L'Academie*, enjoying watching characters go to increasingly unconventional lengths in pursuit of sexual pleasure, this condemnation of sexual excess is at the very least problematic.

Moreover, despite Tullie and Octavie's avowed hostility to male homosex, Chorier-Nicolas devotes an abundance of textual space to pro-homo arguments. History, myth, literature, and law are all mined for supporting evidence. Over and over, talented, famous, or powerful males, historical and mythical (Julius Caesar, Augustus, Socrates, Plato, Aristotle, Virgil, Ovid, Jupiter, Apollo, Hercules) are cited as precedent. Classical defenses of male homosexuality—or rather the love of adolescent boys—such as pseudo-Lucian's *Erôtes* and Achilles Tatius's *Kleitophon and Leucippe* are explicitly invoked (275), enabling readers so inclined to seek them out. When combined with the other examples of, and arguments for, male homosex, especially Tullie's comment that no ancient laws prohibited it, although some prohibited fellatio, the "debate" seems implicitly to suggest that sexual acts are a matter of cultural, historical, and personal taste, rather than immutable law, despite Tullie's explicit assertion of the latter (275–76). At the very least, it becomes unavoidably clear that opinions on the subject differ, not only in distant times and places, but also in Tullie's Europe. For when she declares, "The reasons these Debauchees give in order to justify their dissoluteness do not convince me, although they derive them from the Nature of things, the Examples of the ancients, and even the Manners [*Mœurs*] of the most Wise" (277), readers understand that these "Debauchees" are contemporary proponents of male homosex, not "ancients" themselves.

Moreover, as Turner points out, Chorier-Nicolas "brings out the full bisexual implications of 'natural' desire, which gives men[, in Tullie's words,] '*more* of a penchant for our sex than their own' and *more* appetite for the vagina than 'other places of our bodies'" (330–31). Turner therefore concludes that "[h]aving thus strengthened the substrate of 'natural' arguments, *L'Academie* can then endorse sodomy even less ambiguously than [*Satyra*] had done, evaluating it almost wholly as a source of physical and aesthetic pleasure" (331).

Yet *L'Academie*, I would argue, is still homophobic. For unlike nonprocreative heterosex, both depicted and discussed at length, male homosex is extensively debated but *never* depicted. Notwithstanding the ever-increasing variety of sexual acts and combinations represented, no scene includes two men having sex. When the subject arises, both the visual and narrative element are omitted entirely.[7]

The only near exception occurs in dialogue seven, when Octavie relates a story told by her young lover Alexis. While he was asleep in bed at school, an older student named Patrice entered the room, uncovered the youth's *"Derriere,"* exclaimed over its beauty, sighed, gave him a kiss (the text doesn't specify where), and wanted to go further (II.77). But Alexis rejected these advances, and Patrice begged his pardon and left.

Patrice appears to be homosexual—at first. Upon uncovering Alexis's rump, he exclaims, "Look here... how Jupiter would desire such cheeks in his Ganimede: never did Hercules find such beautiful ones in his Hylas, nor Hadrian in Antinous. Ah! how I would prefer them willingly to all the beauties of Venus?" (II.77). The examples he gives are classical male couples, while Alexis is the name of the poet's male beloved in Virgil's Second Eclogue. Patrice's declared preference for Alexis's buttcheeks (*fesses*) over all the beauties of Venus seems to clinch things.

Yet Patrice is quickly revealed as bisexual (II.78, 89–95). Moreover, the male he fancies is an adolescent boy so pretty that were he dressed in female clothing he'd be mistaken for a girl (which is how he's delivered to Octavie [II.58][8]).

Current historical consensus, as represented most often by Trumbach's work, holds that before the beginning of the eighteenth century, it was widely acceptable for men to sexually penetrate boys, so long as the men also sexually penetrated women (the paradigmatic example: Rochester buggering both whore and page). What this truncated scene thus reveals is that, despite setting up the most culturally acceptable scenario for male-male sex, the author still chooses to halt the action before anything happens. Despite *L'Academie*'s seemingly "anything goes" ethos, and in marked contrast to its explicit portrayal of nonprocreative heterosex, male homosex is off-limits, representationally speaking. In contrast to Rocco's *L'Alcibiade*, or to later texts like Gervaise de Latouche's *Dom B**** and Cleland's *Memoirs*, *L'Academie des dames* will *discuss* male homosex but not *portray* it.[9]

---

[7] On the crucial importance of the visual to pornographic literature, see Goulemot.

[8] See Turner (204–20) on "heteroepheberasty," the form of gender-reversing sexuality that this scene, among others, exemplifies, in which an adult woman undertakes the erotic education of a male adolescent.

[9] On libertine male bisexuality, see Trumbach (1998). I don't dispute his assertion that before 1700 or so it was often more or less culturally acceptable for "normal," if libertine, adult men to penetrate adolescent boys. But I do disagree with his further claims: that this was the only form of male-male sex conceived of or practiced at the time; that it was replaced after 1700 or so by a different, yet also single, conception and practice of male-male sex (namely, effeminate "mollies" with a homosexual orientation attracted to non-effeminate, heterosexual men); and that male homosexuality and effeminacy weren't commonly associated before 1700 or so (see below, 162, n.1). On "the unrationalized coexistence of different models" of same-sex relations during particular periods, rather than "the supersession of one model and the consequent withering away of another," see

And as in *Dom B****, male homosexuality in *L'Academie* equals not just anal sex, but more specifically insertive anal sex. Like Gervaise de Latouche, Chorier-Nicolas quietly but carefully erases the possibility of a man enjoying anal receptivity. *Satyra*'s list of Famous Homosexuals of Antiquity, for instance, contains the following:

> This passion subjected, to King Nicomedes, Julius Caesar, every man's woman as he was every woman's man. (230)

In contrast, *L'Academie*'s "translation" reads:

> King Nicomedes took this pleasure with Julius Cæsar. (269)

The second version omits the famous description of Caesar, which so explicitly and disturbingly states the unspeakable, the inconceivable: a man who allows himself to be penetrated by other men, who not only derives pleasure from the act but engages in it promiscuously, may still prove himself as heterosexually, phallically potent as other men. He may even be a Julius Caesar! And although, in the single, brief sentence that remains in the French, Nicomedes is described as actively taking pleasure, Caesar's relative activity or passivity is rendered ambiguous, further obscuring the unwelcome particulars.[10]

Equally telling is what Chorier-Nicolas leaves unchanged. *Satyra* offers the following paraphrase of a passage from Ovid's *Ars Amatoria*:

> Ovid suffered from the same malady; however, he preferred young girls to boys, because in these amusements he wanted a reciprocal pleasure [*volupté*] and not a selfish delight/orgasm [*jouissance*]. He loved, he said, the pleasure "that ejaculates on both sides," and that is why he was less interested in [*touché de*] the love of boys. (231–32)

L'Academie's version reads:

> Ovid felt the same passion, nevertheless he preferred the love of the sex [i.e., women] to that of Boys, because he wanted sensual pleasure to be common to both parties, and the pleasure of the release to be tasted equally by both. (271)

Although the original has been shortened, and the pejorative "malady" replaced by the neutral "passion," the crucial ideas have been maintained: male homosexuality

---

Sedgwick (1990) 44–48.

[10] See the reference to the Roman emperor Heliogabalus (*Satyra*, 230; *L'Academie*, 270), and the excision of the "Horoscope de Tubero," a prefatory piece in *Satyra* that satirizes its male target, Cotytto, as *cinède* and *pédicon*, penetratee and penetrator in homo-anal intercourse, as well as *irrumator* and *fellator*, suckee and sucker in oral sex (42–43).

is pederasty, and pederastic pleasure is nonreciprocal.[11]

All of which makes one augmentation of *Satyra* quite surprising. In the Latin text, near the end of the digression on anal sex and male homosexuality, after Tullia has condemned both practices and attempted to refute her earlier arguments in their favor, Octavia raises the following objection: "It is all very well; but you have against you [the fact] that these are morals/manners [*mœurs*] approved by long custom, and that illustrious men, in all times, have practiced them" (240). The gist of Tullia's rather lengthy reply is that "as no length of time can diminish infamy, so the glory of the most illustrious men cannot glorify opprobrium" (240). The argument's overall effect is rather ingenious: to portray *condemnation* of anal sex or homosexuality as courageous freethinking, bucking longstanding, irrational convention (rather like opponents of homosexuality appropriating the language of civil rights today).

Be that as it may, the surprise lies in what *L'Academie* does with this exchange. For Octavie has a lot more to say than her prior incarnation:

> In truth Tullie you speak like an Oracle, but permit me to tell you that the reasons you make use of to destroy the arguments you made earlier do not yet appear to me strong enough. Because it is certain that if love is born of likeness, it is more perfect between two boys than between a man & a girl, and if it is true as everyone confesses that that which is agreeable is preferable to that which will be useful, we should not be at all surprised if men scorn our embraces in order to seek a pleasure that they find more perfect in their fellow men. Apart from the fact that those Manners [*Mœurs*] approved by long custom [*usage*], and confirmed by the Example of the greatest Men seem to authorize the practice of this pleasure. (279)

The addition of Octavie's argument, beginning with the premise, "if love is born of likeness," is startling, given that *L'Academie* has transformed male homosexuality into pederasty, a relationship founded, to a significant degree, upon difference (of age and role). Perhaps Nicolas (or whoever translated, adapted, and abridged the Latin text, including possibly Chorier) meant to display his cleverness—but if so, wouldn't he have displayed it further by refuting the argument? Perhaps he meant to amuse, intending the objection as another example of Octavie's naiveté—but if so, why not have Tullie remark upon it, as she so often does? It's as if Octavie's objection, however it ended up in the new version of the text, simply cannot be acknowledged, as if it must be forgotten as soon as it appears. And forgotten it most likely would have been by the text's intended readers: with the end of Tullie's unaltered reply, the digression on anal sex and male homosexuality ends. At Octavie's prompting, Tullie resumes her heterosexual tales.[12]

---

[11] On this passage in Ovid, see below (175–76).

[12] For Turner's comments on Octavie's unexpected argument, see 331–32. It's worth mentioning that *L'Academie*, or at least Tullie, also conflates misogyny and male homosexuality (269, 271–72) even as she offers a misogynist explanation for men's same-

Notwithstanding the space *L'Academie* devotes to arguing the homo side of the case, the text's calm, rational, encyclopedic, yet nonvisual discussion of male homosexuality in history, myth, literature, and law exemplifies what Jean Marie Goulemot would call emotional "distancing," the opposite of the technique, crucial to pornography, of creating visual "distance" between spectator and spectacle, enabling him or her to apprehend it more clearly. Chorier-Nicolas's discussion of male homosexuality simultaneously displays mastery over and denies anxiety. It is characterized by homophobia in its most general sense (hostility toward same-sex sexuality and romantic love), but also by a more specific variety: the homophobia of the man of the world, who distinguishes his stance from irrational prejudice, from the ignorant, insecure panic of the sodomite-burner. Chorier-Nicolas would have us believe his view sophisticated and intelligent, a considered, scientific conclusion.

Such an approach accords with the book's materialist ethos, particularly its libertine ridicule of convention, prejudice, and superstition.[13] It prefigures the shift that was already occurring, and that would accelerate over the next 250 years, from a dominant, religious view of homosexuality as sin to a dominant, medical/scientific view of homosexuality as illness. It may very well be that, as with the text's treatment of heteroanal intercourse, *L'Academie* displays a sexist unwillingness simply and summarily to condemn, and thus curtail, *any* male sexual possibility, in this case even one with which it's uncomfortable. Nevertheless, the contrast between its treatment of male homosex and nonprocreative heterosex is telling: the pros and cons of both are debated extensively, but only the latter is depicted, and thus made inescapably present to the reader's imagination. The possibility of an eroticism based on likeness is momentarily raised, only to be summarily dropped. And the potential pleasure of male receptivity is carefully omitted.

Nonprocreative Sex: Lesbian

Most integral to the text as a whole, however, is Chorier-Nicolas's treatment of sex between women. *L'Academie* is virtually filled with lesbian sex, graphically portrayed. For any reader who wondered what women could do in bed together, what sexual acts they could perform, the text provides detailed suggestions. Consider the following:

---

sex desires: in the countries where male homosex is most popular, women's vaginas are too large to give men pleasure during intercourse (274).

[13] I.288, 291, 293; II.8–9, 11–16, 69–70, 72, 74–80, 86–88, 110–11, 126–27. On the limits of this materialist ethos, see Robinson (1998) 229–46.

Tull. Well, for the first proof of your obedience, give me a kiss, but a kiss that comes from the heart.

Octav. I will grant you not only one, but thousands if you desire them.

Tull. Ah god! what a divine mouth you have? what brilliance your eyes possess? & how the form of your face recalls the beauty of Venus.

Octav. But what? you are throwing off the covers,... look at me all naked in your arms.... How now, Tullie, will Pamphile take hold of my two Tits this way? will he render his kisses as frequent as yours? and will he bite my lips, my neck, & my breast as you do?... Ah? pull back, Tullie, you're putting your hand too low, ah ah ah! you're pinching my asscheeks, ah why are you tickling that part so hard... [the one] at which you stare so fixedly?

Tull. I am Contemplating my Love, with a lively pleasure, the field of Venus, I am admiring its beauty, it is small, it is tight [*estroit,*] it is strewn with roses, and its charms would be powerful enough to make the Gods descend to Earth. (14–15)

Octav. Ah god! what game do you want to play, in stretching yourself out on me in this way? what, mouth against mouth, breast to breast, stomach to stomach, tell me your design in this trifling [*badinage*]? must I embrace you as you squeeze me?

Tull. Yes my little heart, grant me that grace, & do not refuse my caresses, since they can only give you pleasure; open your thighs, & lift them onto mine; now, that's good, you have been as punctual in obeying me, as I have been prompt in commanding you.

Octav. Ah! ah! Tullie, how you press on me, ah Gods! such thrusts? you set me all afire, you are killing me with these agitations....

Tull. My dear Octavie, my Love, embrace me tightly, & receive, ah, ah, ah, I can't take any more, I'm coming ah, ah, ah, I'm dying of pleasure? (19)

In these and many other instances, the text enables, even requires, readers to imagine in detail some of the concrete acts that constitute sex between women.

Granted, *L'Academie* includes apparent condemnation, or at least belittlement, of lesbisex; but as with nonprocreative heterosex, it doesn't hold up under closer scrutiny. To give just one example: while having sex with Octavie, Tullie exclaims, "O Gods! if you wanted to grant me the power, to play here the true role of Pamphile? but alas! I believe your power is limited? since I don't notice a single change in my nature" (14–15), a notion Octavie echoes when she cries, "Ah! ah! ah! how you throw yourself on me, ah! if the Gods had changed your sex, & had metamorphosed you into a man, what wouldn't happen to me?" (23). A staple of anti-lesbian discourse, the idea that sex between women requires a female-to-male sex-change recalls Ovid's "Iphis and Ianthe," in which, while desire between women is possible, sex is not (in *Satyra*, Tullia even quotes a passage from Ovid's tale [61–62]).[14] And yet, since Tullie and Octavie proceed to do many things never mentioned in "Iphis and Ianthe," including bringing each other to orgasm, one might legitimately doubt the seriousness with which *L'Academie* asserts the

---

[14] I thank Turner for pointing out this detail.

impossibility of lesbisex. Likewise, when Octavie states, "I know that from a girl such as I am, you cannot receive a single satisfaction, & I cannot conceive of a single pleasure, with which you could likewise divert me, being of the same sex as I" (16), the statement reads as ingénue ignorance, rather than universal sexual truth. For *L'Academie* quickly proceeds to depict Tullie and Octavie enjoying these very pleasures. It thereby forces the reader to conceive of them.

Strikingly, although Tullie uses lesbisex to initiate Octavie—preparing her for sex with her soon-to-be husband, Pamphile—the two women continue to have sex even after Octavie has begun to emulate Tullie's hetero adventurousness.[15] They seem to believe sex with another woman poses no threat to marriage or female chastity. That's why, when Tullie starts to instruct Octavie in the "usage" of her vagina, Octavie comments, "If I had learned it outside of marriage I would be dishonorable [*malhonneste*], & unworthy of your affection, but do me the favor to instruct me in it..." (17). Apparently, for Tullie and Octavie, lesbisex is neither "outside" nor "inside" marriage. It doesn't count, doesn't signify in relation to the codes regulating heterosexual marriage, fidelity, female chastity, and the like. It is therefore not *malhonneste*. The same thinking is evinced when Tullie urges, "Embrace me then my very dear one, & soothe by your kisses, the violence of the love that I feel for you; do not refuse to my eyes, & my hands, the pleasures that you can grant them, it will do no harm at all to Pamphile, nor to you..." (18). She and Octavie attempt to have things both ways: they engage in acts with each other that produce sexual pleasure (often including orgasm), yet simultaneously maintain that such acts aren't sex, that they don't encroach upon the preserve of the penis.

The question, then, is whether the text as a whole endorses this view, and if so, how. The answer requires examining Chorier-Nicolas's representation of lesbianism more closely, particularly how it accords—or fails to accord—with the lesbian-specific context of *L'Academie*, the ways in which lesbians and lesbianism are typically represented at the time.

Between Texts, Between the Lines: Minding the Gaps

What such an examination reveals is a series of significant absences—four, to be precise. Commonly found elements of content and form in other representations of lesbianism are wholly or virtually omitted from *L'Academie*, while others are significantly downplayed.

---

[15] To see how unusual *L'Academie* is in this respect, one need only glance at other early modern erotic and pornographic texts (such as *La Puttana errante*, *Vénus dans le cloître*, *Dom B****, *Memoirs of a Woman of Pleasure*), in which lesbisex is confined to a virtually *de rigeur* sexual initiation by an older woman, prior to the more satisfying, inevitable experience of heterosex.

We should note, first, that Chorier-Nicolas offers a universalizing rather than minoritizing model of lesbian desire. Lesbian feelings, Tullie claims, are ubiquitous among women:

> *Octav.* ...but please tell me, if other women conceive a similar love for their sex, or whether that malady is particular to you.
> *Tull.* All women my dear Child, burn with the same fire as I, in regard to the youth of their sex; wouldn't one have to be as cold as marble, & as hard as porphyry, to remain insensible at the view of what is most lovable? because what is there more charming than a young girl, beautiful, soft, white, and clean, as you are? (20)

Whereas Octavie voices a traditional characterization of lesbian desire as sickness, as "malady," Tullie implicitly asserts its healthiness: every woman feels it for the most beautiful members of her sex, young girls. The age specification is unusual, recalling the understanding of male homo desire as boy-loving. Nevertheless, what's most important is that Tullie, and through her Chorier-Nicolas, omits any mention of a distinct or separate sexuality that might be called 'lesbianism' or of a distinct or separate sexual minority who might be called 'lesbians.' Instead, she describes sexual desire between women as something "normal," something every woman feels. In the world of *L'Academie,* there is lesbian sex and desire (sex and desire between women), but not lesbian sexual orientation.[16]

In addition to the moment just discussed, the closest the text comes to considering a minoritizing model of lesbianism occurs in a passage in which Tullie comments upon the differences in women's sexual appetite:

> There are those who would like it done to them ten times a week, others would be content with a single time per Month, & finally others don't wish it at all. But it is certain that there are some who naturally have an aversion for it, they flee men, & avoid even finding themselves alone with them. As for me I regard them like Phoenixes, or rather like Monsters of Nature whose most sacred laws they violate, in rejecting the love that she inspires in one sex for the other. (288)

In a text that didn't mention sex between women explicitly, this passage (with its echo of Aristophanes' story from the *Symposium,* and adaptations such as Brantôme's) might easily be considered an indirect allusion to lesbians. But in *L'Academie,* a text that directly and repeatedly depicts woman-only sex, what's striking is that lesbianism is *not* mentioned here, where one would expect it.[17]

---

[16] In Tullie's assertion (quoted earlier) that "this temperament [*cette humeur*] is not particular to me," it's possible to hear suggestions of a minoritizing model of lesbian (or at least bisexual) desire. But Tullie's next words ("the French women, the Italian women, & the Spanish women cherish each other in the same way") reconfirm the universalizing model.

[17] On the homosexual significance of phoenixes and other mythological creatures, see Vanita (1996).

The text's second significant absence is implicit in its presentation of a universalizing model of sex between women: Chorier-Nicolas depicts no women who might be characterized by a specifically lesbian sexuality, no women solely or predominantly attracted to other women, turning away sexually and romantically from men— no lesbians, tribades, fricatrices, or sapphists. The vast majority of sex between women occurs between Tullie and Octavie, yet they also enthusiastically pursue sex with men.

There are, however, three possible exceptions to *L'Academie*'s "no lesbians" rule: the character of Judith in the story of Lucie and Florent (discussed below), and the "friends" Melitte and Cesarie, who appear in the only scene that pits sex between women against sex between woman and man, as well as the one that brings heteromale anxiety about lesbianism closest to the surface:

> *Tull.* A little while ago Cesarie, the sister of Ferdinand, was involved in an amusing [*plaisante*] affair, she had a friend named Melitte[;] it was difficult to say which of the two loved the other the most, there was only one Heart & one soul, & they were as united together as we could be one to the other: Melitte, who couldn't be without her companion for a moment, often passed the nights with her in the same bed in Ferdinand's house; You know that he was himself in love with Melitte to madness, he set traps for her from time to time, but he hadn't yet been able to surprise her. One day when love was tormenting him more than usual, he got up early in the morning, and went down into the garden to walk in the fresh air, he had still made only two or three Turns underneath an arbor that was next to his sister's bedchamber, when he heard her bed shaking with an extraordinary movement: he moved forward in order to hear more distinctly what was going on; & he found the door half-open through the negligence of these poor girls. He entered, & saw Melitte totally nude mounted atop his sister, whom she was shaking/bumping [*secoüoit*] in an amusing/agreeable manner: (the) Love that blinded them, prevented them from perceiving Ferdinand, he hid behind a curtain & after having undressed he threw himself nude between them. Cesarie & Melitte were so terrified, that they didn't even think of withdrawing, Ferdinand took Melitte in his arms, & kissed her. How now, my naughty one, he said to her, you have the recklessness thus to soil my sister by your mad acts? she who is so chaste & so pure? I will myself avenge the injury you have done her, & you will suffer mine as she has endured yours. Ah my Brother said Cesarie, pardon two lovers, & don't render us the laughingstock of everyone. What do you want? he promised them to keep the secret, on condition that he be satisfied, & Cesarie served as madam to her brother & her Friend, & was present at all the blows/strokes/knocks [*coups*] that were given.
>
> *Octav.* Melitte was right to grant Ferdinand what he wished, rather than to give him cause to make known her Triflings [*Badineries*], he still loves her wildly, & by temperament [*de son humeur*] he is not very fickle. I saw at his house a totally nude Venus, for which he had the portrait made in accordance with nature; It was Melitte who served as model, & it was in imitation of her that that figure was drawn. It is one of the best proportioned bodies I have seen. (II.84–86)

Although these loving friends are not called tribades, fricatrices, sapphists, or lesbians, they're nevertheless an unmarried, self-sufficient female couple who refer to each other as lovers [*amantes*] and engage in sex under cover of friendship. A lesbian reader could find much in their story congenial, especially Chorier-Nicolas's choice not to hetero- or bisexualize Melitte by suggesting she really desired Ferdinand or was pleased when he forced her to have sex with him. Lesbian lovemaking, in other words, is *not* presented as leading voluntarily and naturally to the supposedly greater pleasure of heterosex. The only desire the women are said to feel is for each other. On this basis alone, a pro-lesbian reader could easily sympathize with them, and see them (unlike Tullie and Octavie) as a lesbian couple.

But such a reading is clearly not advocated by the text. The women's independence isn't allowed to last long, and they are punished for it: Melitte must have sex with a man for whom she has never shown any inclination, and whom she now has ample reason to hate; Cesarie must prostitute her lover to him, and even witness the very act. As for Ferdinand, who literally jumps in between the lovers to replace a naked female body with his naked male one, he is not just any old man. He represents patriarchy itself, as he asserts the husband-like right of a lover and father-like right of a brother, both of which justify "protecting" Cesarie through control of her sexual behavior.

Despite Tullie's initially likening the two female couples to each other ("they were as united together as we could be one to the other"), neither she nor Octavie evinces any sympathy for the lesbian lovers. Instead, revealingly, Octavie's erotic appreciation of Melitte's body leads her to identify with Ferdinand rather than Cesarie. The text enlists Octavie's pseudo-lesbian desire to bolster a story of the triumph of male hetero over female homo lust and love.

Most tellingly, the reader is invited to laugh at Cesarie and Melitte's expense. In the seventeenth century, *plaisante* (the word I translated as 'amusing': "A little while ago Cesarie, the sister of Ferdinand, was involved in an *amusing* affair") could have an ironic meaning difficult to render in English, but clearly intended here: "causing laughter at the person's expense" (Dubois et al., 383). Thus this *plaisante* affair makes Cesarie laughable. She and Melitte are then mocked by Ferdinand when he uses against them the very language, the very ideology, they must have exploited to conceal the sexual nature of their love. When Ferdinand declares, "you have the recklessness thus to soil my sister by your mad acts? *she who is so chaste & so pure?* I will myself avenge the injury you have done her, & you will suffer mine as she has endured yours," the women's pro-lesbian appropriation of heterosexist and sexist ideology (akin to Behn's "To the Fair Clarinda") is ironically reappropriated by a hetero male for anti-lesbian purposes. As the intended reader laughs along with Ferdinand at the closest thing to a lesbian couple the text presents, Cesarie and Melitte are subjected to the very thing they most feared: they are made laughingstocks.

The third absence to note in Chorier-Nicolas's representation of lesbianism is that *L'Academie* virtually omits any suggestion of masculinity. As Andreadis, Traub, and Wahl amply demonstrate, this is rather unusual for the time and place. Sex between women was typically associated with masculinity, however conceived, in at least one of the women. Of course, as these same critics also document, at least some members of late seventeenth-century British and French society were able to conceive of such behavior occurring between "feminine" women. Nevertheless, in a work such as *L'Academie*, which so copiously depicts sex between women, it's surprising to find only one inappropriately masculine woman who displays lesbian lust.

This character's name is Judith. She appears in a tale Tullie recounts about a young wife named Lucie, who falls in love with one of her young servants, Florent. The feeling is mutual, and the lovers meet secretly while Lucie's husband, Ulric, is away. Unbeknownst to them, however, a female servant named Pelagie is also in love with Florent, and sets a trap. She pierces two or three planks (presumably in the ceiling) to make spyholes, and invites Ulric's sister, Judith, to catch them in the act.

At first the plan works. After watching Lucie and Florent have sex (which, however, Lucie limits to nonpenetrative acts—which she calls *badineries*—because she doesn't want to do anything that would "dishonor" herself [II.46]), Judith rushes in, has Florent locked up, and takes Lucie off to a brothel. There she tells the young wife to resign herself to imprisonment or death. But when she makes Lucie undress, the huntress is caught in her own trap:

> Love softened the Heart of this Tigress, she could not see the beauty of Lucie's body without becoming amorous herself, and as if changed into another person, she throws herself on the neck of that poor afflicted one, and kisses her with an extraordinary ardor. Ah my dear Child she says to her, how pleasing you are even in your sadness, fear nothing more if you want to be mine and to hold Florent in aversion? Lucie promises her all that she wanted, ah how I love you? & how upset I am to have afflicted you so[,] don't think any more of it, dream only of loving me as tenderly as I cherish you. I want to go to bed with you this night, my brother is absent & I will serve as husband to you by occupying his place....
>
> She bedded there indeed, & filled the whole bed with her mad acts [*fureurs*], she gave Lucie a thousand kisses, and tired her more by her thrustings [*secousses*], than she would have been in the embraces of her husband. Judith appeased herself that way, and gave Florent his liberty with the prohibition nevertheless never to enter the bedroom of his mistress.... (II.48–49)

Lucie subsequently informs Florent, "Judith is content, & loves me passionately, although I hold her in aversion; that's why there's nothing more to dread from that quarter" (II.50). Florent, meanwhile, has appeased Pelagie by the same method, claiming to hate "that ingrate" Lucie. The two lovers resume their relationship free from suspicion.

Judith is clearly a Fury—an acceptable figure in classical mythology, perhaps, but in seventeenth-century Europe an inappropriately masculine woman. She's called both a "Tigress" and a "Shrew" [*Mégère*], both of which suggest unfeminine violence, anger, and strength, suggestions borne out in Judith's initial treatment of Lucie. She usurps her brother's place not only by having sex with his wife, but also by spying upon, catching, and punishing the young woman's possible adultery. Tullie explains this odd choice, explains why Pelagie chose to alert Judith and why the latter willingly cooperated, by mentioning that Judith "hadn't wished Lucie at all well for a long time." But that's hardly sufficient. Of course, in one sense, Judith is chosen simply for plot's sake: making the avenger a woman renders the narrative all the more surprising when she succumbs to her victim's charms. Nevertheless, this plot choice masculinizes Judith from the start, giving her the role Ulric ought to play.

Moreover, Judith's very name connotes dangerous female violence: with the help of a maidservant, her apocryphal Biblical namesake severed a man's head. *L'Academie*'s Judith puts horns on one, by having sex with Ulric's wife and by unwittingly furthering that wife's extramarital heterosexual affair (both of which only count as adultery if one considers nonpenetrative sex adulterous—the Bassa question, again). In any case, Judith is the text's only masculinized woman portrayed as desiring and having sex with other women, and the only woman-loving-woman negatively portrayed.[18]

The fourth and final absence in Chorier-Nicolas's portrayal of lesbianism involves women's penetrative capabilities, about which *L'Academie* reveals both fascination and avoidance—with avoidance winning out. On the fascination side, we twice find Tullie vaginally fingering Octavie, with Octavie exclaiming, on the second occasion, "Ah pull out that adulterous finger that sets me all afire" (66), suggesting that, contrary to what Tullie and Octavie maintain elsewhere, lesbisex can indeed count as adultery, at least when it involves penetration. Likewise, at the end of the second dialogue, the idea that women lack the essential equipment to compete with men is brought up, but refuted by the possibility of a dildo (22–23).

On the avoidance side, however, is the fact that a woman penetrating a woman is only briefly suggested; it's neither described nor, like the topic of male-male sex, emphasized. And unlike other sex acts between women, penetration isn't depicted as leading to orgasm. Women's penetrative capabilities seem too threatening to confront head-on, too worrisome to be allowed into the authors' or readers' consciousness for any length of time. Indeed, they seem most clearly to be avoided where one would expect them to be acknowledged, as in the passage (partially quoted above) leading to Tullie's first stretching herself atop Octavie mouth-to-mouth, breast-to-breast, stomach-to-stomach, and with energetic pressing and *secousses* bringing herself to orgasm:

---

[18] Cf. the reference to Judith following a satiric paean to Sappho in *Satan's Harvest Home* (18).

Tull. Embrace me then my very dear one, & soothe by your kisses, the violence of the love that I feel for you; do not refuse to my eyes, & my hands, the pleasures that you can grant them, it will do no harm at all to Pamphile, nor to you: but alas that all my efforts are useless? that they are in vain? and that I am miserable at not being able to extinguish the fire that consumes me.... You are making me then the mistress of the path that leads to the sovereign good, ah! I see its door, but alas? I cannot use the power that you are giving me, I have no Key for opening it, no hammer for knocking, nor any other instrument, which could facilitate entering it; ah Octavie permit me to make an attempt? (18–19)

Tullie and the text seem to have forgotten the penetrative possibilities afforded by fingers, let alone dildos, either of which could surely serve as an "instrument" for "entering" Octavie's vagina. At any moment, in any text, such forgetting would be noteworthy, but here it's particularly strange, since the very language of the text, its word choice and sentence order, seems to suggest the precise possibility—one woman penetrating another—that then fails to occur. When Tullie says, "ah Octavie permit me to make an attempt," it sounds as if she means, "permit me to make an attempt at entering your vagina"—as if the text has once again put forward a staple of anti-lesbian discourse (women's penetrative incapacity) in order to disprove it. Instead, Tullie attempts "to extinguish the fire that consumes [her]" by means of a nonpenetrative act: the type of rubbing known as *frottage*, probably at the root of the two most common seventeenth-century French words for lesbian: *tribade* and *fricatrice*. What's more, this unknowing of the possibility of women vaginally penetrating one another occurs immediately after an assertion that lesbisex is no threat to heterosex, that it will harm neither Pamphile nor his wife Octavie.

This ideologically laden passage thus provides an opportunity to apprehend, at their least disguised, the text's avowed and disavowed notions of, and responses to, sex between women:

> 1. Such sex can give pleasure to its practitioners, all the way to orgasm (in dialogue five, not only does Tullie reach orgasm again from nonpenetrative rubbing, so does Octavie [87]). It's therefore real sex, sex that produces the desired pleasure, even if it doesn't produce offspring.

> 2. Like heterosex, sex between women can also excite and give pleasure to those who imagine it—such as the presumably heteromale readers of *L'Academie*.

> 3. However, imagining sex between women can also cause anxiety for these readers.

> 4. In order to allay anxiety, sex between women is presented as compatible with marriage and with heterosex more generally, which means compatible with men's sexual access to women.

5. To make this presentation convincing, and to reconcile these seemingly conflicting views of sex between women, the text denies its knowledge that, like men, women can penetrate women. Instead, it portrays sex between women as nonpenetrative.[19]

From *Satyra* to *L'Academie*, from Satire to Pornography

As with Chorier-Nicolas's treatment of male homosexuality, changes made to *Satyra*'s treatment of lesbianism support these conclusions. At heart is the difference between a text equally satirical and pornographic, and one primarily pornographic. As Turner puts it, Chorier's *Satyra sotadica* is a "vastly dilated and wholly libidinous parody of women's educational aspirations" (178). And while he's entirely correct to emphasize, "it would be naive to assume that [Chorier's] characters—or any aspect of the text, for that matter—can be wholly determined by the author's controlling intention[;] [t]o show his invention, to indulge his 'salty' genius, Chorier creates figures who exceed his ideological purpose and who hold their 'unnatural' positions with unseemly persistence" (190), nevertheless the anti-feminist satirical intent of the original is important to keep in mind, given how extensively its expression is curtailed in the translation/adaptation.

Not that *L'Academie* isn't markedly anti-feminist. Wahl, for instance, emphasizes the complementarity of the satiric and pornographic treatments of women in both *Satyra* and *L'Academie*:

> Not only does the title *L'Académie des [dames]* make the text seem virtually indistinguishable from other works attacking the *précieuses,* like Chappuzeau's [play] *L'Académie des femmes* [1661], but by simultaneously echoing the title of an

---

[19] Formal choices also help render lesbianism nonthreatening. Whereas *L'Academie*'s female characters have heterosex in virtually all Tullie and Octavie's tales, and whereas virtually all the book's heterosex occurs in these stories, almost all sex between women occurs in the frame-level interaction between the cousins. This combination of dialogue-between-women format and frame-level sex-between-women enables the (presumably heteromale) reader to oscillate between identification with Tullie and Octavie on the one hand, and disembodied, firsthand observation and objectification of them on the other. Woman-woman sex becomes, not just as close to the reader as possible—which might easily increase anxiety—but as reassuringly known as possible. As for the book's actual and intended readership: for evidence that some women had access to pornographic writing in the late sixteenth, mid-seventeenth, and mid-eighteenth centuries, and thus that some lesbians might have read *L'Academie* and other porn, see DeJean (1993), Jacob, Mudge, Toulalan, and Turner. Still, unlike some other early porn (such as *L'Escole des filles* [169–70, 219–20]), *L'Academie* never explicitly hails female readers. My presumption that *L'Academie*'s intended reader is hetero and male is also supported by its treatment of male homosexuality.

anonymous erotic narrative like *L'Escole des filles*, it also represents an implicit breakdown of the distinction between "polite" and "pornographic" modes of satirizing the behavior of women. The text's play on *académie* as a double entendre for sexual knowledge thus renders explicit an association between the education of women and a kind of sexual corruption that more conventional attacks on the *précieuses* had never openly acknowledged. (221)

While not disputing this analysis, which has a great deal to offer, I want nevertheless to suggest that differences between the two versions are also significant, and that they stem from conflict between the genres (or modes) of satire and pornography.

Wahl herself notes "the tension between the… satiric and erotic imperatives" within *Satyra* itself (274). In transforming that text into *L'Academie*, Chorier-Nicolas decisively tips the balance toward the latter. To do so, he removes potentially threatening elements of the Latin version. As Wahl comments, "the subversive appeal of libertine *femmes savantes* like Aloisia and Tullia for an audience of female readers may partially explain why Chorier's French adaptation… excised the prefatory material of the Latin dialogues, effectively silencing Aloisia's narrative voice, as well as suppressing Tullia's impressive command of Latin and Greek and her extensive quotations of classical authors" (261–62). In *L'Academie*, Tullie is much less clearly a *femme savante*. Indeed, as Turner more bluntly states, "the main project" of *L'Academie* is "making Chorier's women stupid" (327).

Wahl also observes that the misogyny of the "descriptions of the female body" in the Latin "is somewhat mitigated in the French translation" (266). This is an understatement. Such misogyny is *decidedly* mitigated. In particular, gynophobic descriptions of Tullia's vagina are omitted in *L'Academie*, which makes sense: disgust and laughter jointly serve the ends of satire, not pornography. *Satyra*'s detailed, anatomical description of female genitalia (69–71)—delivered in a dialogue appropriately entitled "Anatomie"—is likewise dropped in the pornographizing process.

Most importantly for our purposes, Chorier-Nicolas's suggestion that Tullie prefers women sexually (22) turns out to be merely the trace of a much longer, more explicit passage in *Satyra*, in which Tullia explains that Octavia's mother Pomponia "initiate[d her] in this game," which at first she abhorred, but to which little by little she grew habituated, until finally she could hardly do without the older woman (63–64). Tullia then asserts, more or less like Tullie, that "this taste is spread almost throughout the whole universe. The Italian, Spanish, and French women love each other willingly among themselves, and, if shame didn't hold them back, they would throw themselves into each others arms, in rut" (64). But whereas at this point in *L'Academie* the conversation turns briefly to dildos before switching subjects, in *Satyra* Tullia proceeds to deliver a learned disquisition on lesbian history and terminology:

> This practice was especially familiar to the Lesbians; Sappho made its name famous, even better, she ennobled it. How many times Andromeda, Athis, Anactoria, Mnaïs and Girino, her darlings [*mignonnes*], fatigued her flanks! The Greeks call the heroines of this type *tribades*; the Latins give them the names of *frictrices* and *subagitatrices*. Philænis, who devoted herself wildly to this pleasure, is thought to have invented it; by her example, since she was a woman of great renown, she spread among women and young girls the taste of a sensual delight unknown before her. One called them *tribades*, in that alternately they press/fuck and are pressed/fucked [*elles foulent et se font fouler*]; *frictrices*, from the rubbing of the body; *subagitatrices*, from their violent movements of the hips. What more do you want, my dear Octavia? To do and to let oneself be done, it's [for] a woman who isn't stupid and whose heart beats vigorously in her chest. (64–65)

One can, of course, read this passage, like the rest of *Satyra*'s handling of lesbianism, in more ways than one. Turner emphasizes the conflict between *Satyra*'s heteronormative and queer affordances, arguing, for instance, that Tullia "oscillates between two modes of understanding lesbianism[:] ...phallocentric and... philosapphic" (195). He also interprets such passages as "explain[ing] and thereby condon[ing] even those sexual 'mutations' singled out for condemnation" (194). In contrast, I would emphasize the reduction of lesbianism to a curious, titillating, perhaps exoticized, but nonthreatening object of knowledge—precisely the approach taken by Brantôme—complete with specialized terminology, an origin story, and the flaunting of Classical erudition.

Regarding *L'Academie,* my disagreement with Turner is even more a matter of emphasis. Noting the differences in the texts' handling of lesbianism, Turner remarks:

> It seems, then, that the new Académie des Dames teaches a more advanced grade of heteronormativity and subtracts intellectual seriousness from '(per)verse' alternatives like Sapphism. Conceptually, the lesbian bond of the two protagonists is stripped of its erudition and reduced to *badinage*. On the other hand, some of the alterations in *L'Academie* increase the titillating details of woman-woman sex. (328; see 328–29 for the alterations)

Yet it's important not to rush past that "subtract[ion of] intellectual seriousness from... Sapphism." For although Chorier-Nicolas's excision of Tullia's lesbian lecture accords with his overall pruning away of her Greek and Latin erudition, the revised French text, as we've seen, retains Tullia's similar, yet much longer instructional lecture on male homosexuality. The reason for treating sex between women so differently has everything to do with the demands of heteromale pornography. To arouse rather than threaten the intended reader, Chorier-Nicolas depicts sex between women in abundance, but avoids, even unknows, a minoritizing understanding of it, even as an object of contempt.

Perhaps, then, in regard to lesbianism, *L'Academie*'s most telling absence of all is its ostensible absence of anxiety, by which I mean Chorier-Nicolas's choice almost never to discuss sex between women as a problem, but instead "simply" to portray instances of it for the reader's erotic delectation. Given what we know about seventeenth-century French and English discussions of lesbianism and related topics—of tribadism, female friendship, masculine women, passing women, women with enlarged clitorises, hermaphroditism, female marriage-resistance, women in harems, women in convents, and the like—we ought to see Chorier-Nicolas's ostensibly unproblematic presention of sex between women as itself surprising and problematic.

Where sex between women is concerned, the text as a whole endorses—in fact, replicates—Tullie and Octavie's attempt to have things both ways. *L'Academie* presents lesbisex as the quintessential form of *badinerie*, a trifle, a jest, not to be taken seriously. It both *is* sex, and *isn't*. Or to abandon the neat paradox for a less stylish but more accurate formulation, it *is* sex, but not sex that *matters*, not sex that men need worry about, because it won't steal a woman's virginity, won't make a woman pregnant, won't break up a marriage, won't threaten men's access to women, or men's control over women, in any way.

Chorier-Nicolas constructs this view very carefully, by diverging in numerous respects from conceptions of lesbians and lesbianism current at the time. Even the infrequent moments when such conceptions do appear further highlight, as exceptions that prove the rule, the care with which an anomalous and nonthreatening picture of lesbianism has been painted. These exceptions provide a positive example (presence rather than absence) of the hostility the text harbors toward lesbianism, but expresses mostly through erasure and omission.

In sum, Chorier-Nicolas's handling of nonprocreative sex depends upon whether it occurs between women, between women and men, or between men. On the surface, lesbisex and male homosex are polar opposites, with heterosex occupying a midpoint, sharing depictability and implicit approval with the former and discussability and explicit condemnation with the latter. Sex between women is eroticized, sex between men intellectualized. Yet this stark contrast masks an underlying similarity. What we've uncovered are two different strategies for dealing with heteromale anxiety, not unlike some modern-day homophobias. In contrast, the treatment of nonprocreative heterosex, which showed signs of implicit or covert approval, seems more positive than ever. Chorier-Nicolas has written a text that addresses, arouses, reassures, and champions a heteromale reader. In doing so, *L'Academie* not only reflects an already existing, modern heteromale identity, but helps construct and solidify it as well.

Radical Tolerance vs. "pure & innocent Nature"

In discussing *L'Academie*'s handling of male homosexuality, I argued that the book betrays the homophobia of the man of the world, the homophobia of the sophisticate, distinguishing his view from ignorant, irrational prejudice. Such an approach, I suggested, accords with the book's materialist ethos, particularly its libertine ridicule of convention, prejudice, and superstition. And yet even this particular homophobia, like *L'Academie*'s lesbophobia, comes into conflict with libertine ideology.

Of course, one might argue that the text is simply contradictory, that it advocates nothing, that there's no way to determine what statements or actions it endorses. Such a reading would point out textual inconsistencies and contradictions, as I have done, but would rest there. Yet for the most part, *L'Academie*'s contradictions and inconsistencies are neither random nor accidental. They proceed from the conflict between two opposing ideologies: an Enlightenment ethos—libertine, relativist, tolerant, individualist, materialist—repeatedly voiced throughout the book, and a heteronormative and sexist ideology whose traces and effects we have examined in detail. Rather than curtail inquiry by dismissing the text as hopelessly contradictory, or vainly try to resolve and banish its contradictions, I want instead to try to understand them.

Nowhere is an enlightened, libertine ethos expressed more clearly and forcefully than at the end of the book:

> *Octav.* I still believe that this madness of men who treat us with so much rigor, derives greatly from Custom, because there are countries where not only are the women [held in] common, but even where a Husband gives money to him that sleeps with his wife the first night of their nuptials, which couldn't be if jealousy reigned there.
>
> *Tull.* You are right, there is only Custom that governs everything, there is no Just or Unjust in itself, no good or bad in Manners/Morals [*Mœurs*], & custom alone qualifies all things. If these truths were known to an infinity of scrupulous women they would soon renounce their foolish opinions, & examining by the rule of a right reason the natural necessities, they would find much more sweetness in life than they experience from it [now]. To live happy in this world we must remove all the preconceived ideas from our spirit, erase from it all that Tyranny and bad custom could have imprinted there & then conform our life to that which pure & innocent Nature demands of us. (II.110–11)

Despite the final appeal to "that which pure & innocent Nature demands of us," this and similar passages empty out precisely those supposedly absolute and immutable concepts such as "Nature" of any stable, authoritative content. The text does so by repeatedly portraying "natural" behaviors and ideas as culturally and historically contingent, rather than immutable and universal.[20]

As discussed in chapter one, Tullie recommends leading a closeted life (83). Depending on where one draws the line between public and private, and whether her advice applies to men as well as women, this defence of "veiled" sexual deviance has quite radical implications. For instance, among the entertainments one might legitimately enjoy is pornography, later defended in a blatantly self-referential passage:

> *Tull.* ...These superstitious Misanthropes forbid the writing about these sorts of things [the variety of sexual postures], they condemn the figures and the paintings that represent them, & [yet] approve the descriptions of duels and combats, & don't tear apart those images at all. O the Extreme ignorance! of blaming that which leads to the increase of the human species, & of not saying anything against that which destroys it? they would rather see men perish by a thousand artifices, than to see them born by innocent stratagems.... The Lesbians were much wiser, they also were taken to be the most spiritual among the Greeks, because in order to further animate their people to action, they engraved on their coins the most lascivious figures they could imagine. I have seen two of those pieces in Rome in the Orsino house, one of which was of copper & the other of silver, both made in Lesbos. The one represented Sappho totally nude who tightly squeezed in her arms a young girl, nude like her, & one saw in the other a nude man who having one knee on the ground, supported with the other a totally nude girl, whom he cunt-fucked in spreading her legs.
>
> *Octav.* That was rather amusing [*plaisant*]. I remember having seen a Medal [*Medaille*] in Florence that represented Jupiter with Ganimede, with a quite long inscription, of which I could only decipher the words *Amori Vera Lux*. (II.74–75)[21]

This strikingly modern defence of pornography is still used today. And the passage includes the most tolerant mention of homosexuality in the whole book, the single textual moment in which male and female homosexuality are not only presented together, but presented without any negative judgments—and on an equal footing with heterosexuality.

Yet this radical tolerance is quickly contradicted, first by negative comments about lovers of anal intercourse ("*Tull.* They look for a girl in a boy, & a boy in a

---

[20] Among the numerous culturally, historically, and even individually relativist claims asserted in *L'Academie* are the notions that sexual tastes differ from person to person (291, 293), that sexual appetite differs from woman to woman (288), that ideals of beauty differ both culturally (II.8–9) and individually (II.11–16), and that the acceptance or prohibition of nudity varies from culture to culture, as does the value placed upon virginity (II.86–88). The text also contests the authority of medical opinion in regard to sex (II.69–70), as well as challenging the authority of sexual prescriptions, regulations, and rules in general (II.72).

[21] The Latin means, "The light for love is true/truth" or "True light for love"—in other words, "This is an example of, and for, true love." (Thanks to Amy Richlin and Marc Schachter for help with the Latin, here and in subsequent passages.) On the link between this moment and "Italian pro-sodomitic literature" of the Renaissance, see Turner, 325.

girl, & to satisfy themselves they pass the bounds of Nature, & in this way confound the two Sexes" [II.76–77]), and then by the brief narration, discussed above (92), of Patrice's thwarted seduction of Alexis. Interestingly, Chorier-Nicolas seems aware of these contradictions. For when Octavie says, "I know Patrice & I am surprised that he has this foible" (II.78), Tullie responds with what can be read as an attempt at ideological reconciliation:

> *Tull.* Why call a movement of Nature a foible. Banish Love from this world if you wish that it perish, that is an infallible method, because without this God it would not subsist a moment. Do not think, Octavie, that anyone is exempt from that passion, no, it is spread throughout the blood and in the veins of each one, from which it follows that those who are indifferent to the [female] sex, of necessity love Boys, *Genuit Amori Amor homines, & fœminas genuit sibi* ["Love gave birth to (or made) men for Love, and he gave birth to women for himself (as well)"]. It is impossible to escape from the jurisdiction of this Divinity, & if we do not want to taste legitimate pleasures, we go in spite of ourselves towards forbidden ones. You know Mother Justine well..., she wildly loves Scolastique, Constance, Eulalie, & Emerence who are in the same Convent. As she loves she is pleased to be loved. Our houses, she told me the day before yesterday[,] which are believed to be consecrated to Chastity, are not inaccessible to Love.... She was right, Octavie, Love being the food of the soul we cannot abstain from it for long without dying. There exist some who in order to appease their thirst have even drunk their urine, & we have seen some who being famished have torn themselves apart with their teeth, to nourish their own flesh. There are even men and girls when they cannot possess that which their heart desires, willy nilly they will love their own sex [*leurs semblables*]; & try to find in that disordered/dissolute [*dereglé*] love this innocent pleasure, which nature permits them, & which superstition forbids them the use of. One must vent one's kidneys, one must piss! but is it a crime? It makes no difference, there will be no more nor less of it, Love laughs at these forbiddings, and will soil our clothes if we do not present him with the chamberpot. *At mulier matula est* ["Woman is a chamberpot"]. See, Octavie, how one lived in the first ages when Nature, all pure, gave men no laws that were not conformable to their inclination, it is not the same at present & men, in wanting to reform this same Nature, they have entirely corrupted it. (II.78–80)[22]

Early on in this passage, when Tullie says, "those who are indifferent to the [female] sex, of necessity love Boys," it seems some people (at least, some men) just naturally are homosexual. But she soon gives a time-honored, heterosexist explanation for both female and male homosexuality: when no one of the opposite sex is available, either because of a same-sex environment or superstitious, anti-sex prohibitions, people turn to their own sex for an outlet. According to this model, the need for sex is as basic, universal, and irrepressible as the need to drink, eat,

---

[22] Schachter (private conversation) points out that the Latin "At mulier matula est" is a punning reference to the Biblical description of woman as "the weaker vessel" in 1 Peter 3:7. See also Turner.

piss, or shit. Homosexuality isn't unnatural, but rather a natural result of thwarting Nature by heterosexual abstinence. Considering the time and place, this is a relatively enlightened viewpoint. It urges neither suppression of homosexual behavior nor oppression of those who engage in it. But homosex is not really defended, much less advocated. Indeed, if anything is advocated, it's the lifting of restrictions on *heterosex*. Presumably, if everyone were allowed access to the opposite-sex partners he or she desired, homosexuality would wither away on its own, its cause having been removed.

Still, as an attempt to resolve the stark contradiction between *L'Academie*'s defence of pornography and its various condemnations of homosexuality, the passage is unconvincing. Tullie's description of homosexuality as that *amour dereglé* ought to make attentive readers suspicious, since she's already mocked sexual regulation several times. Also, if the Greeks, particularly the Lesbians, were so very sex-positive and so very wise, why were they given to homosexual behavior, both female and male? One might reasonably wonder: could Chorier-Nicolas be *deliberately* undermining Tullie's homophobia?

The Mother Justine story suggests otherwise. As we've seen, although elsewhere *L'Academie* silently converts lesbianism into bisexuality, all the while projecting a confident enjoyment of sex between women, here Mother Justine's wild passion for her nuns is used to exemplify the deviations caused when people can't get the heterosex they naturally need. Earlier, at the only other moment the text explains sex between women, Tullie defends it as entirely natural and universal: all women respond sexually to the most beautiful of their sex. Here, though, lesbisex is lumped together with male homosex and disparaged.

And once again, we hear the would-be man of reason, calmly discussing such topics, with condescending tolerance. What was implicit in the discussion of male homosex becomes explicit in this discussion of lesbisex, male homosex, and sexual repression in general: while denigrating same-sex sexuality, the text nevertheless takes pains to differentiate itself from the forces of sexual repression, forces railing against sin in the hopes of governing private behavior.

Again, these contradictions are not random. The assertion of one of the text's guiding ideologies provokes, in response, the assertion of its other, also guiding but opposing ideology. In this case, as Tullie defends *L'Academie*'s own pornographic practices, she carries its relativist, libertine, Enlightenment logic to its rational conclusion regarding lesbianism and male homosexuality, placing them on an equal footing with heterosexuality, as "natural" variations to which value judgments simply don't apply. But the text immediately recoils and reaffirms its homophobia. It then attempts to reconcile these irreconcilable positions through compromise, ending with a heterosexist tolerance that not only combines elements from each ideology, but disavows its anxious response to the original moment of radical tolerance. In the process, Chorier-Nicolas's conflicting ideological motivations, and his attempt to disguise this conflict, are laid bare.

The Use, and Pleasure, of Anxiety

Although I've been arguing that *L'Academie* evinces particular, complementary forms of disavowed lesbophobia and homophobia, I want to conclude by acknowledging just how little separates my view of the text from Turner's more positive, queer one. Especially given my previous chapters' focus on closeted writing pitched at pro-lesbian and pro-gay readers, I wouldn't want to obscure the uncommonly inviting opportunity Chorier-Nicolas's text would have provided such dissident readers.

It would have done so, most obviously, by so often and so powerfully making the libertine case for the cultural, historical, and individual relativity of sexual tastes and rules. By repeatedly mocking and undermining the authority of traditional, dominant, supposedly natural and universal beliefs about sexuality, the text provides more than ample intellectual ammunition for any reader wishing to apply these ideas to the subject of homosex, even in opposition to *L'Academie*'s own explicit condemnation.

More interestingly, Chorier-Nicolas inadvertently encourages dissident, pro-lesbian reading by choosing appropriation rather than denigration or silence as the text's chief lesbophobic strategy, and making this appropriation so consistent throughout, and central to, the entire work. By repeatedly depicting sex between women in order to colonize it, tame it, exploit it—by transforming lesbianism into a bisexuality that promises men sexual access to all women, involves men in every woman's every desire (including desire for other women), and provides men the illusion of complete knowledge and mastery of female sexuality—*L'Academie* employs a strategy that can easily backfire, enabling readers so inclined to reverse the balance of power, flip the terms of the binary, see lesbisex as dominant and heterosex as subordinate. The precise formal choice Chorier-Nicolas fixes upon to allay heteromale readers' anxiety (repeatedly placing lesbisex in the frame narrative, the dialogues that produce and contain almost all the book's heterosex) especially risks such an outcome. While, as I've argued, through this formal choice, and especially through the series of significant absences in the book's representation of lesbianism, Chorier-Nicolas attempts to press lesbisex into the service of heteromale desire, pro-lesbian readers could see Tullie and Octavie's heterosex stories as fuel for their more important sexual relationship with each other (see Turner, 328–29).

Indeed, even from a nondissident perspective, Tullie and Octavie's swapping of heterosex stories is clearly an extension of their lovemaking, almost like a dildo: a representation the two women can use together, making an actual man superfluous for their sexual satisfaction.[23] The ease with which the text can support such a seemingly dissident, pro-lesbian reading—the apparent recklessness with which it

---

[23] I thank Turner for suggesting this idea.

risks confronting readers with a kind of lesbian supremacy—suggests that the lesbophobic anxiety I've been discussing may not have been quite so aversive to Chorier-Nicolas and his intended readers as one might expect. Much like mid-twentieth-century castration anxiety as theorized by D.A. Miller ([1991] 136), the anxiety exemplified and generated by *L'Academie* may ultimately have been more reassuring than distressing for the text's heteromale subjects, because constitutive precisely of their heteromale subjectivity. In repeatedly evoking the possibility that women could sexually satisfy other women, and thus that men might be sexually superfluous, the text necessitates the repeated introduction of a heteromale sexuality to triumph over this threat, turning potential lesbians into bisexuals, and inserting desire for men, images of men, stories of sex with men into each instance of sex between women.

This text that, almost in passing, unknows the male homosexual who can be penetrated without losing his ability to penetrate, achieves its construction of heteromale subjectivity through the obsessive *de*construction of a lesbian subject, the woman who neither needs nor desires to be penetrated by a man. This deconstructing lesbian, while clearly a variant of Castle's "apparitional lesbian," is a variant specifically fitted to the needs of the reading subject hailed by heteromale porn. She must repeatedly threaten to appear, only to be revealed as no threat, because no lesbian, at all.

Fittingly, *L'Academie des dames* ends with an unresolved evocation of sex between women:

> *Tull.* You don't tire at all of talking & you pay no mind that *voila* now the day [is] over, let's postpone our discussion to another time, kiss me before leaving, Good-bye my Heart.
>
> *Oct.* Ah Tullie I would never tire of such conversations, I would pass days & nights in them without getting bored, & it's only with difficulty that I separate from you, kiss me Tullie.
>
> *Tull.* Ah how playful [*badine*] you are? I believe you don't want to finish at all, Good-bye. (II.112)

As Turner, in response to the earliest version of this chapter, once asked, "Does Tullie push Octavie away, or do they dissolve into an endless kiss over which the credits roll?" The question cannot be answered. But interrupted or not, this final (non)lesbian kiss won't be the last, for the two women will resume their "conversation" another day, an intimation that offers heteromale readers the thrilling prospect of endlessly constructing their ever-threatened subjectivity through the perverse pleasure of imagining unknown lesbian sex.

Chapter 5

"For How Can They Be Guilty?": The Sophisticated Homophobia of Manley's *New Atalantis*

"Ladies... of the new *Cabal*"

In volume two of *The New Atalantis* (1709), Delarivier Manley's unabashedly partisan satire of prominent Whigs' political and sexual misbehavior in late seventeenth- and early eighteenth-century England, Astrea, the goddess of Justice, asks Lady Intelligence, the personification of scandal and gossip, about a group of women riding by in several coaches, laughing "loud and incessantly" (42–43), as if they hadn't a care in the world. Intelligence informs Astrea and her mother, Virtue:

> [T]hese Ladies are of the new *Cabal*; a sect (however innocent in it self) that does not fail from meeting its share of Censure from the World. Alas! what can they do? How unfortunate are Women? if they seek their Diversion out of themselves and include the other Sex, they must be *Criminal*? If in themselves (as those of the new *Cabal*) still they are *Criminal*? Tho' *Censurers* must carry their Imaginations a much greater length then I am able to do mine, to explain this *Hypothesis* with Success; they pretend to find in these the Vices of old *Rome* reviv'd; and quote you certain detestable Authors, who (to amuse Posterity) have introduc'd you lasting Monuments of *Vice*, which could only subsist in Imagination; and can in reality have no other Foundation, than what are to be found in the Dreams of *Poets*, and the ill Nature of those *Censurers*, who will have no Diversions Innocent, but what themselves advance!
>
> Oh how laudable! how extraordinary! how wonderful! is the uncommon Happiness of the *Cabal*? They have wisely excluded that rapacious *Sex*, who making a prey of the Honour of Ladies, find their greatest Satisfaction (some few excepted) in boasting of their good *Fortune*....
>
> The *Cabal* run no such dangers, they have all of Happiness in themselves! Two beautiful Ladies join'd in an Excess of *Amity* (no word is tender enough to express their new Delight) innocently embrace! for how can they be guilty? They vow eternal *Tenderness*, they exclude the Men, and condition that they will always do so. What irregularity can there be in this? 'Tis true, some things may be strain'd a little too far, and that causes Reflections to be cast upon the *Rest*. (43–44)

Intelligence proceeds to describe the Cabal and their escapades at great length (44–58, 206–209). Indeed, no nonpornographic English or French writer in the hundred or so years previous had had as much to say about lesbians and lesbianism as Manley.[1]

More surprising than the sheer volume of lesbian-related material in *The New Atalantis* is its cornucopian variety. Diverse and often contradictory forms, characteristics, etiologies, and estimations of lesbianism, as well as differing narrative and associational contexts for it, abound, suggested by characters' words and deeds. Lesbian desires are ascribed to a hypermasculine woman as well as "normal" feminine women. Lesbians form butch-femme pairs, femme-femme pairs, hierarchical pairs, egalitarian pairs. One woman turns to others by default, rejected by men; others seem always to have been attracted to their own sex; still another indulges in affairs with partners of both sexes, refusing to set limits to her pleasure. Most of these women closet their same-sex desires, marrying or taking a male lover in order to fulfill societal expectations, but others (including married ones) flaunt their same-sex erotic attraction. Some form monogamous relationships, others revel in nonmonogamy or even promiscuity. And while the narrative focuses on numerous, particular relationships, on lesbian couples, it depicts lesbian community as well, also variously represented: as separatist feminist utopia, as cabal or conspiracy, as locus of laughable infighting. Yet whether alone, in couples, or in groups, these lesbians' antics are dramatic. In narratives that range from brief snippets to detailed if still short stories, Manley's women-loving women compete with rivals (both female and male), pursue pretty young things, frequent female prostitutes, fall in love with crossdressing actresses, and crossdress themselves. Their affections are condemned as unnatural, defended as innocent, or dismissed as frivolous, associated with both the height of feminine purity (ideal female friendship) and the depth of masculine depravity (male homosexuality). Their lusts are as old as ancient Greece and Rome, yet wholly unprecedented, wholly new; described at length yet somehow still secret, mysterious, unnameable, unknown.

Manley by no means endorses all these views of lesbianism. She mocks most of the positive ones, representing them as false claims made by lesbians themselves. But the mere fact of their presentation means they were or could be associated in some way with lesbianism at the time (as concept, as lived experience, or both). Manley's text thus demonstrates that far from being unimaginable, or imaginable only in a single, dominant form (*the* hermaphrodite, *the*

---

[1] I've used the 1972 Garland facsimile of the original edition; all page numbers refer to Volume II unless otherwise indicated. I'm grateful to the organizers of the 1998 Eighteenth- and Nineteenth-Century British Women Writers Conference for the opportunity to present an early version of this chapter, and to Rick Incorvati for including a revised (1999) version of the paper (on which his editorial comments were invaluable) in his special issue of *Nineteenth-Century Contexts* (Robinson [2001b]; see http://www.tandf.co.uk). The present chapter extensively revises and expands the latter essay.

tribade, *the* passing woman), lesbianism could be imagined and depicted quite boldly and in an astounding variety of forms in the early eighteenth century. Perhaps even more importantly, for what it suggests about historical continuity in lesbian history, all the forms and characteristics Manley presents are still associated in some way with lesbianism today.[2]

And yet, as suggestive as I find such links between Manley's time and ours, the continuities I wish to trace in this chapter extend backward rather than forward from the eighteenth century. In part by placing *The New Atalantis* in the context of both homophobic and homophilic wrangling over the nature of love, sex, and friendship stretching back all the way to Plato, I hope to answer some deceptively narrow questions: How does the lesbian-related material function in *The New Atalantis*? Why does it feature so prominently in the text? What light might it shed on Manley's self-construction as satirist and female writer? Or to put these questions more simply, and in intentionally intentionalist terms: What is Manley trying to say about lesbianism, how does she say it, and why does she say it?

Most other critics have viewed Manley's portrayal of "the new Cabal" as either predominantly or significantly favorable. Janet Todd, for instance, while noting that lesbianism is presented as "scandalous," adds, "the positive social and psychological side is also stressed" ([1989] 92, citing the "little commonwealth" passage discussed below; see also Ballaster [1992] 140, [1995] 31; Andreadis, 92; Donoghue, 232, 240–41). Even Wahl, who emphasizes *The New Atalantis*'s anti-lesbianism, nevertheless finds "strange outcroppings of utopian discourse" in the new Cabal passages, as well as, at one point, "an oddly sympathetic stance toward the Cabal," which makes Manley's representation of lesbians seem a self-contradictory combination of satiric and utopian elements (127).[3]

Such interpretations, I will later argue, point the way to the text's vulnerability to *dissident* pro-lesbian reading. They also highlight Manley's fascination with the Cabal and her attraction, conscious or unconscious, to elements of these women's lives. Nonetheless, I remain convinced the new Cabal material is intentionally anti-lesbian, insistently and consistently soliciting readers who will recognize the Cabal as lesbian (or in some cases bisexual) and respond negatively to it. And this anti-lesbianism reveals the Cabal's function as a foil or scapegoat, a crucial boundary delimiting feminist readings of the text.

To make this case, I rely upon two rather mundane, even old-fashioned, yet nonetheless invaluable methodologies: close reading and contextualization (the latter, in this case, lesbian- and homo-specific). Critics who painstakingly historicize

---

[2] Lange (226) makes a similar point.

[3] To the best of my knowledge, only three critics wholly share my view regarding Manley's clearly anti-lesbian satiric intentions: Castle (2003) 191; Lange, 94–95, 209–212, 221–27; and Santesso. As for Wahl (ch.3), she departs from this perspective only occasionally, and her analysis of Gallagher's interpretation of the new Cabal accords closely with mine.

and contextualize other aspects of *The New Atalantis*, yet fail to take the same care with female *and male* homosexuality, miss the extent and consistency of Manley's satire of lesbianism, as well as its relation to some of the text's central themes.[4]

"refining upon their mysterious Innocence": *The Symposium*, *The Erôtes*, and Platonic Love

The similarities between *The New Atalantis* and texts that make up a longstanding anti-lesbian and anti-homosexual textual tradition are extensive and fundamental. Like the authors of many of these works, Manley refers to lesbianism without employing a single-word term (e.g., 'tribade,' 'sapphist,' 'rubster,' 'lesbian'); instead, she communicates the idea through indirection, euphemism, allusion. Yet she communicates it clearly. A constellation of words, expressions, characteristics, allusions, practices, and ideas from this tradition reappear in Manley's book: words such as 'vice' ("the Vices of old *Rome* reviv'd"), 'irregularity' ("What irregularity can there be in this?"), 'uncommon' ("the uncommon Happiness of the *Cabal*"), 'tender' or 'tenderness' ("They vow eternal *Tenderness*" [44]), 'friend' or 'friendship' ("that Breach of *Friendship* in the *Fair*" [56]), 'amity' ("Two beautiful Ladies join'd in an Excess of *Amity*"); expressions such as "a too guilty Passion" (46) or "such unaccountable Intimacies" (46); characteristics such as hypermasculinity in women or publicly advertised, and thus suspect, 'virtue,' 'innocence,' and 'chastity'; allusions to

---

[4] Both Ballaster's (1992) and Gallagher's examination of *The New Atalantis* suffers in this regard, each reading the new Cabal for what it might say about generic (hence usually heterosexual) women and their writing, without examining the ways in which lesbianism was conceived of and represented at the time. (Although I disagree with Ballaster's take on most of the texts discussed in "Vices" [1995], there she examines them for lesbian-specific meanings.) *The New Atalantis* is by no means the only lesbo- or homophobic text of the period mistaken for lesbo- or homophilic. The obscene Restoration play *Sodom*, attributed to Lord Rochester, and the anonymous, early eighteenth-century scandal pamphlet *Love-Letters Between a certain late Nobleman and the famous Mr. Wilson* (1723) have both been misread (Weber, Kimmel) as valorizing or documenting male homosexuality rather than satirizing it. On *Love-Letters*, see Robinson (1993); see also Hutcheson (2001b) on "Ahmad al-Tîfâshî's thirteenth-century *The Delight of Hearts*, which in its partial English translation reads as a riotous celebration of gay love, [but] is in essence a scandal sheet whose impact as such depends precisely on heteronormativity remaining the rule" (107 [with macrons not circumflexes]; also 120, n.22). Hutcheson's example, from a text lampooning members of an urban elite, bolsters my argument that the homophobic rhetorical strategies Manley employs are particularly suited to, even mutually dependent upon, the generic requirements of scandalous satire, and strengthens my case for the necessity of reading for continuity and similarity across time and culture. For the importance of taking into account the homoerotics of male friendship when exploring those of female friendship in the seventeenth and eighteenth century, see Robinson (1998), ch.2; also Andreadis (57 & passim). I'm grateful to Andreadis for reading an early (1996) draft of that chapter, and pleased to see its impact on her subsequent work.

Ovid's "Iphis and Ianthe" (49), as well as both classical Greece (Socrates and Alcibiades [45–46]) and Rome; the practices of crossdressing and prostitution (49); the idea of women who turn away from men, of women who court and treat other women as men do (57), of all-female space as a site of lesbian activity, of pastoral retreat as a site of lesbian activity (46), of having a 'favourite' (44, 49, 52) or particular 'Friend' (47, 57), of 'taste' as in 'preference' or 'inclination' ("the *Marchioness*'s and *Ianthe*'s peculiar Taste" [49], "Thus disincouraged by the Men, she fell into the Taste of the *Cabal*" [52]) and 'taste' as in 'good taste' or 'discernment' ("She withdrew those *Airs* of Fondness from a Tasteless undeserving Wretch" [208]), of 'nicety' ("They claim... a right of... *admitting* or *excluding*, in both they are extreamly *nice*" [47]), of newness ("their new Delight," "something so *new* and *uncommon*" [57], "the new *Cabal*"), of esoteric spirituality ("what happy Wretch is it upon whom you bestow my *Rites!*" [45], "admitting [the *Novice*] to their *Bosom*,... initiating her in the *Mysteries* of their *Indearments*" [47]), of philosophy ("such *exalted abstracted Notions* as theirs" [57]), of Nature and the unnatural ("But if they carry it a length beyond what *Nature* design'd" [57], "she did not like those *hugs* and *indearments* from her own Sex, they seem'd *un-natural*" [208]). Such conventional, even stock, words and ideas from English and French anti-lesbian and often anti-homosexual writing permeate Manley's treatment of the new Cabal.[5]

Indeed, Manley employs most of the homophobic rhetorical strategies I've delineated elsewhere under slightly different names: construction of a knowable object (treating lesbianism as a curious subject of inquiry, an unusual phenomenon neither too dangerous to be spoken of, nor ordinary enough to be taken for granted); belittlement; humiliation; demonization; and, especially, mystery-making, via Manley's numerous repetitions of the words 'mystery,' 'secrecy,' and their derivations (e.g., "the Mysteries of the *Cabal*" [47], "the Secrets of the *Cabal*" [49]). Indeed, one of Manley's most important rhetorical strategies— parodic mimicry of the discourses of platonic love and idealized friendship— involves precisely such allegations of esoteric, even Cabalistic mysteries and secrets, and their connection to philosophy and other forms of "higher" knowledge. By means of this parodic mimicry, Manley joins ongoing struggle over the interrelated meanings of love, sex, and friendship stretching back to ancient Greece. By selectively echoing previous texts, Manley signals the self-consciousness of her contribution to this classically derived debate.[6]

---

[5] For many of these links between homophobic rhetorical tradition(s) and *The New Atalantis*, see Robinson (1998) ch.5. On many of the specific terms and expressions, see Donoghue, especially 2–8. On *amity* and *amitié*, see especially Wahl, ch.3. On the pastoral as homoerotic space, see Guy-Bray. The *OED*'s two relevant definitions of 'nice' are "Precise or particular in matters of reputation or conduct; scrupulous, punctilious," and "Fastidious, fussy, difficult to please, esp. with regard to food or cleanliness; of refined or dainty tastes."

[6] On the aforementioned anti-lesbian strategies, see Robinson (1998) ch.1. On

In this, as in so many aspects of Western homosexual history, Plato's *Symposium* is (or has come to be) foundational. For the textual mêlée Manley joins, the two critical speeches are Socrates' account of Diotima's philosophy of love (to which we'll turn in a moment), and Pausanias' defense of male-male sexual "gratification." For centuries, both have profoundly influenced mutually intertwined homophilic and homophobic discourse.

Famously, Pausanias begins by asserting that there are two kinds of love:

[S]ince there are in fact two Aphrodites, there are necessarily two Loves also. And how could there not be two of the goddess? One is older, the motherless daughter of Uranus, whom we call the 'heavenly' Aphrodite, and the other is younger, the child of Zeus and Dione, whom we call the 'common' Aphrodite. It follows, of course, that the Love joined with the latter Aphrodite is rightly called common also, and the other is called heavenly. (22; 180e)[7]

The distinction between the two loves, it turns out, partially involves what we (and many subsequent readers, classical and early modern) would consider sexual orientation:

The Love that accompanies the common Aphrodite is truly common and acts in an opportunistic manner. This is the one whom ordinary human beings love. In the first place, such people love women no less than boys, and they love those they love for their bodies rather than their souls. So, they love the most unintelligent people they can, because they are concerned only about achieving their goal and do not care whether it is done in a noble and beautiful manner.... This Love comes from the younger rather than the older goddess, the one who in her origins shares in both the female and the male.

The Love that accompanies heavenly Aphrodite, first of all, does not share in the female, only in the male—this is love for young boys. Since this Aphrodite is older, she does not participate in outrageous behavior. Those who are inspired by this Love are oriented toward the male, cherishing what is by nature stronger and more intelligent. Anyone would recognize those who are motivated by this Love in a pure way, even in the case of loving young boys. They don't fall in love with boys until they begin to show some intelligence, which starts happening when their beards begin to grow. I believe that those who begin to love boys at that stage are ready to be together with them for their entire lives and even to live with them. Such lovers are not going to be

---

Manley's self-conscious engagement with classical writers, see Santessso. In contrast to Ballaster and others who situate *The New Atalantis* primarily in a "feminocentric tradition" ([1992] 2), Santesso persuasively argues that Manley "imagines herself as writing in the classical satiric tradition" (193), specifically the "Varronian" one derived from Lucian. On some of the classical texts I'll be discussing, and their centrality to male homosexual desire in Shakespeare's England, see Bruce Smith (1991).

[7] The first page numbers refer to Cobb's translation, the second to the corresponding section of the Greek text (according to Cobb).

deceivers, taking on someone when he lacks understanding because of his youth and then contemptuously abandoning him later on to run off after someone else. (22; 181a–81d)

Common love is undiscriminating. It doesn't distinguish between unworthy and worthy objects—between women and stupid boys on the one hand, and intelligent boys on the other. It's an ordinary person's love, not a philosopher's, and carnal rather than spiritual.

Not that heavenly love may not include sex. But certain conditions must be met "if the darling intends to gratify his lover in a noble and beautiful manner." According to Athenian custom, says Pausanias,

When a lover and his darling come together, each has a rule: The lover is justified in performing any services he can perform for the darling who gratifies him, and the beloved in turn is justified in providing whatever services he can for the one who is making him wise and good—assuming the former is able to introduce the other to prudence and other virtues, and the latter does want to acquire an education and other skills. When these two rules come together as a single principle, then and only then does it come about that a darling's gratifying a lover is a noble and beautiful thing. (25; 184d–184e)

Of course, as with the rest of Plato's *Symposium* (cf. Halperin [1992b], Carnes, Martha Nussbaum), it's difficult to know how seriously to take Pausanias' speech. For one thing, as Thomas Hubbard points out, Pausanias was "[a] student of the sophist Prodicus" (183, n.30); his philosophy might therefore be dismissed as mere sophistry (especially his grounding it on conflicting, mythological accounts of the birth of Aphrodite). More interestingly, as Hubbard also points out, "[s]everal sources related that Pausanias was the long-time lover of Agathon, and went with him to Macedon when life in Athens became unpleasant for them" (183, n.30), while "the tragic poet Agathon, the host of Plato's *Symposium*[,] [was] a character known from many sources to have remained clean-shaven and to have played a boy's role with older men well into adulthood" (87). Pausanias, therefore, has skillfully defended and idealized precisely his own unconventional taste in love: life-long, sexually active, same-sex partnering. Indeed, in recommending that a boy's first beard-growth signal the *beginning* of attractiveness to adult men, Pausanias turns on its head the conventional understanding of such signs of physical maturity as *ending* a boy's attractiveness, signaling the impending completion of his transition to manhood (see Tarán).[8]

---

[8] For Plato's, as opposed to Pausanias's, treatment of sexual appetite and Platonic eros, see Gaca, who argues that in Plato "the sexual appetite is point for point the unregenerate opposite of Platonic eros.[¶] ...[H]owever, the overall human experience of falling or being in love with another person combines the conflicting impulses of the sexual appetite and Platonic eros. This heady experience of being in love is a mixture of the two, not pure

Most interesting of all, however, is a feature of Pausanius' speech William Cobb points out: it contains "the first hint in the dialogue of the existence of social disapproval of homosexuality" (65):

> Actually, there should be a rule... against loving [young] boys, so that a lot of effort will not be squandered on an uncertain prospect. It is unclear how young boys will turn out, that is, whether their souls and bodies will end up being bad or virtuous. Good men willingly set up this rule for themselves, but this sort of restriction needs to be imposed on those common lovers, just as we restrict them, as far as we can, from loving free-born women. These are the people who have prompted the reproach by some who go so far as to say that it is shameful to gratify one's lovers. People who observe these men say this because they see their importunity and injustice, since whatever is done in an orderly and lawful manner surely does not justly bear censure. (22–23; 181d–182a)

As Cobb also observes, "the second speech by Socrates in the *Phaedrus* contains strong caution against engaging in such gratification," and in the *Symposium*, "[t]he behavior of Socrates as reported by Alcibiades... seems to stand in marked contrast to Pausanias' view" (65).

That moment in Alcibiades' remarks is worth quoting, as subsequent writers, including Manley, will allude to it when arguing their case:

> After I had made my statement and heard his reply, and as it were let loose my arrows, I thought I had smitten him. So, I stood up, and not letting him say anything further, I put my own cloak over him, since it was winter. Then I lay down, getting under his own worn garment, threw my arms around this truly daimonic and amazing man, and lay there the entire night. (And you can't say that I am lying about this, Socrates!) After I had done these things, he acted far better than I had; he disdainfully laughed at my youthful good looks, in a quite outrageous manner—and [in this regard I thought I was really something], gentlemen of the jury (for you are a jury, judging Socrates' arrogance, and you know it!). By every god and goddess, I swear I got up after having slept with Socrates in a way that had no more significance than sleeping with a father or an older brother. (55 [with fine-tuning by Richlin]; 219b–219d)

The joke (or one of them) may be on Alcibiades: if he hadn't assumed the role of seducer—or had been less brazen, or less vain—Socrates might have behaved more like a lover and less like a father. Regardless, though, we can be sure Pausanias, whose speech is designed to justify a sexual component to virtuous love between *erastes* and *eromenos*, lover and beloved, would have taken full advantage of Alcibiades' offer.[9]

And yet, if the *Symposium*'s Socrates appears not to endorse male-male *sex*, he does offer an extremely influential exaltation of male-male *love*. The argument

---

Platonic eros, and should never be confused with Platonic eros alone" (37; also 36–40).

[9] Cf. Nussbaum, who argues that Alcibiades' speech reveals the *Symposium*, notwithstanding its many comic aspects, to be as tragic.

forms an integral part of the instruction he claims to have received from the wise woman Diotima. In a formulation central to what would eventually be called "platonic love," Diotima defines love as a series of steps leading from the physical world to the spiritual:

> In the activities of Love, this is what it is to proceed correctly, or be led by another: Beginning from beautiful things to move ever onwards for the sake of that beauty, as though using ascending steps, from one body to two and from two to all beautiful bodies, from beautiful bodies to beautiful practical endeavors, from practical endeavors to beautiful examples of understanding, and from examples of understanding to come finally to that understanding which is none other than the understanding of that beauty itself, so that in the end he knows what beauty itself is. (48; 211b–211c)

But like Pausanias—in fact, more clearly than he—Diotima contrasts what we would call heterosexuals with what we would call homosexuals—or rather, she contrasts heterosexual and homosexual *men*:

> All human beings are pregnant, Socrates, both in body and in soul, and when we come of age, we naturally desire to give birth....
>
> Now, those who are pregnant in body are more oriented toward women and are lovers in that way, providing immortality, remembrance, and happiness for themselves for all time, as they believe, by producing children. Those who are pregnant in soul however... give birth to what is appropriate for the soul [:] Good sense... and the rest of virtue....
>
> Whenever someone who has been pregnant in his soul with these things from youth, and who is reaching adulthood and coming into his prime, desires to give birth and produce offspring, he goes around, I believe, searching for something beautiful, with which he can produce offspring. He... eagerly embraces beautiful bodies rather than ugly ones, and should he happen upon someone who has a beautiful, well-bred, and naturally gifted soul as well, he embraces the combination with great enthusiasm and immediately engages in many conversations with this man about virtue...; thus, he sets out to educate him.... [S]uch men have much more to share with each other and a stronger friendship than that which comes from rearing children, since they share in the rearing of children who are more beautiful and more immortal. (44, 46–47; 206c, 208e–209c)

Drawing on these and related passages in the *Symposium*, subsequent classical, early modern, modern, and even postmodern lovers and theorists of love would construct and deconstruct an interrelated series of binaries, variously defending or denouncing the constituent terms: lust/love, sex/love, physical/spiritual, ordinary/elite, vicious/virtuous, procreative/nonprocreative,[10] love of women/love

---

[10] While Diotima's speech doesn't erect this dichotomy (in her account, although love of women and love of men differ in the type of offspring produced, biological versus intellectual, both are procreative), other texts (including Plato's *Laws*) treat pederasty or

of boys, opposite-sex love/same-sex love. Most importantly, homophobes and homophiles, lesbophobes and lesbophiles, misogynists and philogynists, pornographers and *précieuses* alike would make use of the same terms, appropriating and reappropriating one another's arguments.

Thus, in classical debates on the relative worth of loving women vs. loving boys, women-lovers accuse boy-lovers of concealing their lustful desire and activity behind a mask of pseudo-philosophical, pseudo-spiritual rhetoric. For instance, in a text that influenced Manley, pseudo-Lucian's *Erôtes* ("The Loves" or "Affairs of the Heart"),[11] Charicles, the advocate of male-female love, accuses his targets of such deceit. In Ferrand Spence's 1684 translation:

> Tis true, our modern *Socrates'es*, to abuse weak and shallow Understandings, disguise their filthy Love, under a false Masque of Vertue; and think they have a good plea in saying, that they are not enamour'd of the Body, but of the Mind. But, O venerable Philosophers, why do you thus leave those whom Age and Experience renders more worthy of your Friendship, to become Paramours of a young Fry, that have nothing recommendable, but their Beauty and their Youth? Is it because you believe, that nothing but what is beautifull is worthy of being belov'd, and do you inconsiderately confound Friendship with Love? Or d'ye believe, that the Virtues of the Body, and those of the Mind, are never separated? (67–68)

In rebuttal, the advocate of male-male love, Callicratidas, draws liberally upon both Pausanias' and Diotima's arguments. He thus declares, like the former:

> [T]here are two sorts of *Love*; the one Childish, which cannot be govern'd by Reason, and is only the Work of Nature; the other, Cœlestial and Divine, which only inspires Holy desires, and is no where to be found but in great Personages, who being full of the Good, only approve of that Pleasure which is mingled with Vertue. (75)

Indeed, combining arguments from Pausanias and Diotima, Callicratidas maintains:

> As for Marriage, it was introduc'd out of Necessity, for the preservation of the *Species*; but the Love of Boys, is a Work of Reason. Now, such things as have been invented for Pleasure, or for Decency, are much more Noble, and more Perfect, than those which are done out of present Necessity; as the *Honest* is preferrable before the *Useful* and the *Necessary*. During the Rudeness of the first Age, when Art and Experience had not yet found out the Conveniences of Life, People were contented with Common Things, as not having had the Leisure or the Wit to find out others.... (73)

---

homosexuality as nonprocreative, sterile, unnatural (see Hubbard, Ward; but also Pappas).

[11] On the attribution and dating of this circa third- or fourth-century CE dialogue, transmitted with the circa mid-second-century CE work of Lucian, see Halperin (1992a) 241.

Heterosexuality is here reduced to biological reproduction, a vulgar, common necessity. Homosexuality, in contrast, equals reason, invention, pleasure, "decency" (i.e., "Fitness of form or proportion: comeliness"), nobility, perfection, art, experience, "honesty" (i.e., honor, decency, comeliness), leisure, wit.

Callicratidas concludes his oration by appealing to the authoritative example of none other than Socrates:

> This *Socratical Discipline* is approved of by Oracles, who have judg'd [Socrates] the wisest of all men. For among the other Precepts, he has bequeath'd us for the living well, he approves the Love of Boyes, as a thing useful to the Republick. So that we ought to love 'em after his Example, as he did *Alcibiades*, without consuming our Love in fleeting Joyes, and short-liv'd Pleasures; but extending it even to Old Age, in revering this Sacred Bond.... (80)

Promising that for those who follow Socrates' example, "Life will be sweet and pacifique," their "reputation… will still live after they are dead," and "Heaven according to the Doctrine of Philosophers, will receive 'em at their departure from the Earth," Callicratidas rests his case.[12]

In mock-defending the new Cabal from "reflections" cast upon it by "censurers" who "pretend to find in these the Vices of old *Rome* reviv'd," Manley places part of this last passage from the *Erôtes* in the mouth of Lady Intelligence:

> Such Excursions as these [i.e., a Cabal member's jealous outburst upon surprising her "Favourite" with one of those "detestable Creatures," a man], have given Occasion to the Enemies of the *Cabal* to refine, as much as they please, upon the Misteries of it; there are, who will not allow of *Innocency* in any *Intimacies*. Detestable *Censurers*, who after the manner of the *Athenians*, will not believe so great a Man as *Socrates* (him, whom the *Oracle* deliver'd to be the Wisest of all Men) cou'd see every hour the Beauty of an *Alcibiades* without taxing his sensibility. How did they recriminate for his Affection, for his Cares, his Tenderness to the lovely *Youth?* how have they deliver'd him down to Posterity, as blameable for a too guilty Passion, for his Beautiful Pupil?—Since then it *is not in the Fate of even so wise a Man to avoid the Censure of the* Busy *and the* Bold, *Care ought to be taken by others (less fortify'd against occasion of Detraction, in declining such unaccountable Intimacies) to prevent the ill-natur'd World's refining upon their mysterious Innocence.* (46)

---

[12] Writing in his extreme differentist period, Halperin argued that "the quarrel between Charicles and Callicratidas comes down not to a difference in sexual object-choice, to differing preferences or orientations, but rather to a differential liking for particular human body parts, independent of the sex of the person who possesses them" ([1992a] 254). I find the argument unconvincing on several grounds, especially its overly literal reading of select passages, and its simplistic account of modern conceptions of sexual orientation, both of which produce an exaggerated contrast between past and present.

If this passage were taken at face value, Manley, or at least Lady Intelligence, would seem to be siding with abstemious Socrates over indulgent Pausanias, and reading pseudo-Lucian as endorsing Socrates' chaste understanding of homosexual love in general, and Alcibiades' account of their relationship in particular.

Yet both Manley and Lady Intelligence mean precisely the opposite. They no more credit socratic lovers' professions of chastity than does pseudo-Lucian's Theomnestus, to whom his friend Lycinus has been recounting the Charicles-Callicratidas debate. Commenting on Callicratidas' oration, Theomnestus remarks:

> I find *Callicratides* his Harangue somewhat too grave and serious, and I fancy 'twould be a Penance, loving a handsom Youth, and lyin with him, to remain a *Tantalus*,... with water up to the very eyes, without being able to quench ones Thirst.... (82)

After describing the decidedly physical manner in which a boy should be loved— ascending a "ladder of pleasure" from gazes to light touches to kisses to embraces to heavy petting and so on (an erotic parody of Diotima's "ascending steps")— Theomnestus declares:

> Now may I always love Boyes in this manner. But let them that trifle away their time, about sublime and foolish Speculations, and are only Philosophers in their supercilious Looks, feed the unlearn'd with a company of grave and senseless Words, and continue to enjoy and bask themselves in their Chimerical flame; But for Our parts, let us imitate *Socrates*, who was not content with meerly loving *Alcibiades*, but lay with him; which is not to be wondred at at all, since *Achilles* did the like with *Patroclus*, which may be easily conjectur'd from his extreme sorrow for his Death, and from certain Circumstances of his affliction, which speak his Passion rather than his Amity. Now there are those perhaps will say, that this is something too Smutty and obscene to be spoken, but by *Venus* all is true. (83–84)

Although Lady Intelligence and Manley differ from Theomnestus, and probably pseudo-Lucian, in reproving rather than approving homosex, they share with their classical satiric predecessors a worldly, skeptical take on sublime, passionless, platonic "amity." To fully appreciate Manley's homophobic satire in the Socrates and Alcibiades passage—its send-up of socratic, and by analogy sapphic, pseudo-sophistication— readers must be sophisticated enough to recognize her paraphrase of pseudo-Lucian's text, and to notice and fill in the missing punch line.

Spence himself, translating and editing Lucian's works in 1684, provides an example of the heavy-handed, humorless approach Manley eschews. Introducing "Affairs of the Heart," Spence first warns readers of the author's duplicity, but then, in defense of making such dangerous material available to a non–Latin-literate audience, denies it poses any danger:

> This Dialogue consists principally of Two Harangues: In the One, The Love of Women is maintain'd; and in the Other, that of Boyes; which is the honest or honourable Love

according to the Doctrine of the Platonicks: However, the Author endeavours maliciously & slily under that pretext, to introduce the filthy and unnatural Love; but the other Opinion therein, is so well defended, that none can hereby be corrupted; and it serves rather to shew, that this Vice has only Passion for its Plea: For all its Reasons are Chimerical, and confound Friendship with Love, and Vice with Vertue. (55)

Manley portrays the new Cabal precisely as Spence portrays pseudo-Lucian: slyly introducing filthy and unnatural same-sex love under the pretext of honest and honorable platonic love. But she provokes amusement as well at the obviously anxious fulminating of moralists like Spence.

The Gentlemen of the "confraternity": *La France devenue italienne...*

In parodying the spiritual rhetoric with which an elite group of same-sex lovers attempt to veil their sexual shenanigans, Manley follows in the footsteps of a much more recent satirist than pseudo-Lucian: the anonymous author of *La France devenue italienne avec les autres déréglements de la cour* ("France Become Italian with the Other Disorders of the Court" [1688]).[13] This satiric work depicts a secret clique of sodomitical French aristocrats referred to as both a "confraternity" and "cabal," whose clandestine activities and organization are described in terms Manley will closely echo. According to the author:

> In order not to attract the king's wrath..., they judged it appropriate to take an oath, and to have it taken by all those who joined their confraternity, to renounce all women, for they accused one among them of having revealed their mysteries to a lady with whom he was on good terms.... They even resolved not to admit this man into their company anymore, but, having presented himself to be admitted and having sworn not to see that lady anymore, they forgave him this time, on the condition that if he did it again, there would be no more mercy. This was the first rule of their confraternity.... (119)

Among their other rules:

> That they would take a vow of obedience and chastity with regard to women and that, if anyone violated it, he would be expelled from the company without being able to rejoin it on any pretense whatsoever.
>
> That if any of the brothers married, he would be obliged to state that it was only for the sake of his business or because his parents made him do it or because he needed to leave an heir.

---

[13] Two of the well-known scandal writers to whom the tale has been attributed are Bussy-Rabutin (Roger de Rabutin, comte de Bussy) and Gatien de Courtilz de Sandras. I've used the excerpt provided, in English translation, by Merrick and Ragan (2001). I thank Merrick for making the French text available to me.

That he would take an oath at the same time never to love his wife, to sleep with her only until he had an heir by her, and furthermore that he would ask permission to do it, which could be granted him only for one day of the week.

That as for outsiders, it would not be allowed to reveal the mysteries to them and that whoever did so would be deprived of them himself for a week and even longer, if the grand master to whom he answered judged it appropriate. (121–22).

Manley writes similarly of the new Cabal:

[T]hey meet, they caress, they swear inviolable Secresy and Amity; ...they momently exclude the *Men*, fortify themselves in the Precepts of *Virtue* and *Chastity* against all their detestable undermining Arts, arraign without Pity or Compassion those who have been so unfortunate as to fall into [Men's] Snare: Propagate their Principles of exposing them without Mercy—Give Rules to such of the *Cabal* who are not *Married*, how to behave themselves to such who they think fit they should *Marry*; no such weighty Affair being to be accomplish'd without the mutual consent of the *Society*: At the same time lamenting the custom of the World, that has made it convenient (nay, almost indispensible) for all Ladies once to Marry. To those that have Husbands, they have other Instructions, in which this is sure to be one; to reserve their *Heart*, their tender *Amity* for their *Fair Friend*: An Article in this well-bred wilfully-undistinguishing Age, which the Husband seems to be rarely sollicitous of....

Secresie also is a material *Article*; this they inviolably promise, nor is it the least part of the Instruction given to a *new Bride*, lest she let her Husband into a *Mystery* (however *innocent*) that may *expose* and *ridicule* the *Community*, as it hap'ned in the case of the beautiful Virgin *Euphelia*.... (46–48)

Manley likely read *La France devenue italienne* before writing *The New Atalantis*. The popular collection in which the former first appeared (*La France galante, ou Histoires amoureuses de la cour* ["Gallant France, or Amorous Stories of the Court"]) was republished several times during the late seventeenth and early eighteenth century, and exemplifies the "secret history" genre in which Manley had read so widely and to which *The New Atalantis* explicitly contributes. Yet my point, in demonstrating their strikingly similar portrayal of same-sex communities, is not that the former must have directly influenced the latter, much less that Manley's anti-lesbian humor depends on readers perceiving such an influence, as in the ultra-sophisticated intertextual games she plays with Plato and pseudo-Lucian (games that, by demonstrating Manley's classical knowledge, bolster her authority in a masculine literary and political arena). My point is that Manley's scandal-hungry readership was already primed to read her account of the new Cabal as satire.[14]

---

[14] Satiric portrayal of secret same-sex orders, sects, and societies continued at least to the end of the century. See, e.g., Merrick & Ragan, eds. (2001) 173–85, 192–98, 204–12, as well as Cardon, ed. Stanivukovic briefly discusses an intriguing earlier example: in

Primed not only by *La France devenue italienne*, but by a larger, early modern satiric tradition mocking platonic love in general, and ideal friendship in particular, as concealing unnatural sex. Regarding friendship, Wahl has demonstrated that by the late seventeenth century, *précieuse* language was widely subject to "deliberate (mis)reading... as a kind of code for expressing female-female desire[,] ...subvert[ing] the *précieuse* claims to spirituality" ([1999] 207–208; see also Andreadis [2001], Traub [2002]). Indeed, we've already encountered (ch.1, 13–16), in Brantôme's conversation with Lord de Guast, a late sixteenth-/early seventeenth-century instance of such lesbophobic resistant reading from the tradition of gossip and scandal writing.

In that anecdote, Brantôme and his friend were reading "On the Beauty of Women" (*Dialogo delle bellezze delle donne* [1541; tr. French 1578]), in which Agnolo Firenzuola reworks the other dialogue from Plato's *Symposium* central to the history of Western homosexuality: Aristophanes' explanation of the origin of love as human beings' longing for their missing halves. In the midst of, as Kenneth Borris puts it, "modifying Platonic love theory to serve heteroerotic perspectives," including "advanc[ing] a proto-feminist defense of women" ([2004] 274), Firenzuola has his mouthpiece Celso laud and condemn, respectively, chaste and carnal same-sex love. And once again, Socrates and Alcibiades are enlisted as evidence:

> Those who were male in both halves, or are descended from those who were, wishing to return to their original state, seek their other half, which was another male. They thus love and admire each other's beauty, some virtuously, as Socrates loved the handsome Alcibiades, or as Achilles loved Patroclus, or Nisus loved Euryalus; and some unchastely, as certain wicked men.... And all these men, both the virtuous and the wicked, generally flee the company of you ladies. And I know very well that you are familiar with some of these even in our own day.
>
> Those who were female in both halves, or are descended from those who were, love each other's beauty, some in purity and holiness, as the elegant Laudomia Forteguerra loves the most illustrious Margaret of Austria, some lasciviously, as in ancient times Sappho from Lesbos and in our own times in Rome the great prostitute Cecilia Venetiana. This type of woman by nature spurns marriage and flees from intimate conversation with us men. And, we must believe, these women are those who willingly become nuns and willingly remain so, and they are few, because the majority of women are kept in monasteries by force and live there in despair.

As discussed earlier, Brantôme omits most of the story, and discusses only women,

---

PURITANISME The Mother, SINNE THE DAUGHTER (1633), Benjamin Carrier, a Catholic priest and convert form Protestantism, writes, "In the yeare 1632, there was discovered in London a Society of certaine Sodomites, to the number of forty, or fifty; all of them being... Puritans, who had their common appointed meeting-place, for their abominable Impiety" (Stanivukovic, 184–85; 191, n.42). See Carvajal for molly-like gatherings in mid- (and perhaps early) seventeenth-century Mexico City.

but retains a tripartite organizing structure, dividing women into those who love men, those who love each other's beauty, and those who love each other purely and in sanctity. His fellow reader, however, challenges that third category, sounding rather like pseudo-Lucian's Theomnestus commenting on Socrates' supposedly chaste relations with Alcibiades:

> About that, Monsieur Du Guast criticized the author, saying that it was false that this fair Marguerite loved that fair lady with a pure and holy love: because, since she had attached herself to her rather than to others who might have been as beautiful and virtuous as she, it was to be presumed that it was in order to make use of her for her sensual pleasures, no more or less than others; and, to cover up her lasciviousness, she said and proclaimed that she loved her in a holy way, as we see several like her do, who veil their loves with such words.

Using the metaphors of veiling and leaving in shadow (*ombrager*), Du Guast interprets as closeted lesbianism ardent love between women accompanied by protestations of purity and holiness.

Du Guast disparages Marguerite's love as lasciviousness. Yet in early modern as in classical times, opponents of same-sex sexuality were not the only ones to assert the carnality of supposedly spiritual or platonic eros. Take, for example, the most important early modern proponent of fully sexual love between men, Antonio Rocco, whose graphically sexual *L'Alcibiade fanciullo a scola* ("The Boy Alcibiades at School"; wr. c.1630 or before; pub. Venice c.1651) depicts the seduction/education of the beautiful schoolboy Alcibiade by his teacher Filotomo. As Turner explains:

> [Rocco's] goal is to recorporealize the Platonic doctrine of educational pederasty, exemplified by Socrates in the arms of Alcibiades himself (as memorably dramatized in the *Symposium*). *Orthôs paiderastein* or 'straight' homosexual love of a pupil, according to Plato, must be purified by physical abstention and thereby converted into a vehicle for higher knowledge, leading the acolyte step by step towards transcendence; Rocco cunningly retains the upward cognitive drive but literalizes the Socratic imagery of mental intercourse, pregnancy, and 'birth in beauty'…. The end result is to confirm Lucian's equation of exclusive homosexuality, the 'philosophic spirit', and the aesthetic life removed from mere biological 'necessity'. ([2003] 90–91)

In response to those who privileged opposite-sex love, and those who valued only nonsexual same-sex love, *L'Alcibiade fanciullo* upends Western sexual orthodoxy, as its protagonist strives, ultimately with success, to upend his student. To quote Turner once more, "*L'Alcibiade…* spells out in its fullest form the assumption that flourished throughout the period between Tullia d'Aragona's discussion of the 'Socratics' [1547] and Montesquieu's remarks on *amour philosophique* [1729]: that elite homosexuality provides the only way of reconciling Nature and Art, combining Eros and intellect into the elusive Platonic ideal," even going so far as to demonstrate, by philosophical proof, "that the 'vice against nature' in fact fulfils Nature's dearest wishes for humanity" ([2003] 89, 91).[15]

The Story of Harriat

To portray the new Cabal as female versions of Rocco's Filotomo—or better yet, as speaking like pseudo-Lucian's Callicratidas but thinking and lusting like Theomnestus—Manley relies, as mentioned above, upon parodic mimicry. What some critics have read as Lady Intelligence and Manley's own sentiments are parodies of new Cabal rhetoric, coyly reproduced in the form of free indirect discourse.[16]

Readers need only compare Intelligence's language in the new Cabal section with her linguistic overkill in the immediately preceding story, about the unambiguously villainous, arch-hypocrite Harriat. When Intelligence explains that "[The *Cabal*] have wisely excluded that rapacious *Sex*" (44); that "they momently exclude the *Men*, fortify themselves in the Precepts of *Virtue* and *Chastity* against all their detestable undermining Arts" (46); that, upon being rejected by the actress, "The *Widow* found her *Companion* not of a Taste virtuous enough for the *Mysteries* of their *Union*...[;] [t]he *Comedian* had been vitiated by *Amour!* by *abominable Intrigue* with the *filthy odious* Men*!* and was not therefore worthy the Honour of being admitted into their Community" (208), we ought to hear echoes of the ironic, free indirect speech through which Harriat's hypocrisy is mockingly exposed.

A particularly concise and scathing characterization of Harriat opens her tale. According to Lady Intelligence, she is "*Tall*, *Well-made*, *Genteel*, *Agreeable*, *Precise*, a *Devotee*, fraught with *Precepts* of outward *Honour*, an affectation of Virtue, unfathomed *Hypocrisy*, fire in her Constitution, frost in Conversation" (19). Except for the final phrase, the description could easily apply to a typical Cabal member—especially the term *Devotee*. In *The New Atalantis*, as in other French and British anti-lesbian texts of the seventeenth and eighteenth centuries, women who repeatedly protest their virtue and high-mindedness are not to be believed.

---

[15] For the full text of *L'Alcibiade* in Italian, French, and English, see the 1988, 1995, and 2000 editions, respectively; each includes commentary. For an English excerpt, with commentary, see Borris (2004) 365–71. See also Dall'Orto (1983), N.S. Davidson, and especially Turner (2003) 88–105, and for earlier celebration and defense of sex between men, Vignali's *La Cazzaria* (c.1530).

[16] At its most basic, free indirect discourse is a narrative technique for indirectly reporting a character's thoughts. Among its complex uses and effects, it's particularly well-suited for subtle, ironic humor, enabling a narrator to convey a character's thoughts while simultaneously poking fun at her. As used in the following examples from *The New Atalantis*, it is, as Daniel Gunn characterizes Austen's masterful use of the technique, "a kind of narratorial *mimicry*" (35).

Like a later fictional villainess, Laclos's Madame de Merteuil in *Les Liaisons dangereuses*, Harriat has turned concealment of her feelings, especially sexual feelings, into a pseudo-feminist philosophy. In contrast to her poor cousin Urania, who wears her heart on her sleeve, Harriat rejects "that *Plebeian Vice, Sincerity*," in favor of dissimulation (20). She lies even when propounding this credo, disclaiming the sexual desire she clearly feels:

> *Sincerity* in *Manners* was most abominable; what, wear ones *Motions* as ones *Thoughts?* If one told ones self that such a young *Fellow* was *agreeable*, must ones *Actions* tell the World *so*, and speak ones Approbation? What, let the [tell-Tale Eyes] sparkle out the odious desire one had for the *ridiculous Creature*, that contemptible Animal, Man! How*!* give *them Vanity*, and ones self *Censure!* 'twas unpardonable. If one had *desire* (but how comes one by desire for filthy Reptiles, that grovel at ones Feet) wou'd one acquaint the World with ones *Foible?* Oh how necessary was Dissimulation! how it bought Opinion! 'Twas like a *Veil* to the *Face*, conceal'd all that one wou'dn't have disclos'd to vulgar Eyes, and intirely at ones own pleasure and discretion, when to wear or when to lay aside. (21)

The Cabal members' use of words such as 'detestable,' 'rapacious,' 'abominable,' 'filthy,' and 'odious' when speaking of men and of heterosexual desire, signals the same hypocrisy as Harriat's 'odious,' 'ridiculous creature,' 'contemptible animal,' and 'filthy reptiles.' In both cases, Manley reveals, the women's hyperbolically asserted sexual virtue is a closeting device, "a *Veil*... conceal[ing] all that [they] wou'dn't have disclos'd to vulgar Eyes": their selfishness and sexual sin. Harriet, who "pursu'd her Principles of Good-Nature, in censuring and exposing the Frailties of others" (38), masking her malice with "*Tautalogies*" like "her *Duty!* her *Honour!* her *Religion!* her *Glory!* her adored *Virtue!*" (29), eventually gives birth to an illegitimate child. The women of the new Cabal, who proclaim both loving friendship and chastity, turn out to be selfish, scandalous sapphists.[17]

Mock Ignorance

A satiric snippet from slightly later in the century provides a useful point of comparison with Manley's text. It mirrors her use of parodic mimicry by means of free indirect discourse, but also brings out, by contrast, her principal homophobic rhetorical strategy: mock ignorance. In the *Weekly Journal or Saturday Post* of January 26, 1723 (1724 new style), the following item appeared:

> Not far from hence you see a blended Troop of Gallants, who seem to take an Pride in feminine *Airs*, and who, by their Caresses and Fondness of each other, we should conclude, are those *glorious PLATONICKS*, who have contracted *Friendships* from

---

[17] Manley's italics here, which Ballaster's edition omits, further emphasize the irony implied by her use of free indirect speech.

Sympathy in Virtue, *and are grown enamoured* of *internal* Beauties. Did we know the *secret* debaucheries of these *Intimadoes*, we should be startled at the flagitious Epitome of *Sodom*. The most signal *Difference is, that* these are not *nice* enough to covet the *Conversation* of *Angels*. But let us get off from this Quarter of Impurity. ("Those Glorious Platonicks," ed. Norton, 2000–2004)

In the first sentence, the speaker sounds like Lady Intelligence describing the new Cabal to Astrea and Virtue. The Troop of Gallants presumably use most of the italicized, and many of the non-italicized, words to describe themselves and their relationships, at least to outsiders: 'glorious,' 'Platonick,' 'Friendship,' 'Sympathy,' 'Virtue,' "enamoured of internal Beauty." The same goes, in the next sentence, for 'Intimadoes,' a suitably Italian euphemism for what, as we're about to learn, these men actually are. Yet the speaker chooses to communicate outrage rather than amusement, both by explicitly naming the behavior in question and by piling on condemnation: these men who publicly flaunt feminine airs, mutual caresses, and mutual fondness, secretly indulge in vice, in debaucheries that are not just the epitome, but the "flagitious epitome," of Sodom. Not that the author abandons irony. With a neatly phrased allusion (as Rictor Norton explains) "to the biblical story of Sodom and Gomorrah, when the men of Sodom wanted to have 'conversation' with the angels who came to Lot's house," the speaker not only impugns the Platonicks' self-professed spirituality and discriminating taste, but portrays them as worse than even the original Sodomites—at least *they* lusted after angels!

When relating the story of Harriat, Manley likewise allows Lady Intelligence to slip into explicit condemnation. Harriat is one of "those that with the Mask of *Hypocrisy* undo the Reputation of Thousands" (9); she is "fraught with *Precepts* of outward *Honour*, an affectation of Virtue, unfathom'd *Hypocrisy*" (19); "*Harriat* with a malicious and triumphant Smile follow[ed] [*Urania*], casting an air of pleas'd Disdain, and of delightful Scorn, upon the ruin'd Beauty" (31). Throughout the story, we know precisely how much to credit her frequent declarations of chastity and virtue, since she first appears giving birth in the woods in the dead of night, concerned above all for her "ador'd Reputation" (8). As in the newspaper account of "those *glorious PLATONICKS*," Manley's ironic use of free indirect discourse in Harriat's tale enlivens but doesn't replace an authoritative, moralizing satiric voice.

Not so with the new Cabal. To specify explicitly *what* Lady Intelligence is condemning, and *that* she is condemning it, would spoil the fun enabled by Manley's most important homophobic rhetorical strategy: mock ignorance. Just as Chorier-Nicolas's choices serve the particular needs of libertine male pornography, Manley's tongue-in-cheek naiveté is the homophobic strategy best suited to gossip and scandal writing.

It is, of course, a strategy of indirection (Andreadis, 92), itself an overarching approach central to the discursive history of homosexuality, particularly in the form of euphemism. But mock ignorance is even more closely related to such ironic figures as *aporia* ("a speaker's feigned or true ignorance about circumstances, or the ability to express them" [Adams, 144]), *apophasis* ("pretending to deny what is really affirmed" [Adams, 143]), and *praeteritio* or *paralipsis* ("stating and drawing attention to something in the very act of pretending to pass it over" [Burton]), epitomized by references to the "unnameable" vice or sin. As a specifically anti-lesbian strategy, mock ignorance is related to the longstanding unknowing of lesbianism as *amor impossibilis*, impossible love.[18]

However, in the particular form of indirection I call mock ignorance, author and speaker merge, winking archly at the reader, inviting her to join in the naughty fun of sharing risqué knowledge under the transparent guise of innocence and ignorance. Users of this sophisticated, double-voiced technique laugh at those about whom they're gossiping, but also at those whom such gossip distresses, moralistic innocents shocked at the conduct in question. And when it comes to homosexuality, mock ignorance is the scandalmonger's quintessential pose. As *The New Atalantis* is a quintessential scandal narrative, a prime example of the genre so popular in England and France in the late seventeenth and early eighteenth centuries, it's no accident mock ignorance predominates in Manley's account of the new Cabal.

It predominates as well in Anthony Hamilton's portrayal of a lesbian lady-in-waiting in *Mémoires de la Vie du Comte de Grammont* (*Memoirs of the Life of Count de Grammont*; wr. 1703–1704; circulated in ms; pub. 1713). The first time the narrator introduces "Mistress *H--t*" ("Mademoiselle HUBERT" in French, "Miss Hobart" in later English translations), he begins by stressing her "uncommon" or novel [*nouveau*] character, her lack of attractiveness, her "*irregular Fancy*," and her "*tender Heart*, whose *Sensibility*, some pretended, was in favour [only] of the *Fair Sex*." We are told that "Mistress *B--t*" ("Mademoiselle BAGETT," "Miss *Paget*"), who first merited her "*Affection* and *Fondness*" ["ses *Soins* & ses *Empressemens*"], "answer'd it at first, cordially, and with a good Meaning; but perceiving that all her Friendship was not sufficient to repay that of Mistress *H--t*, she yielded that *Conquest* to the Niece of the *Mother of the Maids* [la *Gouvernante*]; who thought herself much *honour'd* by it, as her *Aunt* thought her self much *oblig'd* by the Care she took of the *young Girl*." But this pairing does not last:

> 'Twas not long before the Report, whether true or false, of [Mistress *H--t*'s] *Singularity*, spread through the whole Court, where *People* being yet so *unciviliz'd* as never to have heard of that kind of *Refinement* in *Tenderness* of *ancient Greece*, some imagined, that the *illustrious H--t*, who was so fond of the *fair Sex*, was something more than she appear'd to be.

---

[18] On the *amor impossibilis* trope, see below, ch.6–7, and especially Traub (2002). For analyses of the other rhetorical figures in relation to homophobic or lesbophobic discourse, see Schleiner (1993), Castle (1982), and Schibanoff (2001b). For a late twentieth-century example of another closely related homophobic rhetorical strategy, see D.A. Miller (1989/1993), esp. 214.

> The *Lampoons* began to *Compliment* her upon those new *Attributes*; and her Companions began to be afraid of her, upon the Credit of those *Lampoons*.

La *Gouvernante*, concerned for her niece's well-being, turns for advice to Lord Rochester, who "thereupon advis'd her to take her from Mrs. H____t's Hands, and manag'd Matters so well, that she fell into his." Fortunately, "The *Dutchess* [of York], who was too generous not to treat as *Chimeras* what was charg'd upon Mrs. H____t, and too just to condemn her upon *Songs*, made her from a *Maid of Honour*, a *Bed-Chamber-Woman*."[19]

Like Manley's account of the Cabal, this episode is a masterpiece of indirection, euphemism, and allusion. Like the satiric ballads he mentions, Hamilton insinuates, speaks in code. Some phrases are almost explicit: she had "a *tender Heart*, whose *Sensibility*, some pretended, was in favour of the *Fair Sex*"; "that kind of *Refinement* in *Tenderness*"—or, in the original French, "upon the Tastes of *Tenderness*" ["sur les Gouts de la *Tendresse*"]—"of *ancient Greece*." But as D.A. Miller observes in a discussion of Hitchcock's *Rope*, homophobic discourses' reliance upon connotation rather than denotation turns every textual detail into a potential signifier of homosexuality: "connotation ... tends to light everywhere, to put all signifiers to a test of their hospitality" ([1991] 125). Thus an otherwise vague phrase such as "an *irregular Fancy*" ["une *Imagination* peu réglée"] recalls the Cabal's "irregularity of Taste" (206) and "that irregular/dissolute love" [*cet amour dereglé*] of which Chorier-Nicolas's Tullie speaks (II.9). Even the remark that Mistress H--t had "*bright Eyes*, which yet were not *killing*" ["beaucoup de *Feu* dans des *Yeux* peu touchans"] reinforces Hamilton's anti-lesbian message, as if a woman must be attract*ed* to men in order to be attract*ive*.

But what makes this passage mock ignorant, rather than merely indirect, is that the narrator himself pretends not to endorse the conclusion he takes such pains to impress upon readers: that Mistress H--t is a lesbian. Instead, he ascribes the idea to unspecified others. The notion that the sensibility of her tender heart was in favor only of the fair sex is offered not as simple fact (like the descriptions of her physical appearance, wit, etc.), but as something that "some pretended" to be the case. In recounting the spread of "the Report... of this *Singularity*," the narrator qualifies "the Report" with the phrase "whether true or false." This mock equivocation is part of the anti-lesbian fun. Like some other forms of unknowing, this one uses humor to present lesbianism as nonthreatening, and therefore the speaker (and likeminded readers) as

---

[19] English quotations are from Hamilton (1714) 234–35, French from Hamilton (1713) 280–81; I've provided the latter where its connotations diverge suggestively, if only slightly, from the translation. On the composition and publication history of *Grammont*, see Hamilton (1994) 378–79, Wahl (318, n.6), Love, and Castle (2003). In terms of lesbian humiliation, the Hubert/Bagett episode prefigures Hamilton's longer, more detailed narrative of Hubert's relationship with Mistress Temple (Fr. 288–317; Eng. 241–64), most of which takes place in the Duchess's bathing "closet."

unthreatened. In contrast to the men and women of Charles II's court, the narrator affects to be thoroughly blasé about sex between women. At the same time, this gossipy rhetorical strategy flatters the reader, gives her the illusion of being in the know, able to recognize and decode authorial hints and suggestions, and thus superior to simpletons who need things spelled out.[20]

In *The New Atalantis,* Lady Intelligence similarly ascribes accusations of lesbianism to unspecified others, all the while communicating and implicitly endorsing them herself. Over and over, she marvels at the Cabal's censurers' charges, and asserts the women's innocence, chastity, and virtue, asking "[H]ow can they be guilty?... What irregularity can there be in this?" Even without knowledge of a wider lesbo- and homophobic discursive context, one ought to suspect that the Lady doth protest too much. Intelligence speaks like a stock fictional gossip pretending not to believe or enjoy the dirt she enthusiastically dishes. But with knowledge of that wider context (above all, the strikingly similar *Grammont*), one *must* recognize this as a pose, a homophobic rhetorical strategy early eighteenth-century readers were expected to know and enjoy. Like gossip columnists today, Lady Intelligence and Manley offer readers the sophisticated pleasure of pretending to be unsophisticated. Rather than either fulminate or fall silent, Manley mocks the loudly laughing ladies of the Cabal with belittling laughter of her own.

Nevertheless, her mockery of straitlaced lesbophobia—so in keeping with the tone of a scandal narrative—doesn't alter the fact that all evidence, both internal and external to the text, suggests *The New Atalantis* presupposes an audience able to conceive of lesbianism, familiar with the longstanding conventions that had governed its representation, and, in keeping with those conventions, thoroughly anti-lesbian in sentiment. This negative stance is evident in the very word Manley uses to refer to the lesbians' network or society: a *cabal* (Santesso, 198). In fact, the term had often been used in anti-feminist, anti-*précieuse* satire (Stanton [1981] 112). And as mentioned earlier, Manley may also have been following in the specifically homophobic footsteps of *La France devenue italienne*, which described a secret clique of sodomitical French aristocrats as, among other things, a *cabal*.[21]

Also telling is Lady Intelligence's identifying the Marchioness de Lerma as "one of the first Founders [of the Cabal] in *Atalantis*." Of all Cabal members described, the Marchioness is by far the most masculine,

> [h]aving something so robust in her *Air* and *Mien*, that the other *Sex* wou'd have certainly claim'd her for one of *theirs*, if she had not thought fit to declare her self by her Habit (alone) to be of the *other*; insomuch, that I have often heard it lamented by the Curious, who

---

[20] For evidence that eighteenth-century writers and readers were aware of this particular pleasure afforded by gossipy satire, see Griffin, 167–68.

[21] The association between cabals and homosexuals is continued in the anonymous *Hell Upon Earth* (1729); rpt. McCormick, 148.

have tax'd themselves of Negligence, and were intimate with her Lord, when living, that they did not desire him to explain upon that *Query*. (48)

In other words, the only thing that keeps men from identifying the Marchioness as a man is her female clothing, and friends of her late husband wish they'd asked him what her true sex was (since he had the opportunity to see her naked). With such a founder, English lesbianism is hardly held up for readers' admiration.

One final bit of evidence deserves mention. When Lady Intelligence returns to the subject of lesbianism, describing a widow who falls for an actress specializing in male roles (known as "breeches parts"), her mock-ignorant mask slips. Near the end of the brief episode—after the actress has rebuffed the widow's "*hugs* and *indearments*," which "from her own Sex… seem'd *un-natural*," and after the widow has pronounced the ingrate "not of a Taste virtuous enough for the *Mysteries* of their *Union*" and "vitiated by *Amour!* by *abominable Intrigue* with the *filthy odious* Men!"— Intelligence informs her listeners:

> When [the widow] was return'd to her House in Town, to show the lurkings of her Malice, or rather her *Detestation* to Vice, tho *but* in *Effigy*, she caus'd the *Comedian's* Picture to be let down, and with her own Hand cut out the Face; so stamp'd upon and abus'd it, sent it back to her whom it represented, at the same time causing her to be told, she had by her *loose Libertine*-Life, made it a Scandal to her House to have such a Picture in it. (208)

While maintaining her credulous pose, the speaker's brief self-correction (a mock version of the rhetorical figure *correctio*) makes explicit the authorially intended interpretation of this and other examples of new Cabal behavior.

From their first appearance (laughing "loud and incessantly" as if life were one endless party) to their last (the rejected widow violently defacing the actress's portrait), the members of the new Cabal are depicted in a decidedly unflattering light. Using a variety of recognizable lesbophobic and homophobic conventions, particularly the rhetorical strategies of mock ignorance and parodic free indirect discourse, the text solicits an anti-lesbian reader.

"The mimick Leachery of Manly Loves": Juvenal and Dryden

I don't mean simply to condemn *The New Atalantis*, or to criticize its present-day defenders. The text undeniably contains feminist elements. It can be read, at least in part, as a response to Juvenal's ferociously misogynist *Satire 6*, what Felicity Nussbaum aptly calls "an unrelieved diatribe against Roman women," which was, for the early eighteenth century, "*the* original antifeminist satire" ([1984] 77, 80). Although Manley doesn't explicitly register discomfort with Juvenal's misogyny, *The New Atalantis* implicitly refutes his portrayal of the horrors women inflict on men. True, she depicts some women negatively. But for the most part, men in *The New*

Atalantis are the victimizers, women the victims.

Yet one element of Juvenal's satire Manley does *not* refute is his anti-lesbianism, momentarily perceptible in the Latin original, and registered in seventeenth-century English translations, including Dryden's influential one (1693). On their way home from a drunken midnight feast, three women (one, interestingly, named Tullia) stop at an altar to the goddess Chastity to relieve themselves. The ensuing action is translated similarly by both Robert Stapylton (orig. 1644, rev. 1660) and Barten Holiday (1673):

> ...they doe theire distill,
> And the carv'd Goddess with long spoutings fill:
> They mount by courses in the Moon's chast sight[.] (*ll*.323–25)

> ...here they staine
> The Goddess, whiles her statue they prophane.
> Here mutually they're vile; and yet although
> 'Tis night, the Moon sees all. (97)

Dryden, however, replicates Juvenal's bluntness, at least in manuscript versions of his translation:

> They straighten wth their hands y[e] nameless place
> And Spouting thence bepiss her venerable face:
> Before the Conscious moon they get astride;
> By Turns are ridden & by Turns they ride. (173)

His published version omits these lines, but transfers their anti-lesbian satire to the next scene, in which participants at the annual all-female worship of the Bona Dea, the Good Goddess, their lust incited by music and wine, hold an impromptu erotic-dance competition (think "hoochie coochie" or "bump and grind"), until the crowd grows so excited they cry for men, any men, to be admitted, and an orgy ensues (*ll*.331–35). Once again, Dryden's manuscript and published versions differ. But this time both refer to lesbian sex, although, once again, the lines that appear only in manuscript (marked here with an asterisk) are bluntly colloquial:

> *Laufella* lays her Garland by, and proves
> The mimick Leachery of Manly Loves.
> * Provokes to Flats some batterd household whore
> * And heaving up the rubster does adore.
> Rank'd with the Lady, the cheap Sinner lies;
> For here not Blood, but Virtue gives the prize.
> Nothing is feign'd in this Venereal Strife;
> 'Tis downright Lust, and Acted to the Life. (175, *ll*.436–41)

As mentioned earlier, 'flats' or 'the game of flats' was an early eighteenth-century term for sex between women. As for 'rubster,' it translates *tribas* and *frictrix*, both of which Dryden would have found in seventeenth-century Latin commentary (Juvenal [1684] 200) on the preceding scene (in which women piss on Chastity and mount one another). Yet even without the manuscript's more graphic terminology, Dryden's printed version of Juvenal's *Satire 6* communicates the doubly debased nature of sex between women. It is lechery, rather than love—and not even original or genuine lechery, but mere mimicry of manly lust.

Interestingly, Dryden issues a disclaimer, assuring readers that contemporary Englishwomen do not engage in the practices Juvenal describes:

> Whatever [Juvenal's] *Roman* Ladies were, the *English* are free from all his Imputations. They will read with Wonder and Abhorrence, the Vices of an Age, which was the most Infamous of any on Record. They will bless themselves when they behold those Examples related of *Domitian's* time: They will give back to Antiquity those Monsters it produc'd: And believe with reason, that the Species of those Women is extinquish'd; or at least, that they were never here propagated. (146)

Dryden, it would seem, is not a censurer who, as Lady Intelligence puts it, "pretend[s] to find... the Vices of old *Rome* reviv'd" in modern Englishwomen. Yet his gallantry is hardly convincing. As Nussbaum points out, Dryden updated *Satire 6* "to include Englishwomen's French affectations, references to the mall, park, and theatre," and other contemporary details (80). In the case of lesbianism, the disclaimer is implicitly contradicted by his manuscript use of the up-to-date English slang-word 'flats' to refer to lesbian sex. In any case, Manley far surpasses both Juvenal and Dryden's incidental anti-lesbian slur against woman-only space, offering a copious depiction of the new Cabal as a thriving, if ridiculous, hotbed of early eighteenth-century English lesbianism.[22]

"But when we look with true regard to the World": Feminist Intentions?

The question therefore arises, why does Manley choose to expend so much anti-lesbian textual energy? An answer begins to emerge when we notice Manley justifies

---

[22] Juvenal's apparent use of horse- or horseriding-related language in both passages, as well as, in the latter, his ambiguous assertion that there's "No make-belief here, no pretence/ Each act is performed in earnest" (*Nil ibi per ludum simulabitur, omnia fient/ Ad verum* [324–25; tr. 1967, 139]) are probably what led Stapylton, Holiday, and Dryden to read the scene, like the preceding one, as referring to lesbian sex (cf. Brooten, 48, n.93). On Dryden's use of various translations & commentary, see Dryden (1974) 586–96. I thank Turner for informing me of the difference between Dryden's printed and manuscript versions and for pointing out the implications of his use of the term *flats,* and Richlin for alerting me to oddities in Dryden's rendition of the second passage. For discussion of eighteenth-century translations and interpretations of the passage, many of which read it as lesbian-specific, see Donoghue.

her lesbophobia in part with a feminist argument. When Astrea passes judgment on the Cabal, her first objection is neither feminist nor anti-feminist: she implies that lesbianism is "beyond what *Nature* design'd." Her second objection is definitely anti-feminist: "if they... *fortifie* themselves by these new-form'd *Amities* against the *Hymenial Union*, or give their *Husbands* but a second place in their *Affections* and *Cares*; 'tis wrong and to be *blam'd*." But her third objection at least sounds feminist:

> Thus far as to the *Merit* of the *Thing* it self. But when we look with true regard to the World, if it permit a shadow of *Suspicion*, a bare *Imagination*, that the *Misteries* they *pretend*, have any thing in 'em contrary to *Kind*, and that strict *Modesty* and *Virtue* do not *adorn* and *support* their *Conversation*; 'tis to be avoided and *condemn'd*; least they give occasion for *obscene Laughter*, new invented *Satyr, fanciful Jealousies* and *impure Distrusts*, in that nice unforgiving Sex: Who *Arbitrarily* decide, that Woman was only created (with all her *Beauty, Softness, Passions* and compleat *Tenderness*) to adorn the *Husband's* Reign, perfect his *Happiness*, and propagate the *Kind*. (57–58)

In other words, in addition to being intrinsically bad, any woman's lesbianism harms all women because it incites laughter, satire, jealousy, and distrust from men, who are sexist enough to begin with and shouldn't be given more ammunition in their attempts to make women wholly subservient.

The contradiction between Astrea's second two objections—one anti-feminist, one quasi-feminist—marks this passage as a moment of ideological stress, a place where the text becomes temporarily incoherent and its contradictions are exposed. If there is any Cabal moment where Manley's loyalties might seem uncertain, where one might even question the degree of her lesbophobia, it is here.

One might argue, for instance, that the conclusion of Astrea's judgment could be read as a covert authorial signal that men control the discourse, and that Manley is forced to parrot their lines, unable to risk honesty. Not that her honesty would be lesbian-affirmative—there are no such textual indications—but perhaps she wouldn't be as quick as Astrea to use arguments about "what *Nature* design'd" and what is "contrary to *Kind*," since men use them so often to denigrate and control women (reducing women, for instance, to "propagat[ing] the *Kind*"). Perhaps she wouldn't go so far as to put spousal relationships before female friendship. The contradiction between that completely regressive statement and Astrea's final remark about the "nice unforgiving Sex" (word choice that portrays men much like the women of the Cabal) might hint that Manley's endorsement of putting husbands first may simply be a concession to male power, and that whatever the nature of female separatist communities might be, they're impossible in this male-controlled society. Like it or not (and overall the book suggests Manley does *not* like it) men are and must remain central to women's lives.

Nevertheless, even if we read the passage this way, at best it suggests Manley views *nonsexual* female friendships positively. It doesn't suggest covert sympathy for lesbian relationships. On the contrary, her idealization of female friendship would more likely compound her hostility to lesbians, whom she represents as perverting the language of friendship, cynically manipulating it in order to conceal and further their sexual activities, their use of one another for sensual pleasure (as Monsieur Du Guast says of Margaret of Austria). By sexualizing female friendship, the Cabal drags down relations between women to the level of relations between women and men.

Much like Behn in "To the Fair Clarinda" (see above, ch.2). Of course, Manley presents the women-loving women she parodies as far more earnest and humorless about their supposed innocence than Behn's speaker—although, it's worth recalling, they do first appear "laugh[ing] loud and incessantly," as if they hadn't a care in the world, as if enjoying a private joke for which the text proceeds to punish them. Either way, the loophole-exploiting strategy exemplified by Behn's poem, which manipulates anti-lesbian ideology for pro-lesbian ends, is a primary target of Manley's double-voiced satire, as we shall see in just a moment.

"mutual *Love* bestows all things in *common*": the Cabal's "little *Commonwealth*" and Dissident Reading

First, however, I'd like briefly to return to other critics' predominantly or partially positive readings of Manley's intentions toward the Cabal. These interpretations are more understandable once one recognizes the rich, pro-lesbian, dissident reading possibilities offered by these sections of the text. The great length and detail of *The New Atalantis*'s representation of lesbians—above all its ventriloquized lesbian voices—makes it particularly vulnerable to dissident interpretation, as in the passage with which Lady Intelligence concludes her primary description of the Cabal members and their adventures:

> There are others of the *Cabal*, that lavish vast Sums upon their *Inamoretto's*, with the *Empresment*, *Diligence* and *Warmth* of a beginning *Lover*. I could name a *Widow* or *two*, who have almost undone themselves by their Profuseness: So *sacred* and *invincible* is their *Principle* of *Amity*, that Misfortunes cannot shake. In this little *Commonwealth* is no *Property*; whatever a *Lady* possesses, is, *sans ceremone*, at the service, and for the use of her *Fair Friend*, without the vain *nice* scruple of being oblig'd. 'Tis her *Right*; the other disputes it not; no, not so much as in *Thought*, they have no reserve; mutual *Love* bestows all things in *common*; 'twould be against the *Dignity* of the *Passion*, and unworthy such *exalted abstracted Notions* as theirs. How far *laudable* your *Divinities* will conclude of these tender *Amities* (with all possible submission) I refer to your better Judgements, and undisputed *Prerogativ[e]* of setting the Stamp of Approbation, or Dislike, upon all things. (57)

In arguing that Manley presents the new Cabal in at least a partially positive light, Todd, Ballaster, and Wahl all draw attention to this passage as a utopian moment in the text (Wahl noting, as mentioned earlier, that it demonstrates "an *oddly* sympathetic stance toward the Cabal," making it one of what she calls the "*strange* outcroppings of utopian discourse" in the otherwise satiric portrait of these women).

On the one hand, I'm convinced the author's intent here is still to satirize lesbians. For one thing, while Manley clearly conveys the idea that heterosexual relations as a rule involve men treating women as property (Ballaster [1992] 139), that doesn't mean she makes the leap to endorsing the Cabal's proto-communist, anti-private property rhetoric. Why would Manley, an ardent Tory, present a semi-communistic "commonwealth" as an ideal community? It's far more likely she's evoking the long anti-feminist satiric tradition portraying commonwealths or parliaments of women, a tradition given new life in England in the mid- and late seventeenth century.[23]

And even if Manley *did* idealize such a vision of female community, it would be an ideal the Cabal members clearly fail to live up to. Sexual desire motivates them, the same desire Manley repeatedly reveals motivating men to seduce and betray women. Notwithstanding their communitarian rhetoric, the Cabal are, by and large, as jealous and possessive in their amities as men in their amours (e.g., Armida [44–45], the Marchioness of Lerma [48], and Zara [52–56, esp. 56]). The Cabal's rhetoric is mere lip-service, a cover-up for their actual motives and behavior. As elsewhere in the Cabal passages, Manley portrays the women as insincere and hypocritical.

And setting aside the word 'commonwealth' and the new Cabal's economic philosophy, the overwhelmingly ironic tone of *The New Atalantis* has not been abandoned here. Once again, Manley employs free indirect speech, so often used to turn a character's words against her while maintaining a humorous pose of neutrality. *Sans ceremone* sounds like a garbled (and hence doubly laughable) version of the sort of French phrase a pretentious Englishwoman might affect, while *Inamorettos* adds to such foreign-inflected affectation the same whiff of sodomitically suspect Italian as the Glorious Platonicks' *Intimadoes*. The phrase "the vain *nice* scruple of being oblig'd" calls attention to the more commonsensical opinion that being "oblig'd," being grateful, is a virtue. Moreover, the sentence is overblown, an impression only heightened by what follows: "the other disputes it not; no, not so much as in *Thought*, they have no reserve." The language is repetitive, strained, high-flown—exactly the kind of awkward, self-important, pseudo-heroic language Manley mocks elsewhere. Indeed, she repeatedly puts such bombast in the mouths of characters vaunting unconventional sexual arrangements the text clearly condemns (e.g., Hernando's defense of polygamy [I.219–20], Polydore's justification of incest [II.22–23], Zara's vindication of cohabitation [I.232]).

On the other hand, if one's sympathies are pro-lesbian, pro-communal, and progressive, these supposed Cabal ideals sound admirable. The reader need only disregard the text's signals and take as serious what's offered as ridiculous, take as positive what's offered as negative. Todd, Ballaster, and Wahl's pro-lesbian interpretations of this passage demonstrate the susceptibility of Manley's text to

---

[23] See Turner (2002) 96–106, 261–74, & passim.

dissident reading. By representing lesbians at such length and in such detail, and especially by lending them voices, Manley gives these characters a life of their own. Consequently, some readers' identifications and interpretations are sure to elude her control, allowing them to derive pro-lesbian meanings from an anti-lesbian text.[24]

Self-Satirizing, Scapegoating, and the Limits of Manley's Feminism

I suggested earlier that *The New Atalantis*'s mocking portrayal of the new Cabal can be understood as an attempt to dissociate female friendship from the contamination of lesbian sexuality. A complementary explanation for the text's lesbophobia is that Manley satirizes lesbians to fend off misogynist criticism of her novel as itself too feminist, too man-hating, even too lesbian. She thus anticipates and attempts to preempt exactly the sort of sexist attack to which, Astrea claims, lesbianism makes women vulnerable. Without the Cabal section, *The New Atalantis*—which depicts women seduced and betrayed by men in episode after episode—might easily lead its readers to conclude that women should separate from men and turn to each other for love and sex. The anti-lesbian episodes make clear, however, that Manley advocates no such thing, thereby fending off "*obscene Laughter*, new invented *Satyr, fanciful Jealousies* and *impure Distrusts*, [from] that nice unforgiving Sex."

And yet, in maintaining that Manley's intentions regarding the new Cabal are knowable, I might seem to be taking a retrograde, anti-theoretical position. Late twentieth-century literary critics emphasize the impossibility (and irrelevance) of divining authorial intention, as well as the radical instability of textual meaning. Theorists of satire view satiric texts as especially unstable, offering clear targets and coherent standards only to theoretically unsophisticated readers. Yet my intention, if readers will pardon the expression, is not to deny or underplay the complexity of Manley's satire in *The New Atalantis*, its frequent tendency toward self-subversion, particularly in refusing the reader a comfortable moral standard by which to judge characters' behavior. Manley is clearly aware of the notoriously self-undoing, self-incriminating potential of satire, the way the satirist's motivations and methods quickly become suspect: Is the moralist actually a sadist? Is he wallowing in filth rather than cleaning it up? Rather than ignore such pitfalls, Manley employs remarkably ingenious ways of circumventing them, or even using them to her advantage.[25]

---

[24] See Turner (2002) 265–66 on dissident effects of parliament-of-women satires, which the texts struggle to contain.

[25] For a brief but helpful overview of satire's numerous contradictions, and the history of satire criticism in English, see Connery & Combe. See also Griffin's book-length refutation of the critical consensus achieved in the 1950s and 60s on the straightforward nature of satire. For a particularly good example, drawn from Swift's work, of satirists' own awareness of the risk of self-incrimination, see Griffin, 49.

Appropriately, at the start of Lady Intelligence's account of Harriat, who hypocritically censures the behavior of others, Manley brings such issues to the fore, as Astrea and Virtue challenge their informant's conduct and intentions. After Intelligence identifies "this miserable Woman" (8) alone in the woods at night in the throes of labor, awaiting the return of her lover with a midwife, the following exchange takes place:

> *Intell.* ...I'll tell you their *History.*
> *Virtue.* But first will it not be necessary to offer our assistance to the Lady in pain?... Shall we not appear, and offer her our assistance in her Misery? Her crys and groans pierce my Heart....
> *Intell.* If your *Mightiness* please to hear me; I know the Lady so well, her Spirit is so haughty, and her affectation of Vertue so high, that should she see us, it would certainly cost her her life, in apprehension of being discover'd.
> *Virtue.* My Lady *Intelligence* finds Reasons why her Story is not to be deferr'd: Is Scandal so bewitching a thing in your Court, that you cannot delay divulging what you know, tho' at the expence of Danger?
> *Intell.* Alas, your Excellencies! is it Criminal to expose the pretenders to *Vertue?* those who rail at all the World, and are themselves most guilty? Did I wrong the Good! accuse the Innocent! That indeed would be blameable; but the *Libertine* in Practice, the *Devotee* in profession, those that with the Mask of *Hypocrisy* undo the Reputation of Thousands, ought pitilessly, by a sort of retaliation, to be expos'd themselves; and which I beg leave to appeal to the Divine *Astrea*, whether it be not *Justice?*
> *Astrea.* Something very near it; but I am not satisfied however at not assisting the Lady—O *Lucina* be propitious!... O! how piercing are her Cries!—The Coach returns. I hope there is necessary help, that we may not put her to the Confusion of seeing us.
> *Intell.* There's the *Midwife* [Mrs. *Nightwork*], I know her, she that brought a certain Lady to Bed with her Mask on. Let us observe a little; by the extremity of her Pains it can't be long before they be over, and then I'll tell you the rest. (9–10)

Even if one agrees that censorious hypocrites ought to suffer retaliation in kind, it's difficult not to fault Intelligence as she listens untroubled to the agonized cries that pierce both Justice and Virtue's hearts. It's difficult, as well, to dismiss Astrea's suspicion that Intelligence is motivated above all by love of scandal rather than justice. But what, then, of Manley, who wrote this scandal-filled text? What of us, who enjoy reading it?

Catherine Gallagher's analysis of the strategies Manley and Behn employ to succeed in the difficult enterprise of being, not just authors, but female authors, in the late seventeenth and early eighteenth century, explores precisely such questions. She argues convincingly that neither Manley nor Behn openly or directly opposes anti-feminist ideology—particularly in regard to female authorship, and most particularly in regard to such authorship's sexual connotations—but instead enthusiastically adopts the degraded labels and personae anti-feminist ideology foists upon female authors (and authors in general), in order to exploit the unexpected freedom and agency these labels and personae afford when taken to the extreme. As Gallagher explains, "The more writers actually relied on scandal, the more they sought figures onto whom they could project the opprobrium of discrediting, the scandal of scandal. Manley was in many ways perfect as a receptacle for the disgust due a writer who published the misdemeanors of the great for the delectation of all classes" ([1994] 132–33). Rather than adopt the high-minded, ultra-respectable stance of a Mary Astell, "[Manley] includes herself in her satire..., [becoming] almost a willing scapegoat, a flamboyantly scandalmongering hack" (130). Potentially suspect as a satirist, unavoidably suspect as a woman author, and even more so as a woman of soiled reputation (because of a bigamous marriage), Manley decided to make anti-feminist ideology work for rather than against her, by exploiting this ideology's loopholes.

She employs this self-satirizing strategy with particular subtlety in *The New Atalantis*. By adopting admittedly compromised satirist personae (the somewhat disreputable Lady Intelligence; the even more dubious Mrs. Nightwork; the openly autobiographical, "fallen" Delia); by depicting an unambiguously objectionable, immoral, censorious gossipmonger for comparison and contrast (Harriat); and by all the while providing a pair of morally untainted, reliable reader/judge figures with whom to identify (Astrea and Virtue), Manley counteracts the potentially destabilizing effects of the "satirist satirized" or "scandal of scandal" problem. Her solution may not be morally satisfying (it's an unusually clever attempt to have one's cake and eat it too), but it's psychologically effective, enabling nuanced readerly denial of moral difficulties, by *both* distancing *and* identification, instead of either approach on the one hand, or complete ambiguity on the other.

Granted, Manley sometimes takes a more straightforward approach, even when addressing sexuality and gender. In the Restoration and early eighteenth century, dominant ideology on sex, gender, and sexuality was hardly monolithic, and there are elements of it Manley openly contests. Most significantly, on the subject of female sexual desire, she's very much a Restoration rather than eighteenth-century writer. Although the ideal of female chastity as asexuality was swiftly gaining ground, in Manley's work—as in Behn's, most Restoration drama, and the French *chroniques scandaleuses* that so influenced Manley (including Mme de Murat's)—female sexual desire may sometimes be excessive or ill-controlled, but it's still largely taken for granted: "normal" women do feel lust. In Manley's work, particularly *The New Atalantis*, the danger is mostly that men exploit such feelings in order to seduce, manipulate, and betray women; men's behavior, rather than women's desire, is primarily at fault. This challenge to the asexual ideal of femininity is one of the most powerful, and most feminist, elements of Manley's book. But she portrays only *heterosexual* desire as natural. Lesbian lust, in what from this perspective again seems like a defensive, scapegoating maneuver, is repudiated.[26]

---

[26] For Manley's challenge to the asexual ideal of femininity, see, for example, the Charlot episode (50–84), and Jane Spencer's commentary on it (114–15). Not that Manley is entirely consistent in this stance (e.g., the Delia episode [II.180–94]).

But to return to and extend Gallagher's argument regarding Manley's nonconfrontational, subversive embrace of anti-feminist ideology—which, despite the author's treatment of female heterosexual desire, is indeed her predominant strategy—this analysis of Manley's public persona refines our understanding of her lesbophobia once we notice that, like their author, the lesbians whom Manley satirizes also attempt to exploit the contradictions of sexist ideology. The clearest example occurs in the story of "the witty Marchioness of *Sandomire*,"

> [who] us'd to Mask her Diversions in the Habit of the other Sex, and with her female Favourite *Ianthe* wander thro' the Gallant Quarter of *Atalantis* in search of Adventures. But what Adventures? Good Heaven! none that could in *reality* wound her Chastity! Her Virtue sacred to her Lord, and the Marriage Bed, was preserv'd Inviolable! For what could reflect back upon it with any Prejudice, in the little Liberties she took with her own Sex? (49)

Intelligence here mockingly repeats the argument the Marchioness presumably uses to defend her lesbian diversions and adventures, the very same argument the speaker of Behn's "To The Fair Clarinda" employs: since, according to patriarchal logic, sex necessarily involves a penis, nothing two women do together counts as sex; therefore, nothing the Marchioness does with "her female Favourite" or the "Creatures of Hire" they visit counts as adultery, as something "that could in *reality* wound her Chastity." Rather than challenge phallocentric unknowing of lesbian sex as non-sex and nonsense, the Marchioness (like the rest of the Cabal) enthusiastically embraces it to turn it to her own advantage, deriving a kind of freedom by exploiting its loopholes.

But here, in interpreting the text's treatment of such lesbian appropriation of anti-lesbian logic, I part company with Gallagher. She uses the story of the Marchioness to argue, "The women [of the Cabal], it turns out, are indeed erotically entangled with each other, but their eroticism is in its essence phantasmic," explaining:

> Even if the assurance [of the Marchioness's inviolable virtue] is read as an ironic comment on phallocentric literal-mindedness, it is also a claim that female erotic pleasure is by its very nature potentially irrelevant to the referential norm of heterosexuality that rules 'the marriage bed.'... This absurdly strict phallocentrism implies a vast area of inconsequential liberty; the narrator can barely find words to indicate sexuality without penises, cannot make such sexuality significant, and hence asserts its meaningless innocence. The Marchioness's pleasure can only be credited as something outside the referential rules that give sexual activity substance and sense; that is, it can only be credited as fictional. (139–40)

Gallagher's analysis of the potential implications of phallocentric logic are right on target, as is her suggestion that the passage can be—I would say *should be*—"read as an ironic comment on phallocentric literal-mindedness." But Lady Intelligence's irony is two-pronged, and Gallagher overlooks the second, more important, jab: parodic mimicry of lesbians who try to exploit such ridiculous logic.

In other words, in response to the Cabal's appropriation of anti-lesbian rhetoric for pro-lesbian ends, Manley reappropriates this pro-lesbian twist for once again anti-lesbian purposes. Lady Intelligence does *not* assert the Marchioness's innocence; she *mock*-asserts it, utilizing the well-recognized, homophobic rhetorical strategy of mock ignorance. Humorously *pretending* she "can barely find words to indicate sexuality without penises, cannot make such sexuality significant," the narrator (and Manley) satirically reproduces, in order to debunk, the claims to innocence behind which such lesbians hide. She asserts the opposite of what Gallagher suggests: the supposedly innocent, fictional, fantastic, imaginary erotic behavior of the Marchioness (and other Cabal members) is actually quite guilty, unchaste, criminal, real.[27]

Nevertheless, despite this disagreement, I want to emphasize that Gallagher's analysis of how Manley exploits anti-feminist ideology accords with what I consider the most convincing explanation of why *The New Atalantis* satirizes lesbians at such length: the women of the Cabal are threateningly similar to Manley herself. Like her, they enthusiastically adopt and exploit patriarchal definitions of women. Indeed, they take this strategy to a more daring extreme. As we saw in Astrea's judgment on the Cabal, despite a clear-eyed critique of men's misogyny the text compromises, perhaps reluctantly, by requiring that women make men central in their lives. In contrast, the Cabal spurn men and exalt bonds between women. The close resemblance between the lesbians' and Manley's own response to anti-feminist ideology, as well as the critique of her approach this resemblance implies, clearly fascinates Manley, and even more clearly threatens her. Her response is to attack lesbianism at length, all the while affecting lighthearted, untroubled amusement.

Manley's treatment of lesbianism thus helps illuminate the contours and limits of *The New Atalantis*'s feminism. The moment in which Astrea renders her verdict on the Cabal proves even more revealing than we realized. Like Astrea, Manley may very well valorize female friendship, but if so, only as an impossible ideal (on which see Kernan, 10–11). Both author and character unambiguously repudiate lesbianism. Both accept that women must devote their primary energies to men, and both contradict, undercut, or at least qualify this stance by sharp critique of men's mistreatment of women. Yet despite the close similarity between Manley's feminism

---

[27] Gallagher's discussion of the Cabal is only a final, supporting detail in a much larger argument regarding the genre of scandal-writing, according to which Manley steers a middle-course between satiric/allegorical referentiality (in which each character refers to a single real person) and pure fiction. Viewed through this lens, the Cabal's amorous exploits are analogous to fiction: just as fiction lacks the referent of a real person, lesbianism lacks the referent of a penis, the necessary component for "real" sex, phallocentrically speaking. This approach renders visible important aspects of the text—and of early eighteenth-century fiction in general—masked by the common belief that *The New Atalantis* and similar works are "simply" transparent political satires. But just as it's not suited to exploring where *The New Atalantis* does lampoon particular, identifiable people, neither does it help register the text's place within a long discursive tradition that, according to its own "logic," ought not to be worried about lesbianism, but nevertheless is.

and Astrea's, this passage also reveals their primary difference: Manley has a sense of humor. She thus offsets the seriousness of Astrea's verdict by making the latter genuinely unable or prudishly unwilling to conceive of lesbianism: asked by Intelligence to judge "these tender *Amities*" and "set… the Stamp of Approbation, or Dislike, upon [them]," Astrea declares, "It is something so *new* and *uncommon*, so *laudable* and *blameable*, that we don't know how to *determine*; especially wanting *light* even to guess at what you call the *Mysteries* of the *Cabal*" (57). Readers can thus feel superior to Astrea, more sophisticated and less uptight than this supposedly superhuman judge.

Consequently, although I recognize the feminist force of elements of *The New Atalantis*, I have argued here that Manley explicitly values only female *heterosexual* interests, and explicitly repudiates lesbian ones, portraying the latter as a threat to the former. Manley undermines her sophisticated feminist project with sophisticated lesbophobia, providing an instructive contrast to the more daring Behn. As Gallagher maintains, neither writer sets out to overturn patriarchal ideology, each choosing instead to exploit the unexpected freedoms it offers when taken to an extreme. But whereas Behn applies this approach even to phallocentric anti-lesbianism, Manley uses lesbianism as scapegoat and foil, effectively telling readers: "I'm a scandalmonger, a gossip, a hack. I'm a loose woman. I admit all this freely. But at least I'm no rubster, no tribade, hypocritically concealing my unnatural activities beneath a veil of innocence, virtue, and chastity." By taking this approach, she fails to grasp the extent of—indeed, reinforces and colludes in—men's control of women and their lives. And yet, despite this failing, or perhaps because of it, *The New Atalantis* is a crucial text for understanding seventeenth- and eighteenth-century British and French representation of lesbianism, and for recognizing a particular form of worldly homophobia, directed at both women-loving women and men-loving men, and reaching back, via anti-platonic discourse, all the way to the classical world.

"Pleasures… too refined"? Homo-Elitism, Homophobia, and "Cloe to Artemisa"

For trying to determine authorial intention, Manley's text gives us a great deal to go on: it's a long work, by a well-known author, with much to say about lesbianism. But the methods I've used to analyze *The New Atalantis*—close reading and homo-specific contextualization—can shed light on even far shorter works about which we know very little. I'd like to examine a single such work: a short anonymous sonnet entitled "Cloe to Artimesa," closely related to *The New Atalantis*. The poem appeared in A. Hammond's *A New Miscellany* (1720), a collection that included work by Manley (Lanser [1998–99] 183). It reads:

> While vulgar souls their vulgar loves pursue,
> And in the common way themselves undo;
> Impairing health and fame, and risking life,

> To be a mistress or, what's worse, a wife:
> We, whom a nicer taste has raised above
> The dangerous follies of such slavish love,
> Despise the sex, and in our selves we find
> Pleasures for their gross senses too refined.
> Let brutish men, made by our weakness vain,
> Boast of the easy conquest they obtain;
> Let the poor loving wretch do all she can,
> And *all* won't please th'ungrateful tyrant, Man;
> We'll scorn the monster and his mistress too,
> And show the world what women ought to do.[28]

So far as I know, only two critics, Lanser and Castle, both of them painstaking and thoughtful investigators of eighteenth-century discourses of lesbianism, have commented on this text, albeit briefly. Each takes the poem at face value. Lanser writes, "This anonymous verse… not only underscores the contrast between female-female and male-female relationships, but advertises its defiance by setting female exclusivity as a model for women everywhere," adding, "[t]his elevation of the 'nicer taste' calls on women not only to prefer one another but to reject men entirely, and herein lies its dangerous difference" ([1998–99] 182). Castle calls the poem "a provocative brief in favor of female (erotic?) bonding," observing that "[i]n the confident assertion that love relations between women are more civilized than those between women and men… the speaker articulates a fantasy about female homoeroticism that would be put forward again by Natalie Clifford Barney, Renée Vivien, and other sapphic chauvinists in the late nineteenth and early twentieth century" ([2003] 235). Of course, certainty about the intentions of the unknown author of this single sonnet is impossible. And, indeed, both Castle and Lanser subtly sidestep the question, the former attributing agency to "this anonymous verse" and "this elevation of the 'nicer taste,'" the latter referring to what "the speaker" articulates. Yet clues both internal and external strongly suggest satiric, anti-feminist, anti-lesbian intentions.

"Cloe" echoes the arguments and even wording of such early eighteenth-century feminist writers as Lady Mary Chudleigh and Sarah Fyge Egerton. Both "Cloe to Artimesa" and Chudleigh's "To the Ladies" (1703) urge women not to marry; the speaker of "Cloe" writes, "We… Despise the sex, and in our selves we find" more refined pleasures, while Chudleigh's speaker commands, "Value your selves, and Men despise" (*l*.23); "Cloe" calls women who love men "the poor loving wretch[es]," Chudleigh calls marriage "that wretched State" (*l*.21). All three poets are linked by their choice of political metaphors: "Cloe" speaks of "slavish love," and "th'ungrateful tyrant, Man"; Fyge Egerton, in "The Emulation" (1703), refers to "Tyrant Custom" (*l*.1) and "The Husband with insulting Tyranny" (*l*.8),

---

[28] The poem, reprinted by Lonsdale, is also included in Castle (2003). I'm grateful to Rick Incorvati and Simon Stern for independently bringing it to my attention.

submission to whom constitutes "the last, the fatal Slavery" (*l.*7), although "Poor Womankind's in every State, a Slave" (*l.*4); Chudleigh compares a husband to "an Eastern Prince" (*l.*9) and declares, "Wife and Servant are the same" (*l.*1).

Yet, notwithstanding such echoes of early eighteenth-century feminist writing, the speaker of "Cloe to Artimesa" focuses far less on power politics than her predecessors. Chudleigh witheringly portrays the absolute imbalance of power in marriage and the tyranny to which it gives rise:

> For when that fatal Knot is ty'd,
> Which nothing, nothing can divide:
> When she the word *obey* has said,
> And Man by Law supreme has made,
> Then all that's kind is laid aside,
> And nothing left but State and Pride:
> Fierce as an Eastern Prince he grows,
> And all his innate Rigor shows:
> Then but to look, to laugh, or speak,
> Will the Nuptial Contract break.
> Like Mutes she Signs alone must make,
> And never any Freedom take:
> But still be govern'd by a Nod,
> And fear her Husband as her God…. (*ll.*3–16)

Chudleigh measures Englishmen by their own ideals (freedom; government by reasonable law) and finds them guilty of the very things they decry (tyranny, government by fear). Fyge Egerton makes similar observations about marital tyranny (even pointing out, "*Moses* who first our Freedom did rebuke,/ Was Marry'd when he writ the Pentateuch" [*l.*12]), before proceeding to her main argument: women should not allow men to make the *intellectual* realm a masculine preserve (*ll.*19–22, 29–33). In contrast, notwithstanding her reference to male-female relationships "[i]mpairing health and fame, and risking life," "Cloe" asserts the superiority of female-female bonds primarily on the grounds of superior taste, spouting much the same line as Manley's new Cabal on love between women, or Plato's Pausanias and pseudo-Lucian's Callicratidas on love between men: opposite-sex lovers are vulgar, common, gross, brutish; same-sex lovers have nicer (more discriminating) taste, more refined pleasures (cf. Turner [2003] 191).

Not that such homoelitism is necessarily homophobic invention. A snippet from the 1709–12 secret diary of colonial Virginian William Byrd II suggests some homo-oriented individuals of the time may have held, and even privately voiced, similar views. According to Byrd, whose diary reveals intense curiosity about, and tolerance for, sexual practices far more varied than those considered licit at the time, the following exchange took place between a decidedly worldly pair of brothers:

S[i]r R.S. haveing learnt in Turky to prefer the pleasure of the male sex, to those of the Female, reprovd his Brother the Br...r, for getting drunk continually & runing after vile Harlots, to the imminent danger of his health. Your concern is very obligeing Brother, said the Br...r, but my Carcase is very safe, for I never attack the Strumpets in Front, but in Rear. I'm very glad to hear that, replyd Sr Robt, for no harm can follow from a tast so innocent and refind as that is. (134; quoted in Berland, 3)

Although, as Kevin Berland observes, "this anecdote establishes nothing certain about Byrd except that he was apparently amused by the homosexual's assumption that his brother had adopted the 'innocent and refind' practice of buggery" (3), it suggests that some of Manley's contemporaries who preferred the pleasures of their own sex may have held views about their sexual practices much like those attributed to them by the author of *La France devenue italienne,* Manley, Hamilton, Smollett, and other homophobic writers.

Yet Byrd's Sir Robert praises buggery in private. And *La France devenue italienne,* Manley, Hamilton, and Smollett all mock their homosexual characters. Even Pausanias' and Callicratidas' homochauvinist arguments are placed within frameworks that invite laughter—although not necessarily homophobic laughter. The burden of proof regarding "Cloe to Artimesa," therefore, lies with those who take it at face value. After all, the 1720s were not the Restoration, when poems such as Behn's "To the Fair Clarinda" circulated in a self-consciously libertine milieu. Although not impossible, it's highly unlikely "Cloe to Artimesa" would have been included in Hammond's *Miscellany* had it been understood as a lesbian-feminist call to arms rather than anti-feminist, anti-lesbian satire.

The anonymous poet's choice of vocabulary reinforces this satiric reading. The word 'refine' and its derivatives lent themselves to precisely the homophobic accusation we've been examining: concealing base desire and activity beneath a veil of spirituality. 'Refined' could mean 'purified'; it could also mean "devoid of... rude, gross, or vulgar elements," as well as "[c]ultivated, polished, elegant." It thus risked conflating purity with more worldly questions of taste and manners, giving rise to ambivalence about refinement itself, reflected in yet another sense of the word: "[h]aving or affecting a subtlety of mind or judgment." Those who lay claim to greater refinement provoked suspicions of affectation, of deceit, of sophisticated manners masquerading as superior morals. Thus Hamilton refers, ironically, to "that *Refinement* of *ancient Greece* upon the Tastes of *Tenderness*" ([1713] 233). And thus Manley, more subtly, has Lady Intelligence mock-accuse "the Enemies of the *Cabal*" of "refin[ing]... upon the Misteries of it," and "the ill-natur'd World... [of] refining upon their mysterious Innocence" (46). In the latter case, the joke is that those who censure the Cabal do in fact possess "a subtlety of mind or judgment," insofar as they perceive the impurity, grossness, and carnality beneath the Cabal's mask of refinement.

Revealingly, while "Cloe," like the women of Manley's Cabal, loudly proclaims her nicer taste and refined pleasures, in contrast to vulgar souls who pursue vulgar loves to gratify their gross senses in the common way, Fyge Egerton portrays such pseudospiritual elitism as an age-old ruse in the service of domination. Today, she writes, Men "[k]eep us Fools to raise their own Renown," while in the past,

> ...Priests of old their Grandeur to maintain,
> Cry'd vulgar Eyes would sacred Laws Profane.
> So kept the Mysteries behind a Screen,
> There Homage and the Name were lost had they been seen. (*ll.*23–26)

The contempt for "vulgarity" emphasized so excessively by "Cloe" is a target rather than attribute of the feminist defiance Fyge Egerton exemplifies. The anonymous author of "Cloe to Artimesa" parodies such poems as "The Emulation" and "To The Ladies," discrediting their feminism as covertly lesbian.

Satirists Agree Wondrously Well Among Themselves: Lancaster's *The Pretty Gentleman*

I'd like to conclude this chapter, and these first two parts of my book, by looking at a homophobic text that utilizes many of the rhetorical and thematic conventions we've seen, but manipulates those conventions in especially subtle ways: Nathaniel Lancaster's *The Pretty Gentleman: Or, Softness of Manners Vindicated From the false Ridicule exhibited under the Character of William Fribble, Esq.* (1747).

Garrick's homophobic farce *Miss in Her Teens* resulted in the publication of his friend Lancaster's satiric pamphlet, purporting to defend the effeminate sort of man represented onstage by Garrick himself as Fribble. The author of the piece, "Philautus" (meaning, "loves himself"), mock-criticizes Garrick's performance:

> BELIEVE me, Sir, you have fallen most miserably short in your Attempt. And how should it be otherwise? You *pretend to exhibit a Representation of* The Pretty Gentleman, *who are by no means an* Adept *in the Character!* You! *that are an entire Stranger to those fine Sensations, which are* requisite *to give a thorough Notion, and true Relish of the Enjoyments it affords! How should you paint what Nature has not given you Faculties to feel? As far as* She *leads you by the Hand, you may perhaps succeed: But to leave her* behind, *and tread those secret Paths to which her Guidance never points;* This, *Mr.* Garrick, This *is far beyond the Power of your limited Genius.* (iv)

Garrick, we are to understand, cannot accurately represent Fribble and his ilk because, unlike them, he hasn't engaged in—doesn't even possess the requisite faculties for enjoying—anal intercourse ("*to leave [Nature] behind, and tread those secret Paths to which her Guidance never points*").

Like *The New Atalantis, Grammont,* and "Cloe to Artimesa," *The Pretty Gentleman* targets supposed refinement (e.g., "that *mollifying Elegance* which manifests itself with such a bewitching Grace, in the *refined* Youths of this *cultivated Age*" [6]). As in Charke's *Henry Dumont* (probably influenced by *The Pretty Gentleman*), such refinement includes abominable spelling ("*I Expected yu wud ha' retorted upon that brootal Monstir, who atak'd yu last Nite at Lady Betty's*" [23]) and modishly affected vocabulary—especially the phrase "filthy Creter" (spelled "filty creter" in Charke's novel), to which Lancaster devotes a mock panegyric:

> The Epithet *filthy*, as it appears upon Paper, may seem somewhat coarse and unclean: But were you to hear how he liquidates the Harshness of the Sound, and conceals the Impurity of the Idea by a sweetned Accent, you would grow enamoured of his Address, and admire the enchanting Beauties of refined Elocution. *Oh! fie! ye filt-hy Creter!* How easy, how gentle, how humane a Chastisement for the highest Offence! (14–15)

Like the texts we'll examine in chapters six and seven, this one links homosexuality with sex-changing metamorphosis (33); like texts we've already examined, it associates homosexuality and gender-deviance with foreign influence, in this case French (33). And like Manley, Lancaster insinuates his targets' homosexuality by means of mock-ignorant protestation, although with an unexpected twist:

> It is to attain these and such like Accomplishments [i.e., swooning, hysterics, screaming in fright], that they make frequent Visits to the Ladies; though some slanderous Persons would make us believe, that they have another Motive, and intimate I know not what, *vitious* Designs, that are too indecent even to be mentioned. But I can assure the World, there is not the least Foundation for the base Suggestion. This Attendance, I know, takes its Rise from Causes, with which the Appetite for *That* Sex has no Manner of Connexion. So pure are their Morals! So inviolable their Modesty! Amazing Continence! (29)

Pretending not just to credit but to marvel at the Pretty Gentlemen's purity, modesty, and continence—like Manley's Lady Intelligence exclaiming over the "laudable!... extraordinary!... wonderful!... uncommon Happiness of the *Cabal*" —Lancaster offers a witty variation on Manley's example. Whereas she mock-defended the Cabal from censurers' charges of *homosexual* behavior, he mock-defends the Pretty Gentlemen from *mock* charges of *heterosexual* behavior. When Lancaster assures the world the Gentlemen's attendance upon the Ladies "takes its Rise from Causes, with which the Appetite for *That* Sex has no Manner of Connexion," he amuses his readers with the ludicrous notion that these effeminate creatures could ever be suspected of heterosexual desire, ludicrous because their effeminacy is rooted in an appetite for their own sex.

Finally, as in *The New Atalantis*, Lancaster's mock defense of a community of same-sex–oriented individuals whose behavior he pretends to admire, and whose platonic professions he pretends to believe, is seasoned with key classical allusions:

> Now the better to carry on this glorious Scheme of Reformation [i.e., polishing British manners], these Gentlemen have erected themselves into an amicable Society, and from the Principles, on which it is founded, have very pertinently stiled it,
>
> The Fraternity of PRETTY GENTLEMEN.
>
> As no associated Body can possibly subsist, unless they are cemented by an Union of Hearts, the grand Principle of this Fellowship is mutual Love, which, it must be confessed, they carry to the highest Pitch. In this Respect, they are not inferior to the '$Ιερα\ φαλανξ$' [sic], *The sacred* Theban *Band,* so illustrious in Story. Such an Harmony of Temper is preserved amongst them, such a Sameness is there in all their Words and Actions, that the Spirit of *One* seems to have passed into the *Other*; or rather, they *all* breathe the *same* Soul. This is the secret Charm, that the *Platonists* talk of, the intellectual Faculty, which connects one Man with another, and ties the Knot of virtuous Friendship. But I need not dwell any longer on a Subject, which can admit of no Debate; the Notoriety of the Fact is even become *Proverbial* amongst us, and every one cries out,
>
> *Magna est inter* MOLLES *Concordia!* (9–10)

The speaker twice characterizes the bonds among Pretty Gentlemen as platonic, once using the term itself, and once likening their "fraternity" to "*The sacred* Theban *Band*," the renowned company of warriors composed, according to Plutarch, of pairs of platonic lovers (an idea proposed in yet another speech from the *Symposium*, this one by Phaedrus [178d–179b]), about whom their vanquisher, Philip of Macedon, weeping over their corpses, declared, "Perish any man who suspects that these men either did or suffered anything that was base." But unlike these valiant soldiers, the Pretty Gentlemen spend their time "in the pretty Fancies of Dress, in Criticisms upon Fashions, in the artful Disposition of *China* Jars and other Foreign Trinkets; in sowing, in knitting Garters, in knotting of Fringe, and every gentle Exercise of Feminine Oeconomy" (12). Lancaster's comparison of such effeminates with an almost invincible band of legendary warriors is, of course, intentionally ridiculous.

The climax of the passage, however, is the "proverbial" saying, "*Magna est inter* MOLLES *Concordia!*," a slight misquotation of Juvenal's *Satire 2*. As mentioned in chapter one, Juvenal charges his effeminate targets not with pederasty but with receptive anal intercourse, excoriating them for concealing unmanly desire and activity behind an outward appearance of masculine virtue. The line in question (*magna inter molles concordia*), spoken by a woman named Laronia, means, "Male effeminates agree wondrously well among themselves." As

Amy Richlin explains, "the hypocritical passives who are the target of Juvenal 2 have been calling on the Julian law against adultery, in order to castigate women for promiscuity; the figure of Laronia responds by suggesting that these men are in no position to cast the first stone, and later... goes on to describe them at some length as *molles*" ([1993b] 570). The lines immediately preceding and following *magna inter molles concordia* leave no doubt as to Laronia's true feelings about effeminate men's mutual solidarity:

> [M]en do more wicked things than we do, but they are protected by their numbers, and the tight-locked shields of their phalanx. Male effeminates agree wondrously well among themselves; never in our sex will you find such loathsome examples of evil.... ([1967] 45–48)[29]

As with Manley's use of pseudo-Lucian, the humor here depends upon familiarity with a classical intertext, one that makes explicit what the eighteenth-century speaker feigns ignorance of. To fully appreciate Lancaster's homophobic satire—his send-up of the Pretty Gentlemen's pseudoplatonic refinement and sophistication—readers must themselves be sophisticated enough to recognize the source of the Latin quotation, and to fill in the rest of the passage from which it derives.

Another classical allusion concludes *The Pretty Gentleman*. Yet, surprisingly, this one potentially undermines the otherwise unmistakable homophobia of the rest of the text. As in the preface, Lancaster once again contrasts Garrick to the effeminates he parodies:

> Unhappy indeed for the Sons of Elegance! For what can the most Sanguine expect from one [i.e., Garrick], who has made it the Business of his Life, to bring into Repute the false Refinements of ancient *Greece* and *Rome?* Will a Person of his *Masculine* Talents become the Patron of soft and dulcified Elegance? Will *He* give up that *Attic Wit*, which has gained him such high Applause, and made him the Delight of a mis-judging World, to cultivate Qualities, in which he is not formed to excel? (35–36)

As Paul Hammond remarks, Lancaster portrays the Pretty Gentlemen's "devotion to feminine pastimes [as] a substitute for the pursuit of masculine knowledge.... True knowledge—obtained with effort and deployed to the public benefit—is rejected by such people" (105). In contrast, Garrick, with his "*Masculine* Talents," especially his "*Attic Wit*," exemplifies the best of the West's classical inheritance, the "Refinements of ancient *Greece* and *Rome*" that equal nothing less than Civilization.

But how can Lancaster so unproblematically align classical Greece and Rome with masculinity, given his previous allusions to classical homosexuality and effeminacy? Not that homophobic and sexist discourses are known for logical

---

[29] Note Laronia's erasure of lesbianism.

consistency. A sudden, massively contradictory attempt at homophobic unknowing would scarcely be unheard of—particularly at the end of a text, when ideological as well as narrative closure is often sought. Yet it hardly seems plausible that, having striven so skillfully to bring to mind the Theban army of lovers and Juvenal's anal-receptive effeminates, Lancaster would so clumsily pretend the classical world contained no such examples of homosexuality and effeminacy.

Could this final classical allusion be a covert pro-homosexual joke? Are Lancaster and Garrick sharing a private laugh at the expense of those who equate homosexuality with effeminacy? Have Garrick and Lancaster (in *Miss in Her Teens* and *The Pretty Gentleman*) intentionally reinforced such an equation in order to free appropriately masculine, non-Fribblish men such as themselves from the suspicion of homosexuality? It's an intriguing possibility, especially given Garrick's later theatrical association with playwrights Isaac Bickerstaff and Samuel Foote, both of whom were probably sodomites, and given that Garrick himself would eventually be accused of having a secret love affair with Bickerstaff.[30]

But for such a gambit to work, readers would still need not only to equate homosexuality with effeminacy, but also entirely to forget classical homosexuality, knowledge of which has been crucial for appreciating the text's satire. Yet rather than switch suddenly from *mock* to *genuine* ignorance—a clumsy about-face at which his sophisticated, classically educated audience would surely balk—Lancaster disguises his act of forgetting as an act of remembrance. He's engaged in an act of ideological obfuscation, but a far subtler, far more camouflaged one than bald-faced denial.

To enlist the classical world on the side of masculinity, Lancaster need not forget Greek and Roman homosexuality; he need only remind readers that the real men of the ancient world, men such as Juvenal, knew how to deal with the problem: they ridiculed the deviants. If the ancient world had its vices, its false refinements in love, Garrick, with his "Attic Wit," follows in Juvenal's footsteps, exemplifying Antiquity's true refinements. *The Pretty Gentleman* would have us believe that in Garrick and his champion Lancaster we see the *virtues* of old Rome revived.

But what Lancaster seeks to obscure is that Juvenal's *molles* were not the only ancients to engage in practices the eighteenth century considers unnatural, ones that leave Nature behind. For all the obvious differences between the Pretty Gentlemen and the sacred Theban band, both are lovers of their own sex who express their love physically (the *Symposium*'s Phaedrus, unlike Diotima, says nothing about lovers abstaining from sex).

Even closer to home, Lancaster seeks to obscure the potentially troubling implications of Garrick's talent for mimicking Fribbles both on the page and in the

---

[30] On Garrick, Bickerstaff, Foote, and the homophobic accusations, scandals, and trials in which they were enmeshed in the early 1770s, see Franceschina, McCormick, Norton (http://www.infopt.demon.co.uk/1772sodo.htm), Senelick, and Straub (1992).

flesh. *The Pretty Gentleman* serves the same project as Garrick's own work, as described by Kristina Straub: "to construct Garrick in opposition to ambiguous or suspect forms of masculinity" by means of a "defensive homophobia" ([1992] 61, 68). Garrick is sexually suspect on Platonic grounds, for as Plato famously argued in the *Republic* (Book III), when deciding whether to permit poetry and theater in his ideal state, "no one man can imitate many things as well as he would imitate a single one." The guardians of the state, its just and good men, must not be actors:

> [I]f they imitate at all, [good men] should imitate from youth upward only those characters which are suitable to their profession—the courageous, temperate, holy, free, and the like; but they should not depict or be skilful at imitating any kind of illiberality or baseness, lest from imitation they should come to be what they imitate. Did you never observe how imitations, beginning in early youth and continuing far into life, at length grow into habits and become a second nature, affecting body, voice, and mind?

Rather than acknowledge, much less directly counter, such longstanding views, and their implications for those who, like Garrick and himself, imitate effeminate homosexuals so well, the author of *The Pretty Gentleman* affects the sort of untroubled amusement we saw in Manley's *New Atalantis* and Hamilton's *Grammont*. As he mocks the members of the "fraternity" for their uncloseted effeminacy and closeted homosexuality, Lancaster conceals his anxiety that these men, whose manners, speech, thoughts, and feelings he appears to know so intimately, may not be so very different from Garrick and himself.

Sophisticated Ladies (and Gentlemen)

This chapter has examined several strands in a very long discursive tradition on same-sex love, in which the homophobic and homophilic, male and female, classical, early modern, and eighteenth-century are thoroughly intertwined. Yet despite all this intertextuality, all this quotation and allusion, borrowing and stealing, mockery and parody, the result is *not* simply, or even primarily, ambiguity, polyvocality, or queerness. There's much to gain from queering or deconstructing these and similar texts, revealing the fissures and gaps, the deviations and complications that undermine a single, fixed meaning, especially when that meaning is heteronormative. But such endeavors should not come at the expense of understanding what these texts—which is to say, what their authors—were trying to communicate. And with *The New Atalantis*, *The Erôtes*, *La France devenue italienne*, *Grammont*, "Cloe to Artemisa," *The Pretty Gentleman*, and similarly satiric texts, sharing fully in the fun requires equal sophistication. Above all, it requires sensitivity to their intertextual nuance, to their urbane engagement with rhetorical and discursive tradition.

PART 3
Continuity

Chapter 6

Metamorphosis and Homosexuality I: Ovid's "Iphis and Ianthe" and Related Tales

Throughout the previous chapters, I have argued for renewed focus on authorial intention, in order to uncover partially concealed or disavowed homophilic and homophobic meanings in early modern and eighteenth-century texts. It has been my contention that both external and internal clues strongly signal authorial intention, at least for readers familiar with some of the well-established conventions for representing same-sex sexuality. In chapters two and three, I argued that critics today have missed the deliberately coded, pro-lesbian and pro-sodomitical meanings authors such as Philo-Philippa, Murat, and Cleland surreptitiously offered their homosympathetic readers. In chapters four and five, I argued that Chorier-Nicolas and Manley employed forms of homophobia specifically suited to their texts' generic needs—pornography in the former case, scandal-writing in the latter—even as they attempted, in differing ways and to differing degrees, to disavow homophobic anxiety or antipathy. In chapter five, as in chapter one, I emphasized continuities in the representation of same-sex sexuality stretching from the classical to the early modern and eighteenth-century world, as well as the interrelation of male and female homosexuality in this long discursive tradition. While in my final two chapters authorial intention and the possibility of closeted writing remain active concerns, long-term continuity and male-female interconnections now become paramount.

As I wrote in my preface, contemporary LGBT theory, history, and criticism often seem to proceed from an *assumption* of diachronic change, in the process oversimplifying the past, the present, or both. One example will have to suffice. In a series of important articles over the past decade, Susan Lanser has been exploring the representation of "sapphic" and otherwise deviant women in eighteenth-century Europe, attending carefully to a variety of intersecting concerns (including class and nationality), and drawing thoughtfully upon an unusually diverse range of LGBT and feminist work, produced by scholars working in quite different theoretical traditions. And yet, even she overstates the degree and consistency of diachronic change in understandings of female homoeroticism. Thus, while offering nuanced analyses of eighteenth-century representations of "sapphic" women, in a recent article she nevertheless contends that before the eighteenth century, female masculinity was typically associated with "unlicensed sex with men" rather than with women, and that "the modern link between sexuality and gender had not yet been forged" ([2003b] 25). Similar assertions have been made about associations between male homosexuality and effeminacy (e.g., Trumbach [1998]). Yet it would be more accurate to say the link had not been as *securely* forged as it would later come to be, and thus that female masculinity, like male effeminacy, *sometimes* had homoerotic, sometimes heteroerotic, and sometimes omni- or hypererotic connotations.[1]

In exploring what seems to be new in a given period, it's crucial not to overstate the case. The metaphor of invention is far less appropriate than its ubiquity in contemporary history, criticism, and theory would suggest. Far more appropriate are metaphors of *re*invention or renewal (cf. DeJean [2002]), or even, as in these next two chapters, claims of persistence and continuity.

"There are continuities and connections in the Western world, after all."

To conclude Book IX of the *Metamorphoses* (2 BCE–8 CE), Ovid relates a story (*ll*.666–797) in which what we would call lesbian desire—the sexual and romantic love of one woman for another—is the central issue that leads to metamorphosis. As briefly related in chapter two, the story goes as follows: Ligdus, a poor but upright man of Crete, tearfully tells his pregnant wife Telethusa that, because of their poverty, if their child is female, it will have to be killed. Just as Telethusa is about to give birth, the goddess Isis appears and instructs her to care for the child whatever its sex—even if it means disobeying her husband—and trust that she, Isis, will take care of everything. With only a nurse as witness, Telethusa gives birth to a girl, but passes her off as a boy. As luck or Fate would have it, Ligdus,

---

[1] In the same essay, Lanser writes that before the eighteenth century, "female homoeroticism [was not] yet connected with the other (intellectual, moral, political) usurpations of male prerogative that charges of female masculinity signified in early modernity" (25), to which I would offer, as counter-examples, Brantôme's ruler Marguerite of Austria and poet Laodomia Forteguerra, the poets Philo-Philippa and Philips/Orinda, Cavendish's Empress and Duchess in *The Blazing World,* Chorier's *femme-savante* Tullia in *Satyra Sotadica* (Turner [2003] ch.4), Chorier-Nicolas's Judith in *L'Academie des dames,* John Crowne's Psecas in *Calisto: or, The Chaste Nimph* (Robinson [1998] ch.1), and the French *précieuses* (Wahl). Moreover, Lanser follows Traub in overstating the distinction in the seventeenth century between what was considered tribadism and what Traub calls "femme-femme love" (cf. Borris, 19). As for effeminacy, notwithstanding the influential claims of Bray (1982), Goldberg (1992, citing Bray), McIntosh, and Trumbach (1987b), effeminacy and male-male sex *were* linked prior to the late seventeenth century. For some of the many classical, medieval, and early modern texts in which such linkage can be found, see, for a start, Cady (1996), Carvajal, Hubbard, Keiser, Kuefler, Leibacher-Ouvrard (2000), Poirier (1996a and b), Richlin (1993b), Saslow (1986), Bruce Smith (1991), and Young.

naming the child after its grandfather, chooses a gender-neutral name: Iphis. The girl is then raised as a boy (without difficulty, it would seem) until she reaches the age of thirteen, when Ligdus betroths her to her schoolmate Ianthe. For the two girls have fallen in love, Ianthe not suspecting Iphis's true sex. Telethusa postpones the wedding as long as she can, but eventually the day is fixed. The night before the ceremony, the disguised girl and her mother shut themselves in Isis's temple and pray for help. The goddess transforms Iphis into a boy. The next morning the newly opposite-sex couple is married.[2]

Critics and scholars have offered widely divergent interpretations of the tale's, and Ovid's, attitude toward lesbianism. For instance, Judith Hallett argues, "Iphis's revulsion at female homoerotic passion must not be confused with the view of Ovid himself. Indeed, Ovid's narrative displays immense sympathy with Iphis's plight, a sympathy contrasting to Iphis's own self-condemnation and negative view of female homoeroticism" ([1997] 263). John Makowski argues the opposite: the tale constitutes "Ovid's most damning denunciation of homosexuality" (30). Most recently, in an especially thoughtful and illuminating essay (to which I'll return), Diane Pintabone steers a middle course, contending that "Ovid, as is common in his works, has it almost all ways: he manages to present both a positive and a negative portrait of woman-for-woman… passion—suggesting that it is both natural and unnatural—precisely by simultaneously overturning stereotypes and reinforcing them. He provides no firm judgment of his own (i.e., as narrator), either for or against female homoeroticism" (259). Such divergent response to "Iphis and Ianthe," and to the web of stories within the *Metamorphoses* concerning sex-change, strange or forbidden love, or both, is nothing new. For centuries, and particularly during the early modern period, European writers have reworked "Iphis and Ianthe," "Narcissus and Echo," "Salmacis and Hermaphroditus," "Byblis and Caunus," "Caenis/Caeneus," and related Ovidian tales in order to ponder and play with possibilities for sex, gender, and sexuality.

Yet running beneath, or through, these varied stories are striking similarities, striking continuities among the Ovidian originals, early modern adaptations, and present-day patterns of thought and representation. Notwithstanding the flux and

---

[2] This chapter and the next extensively expand and revise Robinson (2001c). I'm grateful to Chris Mounsey for his helpful comments on that earlier work. I refer to particular tales from the *Metamorphoses* by the names of their protagonists, in quotation marks. English quotations from the *Metamorphoses* are from Sandys's 1632 translation or Hill's modern one, unless indicated. All Latin quotations are from Hill. Quotations from Sandys are identified with the letter 'S' followed by the page number in Hulley and Vandersall, from Hill by 'H' followed by the volume and page number, from Ovid's Latin by book and line number. Ovid's Latin text, as well as several translations (including Sandys) can be found online at <http://etext.lib.virginia.edu/latin/ovid/index.html>. On the significance of Iphis's name, especially in relation to sex and gender ambiguity and female homoeroticism, see Wheeler.

transformation to which the word 'metamorphosis' itself refers, these classical and early modern stories reveal as much about continuity and likeness as about discontinuity, rupture, difference, and change, within and across times and cultures. Confronted with these texts' schema for ordering sex, gender, and sexuality, I find myself experiencing the "surprising lack of surprise" noted by Jonathan Walters in his examination of Roman ideologies of masculinity, which he attributes in part to "the effect on the modern reader of cultural assumptions that are common to both our society and that of the Romans" (33).[3]

In contrast, the past two decades' most influential work on the history of sexuality has argued not simply that historical difference must be better appreciated, but that resemblance or similarity is merely superficial, while difference is real, fundamental, essential. Famously, John Winkler and David Halperin (both 1990) took such an approach to sex, gender, and sexuality in ancient Greece. Explicitly following in their footsteps, Craig Williams has recently made the case for the radical alterity of ancient Rome, arguing that "the prime directive of masculine sexual behavior for Romans" was that "a self-respecting Roman man must always give the appearance of playing the insertive role in penetrative acts, and not the receptive role: ...he must be the 'active,' not the 'passive,' partner" (18). As Williams elaborates at the start of his chapter on "Sexual Roles and Identities":

> [W]hile the importance of the insertive/receptive dichotomy has been recognized, I wish to insist on its utter centrality. The question "Who penetrated whom?" lies behind practically every surviving ancient allusion to a sexual encounter, even between women....
>
> This chapter thus argues that, rather than being endowed with a deeply entrenched sexual identity as heterosexual, homosexual, or bisexual, based on the sex of the sexual partners to which he was oriented, a Roman man was normally assigned to one of two identities, 'man' (*vir*) or 'non-man'; and that when these identities were embodied in specific sexual practices, the sex of the man's partner was irrelevant to his own status....
> In the end, my object in this chapter is to probe the discontinuity between ancient and modern modes of categorizing male sexual agents: the ancient as observably inclined to engage in certain sexual practices, the modern as erotically oriented toward persons of one or the other sex, or both. (160–61)

On the one hand, in his important book Williams convincingly demonstrates very real, often startling differences between dominant ideologies of sex, gender, and sexuality in ancient Rome and the modern West. On the other, he underplays or ignores similarities between then and now, including similarities to which some of his own findings attest. To give just one example: in arguing that the Roman word

---

[3] See Richlin's conclusion (1993b) and Fradenburg and Freccero's "Introduction" for particularly thoughtful expressions of the importance of perceiving both continuity and discontinuity, similarity and difference, between past and present.

cinaedus designated something different from the modern word 'homosexual' or even the concept 'passive homosexual,' he makes much of the fact that "*cinaedus* [was] capable of being used in contexts other than those referring to penetrated males" (178). And yet the same can be said of the modern terms 'faggot' and 'gay.' The former can be used to charge a man with effeminacy or unmanliness, even when same-sex sexuality isn't intimated; the latter can be used to mean 'bad' or 'uncool,' as when adolescents or children derisively exclaim, "That is *so* gay!"

Like other differentist historians of premodern sexuality, Williams tends to write as if modern homophobia were directed solely or primarily against same-sex object choice, in contradistinction to gender deviance. Yet modern homophobia*s* seem, at least to me, focused as much upon the latter as the former. In many cases, perhaps most, untangling concerns about sexual orientation from those about gender is impossible (again, think of the terms 'faggot' or 'dyke'). True, the ancient conception of proper sexual behavior for (adult citizen) men consisting above all of sexual "activity" does seem to have been replaced by one consisting above all of men desiring and having sex with women. Yet in both cases the issue is gender, specifically manliness, as expressed through sexual behavior or desire. One could easily, and plausibly, make the case that men who desire other men are vilified today, not on account of this desire in and of itself, but instead precisely because they demonstrate desire in the way "women" are supposed to: toward a man. But one needn't go to this opposite extreme to recognize that contemporary homophobias target—and usually conflate—same-sex object-choice and gender deviance: gender deviance is routinely interpreted as a sign of homosexuality, homosexuality as a sign of gender deviance (not being a "real man" or "real woman"). And when one considers the frequency with which all gay men are assumed (incorrectly) to want to be penetrated, whether anally or orally (the reason 'cocksucker' and 'faggot' are typically synonymous), the ancient focus upon an active/passive, penetrator/penetratee dichotomy seems a good deal less strange, foreign, or outmoded than Williams and others make it out to be.

Or consider the much-remarked-upon "fact" that a man today who conforms in every other way to dominant conceptions of masculinity is nonetheless considered homo or bi if he has sex with other men, regardless of the specific sex acts. As Williams, Halperin, Holt Parker, and others remind us, such categorization would have made no sense in the ancient world. To the ancients, such a man was normal and respectable, so long as he penetrated (or was believed to penetrate) his sexual partners; so long as these partners were socially inferior to him; and so long as he seemed in control of, rather than controlled by, his sexual desires. At worst, if he evinced no sexual attraction to females, he might be deemed eccentric, but not perverted or degraded, nothing akin to a *cinaedus* or *faggot*.

And yet in certain public cruising spots (such as public bathrooms and parks); in safer-sex workshops and brochures designed for "men who have sex with men"; among Black and Latino men "on the down low"; in the personals section of weekly gay "bar rags"; and in innumerable online venues, men who consider themselves or wish to be considered straight seek out other men to be blown by or to fuck. Of course, sexual-object choice is still a relevant, even crucial, factor: a man who regularly let other men suck him but who never had sex with women would be considered a closeted homosexual by most people today, straight, gay, or bi. My point, however, is that there are multiple, often contradictory ideologies of sex, gender, and sexuality operating in even contemporary Western urban centers with large gay communities. In order to assert the overwhelming difference between ancient and modern conceptions of homosexuality, differentist historians erase all this messy multiplicity and contradiction, replacing it with a monolithic—and fictional—"modern homosexuality."[4]

Sedgwick made this point brilliantly almost fifteen years ago, in *Epistemology of the Closet*, with her axiom, "The historical search for a Great Paradigm Shift may obscure the present conditions of sexual identity" (44–48). She argued that in "radically defamiliarizing and denaturalizing the past," in asserting that past same-sex practices are fundamentally different from "the homosexuality 'we know today',... such an analysis... has tended inadvertently to *re*familiarize, *re*naturalize, damagingly reify an entity that it could be doing much more to subject to analysis...[,] counterposing against the alterity of the past a relatively unified homosexuality that 'we' *do* 'know today'" (44–45). In contrast, she proposed a different approach: "to show how issues of modern homo/heterosexual definition are structured, not by the supersession of one model and the consequent withering away of another, but instead by the relations enabled by the unrationalized coexistence of different models during the times they do coexist" (47; cf. Lloyd).

But whereas Sedgwick defamiliarized the present, in this chapter and the next I aim to refamiliarize the past, both classical and early modern. My contention is simple: an examination of, on the one hand, Ovid's "Iphis and Ianthe" and closely related tales from the *Metamorphoses*, and, on the other, early modern dramatizations of these tales, reveals strikingly similar ideologies of sex, gender, and sexuality, communicated through the invocation and linkage of a common set of topics intended simultaneously to repel and attract—lesbianism, male homosexuality, sex-change, crossdressing, effeminacy, aggressive female sexual desire, narcissistic desire, incest, twinning, misogyny, and patriarchal tyranny—topics that together delineate boundaries of the normal, the natural, the approved. And these boundaries, while somewhat different from those dominant today, are also rather familiar, certainly far more so than recent histories of sexuality would have us believe.

I do not mean to imply that work emphasizing the disjunction between ancient and modern conceptions of sex, gender, and sexuality is wrong. Particularly as a corrective to popular assumptions of the universality of dominant modern Western

---

[4] See Frier for a similar critique of Williams's book, and Chauncey for such issues in late nineteenth- and early twentieth-century New York gay life.

ways of thinking, such work continues to be invaluable. Yet among academic historians of sexuality and those who have followed their work over the past two decades, insistence upon the radical alterity of past sex, gender, and sexuality systems has led historians and critics to overlook the ways in which past and present systems are also similar, to the point that, as we shall see, material that might challenge the prevailing theoretical paradigm is cited instead as further support, its meaning predetermined by scholars' prior expectations.

Focusing intently on a limited number of texts, I hope in these final two chapters, as in previous ones, to reawaken sensitivity to the familiar in a past we've learned to see as fundamentally unfamiliar, fundamentally Other. My aim is perhaps best expressed by the declaration of purpose from Margaret Anne Doody's dazzling exposition of connections among ancient, medieval, modern, and postmodern prose fiction, *The True Story of the Novel*:

> It is my purpose in *this* book to deal with continuities and to make a point of connectedness. Such an interest does not preclude a respect for difference. It is simply that difference is not my subject here; I write because I feel our comments on some kinds of differences have recently tended to obfuscate connections and to blot out continuities. There are continuities and connections in the Western world, after all. (9)

The rest of this chapter explores some of these continuities and connections, involving sex, gender, and sexuality.[5]

Sex-as-Penetration and Other (Im)Possibilities

The centerpiece as well as longest section of "Iphis and Ianthe" (taking up almost a quarter of its length) is Iphis's lament, the three interconnected themes of which are her desires' utter uniqueness, their unnaturalness, and the impossibility of fulfilling them. Iphis believes she's not only the sole woman but also the sole living creature ever to experience these "new, unknowne, prodigious loves" (Sandys, 421):

---

[5] For excellent classicist essays on historical continuity and discontinuity, see Golden and Toohey, eds., especially Richlin's contribution. For an encouraging sign that the Age of Alterity may be drawing to a close, compare the treatment of the figure of the *kinaidos/cinaedus* in the original and revised versions of Halperin's "Forgetting Foucault" (1998; 2002a). And see Halperin (2002b), especially his discussion (10–13) of the Sedgwick passage quoted above, in which he admits, "It has taken me nearly ten years to get my mind around Sedgwick's objection, to absorb it into my own thinking" (12). Although I can't help but note that the process might have been considerably accelerated had the work of other scholars who questioned differentist orthodoxy been more widely read, taught, cited, and anthologized—in short, more seriously considered—by Halperin and others these past two decades, this evolution in Halperin's perspective bodes well for the field as a whole.

No Cow a Cow, no Mare a Mare pursues:
But Harts their gentle Hindes, and Rammes their Ewes.
So Birds together paire. Of all that move,
No Female suffers for a Female love. (S421)

William S. Anderson is probably correct to read this mistaken belief as an indication of Iphis's innocence, and to assert that "all this emphasis on novelty must have amused [Ovid's] Roman audience" ([1972] 469). For as Bernadette Brooten demonstrates, "Whereas pre-Roman-period Greek and Latin literature contains very few references to female homoeroticism, the awareness of sexual relations between women increases dramatically in the Roman period" (1; see also Hallett [1997], Pintabone, Boehringer).

Yet by leaving undisputed, both in this story and elsewhere, Iphis's belief that her desires are unprecedented, Ovid's text colludes in establishing what will become a staple trope of anti-lesbian Western discourse: newness. For example, crediting Sappho with the "invention" of lesbianism, as do so many seventeenth- and eighteenth-century British and French writers (Donoghue, 253–68), doesn't preclude—indeed goes hand in hand with—describing lesbianism in the writer's own time and place as something new. Thus, as we've seen in the *Vies des dames galantes*, after remarking that "It is said that Sappho of Lesbos was a very good mistress of this trade, indeed, they say, that she invented it, and that (ever) since the lesbian ladies have imitated her in it, and continued to this day; just as Lucian says: that such women are the women of Lesbos, who do not want to endure men, but approach other women just as men themselves (do)," Brantôme still feels compelled to account for lesbianism's existence among his contemporaries. He therefore soon adds, "In our France, such women are quite common, and yet it is said that they have not long been mixed up in it, even that the practice of it was brought from Italy by a lady of quality whom I will not name."[6]

According to Iphis, however, lesbian desire isn't only new, it's also unprecedentedly strange and unnatural—even bestiality seems normal in comparison. The latter, she asserts, is always heterosexual: Pasiphae fell in love with a bull, but at least "They [were] male and female" (S421). Her feelings for Ianthe, one girl's love for another, are "farre more full/ Of uncouth fury!" (S421). As with Iphis's belief in the uniqueness of her desires, Ovid seems not to endorse this part of her lament. Certainly, as Pintabone astutely observes, if readers think through the comparison between Iphis and Pasiphae, they're likely to judge the former far more positively. For the very words Ovid has Iphis use to refer to Pasiphae's behavior liken the latter to a rapist: *passa bovem est, et erat qui deciperetur, adulter* (740; ["She had sex with/endured the bull, and it was he, the adulterer, who was deceived"] [Pintabone, 268]). Although Iphis emphasizes

---

[6] As we shall see when discussing Ovid's "Orpheus," male homosexuality is also represented as an invention.

Pasiphae's having taken the proper, receptive, female role in the actual sex act, "In effect," Pintabone demonstrates, "Ovid has Iphis say that while Pasiphaë 'endured' the bull, it was really she who raped him, by tricking him with her animal disguise" (269). But unlike Pasiphae, and unlike other females in the poem who aggressively pursue the objects of their sexual desires (several of whom we'll consider below), "Iphis maintains the passivity associated in Roman thought with [virtuous] women" (275).

Yet if Ovid invites us to laugh at some of Iphis's notions, and perhaps at her entire predicament, he and his character agree about the lament's chief assessment of love between women: it is vain, hopeless, *impossible*. Not for the typical reasons: a watchful guardian, jealous husband, strict father, unloving beloved. No, Iphis and Ianthe are both unmarried, both in love, their fathers both approve, indeed are hastening the match. The very gods have done all in their power to bring it about: "What they can give, the easie Gods afford" (S421). But an unconquerable, unbending opponent makes this pairing impossible: "What me, my father, hers, her selfe, would please,/ Displeaseth Nature; stronger then all these./ Shee, shee forbids" (S421). As we shall soon see, other characters in the *Metamorphoses* are willing, even able, to brave Nature. Iphis, though, doesn't even consider the possibility. She, and the story as a whole, ultimately treats lesbian sex as unnatural not merely in the sense of going against what Nature intended, but in a far more absolute sense: lesbian sex is an oxymoron, it cannot happen, it is literally, physically impossible.

One might, of course, argue that far from posing a puzzle, Ovid's tale provides further evidence that sex for the ancient Greeks and Romans was all about power and hierarchy. As Foucault wrote in *The Use of Pleasure*:

> [S]exual relations—always conceived in terms of the model act of penetration, assuming a polarity that opposed activity and passivity—were seen as being of the same type as the relationship between a superior and a subordinate, an individual who dominates and one who is dominated, one who commands and one who complies, one who vanquishes and one who is vanquished. (215)

Such a schema, of course, was thoroughly gendered. Masculinity—indeed maleness—and penetration were conceived of as mutually defining, even synonymous; so, too, femininity/femaleness and being penetrated. Two women having sex would have been literally inconceivable.[7]

Notwithstanding its popularity among historians of sexuality over the past two decades, this neat schematic view of ancient Greek and Roman sex, gender, and

---

[7] Writers on ancient sexuality have tended to take Foucault's remarks here out of context (e.g., Halperin [1990], 30–32; 165, n.68). Foucault himself, in the sections of *The Use of Pleasure* devoted to sex and love (185–246), presents a far more nuanced, and explicitly limited, argument (e.g., 193–203).

sexuality is decidedly oversimplified. Indeed, James Davidson maintains "that the picture of ancient sex and sexual morality as a plus-minus 'zero-sum game', where one party can only 'win' at the expense of the other, is not only unsubstantiated, but contradicts what evidence there is" (7). And one needn't go quite so far in order to recognize that in any particular culture—let alone a roughly twelve-hundred-year-long, up to two-and-a-half-million-square-mile, multicultural collection of societies and civilizations such as "Classical Antiquity"—there's sure to be more than one way to think about such issues.[8]

Of course, even some scholars who espouse the dominant view acknowledge a greater range of ancient thought, feeling, and behavior than the active/passive, penetrator/penetratee schema would suggest. Winkler, for example, makes such an acknowledgment:

> It would of course be wrong to read this interpretive system as a phenomenology of actual desire and behavior.... We might refer to this set of protocols as "what will the neighbors think." They are not moral rules determining one's conduct, except insofar as that conduct will be available to and assessed by the community. Knowing them gives us a firm idea of community values, but not necessarily an account of individual or private behavior. (40–41)

Such a position is a good deal subtler than the blanket equation of ancient sexuality with penetration and power still made by otherwise thoughtful historians and critics.[9]

Nevertheless, this somewhat more nuanced view strikes me as still too absolute, assuming too great a uniformity and consistency in "community values," as well as too easy and uncomplicated a distinction between public and private. Too often ignored, or briefly acknowledged only to be forgotten, are the signs that in the ancient world, as in the modern and postmodern ones, dominant ideology was *contested*. Not just contradictory, or unstable, or "precarious" (Raval, 168), but actually challenged by other ways of thinking and acting, other ways of understanding and experiencing the world. Subversive views were not only possible in the privacy of one's own head and bed, but were audible and visible in a variety of semi-public and public representational, discursive, and even real-life embodied realms.[10]

---

[8] Most convincingly, Davidson argues that the work of K.J. Dover in *Greek Homosexuality* (1978), a foundational text for constructionist gay historiography, was deeply flawed (particularly its reliance upon the explicitly homophobic work of George Devereux). See also Hubbard (7–8), Barkan's response to Halperin (21–24), and Sissa.

[9] Williams takes care to make this sort of distinction between ideology and experience repeatedly (e.g., 9–11). In a footnote, Halperin ([1990] 32) offered a similar caveat.

[10] See Richlin (1993b); also Frier, Gleason, Taylor. Studies of Sappho's poetry have proven particularly useful for discussing resistant or alternative sex/gender/sexuality ideologies in antiquity; e.g., Snyder; duBois; Greene, ed. See also Hallett and Skinner, eds.;

Moreover, along with ignoring or minimizing the existence of divergent conceptions of sex, gender, and sexuality, the sex-as-dominance model often erases classical ambivalence about even "approved" sex. For the Greeks and especially Romans, self-mastery was a fundamental masculine ideal. As Alison Sharrock explains,

> One of the oddest aspects of Roman sexuality to modern eyes is that male love, even in its most conventional manifestations, is not unproblematically masculine for the Romans. Masculinity is predicated not only on sexual performance but also on autarky, control of the self both internal (in the emotions) and external (in political liberty).... If the very thing that makes a man (sexual power) also unmakes him (by undermining his autarky), then gendered categories are never going to be easy and stable. ([2000] 98)

Eros of *any* sort, even if it provided an opportunity to reinforce social hierarchies, also threatened to undermine masculine self-mastery. Over and over, surrender to the beloved, to sexual desire, to Eros is portrayed as both pleasurable and painful, delightful and dangerous.[11]

Finally, the sex-as-dominance model, while presented as nothing if not ideologically constructed, can nevertheless obscure much of the *work* that a word such as 'construction' would seem to imply: the selection and exclusion of material, and the laboring to build, through a combination of planning and accident, a finished structure, with attractions highlighted and flaws concealed. In the case of the *Metamorphoses*, if we remain alert to traces of stories that could have been told, but were not, we quickly realize that Ovid's handling of Iphis's love for Ianthe forms part of a much larger set of choices—rather than inevitabilities—about the representation of sex, gender, and sexuality in the poem as a whole.

Familiarity with the representation of love and sex among women in other periods of Western history also helps reveal the ideological work involved in treating lesbian sex as "impossible." As Traub argues, "The trope of impossibility, signified by Ovid's story of Iphis and Ianthe, epitomizes the fate of female-female love up to the end of the eighteenth century.... The *amor impossibilis* is a thematic convention within a long literary heritage" ([2002] 279). Far from exemplifying a simple belief about the mechanics of sex, this tradition reveals a complex response to the intermingling of sexual acts, sexed bodies, and societal structures. To quote Traub again, "The solution of sex transformation mandates neither the eradication

---

Rabinowitz and Auanger, eds.; Hubbard, ed.; Clarke; Culham; Goldhill; Kilmer; Konstan. Of radically differentist scholars, Williams devotes the most attention to oppositional or dissident possibilities (e.g., 153–59; 195–97); nevertheless, they remain peripheral, even expendable, for his study as a whole, which focuses overwhelmingly (and intentionally) on dominant ideology.

[11] Again, among differentists Williams is notable for attention to such complexities.

of desire nor its redirection toward a different object, but a change in the desiring subject's body. Even as it concedes to a system of eroticism linked to gendered bodies, it performs, if unwittingly, an implicit disarticulation of the body from desire" (288). In "Iphis and Ianthe" and many subsequent texts, social prohibition is unknown as Nature, as physical impossibility. Yet the eventual violation through sex-change of the laws of possibility (or probability), further undermines the stability of the sex/gender/sexuality system the story appears to reinforce.[12]

But I'm getting ahead of myself. It's enough to notice here that in a text such as Ovid's, premised upon the impossible happening—upon miraculous metamorphoses—an assertion of impossibility cries out for scrutiny. In this case, we're supposed to find plausible (at least within the fictional realm of the poem) a goddess's transformation of a girl into a boy, but not two girls having sex. This assertion of lesbianism's impossibility attempts to conceal a rather glaring faultline, or set of overlapping, multiply intersecting faultlines, regarding sexual ideology.

Boy-Loving, Homosexuality, Homophobia?

The contours of these faultlines become clearer if we examine other stories within the *Metamorphoses* with which "Iphis and Ianthe" is linked by theme, content, form, placement, or language. The most obvious, "Byblis," immediately precedes "Iphis and Ianthe." Byblis falls in love with her twin brother Caunus, unsuccessfully attempts to seduce him, and ends up transformed into a fountain, weeping everlastingly. As William Brewer notes, Byblis's incestuous and Iphis's lesbian love are implicitly likened—as "abnormal passions"—yet they are also contrasted (294). Most importantly, at least for our purposes, although Byblis's desires are represented as abnormal, they are not portrayed as impossible. The story therefore opens with a clear, admonitory moral: "Byblis is a warning that girls should love what is permitted" (H.IX.29). There would be no need to warn against an "impossible" passion. But what Byblis desires—however lawless, out of the ordinary, even wondrous/monstrous/unnatural (*monstri* [IX.667])—is all too possible.

Like Iphis, Byblis laments her predicament at considerable length. But she finds, comparing her situation to that of others, both divine and human precedent:

---

[12] I intend the phrase "sex/gender/sexuality system" as an expansion of Gayle Rubin's "sex/gender system" (1975), distinguishing between gender and sexuality as Rubin herself suggested in subsequent work (1984/1993). On Roman beliefs about actual, as opposed to mythical, sex-changes, see Pliny the Elder's *Natural History*, VII.IV.36–37, and Brisson. It should be remembered, however, that in the *Metamorphoses*, sex-change is presented as supernaturally rather than naturally caused, akin to the transformation of humans into animals, vegetables, minerals, etc.

> ...Gods their Sisters wed.
> *Saturne* and *Ops* had both one womb and bed.
> So *Tethys* with *Oceanus*; so *Jove*
> Combines with *Juno* in eternall love. (S414–15)

Byblis sets out to follow such examples.

In the succeeding book, Ovid depicts another woman tortured by abnormal but not impossible passion: Myrrha, in love with her father, Cinyras. Her story, like "Byblis," opens with unequivocal moral condemnation, although expressed at significantly greater length (X.300–307). More importantly, as both Brewer and Anderson (1972) note, Myrrha delivers a lament strikingly like the plaints of Iphis and Byblis. Like Iphis, Myrrha examines the animal kingdom for precedent; unlike Iphis, she finds it:

> Horses their fillies back, sires Heifers beare;
> Gotes kids beget on those whose kids they were:
> Birds of that seede conceive, whereof but late
> Conceiv'd themselves: nor they degenerate. (S462)

Like Byblis, she finds precedent also in the human world:

> There is a Nation... to their blood more kind;
> Where sons their mothers, fathers daughters wed;
> Affection doubled by their birth and bed.
> Woe's me, that there I was not borne! the place
> Makes this a crime. (S463)

Here and elsewhere, the forbiddenness of Myrrha's desires is made clear. So is their horrifying possibility, even more so than Byblis's: Myrrha actually has sex with her father, repeatedly. The links between "Myrrha" and "Byblis" on the one hand and "Iphis and Ianthe" on the other are clear, and to be expected: incest, like lesbianism, threatens to erase the power-distributive distinctions between people so fundamental to a patriarchal society such as Ovid's Rome.

"Myrrha" is immediately preceded by "Pygmalion," the story of a man who falls in love with his own creation, a beautiful statue of a woman, and whose desires are fulfilled when Venus brings the statue to life. The links between "Pygmalion" and "Myrrha" are numerous, as other critics have demonstrated and as I shall discuss below. But its direct link to "Iphis and Ianthe" is single: Pygmalion's love, like that of Iphis, is seemingly impossible to consummate.[13]

---

[13] On links between "Pygmalion" and "Myrrha," see especially Sharrock (1991). As for whether Ovid presents Pygmalion's passion for statuary as normal or abnormal, over the past few decades critical opinion has swung toward the latter view, away from earlier readings that stressed Ovid's celebration of and identification with the artist enamored of his

The *Metamorphoses*, however, provides another famous story of impossible love, one that, like "Byblis" and "Myrrha," is multiply linked to "Iphis and Ianthe": Book III's "Narcissus and Echo," itself preceded by a brief story of sex-changing ("Tiresias") in which a man is transformed into a woman, and then, seven years later, back into a man, and in which, as in "Iphis and Ianthe," sexual pleasure and fulfillment are explicitly at issue.

As for "Narcissus and Echo"—or "Narcissus," the portion with which we're concerned—it is, as just mentioned, a story of impossible love: beautiful, sixteen-year-old Narcissus, having proudly spurned the many youths and maidens who amorously pursued him (most notably, the nymph Echo), is, at the angry prayer of a rejected youth, made to fall in love with his own reflection in a pool, which he recognizes too late to prevent his death (from pining) and metamorphosis (into a flower).[14] Like Iphis, as Brewer notes, Narcissus delivers a lament focused on his love's impossibility, notwithstanding "that the usual barriers [to love] were absent" (299):

> What grieves me more; no Sea, no Mountayne steep,
> No wayes, no walls, our joyes a-sunder keep:
> Whom but a little water doth divide;
> And he himselfe desires to be injoy'd. (S139)

Once Narcissus realizes he's fallen in love with his own image, he sums up the odd and lamentable circumstances with a paradox, as Iphis will later do: "Shall I be woo'd, or wooe? What shall I crave?/ Since what I covet, I already have./ Too much hath made me poore!" (S139), an idea recalled when Iphis exclaims, "Look, the longed for time is coming/ the wedding morn is at hand and now Ianthe will be mine—/ but she will not be given to me; we shall be thirsty in the middle of waters" (H.IX.41).

A reader today might also notice that both stories focus on same-sex love: Iphis falls in love with another woman, Narcissus with what he mistakes for another man. But is such an observation anachronistic? Are we misreading if we draw attention to Sandys's virtually identical encapsulation of each character's predicament ("Himselfe, himselfe distracts" [138], "a maid, a maid affects" [421]), or argue that in condensing and intensifying the similarity of the Latin wordplay—*se cupit imprudens et, qui probat, ipse probatur,/ dumque petit, petitur, pariterque accendit et ardet* (III.425–26; "Unwittingly, he desired himself and both praised

---

work. Elsner cites several examples of each view, then offers his own persuasive reading of Pygmalion as viewer/reader.

[14] For versions of the story upon which Ovid may have drawn, as well as ones he most certainly influenced, see Vinge. On contrasts between Ovid's version and earlier ones, see also Richard Spencer, 30–31. For the Narcissus myth in Romantic through Modernist homosexual writing, see Bruhm (2001).

and was himself the praised one,/ and while he sought, he was being sought, and he was at once both burning and igniting" [H.III.111]; *ardetque in virgine virgo* (IX.725; "maiden... on fire for maiden" [H.IX.39])—Sandys sensitively picks up on meanings already present in the original text, making nearly explicit what is nonetheless implicit in Ovid?

To make the case that this is indeed misreading, that male homosexuality is not at issue in "Narcissus," one would probably point out three things: First, the narrator explicitly says the beautiful youth is punished for excessive pride and self-love, the character traits we've therefore come to call 'narcissism.' Second, male homosexual desire is treated positively elsewhere in the story. As already mentioned, Narcissus is loved by other youths as well as maidens, and it's a *youth*'s angry prayer that costs the beautiful boy his heart and life. Third, some readers might even add that love between men is handled sympathetically later in the *Metamorphoses*, in Book X's "Apollo and Cyparissus," "Jupiter and Ganymede," and "Apollo and Hyacinthus," the latter two recounted by the boy-lover Orpheus, soon to be martyred for homosexual love (at the start of Book XI), and who, as supremely gifted bard, is an obvious stand-in for Ovid.

Yet none of these objections—most of which, in fact, Williams offers in proof of his differentist assertion that "to this poet, as to his readership, there seem to have been no significant parallels, no meaningful common ground, between sexual practices between men and boys on the one hand and between women on the other: they did not both constitute embodiments of the overarching concept 'homosexuality,' with the subsets 'male' and 'female'" (8; 262, n.29; 234; 359, n.11)—none holds up under closer examination. In response to the first objection, I'd offer the rather obvious reminder that a text can imply more than it directly states; moreover, such indirection is an age-old rhetorical staple of homophobic (and homosexual) discourses. In response to the second, I'd point out that despite a semblance of equality in the treatment of the youths' and maidens' love for Narcissus, the representation of the former is kept to the absolute minimum necessary to advance the plot: "till one of those he had disdained raised his hands up towards the ether/ and said, 'So may he too love, so may he not gain/ what he has loved!'" (H.III.109). The youths' love for Narcissus is mentioned rather than represented. In contrast, the representational red carpet is rolled out for the maidens' love, via the story of Echo. As for the third objection, a closer reading of the boy-love stories suggests a more negative portrayal of love between males than one might at first assume, one more in keeping with the speaker's comment in Ovid's *Ars Amatoria* ("The Art of Love") that "he hate[s] sex that doesn't gratify both partners,/ And that is why [he is] less enthralled with boys" (3.437–38; tr. Hubbard, 373).[15]

---

[15] It's worth noting, as Richard Spencer does, that in a version of the Narcissus myth roughly contemporary with Ovid's, written by the Greek mythographer Conon, "Narcissus rejects a [male] lover, Ameinias, who kills himself at Narcissus' door and begs Eros to

To begin with, as others have noticed, there's the grouping together of the boy-love material in Book X, to which Orpheus calls attention when he announces, "Now, in a lower tune, to lovely boyes/ Belov'd of Gods, turne we our softer layes" (S457). Orpheus (and through him Ovid) makes sure we realize these aren't just stories that happen to involve boy-loving as an incidental feature; we're being asked, even forced, to conceive of the category or phenomenon "boy-loving," which these stories will then illustrate.

Yet we're not meant to contemplate the category in isolation. Instead, it's immediately yoked to a second topic: "women well deserving punishment,/ On interdicted lust, with fury bent" (S457). The pairing of these two topics strikes me as suspicious if boy-loving is presented in a positive light. Readers might easily see both sets of tales as cautionary, both types of love as deviant and immoral, rather than favorably contrasting one to the other.

Then there's the origin story for boy-loving Ovid has just provided. Having twice suffered the death of his beloved wife Eurydice, for whom, after her first death, Orpheus literally went to hell and back,

> ... Orpheus... shunned all
> Venus with women, either because it had turned out ill for him,
> or because he had given a pledge. Yet many women were gripped by a burning desire
> to join themselves with the bard; many grieved when rebuffed.
> He was even the instigator [or *author, inventor* (*auctor*)] among the people of
>   Thrace of transferring
> love to tender males and of plucking the first
> flowers of the brief age of spring before young manhood. (H.X.47)[16]

The first thing I want to emphasize about this passage is that it conflates male

---

vindicate him. His prayer is answered and Narcissus dies realizing his death is just retribution for his *hubris*..." (30).

[16] Note that Sandys's commentary on his rendition of the boy-love reference ("Who beauty first admir'd in hopefull boyes" [456]) reads, "Not rendering the Latin fully; of purpose omitted" (456, n.21). Arthur Golding (whose 1567 translation of the *Metamorphoses* influenced a host of English Renaissance writers, most famously Shakespeare) had no such scruples, translating the lines on boy-loving as, "Orphye... did utterly eschew/ The womankynd.... He also taught the Thracian folke a stewes [brothel] of Males to make/ And of the flowring pryme of boayes the pleasure for to take" (X.87–92). On precedents for Orpheus as the first Thracian man to love other males, see Segal, 57. Schibanoff insightfully suggests, "Orpheus's interest in boys may constitute his metamorphosis: the former devotee of Eurydice now gives his sexual attention to young men" (42); but see below, n.21, on problems with Schibanoff's reading of "Orpheus." As Marc Schachter pointed out to me, the use of *auctor* here, one of the meanings of which is *inventor*, potentially links Orpheus to the legendary inventor Daedalus, and to Iphis's naive belief that even he couldn't have invented a means for one woman to have sex with another (IX.742–43; see below, n.43).

homosexuality—rejection of the love of women, turning to the love of men—with adult male boy-loving, even though we've already seen, in "Narcissus," that males of the same age (at least male youths of the same age) can desire one another. This ideological sleight-of-hand (to which I'll return below) is easy to miss, especially since most modern accounts of homosexuality in the ancient world speak only of age-differentiated relationships, as if age-equivalent ones were nonexistent, unimaginable, or insignificant. For even if Foucault were correct—and I think he isn't—that same-age same-sex relationships between males were simply "not an object of moral solicitude or of a very great theoretical interest" in the ancient world ([1985] 194–95), historians (including Foucault) have tended to replicate rather than interrogate this apparent lack of interest.[17]

The second thing I want to point out is that Ovid clearly presents boy-loving as Orpheus's second choice, consolation for the failure of his hetero relationship or an expedient to allow him to enjoy erotic activity without truly committing his heart (since by its very nature boy-loving is relatively short-lived, ending when the boy becomes a man). Add to this the passage's emphasis on shunning womankind, repulsing women's love, and it pretty much depicts boy-loving as misogynist sour grapes. Indeed, Orpheus's declaration of the intended subject of his song—lovely boys beloved by Gods and lustful women deserving punishment—sounds just like what one would expect from, as Makowski puts it, "an effeminate, gynophobic pederast" (27).[18]

Other critics have noted Orpheus's misogyny and its linkage to his boy-loving. Sharrock, for instance, advises us to "remember that the internal narrator [Orpheus] sings precisely out of his misogyny: [His] reaction to the loss of his wife is to avoid heterosexual love" ([1991] 174), later adding, "It was by his own fault that he lost Eurydice…, yet his misogynistic reaction is implied accusation of his wife" (179). Similarly, Harry Berger stresses "the significance of… Orpheus' response to the loss of Eurydice":

> that he shuns the love of women and turns to that of boys; that he resolves to "sing of boys beloved by gods, and maidens inflamed by unnatural love and paying the penalty of their lust"…; and that he tells in addition the tales of Pygmalion and Venus and Adonis (within the latter of which Venus tells of Atalanta)—these preferences compose into a fairly consistent pattern. Antifeminism, promiscuous homosexuality, and

---

[17] E.g., Cantarella, viii. Williams at least devotes an appendix (245–52) to one form of same-age same-sex relationship—male marriage—although it's decidedly beside the point of his book.

[18] See Makowski and Segal for critics' widely varying reactions to "Orpheus." For Orpheus as object of Ovidian mockery or parody, see also Richard Spencer. For a different view, see Hardie. And for a reading of "Orpheus," along with the myths of Ganymede and Hylas, as "provid[ing] Renaissance writers with a common vocabulary for alluding to [the] conflict between male homoerotic desire and chaste marital (hetero)sexuality," see DiGangi's important book (1997), 23–24.

antieroticism are all defenses against the kind of commitment Orpheus made and the consequent pain of the loss he incurred. (32)

Both critics, in other words, not only note Orpheus's directly expressed misogyny, but also read the tales he tells as expressing it. Thus Berger points out, "Pygmalion's disgust at the shameless Propoetides [the first women to become prostitutes] is quickly generalized to 'the faults which in such full measure nature had given the female mind' [X.244–45], and [his statue] is both the product and the symbol of his misogyny" (32; also Sharrock, 170).

Berger and Sharrock also discuss the misogyny of "Myrrha" and its multiple connections to "Pygmalion": Myrrha and her Nurse are made entirely responsible for the father-daughter incest, despite, as Sharrock points out, "plenty of hints in the text that he is involved in its incestuousness, if not quite consciously" (177); Cinyras and Myrrha are, respectively, Pygmalion's grandson and great-granddaughter; Pygmalion is the father (and mother) of his statue, given that "One very obvious form of creation is procreation, and one metaphor for the relationship between the artist and his creation is that of parent and child, or rather, specifically *father* and child" (Sharrock, 176).

Berger also draws our attention to "Venus and Adonis," in which "Myrrha's son Adonis... unwittingly 'avenges his mother's passion'... by arousing that of Venus." As Marc Schachter suggests, the desire for revenge against Venus would seem to be Orpheus's, revenge not for the disastrous passion with which she inspired Myrrha but for the disastrous passion with which she inspired him—his love for Eurydice.[19] One might also observe the tale's implicit continuation of Ovid's incest theme, representing another primary, as yet omitted, intrafamilial possibility: mother-son. Venus conceives her passion for the adolescent Adonis as a result of metaphoric sexual intercourse with Cupid: "For while the quivered boy was giving kisses to his mother,/ he unwittingly grazed her breast with a protruding shaft" (H.X.65). As in "Myrrha," it's the child rather than parent who dies; but whereas Cinyras is portrayed as blameless for his daughter's death and transformation, Venus is made more or less responsible for Adonis's, as Eleanor Leach argues (122–23). Although Leach doesn't pursue the point, the effeminizing, even castrating effects of Venus's love, a woman's love, are very much at issue, not least in the description of Adonis's fatal wounding: "[the boar] buried all its tusk/ in his groin and sent him sprawling on the yellow sand in his death throes" (X.73). As in "Pygmalion" and "Myrrha," the misogyny of this inset tale reflects back upon its teller.[20]

Yet while interrogating and challenging Orpheus's misogyny, Sharrock and

---

[19] Personal communication, 1999.

[20] See Bate. As Berger mentions but doesn't explore, "Venus and Adonis" itself includes an inset tale, "Atalanta and Hippomenes," recounted by Venus to Adonis, that echoes in intriguing ways the stories I've been discussing (see Hallett [1978]).

Berger miss the homophobia in Ovid's construction of the once woman-loving, now boy-loving bard. Indeed, in the passage quoted above, Berger virtually replicates Ovid's homophobia when he states, "Antifeminism, promiscuous homosexuality, and antieroticism are all defenses against the kind of commitment Orpheus made and the consequent pain of the loss he incurred." Berger's slippage from "the love of boys" to "promiscuous homosexuality" aside, he and Sharrock fail to consider the fact that boy-loving's seemingly unproblematic alignment with misogyny, boy-loving as an outgrowth of misogyny, is constructed *by Ovid*. In contrast, this is precisely the point Schachter (1997) highlights: "Ovid's Orpheus is an extremely complex and ambivalent figure in part set up—and perhaps conspicuously so—to represent a misogynist pederasty. If Orpheus introduced pederasty to the Thracians, it is Ovid who introduces this Orpheus to us." When Sharrock rightly claims, "[Myrrha] is a scapegoat...[, onto her] is focused all the fear of the female subliminally expressed and pre-figured in Pygmalion's act of creation" (181), what she overlooks is that the boy-lover Orpheus is scapegoated for this scapegoating, scapegoated for this misogyny.[21]

This ascription of misogyny to a boy-loving man is mirrored by the text's ascription of homophobia to the heterosexual women who then murder him. Book XI begins, in Sandys's translation:

> THUS while the *Thracian* Poet... with his songs
> Beasts, Trees, and Stones, attracts in following throngs:
> Behold, *Ciconian*... dames (their furious brests
> Clad with the spotted skinnes of salvage beasts)
> The sacred Singer from a hill espy'd,
> As he his dittie to his harp apply'd.
> Of these, One cry'd, and tost her flaring haire;
> Lo he who hates our sex!...
> Him, holding up his hands, who then in vaine
> First spent his breath, nor pitty could obtaine,
> That Rout of sacrilegious Furies slew! (497–98)

Once again, through intensification, Sandys takes implicit elements of the text and makes them explicit. *Nostri contemptor*, which he translates as "he who hates our sex," literally means "he who scorns us." Likewise *sacrilegae*, which he translates as "That Rout of sacrilegious Furies," is simply "the sacrilegious women." Yet Ovid does portray them as Furies: horrifying, bestial, murderously violent females. But the text disavows this misogyny, projecting it onto the woman-hating boy-

---

[21] Weber and Kimmel, respectively, miss this dynamic in Rochester's *Sodom* and the anonymous *Love-Letters Between a certain late Nobleman and the famous Mr. Wilson*. Both Bate and Schibanoff read "Orpheus" much as Berger and Sharrock do. Anderson (1982) correctly identifies the homophobia of "Orpheus" and the stories Orpheus sings (44–46); unfortunately, he shares the sentiment.

lover, just as it disavows homophobia, projecting it onto the homo-hating women. Ovid is waging ideological warfare, but covertly.[22]

Boy-Loving, Homosexuality, Homophobia!

We may seem to have strayed rather far from "Iphis and Ianthe," but in exploring these densely interrelated tales ("Iphis and Ianthe," "Byblis," "Myrrha," "Pygmalion," "Tiresias," "Narcissus," "Venus and Adonis," "Orpheus"), we've returned almost to where we started, literally and thematically. "Orpheus" immediately follows "Iphis and Ianthe." Orpheus's lyre and severed head, borne out to sea by the river Hebrus, come to rest on the shores of Lesbos. As Schachter observes, "'Iphis and Ianthe' and Lesbos frame Orpheus's story, suggesting a curiously sustained meditation on homosexuality—Lesbos is associated obviously with Sappho, and also with Alcaeus, known for writing about pederasty."[23]

In light of this reading of "Orpheus," my earlier observation that both "Iphis and Ianthe" and "Narcissus" focus on same-sex love seems less anachronistic, as does the suggestion that, notwithstanding the seemingly positive, if exceedingly skimpy, treatment of other youths' love for Narcissus, his story represents same-sex love homophobically. Indeed, since "Narcissus" (like "Iphis and Ianthe") represents *same-age* same-sex love, one ought to expect a negative portrayal, given the centrality—and *precariousness*—of the Roman sex-as-dominance ideology, reflected in story after story in the *Metamorphoses*. True, Ovid's playful, ambiguous poem is a good deal less disciplined than many sexually conservative texts, seeming often invested as much in depicting as in condemning sexual and gender aberrance (see Richlin [1992b] on Ovid's rapes and [1983] on Roman satire more generally, especially Juvenal). Nevertheless, it's a mistake to see in the *Metamorphoses* simply "a delight in the polymorphousness of both narrative art and sexual desire" (Burrow, 305). Closer attention reveals subtle differences in Ovid's handling of various deviations from the patriarchal Roman rule.

For instance, as threatening as it is, incest is depicted in the *Metamorphoses*; for Ovid at least, it needn't be represented as impossible, erased through ideological sleight-of-hand—like lesbianism, and like male homosexuality if not expressed as boy-loving. Consider the *Metamorphoses*' other tale of female-to-male sex-change, "Caenis/Caeneus." Like Narcissus, Caenis is famously beautiful ("the fairest maiden of the daughters of Thessaly" [H.XII.113]). Like him, she spurns all who come a'courtin' ("vainly desired in the prayers of many suitors…[,] Caenis did not enter into any marriage" [XII.113–14]). She's then raped by

---

[22] Not that Sandys attempts to expose and contest Ovid's misogyny; he quite clearly shares it, as witnessed by his commentary on the believability of female-to-male sex-change (449–50).

[23] Personal communication, 1999.

Neptune, who, when finished, offers to grant her a single wish. "'This wrong,' said Caenis, 'makes for a great prayer/ that from now I can suffer no such thing. Grant that I be not a woman,/ and you will have provided me with everything" (XII.115). Neptune makes her a man, and throws in an added bonus: "that he could not be/ hurt by any wounds or fall to the sword" (XII.115). Caenis, now Caeneus, becomes a nearly invincible soldier (see Delcourt [1958], Brisson).

The story exemplifies the fundamental Roman construction of the genders "woman" [*femina/puella*] and "man" [*vir*]: woman is penetrated, man penetrates.[24] Caenis, the woman who resists lawful penetration (by a husband), is punished with unlawful penetration (rape by a male not her husband). The only way she can escape penetration is not just to cease being a woman (what she requests), but actually to become a man (what Neptune makes her). Yet the fault in this logic ought to be obvious: men, too, can be penetrated and raped. Tellingly, as Walters points out, "In Latin, when a male was sexually penetrated by another, a standard way... of describing this was to use the expression *muliebria pati;* that is, he was defined as 'having a woman's experience,'" suffering as a woman (30). Ovid unknows this possibility, replacing it with a near equivalent: wounding by weapons, especially swords.

In doing so, he addresses a genuine source of Roman masculine anxiety. As Walters explains, the Roman male ideal, the *vir*, is defined by his ability "to defend the boundaries of [his] body from invasive assaults of all kinds" (30). The Roman soldier, however, is an exception to this rule: "[A] soldier's wounds are honorable, not dishonoring" (40). And yet "the situation of the soldier is dangerously close to the edge in terms of social status: the exception that highlights the rule" (40). The fantasy-figure Caeneus embodies the soldier's aggressive, masculine qualities without his anxiety-provoking propensity (inherent in the definition of a soldier) to be penetrated by other men's weapons. In other words, the creation of Caeneus soothes the anxiety generated by the soldier's fundamental contradictions.

Yet soldiering was not the original source of anxiety in the story; it was a woman who refused to submit to marriage and sexual penetration. And the restoration of the dominant order (via rape and sex-change) generated a faultline: men can also be penetrated and raped. Ovid replaces the notion of the raped man with the less threatening figure of the soldier. The anxiety the latter generates is clearly tolerable, for the unabashedly wish-fulfilling figure of Caeneus alludes to as much as evades the reality that *viri*, no matter how virile, can be wounded, can

---

[24] By 'woman' and 'man' here, I'm referring to gender rather than sex. For classical Rome, *femina/puella* and *vir* refer only to respectable or high-status women and men. Disrespectable or low-status women may be penetrated by men other than their husbands; disrespectable or low-status men may be penetrated by other men; slaves of either sex may be penetrated by anyone, of either sex; and so on (see Walters, 30–37, for a brief but excellent explanation of this particular sex/gender/sexuality system; for extended analysis, see Williams).

be penetrated, by weapons—an unpleasant thought, but one clearly less disturbing than men's penetrability by penises.[25]

One final point about "Caenis/Caeneus": its unknowing of men's vulnerability to rape/penetration implies a further unknowing, one I mean to signal precisely by conflating rape and penetration, thereby erasing the possibility of consent. By definition, a *vir* cannot consent to anal or oral penetration. Were he to do so, he would cease to be a *vir*. He would be (would become? would always have been?) a *cinaedus*. By changing Caenis into a man, Neptune not only preserves her from future rape, but also assures she will remain what she ever was: a person with no desire to be penetrated. Or so the text would have us believe.[26]

Yet setting aside the clearly abhorrent notion of a *vir* being penetrated, what the neighbors would have thought of even age-differentiated, man-penetrates-boy sex was by no means certain in Ovid's day. Even more than the Greeks, the Romans were ambivalent about boy-loving. As Marilyn Skinner explains:

> From the perspective of an adult male, boys are legitimate objects of sexual pleasure. Yet the freeborn youth's future responsibilities to the civic community preclude his identifying with the passive role…. Roman society attempted to surmount this problem by forbidding relations with citizen boys; thus the literary *puer delicatus*, "boy-favorite," is normally a slave or ex-slave, often of foreign extraction…. ([1997] 135)

Or as Walters puts it, "If we look at the case of the *praetextatus*, the freeborn male youth who is not yet an adult man, we see that he occupies an ambivalent position, and is an object of special concern, precisely because the Roman protocols of sexuality place him in a marginal state in the pattern of 'gender' and wider social status" (33). The sexual subordination, and thus effeminacy, of the penetrated youth threatens to contaminate masculinity itself: both the masculinity of the man he'll eventually become, and the masculinity of his partner, who was himself once a penetrable boy and could thus somehow become—or could already be—a penetrable man. "Orpheus," I'm arguing, while not necessarily impugning the masculinity of the bard or the boy-loving gods of whom he sings, draws from and contributes to this anxious ideological matrix, constructing a misogynist, sour-grapes pederasty.[27]

---

[25] Part of the subsequent battle scene (XII.443–535) responds to a slightly different aspect of the same anxiety-provoking notion: the fearful knowledge, discussed below, that all "men" were once boys, and thus penetrable.

[26] On the figure and possible reality of the *cinaedus*, see Gleason; Richlin (1993b); Taylor; Williams (esp. ch.5); and Halperin, "Forgetting Foucault" (2002a). For the best-known Roman portrayal of such men, see Juvenal's *Satire 2* (discussed above, ch.1).

[27] Again, see Makowski for critics who read Ovid's Orpheus as effeminate. Some even see "Iphis and Ianthe" responding to this anxiety over masculine adolescence, or adolescence more generally (e.g., Viarre; Sharrock [2002]). For more on the disturbing implications of Greek or Roman adolescent boys' penetrability, see Foucault (1984/1986)

Moreover, as Schachter astutely demonstrates, even "Apollo and Cyparissus" and "Apollo and Hyacinthus"—usually seen as positive portrayals of boy-loving—reinforce the homophobia of "Orpheus." The gist of his argument is that "Apollo and Cyparissus," recounted by the narrator, comments ironically on "Apollo and Hyacinthus," recounted by Orpheus. Cyparissus loves a stag, Apollo loves Hyacinthus; Cyparissus accidentally kills the stag with a javelin, Apollo accidentally kills Hyacinthus with a discus; grief-stricken Cyparissus resolves to die, grief-stricken Apollo wishes to die; Cyparissus wishes to mourn forever, Apollo pledges to mourn forever; and so on. The irony, of course, is that Cyparissus grieves for a stag, a decidedly unworthy and strange love-object. His grief seems excessive, as Apollo himself points out: "How he urged him to grieve slightly/ and proportionately!" (H.X.49). By analogy—an analogy meticulously constructed by the text: Apollo is to Hyacinthus as Cyparissus is to stag—Apollo's love for Hyacinthus is also strange, his grief also excessive. In the context of "Orpheus," which explicitly makes boy-loving an issue and sets it in opposition to heterosexual love, the analogy serves to undercut Orpheus's love of boys and the stories of boy-loving he relates.[28]

Still, although age-differentiated male homosex is undercut by the text, it's not represented as impossible (as are both same-age male and female homosex). This is so, I would argue, not only because it accords, at least on the surface, with the idea of sex as an expression of difference and dominance (and is thus at worst disapproved of rather than taboo), but also because it has a kind of built-in impossibility, mentioned briefly above: by its very nature, boy-loving is short-lived, ending when the boy becomes a man—hence Orpheus's supposed instructions to the Thracians to "pluck... the first/ flowers of the brief age of spring before young manhood." To adherents of boy-loving this evanescence only adds to

---

193–203; Konstan (2002); MacMullen; Richlin (1983) ch.2 and appendix 2; and Williams, 185–88.

[28] Schachter (1997) and private communication (1999). For a similar reading, see Makowski, particularly on Orpheus's allusion to self-castrating Attis [X.104] (Ovid recounts Attis's story in the *Fasti* [4.223–46]; see Shane Butler, Konstan [2002], Skinner [1997], Williams). As for "Jupiter and Ganymede," the other tale of divine boy-love about which Orpheus sings, and the only one to end with an intact male couple (at the expense, moreover, of male-female coupling), I find it suggestive that Ovid has Orpheus abbreviate the myth, briefly relating the abduction, and merely alluding, even more briefly, to its outcome (X.155–61). On other versions, treated much differently, see Boswell (1980), DiGangi (1997), Richlin (1983) ch.2 and 5, Bruce Smith (1991, 1995), Williams, and especially Saslow (1986) and Barkan. Williams also points out (359, n.11) that Ovid mentions another male-male couple, "the beautiful sixteen-year-old Indian boy Athis and his Assyrian lover Lycabas" (V.47–73). I agree the text doesn't appear to criticize either character or their relationship. Yet of all possible male-male pairings, this one is most easily assimilable to Roman notions of honor: Athis and Lycabas are age-differentiated soldiers, depicted dying bravely in battle (cf. Virgil's account of Nisus and Euryalus [*Aeneid* IX]).

its poignancy, and to what might be called its truthfulness: since all of life is transitory, and everything we love we will lose, a love that never allows us to lose sight of its ending is the truest kind, both obeying and revealing the nature of life. Conversely, heterosexual love is rebellious and deceptive, with its promise of happily-ever-after. But to critics of boy-loving, its evanescence denotes triviality: it is love of the superficial, of outer beauty that fades rather than inner beauty that remains. True love should last as long as life, and then some, an ideal exemplified by the end of "Orpheus":

> His shade went under the earth, and he recognized all the places
> he had seen before and, seeking her through the fields of the pious,
> he found Eurydice and embraced her with eager arms.
> Here they both stroll, sometimes side by side,
> or he follows as she goes ahead, or he goes in front to lead the way,
> and Orpheus, safely now, looks back on his Eurydice. (H.X.77)

Boy-loving was only a stopgap, a detour, an aberration. It is left behind and forgotten. Everlasting, ever-happy hetero love remains.[29]

Same-age same-sex love, though, is even more threatening than boy-loving to a social order based on difference and hierarchy, because its primary feature, when viewed through this lens, is sameness, indistinguishability, equality. Thus Ovid makes Iphis and Ianthe noticeably twin-like: "Like young, like beautifull, together bred,/ Inform'd alike, alike accomplished" (S421, driving home the "like"-ness). And thus Narcissus, who falls in love with a youth his own age, turns out to have fallen in love with himself, the ultimate erasure of difference. In both cases, this system-destroying love-as-sameness is conjured up only to be revealed as fantastic, impossible to act upon or fulfill.

Still, if lesbianism and same-age male homosexuality are so threatening, why does Ovid treat them so lightly? For Anderson is right to argue for a humorous reading of "Iphis and Ianthe." He points out that the story's beginning, "The decision of the poor man that a female child must be exposed[,] constitutes one of the stock motifs of New Comedy" ([1972] 466). And his characterization of Iphis's complaint as her "tearful, but untragic, soliloquy" is apt (469). As mentioned earlier, her belief in the utter uniqueness of her desires surely amused Ovid's original readers. And what Anderson calls her "argument from animals to men"—*nec vaccam vaccae, nec equas amor urit equarum:/ urit oves aries, sequitur sua femina cervum./ sic et aves coeunt, interque animalia cuncta/ femina femineo conrepta cupidine nulla est*—"[makes her] appear more witty than pathetic, so that we may enjoy this speech without engaging our emotions in this pseudo problem.

---

[29] Reality, of course, could belie ideology, and boy-love could continue beyond the beloved's boyhood, as recommended by the *Symposium*'s Pausanias (discussed above, ch.5).

The word order of 731 and 732, the five quick dactyls of 732, and the alliteration of 734 keep the tone light" (470).[30] And, of course, all ends happily for Iphis. As for Narcissus, although his tale ends *un*happily, his basic predicament invites amusement:

> He too wants to be held;
> for, whenever I have stretched my lips down to the clear waters,
> each time he has strained towards me with upturned mouth.
> ...Why do you deceive me, matchless boy,
> when I reach for you, where do you go?...
> There is some sort of hope you offer me with your friendly look,
> and when I stretch my arms to you, you stretch yours back in return.
> When I smile, you smile back; when I nod too, you return the sign
> and, as far as I can guess from the movements of your beautiful mouth,
> you answer me with words that do not reach my ears. (H.III.111)

To appreciate the humor of the scene one need only pause to visualize it, as the extended description virtually requires. Of course, we may also feel compassion, particularly as Narcissus dies, although the news that "after he had been received by the place below, even then/ he would gaze upon himself in the water of the Styx" (III.113) might complicate this compassion—does one pity or condemn (or both) such eternal self-absorption? But during most of the story, we surely share the narrator's rather amused assessment of Narcissus and his situation: "Naive one, why do you vainly clasp at fleeting images?/ What you seek is nowhere; turn away, and you will lose your beloved" (III.111). Thus I repeat: if lesbianism and same-age male homosexuality are so threatening, why are they treated so lightly in "Iphis and Ianthe" and "Narcissus"?[31]

Fathers, Freaks, and the Phallus

To answer this question, we need to take one more tour through related tales in the *Metamorphoses*, tales in which appearances of disapproval and approval, horror and amusement are also frequently deceiving. "Myrrha," for instance, with its extended, condemnatory opening, would appear to be unambiguously negative. It's a story of "dreadful things" (H.X.57; *canam* [X.300]) about the "crime," the

---

[30] On the rhetorical rather than factual value of appeals to animal behavior in Ovid and other Roman writers, see Williams, 232–34 (also Boswell [1980] 152–56, for the Christian middle ages).

[31] For "Narcissus" as humorous, see also Richard Spencer. Of course, to some extent, Ovid treats everything as a joke (see Richlin on Marsyas [1992b]); however, that doesn't negate any particular treatment's importance, nor its distinctive features (cf. Richlin [1983] ch.3, on cuing and the content of jokes).

"wickedness" (H.X.57; *sinit, nefas, crimine, scelus* [X.304, 307, 312, 314, 315]) of father-daughter incest. Yet as mentioned above, only the daughter is punished. Father gets off (in both senses) scot-free: he's faulted neither for cheating on his wife nor for spicing up adulterous sex with incestuous fantasy (addressing as "daughter" [*filia*; X.467] the girl who's been brought to his bed). Unlike Venus, mother-figure in her metaphorically incestuous relationship with Adonis, Cinyras barely suffers or grieves. At the moment when his sex partner's identity is revealed, he is speechless, "words held back by grief" (H.X.63)—that's all the suffering we see, and it's followed by, as Sharrock (1991) points out, his immediately "whip[ping] out his sword in a passage replete with sexual overtones: *pendenti nitidum uagina deripit ensem* ('he whips his shining sword from its sheath' [X.475])" (182, n.29). One might sum up the consequences of parent-child incest in the *Metamorphoses* as "Children die, mothers grieve, fathers get away with it."[32]

Not that Father is painted in entirely rosy hues; arguably, a main target of the poem is abuse of patriarchal power. As one would expect: the possibility of patriarchal tyranny was an enormously important, enormously dangerous topic in the Rome ruled by Augustus (known as *pater patriae*). Indeed, in some ways, tyranny seems to be the central problem for all patriarchal societies: so long as masculinity is defined by the right and ability to wield power over others, the danger posed by that power, that it will be wielded unjustly and destructively, is always present. Predictably, a great deal of energy in patriarchal societies goes toward denying that patriarchal masculinity is the problem, and toward scapegoating women, effeminate men, the lower classes, foreigners, people of different nations or skin tones, and various other "Others."

Nevertheless, fathers in the *Metamorphoses* are required to show some respect to the feminine, the nonmasculine, or the gender-blurring. In "Iphis and Ianthe" this power is Isis, to whom Ligdus ought to have turned before the birth of his child, rather than resolving on infanticide if his wife bore a daughter. In the story following "Narcissus" and concluding Book III, it is Bacchus, the "boy with a maiden's beauty" (H.III.119), whose followers are mostly women, youths, and old men. In this story, Pentheus, too masculine for his own good, makes war on the cult of what he considers an effeminate pseudo-god, "an unarmed boy/ who enjoys neither wars nor weapons nor the use of horses,/ but hair drenched in oil of myrrh, soft garlands/ and purple and gold woven into the decoration of his clothes" (III.117). Pentheus's attempt to assert masculinity's total dominance over its Others—the feminine, effeminate, vulgar, irrational, out-of-control—results in a truly horrifying inversion of the "natural" order he believes he's defending: in a sort of reverse incest, the opposite extreme of unnatural familial relations, his

---

[32] For an argument that Ovid evokes some sympathy for Myrrha, see David Hopkins; see also Richlin (1992b).

mother, sister, and aunt tear him limb from limb.[33]

And yet, if "Pentheus" is a cautionary, fearful fantasy about taking Father Power too far, "Pygmalion" is a wish-fulfilling fantasy of paternal omnipotence. At first glance, Female Power might appear triumphant, since Pygmalion is the victim of an impossible love until Venus grants his prayer and brings the statue to life. But was his love really impossible? Can't a man have sex with a statue? Pygmalion possesses a penis, the sine qua non of "real" sex (hence the "impossibility" of lesbian sex). All that's missing is an orifice or two to penetrate, which the sculptor could easily drill, making his statue the perfect sex object (cf. pseudo-Lucian's *Erôtes*).

Indeed, in bringing the statue to life, Venus seems to accomplish almost nothing at all. As Sharrock (1991) observes, "In the final metamorphosis [the statue] becomes even more like an automaton: [S]he now really does move, and gives birth, but she seems barely more alive than she was as a statue" (174). The live woman, like the statue, has no name, never speaks, and is thoroughly passive. She is kissed, but not described as kissing back. Her "activity" consists of feeling the kisses, blushing, lifting up her eyes, and seeing "the sky and her lover together" (H.X.55). Nine months later, we're told, she bore a daughter, Paphos. Yet even this accomplishment seems more Pygmalion's than hers, as Sharrock argues: "Even [the statue's] fertility is no more than an extension of Pygmalion's creativity.... Pygmalion has fulfilled the fantasy of reproducing without another's agency: that is, without a woman's agency. For since he himself made the mother of his children, their entire being comes from him" (169).

Admittedly, this fantasy of paternal omnipotence is somewhat critiqued. Surely, the descriptions of Pygmalion kissing his statue, grasping it, speaking words of love to it, bringing it gifts, dressing and accessorizing it, and laying it, unadorned, "on coverlets dyed by the Sidonian shell-fish[,]/ ...and set[ting] her neck/ leaning on soft feathers as if she would feel them" (H.X.55) make him look rather silly (Berger, 32–33).

Nevertheless, unlike Narcissus, Pygmalion doesn't suffer as a result of his laughable passion—quite the opposite. And his successful attempt at virtually womanless procreation echoes an earlier one, accomplished by no less a personage than the king of the gods. In "The Birth of Bacchus," upon the death of Semele, "Her baby, still not fully formed, was snatched from his mother's/ womb and the delicate child was sewn (if it is to be believed)/ into his father's thigh to complete his mother's term" (III.105). Granted, a woman is needed for conception, and others for nursing, but Father is able to perform the defining maternal function: giving birth.

Immediately afterward comes "Tiresias," a brief story that, to some extent,

---

[33] *Sparagmos*, the tearing apart of the body, is likewise the punishment for Actaeon (explicitly alluded to by Pentheus [III.721–22]), who intrudes upon Diana bathing with her nymphs (III.138–252), and for Orpheus, who spurns the love of women.

expresses attraction to gender fluidity. Yet following "The Birth of Bacchus," it reads as another male appropriation of female experience. Not only does Tiresias start and finish his adventure male, he also enlists his female experience in the service of men against women: asked to arbitrate a dispute between Jove and Juno over whether women or men enjoy greater pleasure in love—Jove says women, Juno men—Tiresias, who "had known both Venuses,... confirmed the words of Jove; Saturnia, they say, was upset/ more seriously than was fair and out of proportion to the issue, and/ she condemned the eyes of their judge to eternal night." As partial compensation, "the almighty father"—perhaps an ironic appellation here, given that, like his fellow divinities, Jove is unable "to nullify the actions of a god"—grants Tiresias the gift of prophecy (H.III.105).[34]

Both the scenario and its outcome are misogynist. A man is made the uniquely qualified authority on the sexes; the question posed is loaded only for women (since dominant ideology in the ancient world was profoundly ambivalent about female sexual desire, regarded as perilous because always potentially excessive); his judgment insults respectable women; and Juno's response makes them look humorless, hypocritical, and vengeful.[35]

Nonetheless, safeguarded by this misogynist narrative, and by the reassuring foreknowledge that Tiresias will end up unambiguously male, readers are free to imagine gender fluidity as enjoyable. Tiresias's seven years as woman are an unnarrated blank for the reader to fill in any way he—and I do mean *he*—chooses (whatever the actual sex of Ovid's readers, "Tiresias" expects them to adopt a male point of view). The sex-changes are presented as valuable, for they give Tiresias knowledge no other man possesses: knowledge of Woman *from the inside*. To get inside a woman through sexual penetration is to know her only from the outside. No matter how often men penetrate women, they never apprehend their experience. Tiresias, by becoming a woman, gains this mysterious, unattainable knowledge. He pays for it: Juno blinds him. But Jupiter "allowed him to know the future,/ in place of his eyesight now removed" (III.105), as if confirming or extending Tiresias's already acquired comprehension of the unknown.[36]

---

[34] For a brief, but astute, analysis of the tale, see Hirschfeld; the article itself explores the relevance of "Tiresias" to a crucial text for the study of early modern crossdressing and female same-sex sexuality: Middleton and Dekker's *The Roaring Girl* (1611). For several versions of the Tiresias myth, see Brisson.

[35] On Roman male views of female sexuality, see Sharrock (1991), who highlights contradictions between respectable and racy Roman sexual discourse (172), and Joshel.

[36] As mentioned above, Actaeon's forbidden knowledge of Woman—his glimpse of Diana and nymphs bathing—results in his violent death. Jupiter, however, intrudes upon this chaste female community and emerges unscathed. In "Callisto" (II.409–530), his passion kindled for Diana's favorite nymph (who goes unnamed in the poem), Jupiter disguises himself as Diana, joins Callisto when she's alone, and rapes her. Once sated, he leaves her (and the baby she eventually bears) to suffer all the repercussions of his act. On how, in Ovid's version and early modern dramatic, operatic, and graphic renditions, this story both

In contrast, Book IV presents a nightmare (although still comic) vision of sex-change: "Salmacis and Hermaphroditus." The story purports to explain "Why Salmacis is thought ill of, how the evil strength of its waters enfeebles and softens the limbs they touch (H.IV.139). Hermaphroditus, the son of Hermes and Aphrodite, comes upon "a pond of water/ gleaming all the way to the bottom" (IV.141). The nymph who inhabits the pool, Salmacis, "saw the boy and, on seeing him, she wanted to possess him" (IV.141). She woos the innocent youth, "endlessly demanding sisterly kisses/ at least" and is "already putting her hands on his ivory-coloured neck" (IV.143), but he rebuffs her. Pretending to leave, she hides in a nearby thicket and watches as the youth disrobes and dives into the pool. Salmacis then pounces:

> "I have won, and he is mine," cried out the Naiad, and she threw
> all her clothing well away from her and rushed into the middle of the waters
> and held him as he fought against her, violently snatching kisses
> and bringing her hands up under him and touching his unwilling breast;
> and now she draped herself around the youth this way and that. (IV.143)

Hermaphroditus resists, but to no avail. Wrapped around him, the nymph prays to the gods:

> "...Oh gods may you so order it, and let
> no day take him away from me or me from him."
> Her prayers were granted by the gods: for their two bodies
> were mingled and joined, and they put on the appearance
> of one...
> so, when their bodies had come together in a clinging embrace,
> they were not two, but they had a dual form that could be said to be
> neither woman nor boy, they seemed to be neither and both.... (IV.144–45)

The youth then utters a prayer of his own:

> [W]hen he saw that the transparent waters, to which he had gone down
> a man, had made him a half-male, and that his limbs had been made soft
> in them, Hermaphroditus stretched out his hands and said,
> but no longer with a man's voice, "Grant your son a favour,
> oh father and mother too, for my name comes from both of you:
> whoever comes into this spring a man, let him come out from here
> a half-man, softened immediately he touches the waters."

---

skirts and inspires consideration of lesbianism, see Heller, ch.5; Simons; Traub (2002); and Robinson (1998) 29–37. See also Mack, Raval, Richlin (1992b), and Johnson, who discusses two Ovidian versions, one in the *Metamorphoses*, the other in the *Fasti* (2.153–92), arguing that they comment upon rather than merely reproduce the ideology of rape.

Both his parents were moved and fulfilled the words of their two-formed
son by infecting the spring with an unholy drug. (IV.145)[37]

The thematic concerns of this story, like its characters at the end, are two-fold and interconnected: excessive female sexual desire, and effeminacy, the former causing the latter. So extremely out of control is Salmacis, "in her madness" (H.IV.143) she rapes—or tries to rape—the object of her desire. As Richlin (1992b) remarks, "Other women in the *Metamorphoses* pursue men out of excessive desire (the maenads, Byblis, Myrrha, Circe), never with good results. But here the poet experiments with a female who has all the trappings of the most forceful rapist, and the interchange of roles here results in a permanent and threatening confusion of gender.... [W]hen a female acts male, the result is the unmanning of all men, and the narrative makes it clear that this is a bad thing" (166). A comparison with "Caenis/Caeneus" is useful: Caenis's unwomanly attempt to withhold herself from penetration is not nearly as threatening as Salmacis's attempt to become a penetrator herself. Caenis's transgression results in suffering for herself alone, immediately followed by the highest possible reward: elevation to the pinnacle of manhood. Salmacis's transgression harms Hermaphroditus and untold numbers of future men, effeminizing every man the nymph/fountain touches.[38]

Aggressive female sexuality isn't the only threat to masculinity here, however. As a beautiful youth, an *ephebe*, Hermaphroditus both embodies endangered masculinity and endangers the masculinity of men who desire him. His sex/gender is uncertain long before fusion with Salmacis, as indicated from this first description: "his was a face in which both mother and father/ could be recognized" (H.IV.140–41). As Anderson argues, although "it might seem that the narrator merely indicates that the boy resembles both his divine mother and father[,...] she is probably referring to that special age of adolescents when, to poet and lover, it was hard to decide whether they were male or female" ([1972] 444).[39] As discussed above, the desirability of such androgynous youths was profoundly

---

[37] For background on the myth and/or ancient treatment of actual hermaphrodites, see Brisson, Shane Butler, and Delcourt. Brisson, interestingly, interprets Ovid's version as an attempt "to explain the origin of passive homosexuality" (42), primarily on the basis of the terms *mollis* and, to a lesser extent, *impudicus* (166–67, n.18). See also M. Robinson's analysis of Ovid's version.

[38] On the terms Ovid uses to indicate hermaphroditism and/or effeminacy (including, among others, *semimarem, semivir, forma duplex, biformis*), see Anderson (1972) 443, 453–56. Salmacis possibly harms herself, too: she seems to disappear as a subject once her prayer has been granted.

[39] Anderson adds, "Ovid has already described the 'virginal appearance' of young Bacchus at 3.607 and the sexual ambiguity of Narcissus (a closer prototype for Hermaphroditus) at 3.351 ff. Later, he will make much of the *facies* of Atalanta (8.322–23) and Iphis (9.712–13) that indicates sexual uncertainty" (444). It's no accident all these characters' stories focus upon challenges to the dominant Roman sex/gender/sexuality system.

troubling to dominant Greek and especially Roman ideologies of sex, gender, and sexuality. Accordingly, "Salmacis and Hermaphroditus" both revels in and recoils from this desirability. When Hermaphroditus disrobes and dives in the pool, the narrative rapidly shifts our attention back and forth between the sight of his "delicate," "naked," "gleam[ing] body" and Salmacis's mounting excitement as she ogles it (IV.143). Reading the passage, men are incited both to participate in the nymph's lustful voyeurism—to imagine with pleasure the undescribed bodily details driving her wild—and to disavow and reject it as the improper lustfulness of one or more bad women (Salmacis and/or Alcithoe, the tale's impious narrator, soon to be transformed into a bat). Masculinity remains threatened, but from without rather than within.[40]

Not that the story is all horror. Quite the contrary, since for all her sexual aggressiveness Salmacis is a *failed* rapist. The best she can do, unaided by the gods, is *circumfunditur* (360), a verb that, as Anderson notes, "reminds us that Salmacis, both water and nymph, can 'pour around' [Hermaphroditus] all by herself" ([1972] 450). But entwining and surrounding are not penetrating. Her desire is impossible for the same reason as Iphis's love for Ianthe: she lacks a penis. Salmacis is masculine, but not phallic.[41]

Indeed, the tale's lack of a phallus—the beautiful Hermaphroditus, unable to fight off the sexual advances of a mere maiden, is hardly more phallic than his attacker—is probably its strongest point of contrast with "Tiresias," oversupplied with phalli. (It's also the point that will return us at last to "Iphis and Ianthe.") Tiresias's sex-changes are accomplished through the conjunction of three phallic symbols:

For while the bodies of two great serpents had been coupling
in the green wood, he had abused them with his staff,
and from a man, he was made (amazingly) into a woman and spent
seven autumns so; in the eighth, he saw the same creatures
again and said, "If the power of a blow on you is
so great that it changes the lot of its perpetrator into its opposite,

---

[40] For a cogently argued psychoanalytic reading of "Salmacis and Hermaphroditus" that accords closely with my own, see Nugent. The tale's many echoes of "Narcissus" (Anderson [1972] 441, 444–46, 448) strengthen my conviction that it's both anxious about boy-loving and anxious to conceal this anxiety. Note also the story's two suggestions of incest (IV.323–24, 334).

[41] Indeed, the verb *circumfunditur* is in the passive voice. Granted, Salmacis wrapped around Hermaphroditus is likened to "a snake picked up by the king of birds/ and snatched aloft (as she hangs from him she binds his head/ and feet and entwines her tail around his spreading wings" (H.IV.143). But the point of the description, as of the entire story, is inversion. What ought to be feminine is masculine, she who ought to be victim is victimizer. Or worse, supposed opposites become indistinguishable: masculine Salmacis can just as easily be read as hyperfeminine ("femme-femme," in Viarre's phrase [237]). For a much more positive reading of "Salmacis and Hermaphroditus," see Bate.

I shall hit you now too." And when he had struck these same snakes,
his earlier form returned and his natural appearance came back. (H.III.105)

Many interpretations of this scene are possible. But in light of what precedes it ("The Birth of Bacchus," in which a male gives birth), it easily reads as a fantasy demonstration of the magical powers of the penis and the superfluity of the female: two copulating penises give birth, upon contact with a third (the staff), to a being paradoxically possessed of gender fluidity and yet still male (even as a woman Tiresias has a staff); none of this being's experiences as female are related, except his/her transformation back into a man, by means of the same copulating penises. The moral of the story might be, "Anything a vagina can do a penis can do better."[42]

Of course, snakes in general, and these snakes in particular, may well have had quite different associations for Ovid and his readers (cf. Brisson). Yet even if one rejects this reading of "Tiresias," the story with which we started and to which, as just promised, I now return, is clearly a story about penis power. The unmistakable focal point of "Iphis and Ianthe" is the penis Iphis lacks and eventually gains. This penis is never directly spoken of, not even at the moment of Iphis's transformation from girl to boy:

> The Mother... returnes from *Isis* shrine.
> Whom *Iphis* followes with a larger pace
> Then usuall; nor had so white a face.
> Her strength augments; her looke more bold appeares;
> Her shortning curles scarce hang beneath her eares;
> By farre more full of courage, rapt with joy:
> For thou, of late a Wench, art now a Boy. (S422)

Anderson instructs us to "Note how Ovid delicately slides over the chief change by which Iphis became a man ready for marriage," contrasting this Ovidian delicacy with an earlier rendering of the scene: "Nicander was only interested in the miraculous new genitals" ([1972] 473). But delicate sliding notwithstanding, Ovid's version is no less genitalia-obsessed. The longer stride, the darker hue, the greater strength, the shorter hair all serve as unmistakable signs of the all-important change that has occurred in Iphis's breeches (or the Cretan equivalent), the only change that could fit her for marriage to Ianthe.[43]

---

[42] A complementary, Freudian reading of "Tiresias" would follow the "technical rule" that, as Nugent remarks, "Freud applied to his own analysis of Medusa's snaky hair, 'according to which a multiplication of penis symbols signifies castration'" (182, n.7, quoting Freud, "Medusa's Head" [1922], *Sexuality and the Psychology of Love,* tr. Strachey, ed. Rieff [Collier, 1963] 212).

[43] Indeed, earlier (IX.742–43) the text prompts readers to imagine not only actual penises but also fake ones: dildos (Pintabone, 267). In fact, the story as a whole, if not this

As we saw in chapter five, this elaborate, urbane, tongue-in-cheek indirection, in which dirtiness naughtily masquerades as delicacy, was to become, like the tropes of invention and newness, a staple of Western homophobic discourse. With its highly self-conscious, self-congratulatory knowingness—"You and I, dear Reader, don't need these things spelled out. Besides, it's so much more fun to be faux naive!"—mock ignorance or innocence is a particularly wily finish for a story premised upon and dedicated to *not* facing facts, to preserving and constructing ignorance, to *unknowing*.

By simultaneously mocking and unknowing lesbianism, by treating it as both a joke and an impossibility, "Iphis and Ianthe" does its part to seal over the faultlines in the conservative sex/gender/sexuality ideology producing and produced by the *Metamorphoses*. "Narcissus" and "Orpheus" do the same, by mocking and unkowing same-age male homosexuality (replaced by boy-loving, through ideological sleight-of-hand, as the only form of homosexuality). In other words (to finally answer the question posed earlier), it is *precisely because* they're so threatening that lesbianism and same-age male homosexuality are treated lightly by Ovid, so lightly they seem not even to exist, or to exist only as impossible desire. For if lesbianism is possible, if it is true, if it is real, then it erases, displaces, dethrones the phallus; if same-age male homosexuality is possible, if it is true, if it is real, it turns the phallus into simply a penis, an organ that no longer functions symbolically, neither conferring power upon its possessor nor subordinating those with whom its possessor has sex. Even to acknowledge such threats is to give them power, to show that our account of the way things are is really an account of the way things ought to be, barely a step away from the way *we* think things ought to be, by which point the towering Absolute has shrunk to the merely Relative, just an opinion, with no greater claim to authority than anyone else's. Better far to unknow such threats; after all, what we don't know can't hurt us.[44]

"Iphis and Ianthe": The Untold Stories

And yet, to stress only the conservative aspects of this tale, and of the others with which it is interwoven, is to miss the complexity, the intricacy, of its ideological labors—its mix of acknowledgment and avoidance, transgression and tradition—which proved so fascinating to subsequent writers, and so conducive to dramatically different reimaginings. Pintabone alerts us to this complexity when

---

specific line, led at least one medieval reader to consider such a possibility (Blumenfeld-Kosinski, 318). Interestingly, Nicander's version of "Iphis and Ianthe," in his *On Changes of Shape* (*Heteroioumena*), didn't include the lesbian love element, which seems to be Ovid's own invention (Anderson [1972], 464–65). For more on the Nicander version, see Raval. Like Anderson, Raval argues for Ovid's lack of concern with Iphis's anatomy.

[44] See Montaigne's essay, "Of the Force of the Imagination."

she underscores the contrast between Iphis and women like Byblis, Myrrha, and Salmacis:

> Ovid's pattern of destroying female aggressors is most pertinent to our Iphis: she differs greatly from these other women who express sexual desire because Iphis simply does nothing.... Passive, she ultimately leaves the whole matter to her mother and to the goddess Isis. By making her passive, Ovid breaks with the notion posited in Roman literature (cf. Hallett's and Brooten's analyses...) that women erotically attracted to women are very aggressive pursuers of their desires. (274–75)

Indeed, as Pintabone then argues, the situation is even more surprising, even more complex:

> In Ovid's story of Iphis and Ianthe, gender is framed in terms of cultural stereotypes that are first shown, then overturned, and then reaffirmed. Ovid's Iphis is raised as a male but thinks and acts, in Roman terms, like a female: although she recognizes her own biological sex (female) and her sexual desire for a woman (which is seen as essentially male in Roman thought), she remains passive (which is seen as essentially female in Roman thought) both by not acting on her desire and by expressing no preference that she be the penetrator in her relationship with Ianthe. The essentializing effect suggests that in her obedience to/acceptance of her 'female nature,' Iphis is rewarded by becoming a male. (276)

Insofar as Ovid portrays Iphis as properly feminine, notwithstanding her masculine upbringing and her sexual desire for Ianthe, he takes a tack that would most likely have surprised his readers. And yet, in the end, I find "Iphis and Ianthe" less unconventional and less approving of the two girls' love than does Pintabone, particularly when she considers the issue, raised by the tale itself, of the naturalness or unnaturalness of Iphis's desires:

> Ovid leaves ambiguous whether love came naturally [to Iphis and Ianthe] or was given by Amor [Cupid], but he suggests the former. Their love seems to be natural, mutual, and equal; Iphis maintains a female self-identification even while she is believed to be male. But consider for a moment if Ovid had written a different story: that although raised as a male, [Iphis] the woman... desires males [Pintabone offers the film *Yentl* as an illustration]. This would suggest that heterosexual sexuality was naturally occurring and arose and remained despite culturally instilled gender roles. Because in this story Iphis was socialized as a male, we might conclude that her passion for Ianthe derives from her upbringing according to male gender roles, suggesting that her passion, then, is culturally created. Yet this is contradicted by Ovid's own story, which suggests a naturally occurring love by a (self-identified) woman for a woman. (277–78)

I disagree. Ovid *does* manage to suggest that Iphis's love for Ianthe is somehow connected with being raised male. For, to use Pintabone's own excellent method of reasoning, Ovid could have written a different story: one about a young woman, raised *female*, who falls in love with her best girlfriend. In other words, he could have made "Iphis and Ianthe" more like "Byblis" and "Myrrha," with no explanation for the perverse desire felt by the female protagonist. But Ovid excludes such a possibility from his poem. Instead, he presents a doubly fantastic story, in which a girl is raised as a boy and then falls in love with a girl. And the two fantastic occurrences are related; indeed, because of their occurring in temporal sequence, the first seems to cause the second.

Or imagine another story Ovid chose not to write: about a girl raised as a boy, who becomes thoroughly and properly masculine, falls in love with a properly feminine girl, and then devises a means of sexually penetrating her (the possibility to which Ovid's Daedalus reference alludes [IX.742]), for which in the end she's punished by the gods with some awful metamorphosis. The poem unknows such possibilities, as it unknows the possibility that "normal" girls—properly feminine, and raised as such—might fall in love with other girls.[45]

Pintabone (who in the end retreats a bit from her positive take on the tale) is right about Ovid *not* masculinizing Iphis, instead presenting the two girls as almost twin-like in their similarity. But by setting this love within the girl-raised-as-boy framework, Ovid makes it a fantastic joke. He can count on his readers "knowing" (from the sort of texts discussed by Brooten, Hallett, and Boehringer) that two women can in fact feel sexual desire for each other, can even have some kind of sex, but that one of them must be masculine. The poem excludes this situation from representation (the poem's masculinized women are all man-chasers). It also excludes the possibility of love and sex between two completely feminine women. Instead, it represents "lesbianism" through an example that combines elements of each but succeeds in being neither—one that, above all, stresses impossibility.

---

[45] Or imagine yet another story Ovid didn't write: a young girl raised as a boy takes to her assigned gender so completely (even falling in love with another girl) that eventually, in order to match her psyche, her body turns male, doing so naturally rather than supernaturally. It's this unwritten story, rather than the actual one, Shilpa Raval appears to be analyzing in her Butlerian reading of "Iphis and Ianthe" as predominantly positive, even subversive. Always interesting and often enlightening (particularly when analyzing other crossdressing tales from the *Metamorphoses*), the essay nevertheless depends in the end on overstating the success of Iphis's "gender performance." For what neither that performance, nor discourse, can accomplish turns out to be the crucial requirement—a physical sex-change—miraculously performed by Isis, not Iphis.

Chapter 7

Metamorphosis and Homosexuality II: Iphis, Ianthe, and Others on the Early Modern Stage

Despite feeling that at times, without quite realizing it, Pintabone is reading "Iphis and Ianthe" resistantly, I agree wholeheartedly when she maintains that "Ovid's story of Iphis and Ianthe both overturns and affirms readers' expectations through the possibility of various, even contradictory, interpretations. Ovid makes the story open to the interpretations of others" (280). Certainly, the abundance of medieval and early modern texts inspired by "Iphis and Ianthe" and related tales bears out that assertion. Whatever Ovid may have intended, subsequent authors drew upon his stories for a variety of purposes, with a variety of results. And yet, as different as these texts are, they are also often strikingly similar, concerned with the same set of ideological flashpoints: lesbianism, male homosexuality, sex-change, crossdressing, effeminacy, aggressive female sexual desire, narcissistic desire, incest, twinning, misogyny, and patriarchal tyranny.

In this final chapter I explore three early modern dramatizations of "Iphis and Ianthe": Henry Bellamy's Latin version, *Iphis* (c.1622–32); Isaac de Benserade's French adaptation, *Iphis et Iante* (perf. 1632; pub. 1637); and Charles Hopkins's English adaptation, *Friendship Improv'd; Or, The Female Warrior* (perf. 1699; pub. 1700). But first I examine three slightly earlier plays—John Lyly's *Gallathea* (perf. 1587/1588; pub. 1592), the anonymous *The Maydes Metamorphosis* (1600), and Francis Beaumont, John Fletcher, and possibly Philip Massinger's *Love's Cure, or The Martial Maid* (wr. c.1605?; rev. c.1625–26?; pub. 1647)—which demonstrate the various, complex, and surprising uses to which Ovidian material could be put.[1]

---

[1] On the dating of Bellamy, Benserade, and Hopkins's plays, see below; of *Gallathea*, see Lyly, v–xi; of *The Maydes Metamorphosis*, see the play's title page; and on the dating and authorship of *Love's Cure*, see Duncan (398, n.10) and Beaumont and Fletcher (1976 and 1992). On a variety of seventeenth-century French translations and adaptations of "Iphis and Ianthe," in prose and poetry, in print and onstage, see Leibacher-Ouvrard (2003). I have chosen to focus on drama because of the pleasures and perils added to Ovidian material by live performance. Of course, a comprehensive examination of the afterlife of the tales would include many other written texts, as well as numerous visual representations (paintings,

"Doe you both being Maidens love one another?": Lyly's *Gallathea*

In *Gallathea*'s paganized England, the inhabitants of Lincolnshire suffer the effects of Neptune's displeasure at their insufficiently worshipful ancestors: every five years, they must sacrifice the community's most beautiful young virgin (tying her to Neptune's sacred oak, from which a monster carries her off), or else perish by flood. At the start of the play, with the day of sacrifice approaching, Tyterus sends his daughter, Gallathea, into the forest dressed as a boy, to escape the terrible fate he fears must otherwise befall her. Separately, Mellebeus does the same with his own daughter, Phillida. In the forest, the girls meet and fall in love, each believing the other to be male. They are adopted, at least temporarily, by Diana and her virgin nymphs. The latter, however, provoke Cupid's wrath by scorning the power of love. In revenge, the god disguises himself as a nymph, infiltrates Diana's band, and inflames the nymphs with love for the two young "boys." Diana, in turn, takes Cupid captive, vowing to prove chastity's superiority to amorous affection. In the meantime, as Gallathea and Phillida fall more deeply in love, the inhabitants of Lincolnshire offer up their second-best virgin. The monster rejects her. At last, Venus and Diana avert Neptune's wrath by asking him to adjudicate their dispute over Cupid. The god of love is released into Venus's custody, and the virgin sacrifice abolished. As for the crossdressed girls, whose true sex has been revealed yet whose love remains constant, Venus offers to turn one of them into a man. Over the protest of their fathers, but with the consent of Diana and Neptune, Gallathea and Phillida accept the goddess's offer. The play ends with universal celebration, as a prelude to sex-change and marriage.[2]

Over the past several years, *Gallathea* has received considerable attention for its treatment of female same-sex desire. Although the play's debt to "Iphis and Ianthe" is obvious, Lyly makes it explicit, having Venus back up her offer of a sex-change by asking, "Was it not Venus that did the same to Iphis and Ianthes …?" (53). For alert spectators and readers, though, this moment underscores the play's difference from, as much as debt to, Ovid's tale: Venus takes credit for the handiwork of Isis (cf. Dooley, 64). Even less-alert spectators would note differences: Lyly has doubled the number of crossdressed girls; each initially

---

drawings, ceramics, medals, sculpture…), and would encompass premodern, modern, and postmodern work. For a start, see especially Bate, Blumenfeld-Kosinski, Borris (2001), Bredbeck, Bruhm (2001), Burrow, Clark and Sponsler, DiGangi (1997, 2001), Ellis, Folkerth, Harley, Holsinger, Keach, Silberman, Bruce Smith (1991), Traub (2002), and Watt (2003).

[2] For several of the following points, I'm indebted to Jankowski (2000), Tvordi, Dooley, and Traub (2002). See also Bate, as well as Wixson, whose concern for "how ideologies of gender, rank, and sexuality overlap and play off of each other" (253) is valuable, although he overstates the play's presentation of Neptune's authority as absolute.

believes she's fallen in love with a boy, but soon begins to suspect he's a girl, like herself; and, unlike in Ovid's tale, the truth is revealed *before* the sex-change occurs. Even more interestingly, after only a moment or two's dismay, Gallathea and Phillida affirm their unshaken love:

> *Galla.* Unfortunate Gallathea if this be Phillida.
> *Phill.* Accursed Phillida if that be Gallathea.
> *Galla.* And wast thou all thys while enamoured of Phillida, that sweete Phillida?
> *Phill.* And couldest thou doate upon the face of a Maiden, thy selfe being one, on the face of fayre Gallathea?
> *Neptune* Doe you both being Maidens love one another?
> *Galla.* I had thought the habite agreeable with the Sexe, and so burned in the fire of mine owne fancies.
> *Phillida* I had thought that in the attyre of a boy, there could not have lodged the body of a Virgine, & so was inflamed with a sweete desire, which now I find a sower deceit.
> *Diana* Nowe things falling out as they doe, you must leave these fond fond affections, nature will have it so, necessitie must.
> *Gallathea* I will never love any but Phillida, her love is engraven in my hart, with her eyes.
> *Phillida* Nor I any but Gallathea, whose faith is imprinted in my thoughts by her words.
> *Neptune* An idle choice, strange, and foolish, for one Virgine to doate on another, and to imagine a constant faith, where there can be no cause of affection. Howe like you this Venus?
> *Venus* I like well and allowe it, they shall both be possessed of their wishes, for never shall it be said that Nature or Fortune shall over-throwe Love, and Fayth. Is your loves unspotted, begunne with trueth, continued with constancie, and not to bee altered tyll death?
> *Gallathea* Die Gallathea if thy love be not so.
> *Phillida* Accursed bee thou Phillida if thy love be not so. (52–53)

Despite Diana and Neptune's objections—appeals to 'nature' and 'necessitie,' and epithets such as 'fond,' 'idle,' 'strange,' 'foolish'—Gallathea and Phillida remain steadfast in their love. Most interesting of all, the play concludes with neither metamorphosis nor marriage having yet taken place.

It's as if Lyly cannot bear to differentiate his twin-like heroines (he even has Venus refuse to specify which of the two will be turned male). Relying upon and reinforcing what Laurie Shannon has dubbed "Renaissance homo-normativity"— "an almost philosophical preference for likeness or a structure of thinking based on resemblance" ([2000] 191–92), including the celebration of equality, similitude, and even sameness as the foundation of an eroticized friendship, one that offered an alternative model of pair-bonding to hierarchal, heterosexual coupling—Lyly makes Gallathea and Phillida virtually indistinguishable in every way: physical sex, gender, age, social station, upbringing, attire, speech, feeling, and predicament.[3]

This near-sameness helps bring out the *male* homoerotic potential of "Iphis and Ianthe" as well, which in Ovid's version only emerged through links with "Orpheus," "Narcissus," and related tales. In *Gallathea*, the heroines spend almost the entire play dressed as boys. And though, as we've seen, when their true sex is revealed, each "girl" remarks upon the clash between appearance and reality, attire and sex, the audience for this performance by the boy actors of St. Paul's Cathedral knew it was watching two boys, dressed as boys, exchange words of love.[4]

Two other aspects of *Gallathea* deserve mention: Lyly includes a passing reference to father-daughter incest (36), and, more significantly, while altering Ovid's family dynamics, he continues the theme of patriarchal tyranny. Unlike Ovid's Ligdus, who plans to sacrifice his own daughter, *Gallathea*'s Tyterus and Mellebeus disobey a patriarchal god and imperil their country to protect their daughters, in rather maternal fashion. Yet as in "Iphis and Ianthe," the legitimacy or illegitimacy of father-figures' behavior is difficult to gauge. The rights of a monarch to obedience conflict with the duties of a father to protect his children. Perhaps in deference to the female monarch in the audience, Lyly lets matriarchal rather than patriarchal authority triumph. Yet such flattery is not unmixed with criticism, irony, or at least ambiguity. In the end, when the play's only mother, Venus, takes charge in support of the loving female couple (53–54), the two human fathers look foolish, while both Neptune and the virginal Diana seem docile.[5]

"Doth kind allow a man to love a man?": Friendship, Love, and *The Maydes Metamorphosis*[6]

While equally Ovidian in its inspiration, *The Maydes Metamorphosis* draws upon different tales than does *Gallathea*. It opens with a maiden named Eurymine led into the woods by two male friends. The ruling Duke, they reveal, has ordered

---

[3] See also Shannon's excellent book (2002), as well as Traub (2002) ch.8; the latter offers a fascinating, if reductive, analysis of the foundational influence of "the rhetoric of erotic similitude in Renaissance literature" (330) on the modern conceptualization of lesbianism and especially on lesbian historiographic practice.

[4] Jankowski (24) explicates the play's multiple, shifting, uncertain erotic possibilities particularly well. As for the sex/gender/sexuality implications of crossdressing on the early modern stage, by actors or characters, some of the many useful titles (through which many earlier titles can be traced) include Barbour, Bly, Steve Brown, Callaghan, DiGangi (1997), Dollimore, Forker, Franceschina, Garber, Greenblatt, Howard, Jardine, Levine, Jo Miller, Orgel (1996b), Radel, Sedinger, Michael Shapiro, Bruce Smith (1991, 1992), Peter Smith, Solomon, Stallybrass, Traub (1992a, 2002), Vélez-Quiñonez, and Zimmerman.

[5] How this might have struck Elizabeth (who might have identified with Diana, Venus, and/or Neptune) is a complex question. See Tvordi for a start, as well as Traub (2002).

[6] The play is divided into acts but not scenes; citations refer to act and line numbers.

them to kill her, because his son, Prince Ascanio, loves her, despite her low birth. After persuading the reluctant executioners to let her escape, Eurymine sets up house in a woodland cottage, with the assistance of a forester and shepherd. Meanwhile, Ascanio and his page Joculo enter the forest to find her. Unbeknownst to them, however, Apollo has also fallen for Eurymine. In a variation on Ovid's "Caenis/Caeneus," she spurns his advances, he threatens to use force, she requests a single wish, and he agrees to grant it. Her wish is to be transformed into a man. Grudgingly, Apollo keeps his word, then allows Eurymine, now male, to continue on his way. Elsewhere in the forest, Ascanio and Joculo seek help from a fortune-telling old wise man, Aramanthus, "Sometime... a Prince of *Lesbos* Ile" (IV.73), but now a recluse, betrayed and exiled by his own brother years before. Aramanthus divines the change Eurymine has undergone, but recounts his discovery in terms that leave Ascanio confused. Back at the cottage, the forester and shepherd come knocking, to learn which of them Eurymine loves. To their surprise, they find a beautiful young man, whom they assume to be a rival, yet who claims to be Eurymine's brother. Doubtful, they take him to Aramanthus for answers. On the way, Ascanio catches up with Eurymine, and after some trouble understanding what has happened, decides to follow Aramanthus's advice and ask Apollo to make her a maiden once more. With the help of several Muses, the prince persuades the god to grant this second petition. In a burst of further generosity, Apollo allows Aramanthus to come live with him, promises him immortality, and reveals that Eurymine is Aramanthus's long-lost daughter, Atlanta. The necessary differences of sex and birth now respectively restored and removed, Ascanio and Eurymine embrace in anticipation of their marriage, and the play ends with a joyful song and dance.

Although modeled on "Caenis/Caeneus," *The Maydes Metamorphosis* follows "Iphis and Ianthe" in foregrounding the trope of impossible love, but in regard to male homosexuality, not female. Thus, after changing Eurymine's sex, Apollo declares:

> And though thou walke in chaunged bodie now,
> This pennance shall be added to thy vow:
> Thy selfe a man, shalt love a man, in vaine:
> And loving, wish to be a maide againe.

To which Eurymine replies:

> *Appollo*, whether I love a man or not,
> I thanke ye, now I will accept my lot:
> And sith my chaunge hath disappointed you,
> Ye are at libertie to love anew. (III.32–36)

The paired assumptions upon which the success of Eurymine's escape plan depend—that the sexually aggressive god will not desire a male victim, and that, besides, men cannot be raped—are borrowed directly from "Caenis/Caeneus."

Yet here they strain credibility even more than in the *Metamorphoses*, precisely because the play relies so explicitly upon Ovid's poem. For Apollo, appearing mysteriously sad in the previous scene (cf. Antonio in *The Merchant of Venice*), had explained his mood as grief occasioned by the anniversary of the death of his beloved Hyacinth:

> This time of yeare, or there about it was,
> Accursed be the time, tenne times alas:
> When I from *Delphos* tooke my journey downe,
> To see the games in noble *Sparta* Towne,
> There saw I that, wherein I gan to joy,
> *Amilchars* sonne a gallant comely boy,
> Hight (*Hiacinth*) full fifteene yeares of age,
> Whom I intended to have made my Page,
> And bare as great affection to the boy,
> As ever *Jove*, in *Ganimede* did joy. (III.51–60)

Having linked his own famous episode of boy-loving with Jupiter's—a link, as we've seen, made by Ovid, too—Apollo then recounts how "[his] lovely boy was slaine" (70).

As it turns out, he's lying: love for Eurymine, not Hyacinth—love for a girl, not a boy—explains his mood. Yet having reminded the audience that adult males can fall for beautiful teenage boys, and that Apollo himself had done so in the past, does the playwright truly expect the audience to accept as unproblematic, as self-evident, the impossibility of Apollo continuing to love or lust after the sex-changed Eurymine? And does the author, or his text, continue in that expectation even after forester and shepherd exclaim, on finding a beautiful young man opening Eurymine's door, "It is *Adonis*" and "It is *Ganymede*" (IV.265–66)?[7]

Apparently so, for the play soon echoes "Iphis and Ianthe," as first Aramanthus, then Ascanio, then Eurymine assert the unnaturalness, impossibility, and insanity of erotic love between men, emphasizing its violation of 'kind,' which meant, among other things, "Nature in general, or in the abstract, regarded as the established order or regular course of things," as well as 'gender' or 'sex' (*OED*). The subject is broached explicitly when Aramanthus, having divined Eurymine's metamorphosis, informs Ascanio, "By proofe of learned principles I finde,/ The manner of your love's against all kinde./ And not to feed ye with uncertaine joy,/ Whom you affect so much, is but a Boy" (IV.143–46). Confronted with this wholly unexpected news, Ascanio bewails his predicament in a manner that recalls Iphis's lament:

---

[7] Cf. Stanivukovic (190, n.40) for a 1633 example of both 'Adonis' and 'Ganymede' as synonyms for 'catamite.'

Asca. I love a Boy?
   Ara. Mine Art doth tell me so.
   Asca. Adde not a fresh increase unto my woe…
As well I might be said to touch the skie,
Or darke the horizon with tapestrie:
Or walke upon the waters of the sea,
As to be haunted with such lunacie. (149–57)

A moment later, Joculo assures his master that Eurymine must simply have changed clothing. Ascanio then pursues his beloved to ask why she flees. In an exchange overflowing with polyptoton, punning, and ploce[8] involving the words 'habit,' 'guise,' 'fancy,' 'strange,' 'change,' 'alter,' 'man,' 'woman,' 'friend,' 'mind,' and, to an extravagant degree, 'kind,' Ascanio asks why a costume change should change Eurymine's affections. Her explanation: their love is now impossible.

   Asca. Eurymine, I pray if thou be shee,
Refraine thy haste, and doo not flie from mee.
The time hath bene my words thou wouldst allow,
And am I growne so loathsome to thee now?
   Eu. Ascanio, time hath bene I must confesse,
When in thy presence was my happinesse:
But now the manner of my miserie,
Hath chaung'd that course, that so it cannot be.
   Asca. What wrong have I contrived? what injurie
To alienate thy liking so from me?
If thou be she whom sometime thou didst faine,
And bearest not the name of friend in vaine,
Let not thy borrowed guise of altred kinde,
Alter the wonted liking of thy minde:
But though in habit of a man thou goest,
Yet be the same *Eurymine* thou wast.
   Eu. How gladly would I be thy Lady still,
If earnest vowes might answere to my will?
   Asca. And is thy fancie alterd with thy guise?
   Eu. My kinde, but not my minde in any wise.
   Asca. What though thy habit differ from thy kind:
Thou maiest retain thy wonted loving mind.
   Eu. And so I doo.
   Asca. Then why art thou so straunge?
Or wherefore doth thy plighted fancie chaunge?
   Eu. Ascanio, my heart doth honor thee.

---

[8] Polyptoton is "repetition of the same root word with different grammatical inflections"; ploce is "a general term used to cover all cases of insistent repetition that fall into no set patterns" (Adams, 115, 116).

> *Asc.* And yet continuest stil so strange to me?
> *Eu.* Not strange, so far as kind wil give me leave.
> *Asca.* Unkind that kind, that kindnesse doth bereave:
> Thou saist thou lovest me.
> *Eu.* As a friend his friend:
> And so I vowe to love thee to the end.
> *Asca.* I wreake not of such love, love me but so
> As faire *Eurymine* lov'd *Ascanio*.
> *Eu.* That love's denide unto my present kinde.
> *Asca.* In kindly shewes, unkinde I doo thee finde:
> I see thou art as constant as the winde.
> *Eu.* Doth kind allow a man to love a man?
> *Asca.* Why art not thou *Eurymine*?
> *Eu.* I am.
> *Asca.* *Eurymine* my Love?
> *Eu.* The very same.
> *Asca.* And wast not thou a woman then?
> *Eu.* Most true.
> *As.* And art thou changed from a woman now?
> *Eu.* Too true.
> *Asc.* These tales my mind perplex: thou art *Eurymine*.
> *Eu.* In name, but not in sexe.
> *Asca.* What then?
> *Eu.* A man.
> *Asca.* In guise thou art I see.
> *Eu.* The guise thou seest, doth with my kinde agree.
> *Asca.* Before thy flight thou wast a woman tho.
> *Eu.* True *Ascanio*.
> *Asca.* And since art thou a man?
> *Eu.* Too true deare friend.
> *Asca.* Then have I lost a wife.
> *Eu.* But found a friend, whose dearest blood and life,
> Shalbe as readie as thine owne for thee:
> In place of wife, such friend thou hast of mee. (V.1–60)

Ostensibly, the cause of Ascanio's confusion is simple: he believes Eurymine merely to have changed clothing, not sex. But the mystery the passage worries and wrestles with is the mystery of sex and its relation to identity. Are they a matter of kind or mind, form or fancy, body or brain? If Eurymine is still Eurymine, if she still loves Ascanio, if she has not changed her mind, then why should their love now be impossible? For if the heart, the mind, the spirit constitute identity ("Why art not thou *Eurymine*?" "I am." "*Eurymine* my Love?" "The very same"), then is not the body merely a form of clothing, an outward *guise*?

As Ascanio circles confusedly round and round the same track, he, and through him the play, seems, perhaps unconsciously, on the verge of asking such questions. Instead, though, after Eurymine's initial "it cannot be," she, and through her the play, reiterates the reply that seemingly brooks no argument: Nature, the body, sex; *kind, kind, kind*. Until at last, when for the umpteenth time Ascanio charges her with inconstancy, Eurymine asks the all-important question: "Doth kind allow a man to love a man?" It's an ambiguous question: 'kind' refers to Nature and the body, and thus to physical possibility or impossibility, while 'allow' (like the earlier 'deny') alludes to human law, to permission and prohibition; as for 'love,' its possible meanings ran the gamut from sexual to nonsexual, and everything in-between (as they do today). Significantly, no one answers the question directly. Instead, it seems to clear the cobwebs from Ascanio's brain. With a rapid-fire series of short questions and answers, he learns the truth: Eurymine *was* a woman but is *now* a man.

At this point, Joculo and Aramanthus catch up and ask Ascanio how things are going. Having come round to Eurymine's way of thinking, he replies:

Both good and bad, as doth the sequell prove,
For (wretched) I have found, and lost my Love.
If that be lost which I can nere enjoy. (V.72–74)

Like Iphis, Ascanio despairs of being able to 'enjoy,' to derive not only pleasure in general but sexual pleasure in particular from a same-sex love. In a reverse of Iphis's trajectory, Ascanio has "lost a wife... But found a friend."

Indeed, the point of the passage would seem to be to clarify the distinction between those two terms by disambiguating the word 'friend.' For early in the exchange, Ascanio had pleaded with his beloved to "be the same *Eurymine* thou wast," that is, "If thou be she whom sometime thou didst faine,/ And bearest not the name of friend in vaine." At that moment, "friend" still meant any and all of the people we would now term 'friend,' 'lover,' or 'spouse.' But moments later the characters restrict the term's meaning:

Asca. ...Thou saist thou lovest me.
Eu. As a friend his friend:
And so I vowe to love thee to the end.
Asca. I wreake not of such love, love me but so
As faire *Eurymine* lov'd *Ascanio*.
Eu. That love's denide unto my present kinde.

Love between same-sex friends now contrasts with love between man and woman. Ascanio therefore finds no comfort in Eurymine's repeated insistence that he's at least "found a friend"; as he repeatedly replies, he's "lost a wife," "lost [his] Love."

And yet, it's unclear whether the possibility of sex between men is being wholly unknown here. For when Ascanio rejects the love of friend for friend as something he "wreacke[s] not of," he is calling it something he cares little for, has little interest in or inclination toward. Perhaps, then, he raises an issue akin to what we'd call sexual orientation or preference. Perhaps, as Eurymine alludes to the *unlawfulness* of sex between men (through words like 'allow' and 'deny'), Ascanio communicates his *distaste* for it. Let other men have their "friends," he wants a woman—perhaps even, more specifically, a wife.

The lines that follow continue to support either interpretation, as Joculo and Aramanthus respond to Ascanio's news, Joculo still believing Eurymine to have merely changed clothing:

> *Jo*. Faith Mistresse y'are too blame to be so coy.
> The day hath bene, but what is that to mee:
> When more familiar with a man you'ld bee.
>   *Ara*. I told ye you should finde a man of her:
> Or else my rule did very straungely erre.
>   *Asca*. Father, the triall of your skill I finde,
> My Love's transformde into another kinde:
> And so I finde, and yet have lost my Love.
>   *Jo*. Ye cannot tell, take her aside and prove. (V.75–83)

Again, the most obvious meaning accords with the Ovidian source and its approach to most homosexuality: because Ascanio's beloved has undergone a sex-change ("My Love's transformde into another kinde"), the prince has found his lover only to lose her as such ("And so I finde, and yet have lost my Love"). But like Eurymine's sex, Ascanio's words refuse to limit themselves to this meaning or that, one thing or another. Behind his despairing encapsulation of the situation, we can hear echoes of other possibilities: his feelings and desires could be transformed from one kind into another. And if he heeds an alternate, seemingly unintended meaning of Joculo's suggestion to "take her aside and prove," Ascanio might not only *prove* Eurymine's sex male or female, but also prove, as in *test*, the truth of the assumption that sex between men is impossible.

Unlike *The Maydes Metamorphosis*, *Gallathea* raises the possibility of precisely such same-sex experimentation, particularly when Phillida says to her beloved, "Come let us into the Grove, and make much one of another, that cannot tel what to think one of another" (III.ii). Although, in subsequent scenes, the girls still seem unsure of each other's sex, the audience is invited to imagine what they did in the forest alone together. *The Maydes Metamorphosis* proffers no such invitation. Instead, the characters hurry off to have Apollo reverse Eurymine's sex-change, thereby banishing all mystery and confusion, putting things back in natural order.

If the play ended there, with the reverse sex-change accomplished (reminiscent of Ovid's "Tiresias," already recalled in the figure of Aramanthus), I'd conclude that notwithstanding its explicit evocation of male-male desire (Apollo and Hyacinthus; Jupiter and Ganymede) *The Maydes Metamorphosis* is, unlike *Gallathea*, uninterested in exploring the possibility, let alone desirability, of same-sex love. But the play closes with a song that begins:

> *Since painfull sorrowes date hath end,*
> *And time hath coupled friend with friend:*
> *Rejoyce we all, rejoyce and sing,*
> *Let all these groaves of* Phoebus *ring.* (V.364–71)

After having disambiguated the term 'friend,' the play ends by *re*ambiguating it, leaving me (and perhaps some of the original audience) to wonder: Does the play mean to suggest same-sex "friends" can "couple" too?

I find the question difficult, perhaps impossible, to answer. Hardly a well-constructed drama, *The Maydes Metamorphosis* easily reads as sloppily contradictory. And compared to *Gallathea*, with its extended treatment of love and desire between two females, both of whom remain female to the very end, *The Maydes Metamorphosis* seems tame and unimaginative. Rather than allow sex-changing or crossdressing to multiply erotic possibilities, its plot hinges upon heterosexist, either/or conventions: if Eurymine is female, Apollo and Ascanio can desire her; if she is male, they cannot. And yet, the homoerotic references are too numerous (Lesbos, Ganymede, Adonis) and too explicit and extended (Apollo's affair with Hyacinthus) for the play to be plausibly read as unaware of lust between men.

Such unconsciousness seems even less plausible in the context of English Renaissance Ovidiana. Consider, for instance, Lewes Machin's "Apollo and Hyacinth," comprising the second two of "Three Eglogs" appended to William Barksted's poem "Mirrha The Mother of Adonis: Or, Lustes Prodegies" (1607). Following "Menalcas and Daphnis," Machin's unabashedly erotic poem of opposite-sex dalliance, his two-part story of same-sex love includes the following:

> So hand in hand, they sat them on the ground,
> Where little birds did make harmonious sound,
> But *Phebus* heart did pant and leape with joy,
> When he beheld that sweete delicious boy.
> His eyes did sparkle, love his heart flamde fire,
> To see this sweete boy smile, is his desire.
> Then with an ardent gripe his hand he crusht,
> and then he kist him, and the boy then blusht,
> That blushing coulour, so became his face
> That *Phebus* kist againe, and thought it grace
> To touch his lips, such pleasure *Phebus* felt,
> That in an amarous deaw his heart did melt.
> and thus he dallied with his amorous kisses,
> Forgetting of the world, that his light misses. (sigs. E5v–E6r)

Although this activity is then referred to as "toying" and "play," it's the same sort indulged in by shepherd and nymph in the previous poem. Moreover, as Mary Bly argues, "[t]he relationship between Apollo and Hyacinth is not only erotic but consummated," noting that "[t]he pun Machin employs for ejaculation (an 'amarous deaw' during which Phebus' heart melts) was a common one (93; cf. Bly's examples from Machin's contemporaries).

And as Mario DiGangi points out ([1997] 11), Machin applies both the language of friendship and the language of heterosexual love to Apollo and Hyacinth's relationship. Upon their separating for the first time, Hyacinth declares, "The parting of true friendes all paines excell" (sig. E6r); later, Hyacinth is designated Apollo's "male paramore" (sig. E6v). Comments DiGangi, "In this poem, the language of friendship comprehends not only the expression of erotic desire but the performance of certain sexual acts" (11). Yet the poem goes even further, echoing pseudo-Lucian's *Erôtes* and other texts that place love of boys and love of women or girls in competition:

> And now *Appollo* wayning towards the west,
> Unteam'd his fierie steedes, and let them rest
> Whilst he discended on this ball of earth,
> To sport with *Hiacinth* strange unknown mirth
> For which the Gods were angrie, and decreed
> They wold remove the cause, the boy must bleed.
> Now *Phebus* for to see his love did hast him,
> Then *Hiacinth* came running and embrac'd him:
> More joy had *Phebus* in this Spartane lad,
> Then heaven borne *Jove* in Phrigian Ganimed:
> His love to *Daphne* (that chaste beautious nimph)
> Was not so great, as to his *Hiacinth*.
> All Female pleasures, which he did adore,
> Are dull to those of his male paramore. (sig. E6v)

It is no accident Machin refers to the "sport" in which Apollo and Hyacinth engage as "strange" and "unknown," recalling Iphis's reference to her love for Ianthe as "strange," "uncoth," and "prodigious" (IX.855 in Golding's 1567 translation) or "new," "unknowne," and "prodigious" (in Sandys's 1632 version). Indeed, the homosexual Ovidian references are multiple: not only the echo of Iphis's characterization of female-female love, but the reference to Jove and Ganymede, as well as, in the lines preceding this passage, an allusion to Narcissus's homoerotic self-infatuation (sig. E6v). The poem comments on same-sex love, registers its competition with opposite-sex love (using the same example Philo-Philippa will later use: Apollo and Daphne), and even registers the violent hostility with which it is met by the Gods, who punish the couple's indulgence in the wrong kind of sport (male-male erotic play) by booby-trapping the right kind of sport (athletics). Most interesting of all, the poem does *not* appear to sympathize with this hostility to Apollo and Hyacinth's "strange unknown mirth." On the contrary, as Bly argues, "The two eclogues relating the love story of Apollo and Hyacinth betray almost none of the anxiety that scholars have noted in parallel works from the period....

Hyacinth's death is presented not as a just reward for strange love, but as a classic love tragedy.... The narrator's lengthy rendition of Apollo's lament emphasizes grief without shame, sin, or guilt" (93–94).[9]

With such a poem as part of the cultural context, as well as the larger body of homoerotic Renaissance Ovidiana, I begin to wonder whether *The Maydes Metamorphosis* really unknows the ideological faultlines to which I've drawn attention. Rather than working to finesse or suppress its contradictions, might it perhaps be flaunting them? Could the playwright be teasing the audience with the prospect of a boy-loving Apollo, expecting them to enjoy the characters' repeated inability to realize the obvious: that friends can also be lovers? Consider that *The Maydes Metamorphosis* was performed by the boys of St. Paul's, the same company that performed *Gallathea* (cf. Bly, on their especial bawdiness). Were the players winking at the audience when they acted as if the once boy-loving Apollo would naturally stop lusting after a girl-played-by-a-boy-actor once she became a boy-played-by-a-boy-actor? Were they smirking when they asked (but never answered) the question, "Doth kind allow a man to love a man?" Were they giggling when the shepherd and forester referred to the sex-changed Eurymine as "Adonis" and "Ganymede," or when at play's end these singing-and-dancing boys sang of friend coupled with friend? In other words, if after Apollo's account of his tragic love for Hyacinth the play unknows male homoeroticism, perhaps, unlike "Caenis/Caeneus," it does so knowingly.[10]

At the very least, the play seems relatively untroubled by its conflicting messages regarding homoerotic versus heteroerotic desire, and about the distinction or lack of distinction between friendship and love. If what Jean Howard calls "the heterosexual imperatives of the marriage plot" ([1992] 175) require same-sex love to function as *amor impossibilis*, the play seems to request no more of its audience than a willing suspension of disbelief. Rather than endorse the homophobia of Ovid's original tales, the play seems at most to reproduce such thinking for practical reasons: it advances the plot.

---

[9] For more on "Apollo and Hyacinth," and especially Machin's homoerotic "literary community, a group of writers who shared an interest in depictions of homoerotic pleasure," the traces of which Bly uses "to discern and reconstruct a community of readers" (87), see Bly, ch.4.

[10] On "the consummate [erotic] appeal of the dancing boy," particularly when cross-dressed, see Zimmerman (44–45). On boy actors in general, and Lyly and his company in particular, see Franceschina, ch.2.

"Nature (though long kept back) wil have her owne": Gender, Sex, and *Love's* (Heterosexual) *Cure*

Beaumont and Fletcher's (or Beaumont, Fletcher, and Massinger's) comedy *Love's Cure, or The Martial Maid* goes "Iphis and Ianthe" two better, doubling the number of crossdressed characters, as in *Gallathea*, and doubling the number of metamorphoses, as in *The Maydes Metamorphosis*. But unlike those earlier plays, *Love's Cure* magically transforms its characters' genders, not sexes.[11]

The plot centers on Clara and Lucio, a sister and brother each raised as the opposite sex, Clara by their father, Don Alvarez (in exile for having killed Don Pedro), Lucio by their mother, Eugenia. In a triumph of nurture over nature, Clara has grown into a valiant and honorable soldier, Lucio into a prattling, timorous housewife. Pardoned by King Philip, Don Alvarez has returned home and reunited his family. But Clara and Lucio must now be re-gendered, a far more difficult task than anyone anticipates. Although they obediently assume gender-appropriate garb, neither Clara nor Lucio feels or behaves, or wants to feel or behave, as socially expected.

Nevertheless, Clara's feelings and gender begin to alter when she falls in love with valiant young Vitelli. Unfortunately, he's the late Don Pedro's nephew, and thus sworn enemy of her father's house. Yet when he defends himself with rare fortitude against two simultaneous opponents (one of whom is her father), Clara leaps to the rescue, earning Vitelli's gratitude, admiration, and—when he learns she's a woman—his love, which she ardently returns. But in addition to the enmity between their houses, their love faces another barrier: Vitelli's amorous entanglement with the devious, mercenary "curtizan" Malroda (II.i.121). Before Clara and Vitelli can be united, she must teach him an important lesson: chastity is a virtue for *both* sexes.

In the meantime, she must learn to think, feel, and act like a woman, something her father's steward, Bobadilla, a crude, hypermasculine soldier, has failed to teach her, as he has failed to teach Lucio to be a man. Other characters join in the attempt at gender re-education, but to no avail. Don Alvarez grows increasingly furious, even desperate, until love finally saves the day: when Clara foils Malroda's plots, Vitelli agrees to marry his two-time rescuer, while she agrees to be—indeed has already become—a properly feminine woman. Lucio, meanwhile, discovers his long-lost manhood by falling in love with Vitelli's sister, Genevora. All that remains is for the men to make peace. Thanks to the efforts of the women, they do so. The play ends with the siblings ready for marriage, correctly gendered and suitably paired.[12]

---

[11] All quotations are from Beaumont and Fletcher (1976).

[12] It's worth mentioning that the pairing off of Clara with Vitelli, and her brother with his sister, adds a not unexpected hint of incest to the story, while the fact that, during her crossdressed childhood, Clara was known as Lucio, adds a hint of twinning.

Love's Cure departs most markedly from the *Metamorphoses*, and from *Gallathea* and *The Maydes Metamorphosis*, in almost completely avoiding the subject of homosexuality whether female or male. As a deviant female, Clara is the opposite of Iphis: Iphis was feminine, Clara is masculine; Iphis loved a woman, Clara loves a man. At no point does the play suggest any possibility of erotic desire between women. As for erotic desire between men, it makes at most a fleeting, shadowy appearance when Clara and Vitelli first admire one another, before the secret of her true sex has been revealed, and before her gender change has begun (as when she comments, "valour, and true resolution/ Never appear'd so lovely" [I.iii.98–99]). If one pauses to ponder the situation, Clara, in terms of gender, is a man in love with another man. But of the possible forms homoeroticism might take, this is the most culturally approved: the mix of desire and identification flowing between soldiers, spurring them to bond with or fight each other (or both).[13]

Moreover, the play does *not* allow us (particularly if watching the action rather than reading it) to pursue such possibilities. No sooner has Cupid's arrow struck than it begins to work its unswervingly heterosexual magic, revealed when Clara soliloquizes:

> ...what new exercise
> Is crept into my breast, that blauncheth clean
> My former nature? I begin to finde
> I am a woman, and must learn to fight
> A softer sweeter battaile, then with Swords.
> I am sick me thinks, but the disease I feele
> Pleaseth, and punisheth: I warrant love
> Is very like this, that folks talke of so;
> I skill not what it is, yet sure even here,
> Even in my heart, I sensibly perceive
> It glows, and riseth like a glimmering flame,
> But know not yet the essence on't nor the name. (II.ii.248–59)

Vitelli, for his part, falls for Clara only upon learning she's a woman.

Given the play's subject (sex-and-gender confusion) and genre (comedy), and the treatment of so many crossdressing male characters on the Elizabethan, Jacobean, and Caroline stage, one would expect at least *some* homoerotic humor centering on Lucio—such as a man making a pass at him. But in *Love's Cure*, the playwrights eschew such situations entirely. Lucio arouses other men's ire, not libido. And nothing in the play suggests the audience should feel otherwise.

As for Lucio's gender transformation, it's a quick, albeit two-step, process, catalyzed by a woman's kiss. Here's step one:

---

[13] On such heroic homoeroticism, see especially Bruce Smith (1991, 1992), as well as DiGangi (1997).

> What strange new motions do I feele? my veines
> Burn with an unknown fire: in every part
> I suffer alteration: I am poysond,
> Yet languish with desire againe to taste it,
> So sweetly it works on me. (IV.iv.12–16)

In an amusing touch, Lucio's description of heterosexual desire recalls Iphis's lament over lesbian feelings: both call their sensations 'strange,' 'new,' and 'unknown.' And the first half of the passage makes Lucio's gender change sound like a sex-change, a bodily change, insofar as he reports physical sensations. Nonetheless, Lucio's veins burn only metaphorically, and any physical change is clearly subordinate to, and resulting from, new emotions—the reverse of Iphis's experience.

Even more interestingly, the new emotions have not, in fact, precipitated a gender change from feminine to masculine. For in the second half of his little declaration, Lucio emphasizes the conventionally and paradoxically *unmanning* effects of love: it's a sweet poison that leaves him languishing, craving, suffering. All three verbs, while technically active, convey a passive state. Hence the final line: something is being done to Lucio, something is *working on* him.

Not surprisingly, we quickly receive proof that his gender change is incomplete. Faced with a rival for Genevora's love, who "ravishes" from him the glove she bestowed as a token of affection, Lucio fails to respond "valiant[ly]," as a man ought (38–52). Angry and disappointed, Genevora spurns him. Only then does the second step of Lucio's metamorphosis take place:

> My womanish soul, which hitherto hath governd
> This coward flesh, I feele departing from me;
> And in me by [Genevora's] beauty is inspir'd
> A new, and masculine one: instructing me
> What's fit to doe or suffer; powerfull love
> That hast with loud, and yet a pleasing thunder
> Rous'd sleeping manhood in me, thy new creature,
> Perfect thy worke so that I may make known
> Nature (though long kept back) wil have her owne. (IV.iv.54–62)

Having learned to suffer, Lucio is finally learning to act. And his first act will be to make known the truth about nature and gender.

Notice the metaphor Lucio employs to describe his transformation, so much deeper than a physical alteration. In striking contrast to *The Maydes Metamorphosis*, where Eurymine's body but not her identity changes ("Why art not thou *Eurymine*?" "I am." "*Eurymine* my Love?" "The very same"), although Lucio's body remains unchanged he speaks as if his very soul were being replaced, as if he were becoming an entirely new person. For this play, gender and sex aren't merely the outward guise in which an ungendered core is clothed; they go right down to, even constitute, the core, the essence, of identity.

The playwrights, meanwhile, make sure we don't miss the story's debt to Ovid. Alvarez, angry that his children, although appropriately dressed, remain inappropriately gendered, asks, "Art not thou *Clara*, turn'd a man indeed/ Beneath the girdle? And [Lucio] a woman thou?/ Ile have you search'd by —, I strongly doubt/ We must have these things mended" (II.ii.152–54). Alvarez intends the questions sarcastically. No search takes place, and gender deviance rather than anatomical change remains the characters' concern. Yet the Ovidian notion of metamorphosis continues to be central, as Marea Mitchell notes (20, fn.). The word itself is spoken moments after Alvarez's sarcastic question, when Vitelli asks, "Are you the *Lucio*, sir, that sav'd *Vitelli*?" and receives the answer, "Not I indeed sir.../ There walks that *Lucio*, metamorphosed" (II.ii.165–67). Most memorably, the term is repeated in the lines with which Vitelli closes the play:

> Behold the power of love: lo, nature lost
> By custome irrecoverably, past the hope
> Of friends restoring, love hath here retriv'd
> To her own habit, made her blush to see
> Her so long monstrous metamorphoses.
> May strange affaires never have worse successe. (V.iii.257–62)

The conventionally feminine gendering of Nature here acquires particular significance: like an errant woman, lost without her modesty—indeed monstrous without her modesty—Nature must be rescued and re-educated by Love, who *must* be male, since he only operates in this play between oppositely sexed individuals. At the same time, the passage treats as *natural* the gender change wrought by love, a mere retrieval of something lost, while portraying the original effects of custom as *supernatural*, a "monstrous metamorphosis." Vitelli thus reinforces a perspective articulated earlier by Alvarez, when he asks in angry disbelief whether "strong habituall custome [can]/ Work with such Magick on the mind, and manners/ In spight of sex and nature?" (II.ii.140–42).

But the text contains an even more explicit, more revealing reference to the *Metamorphoses*, when Lamorall, Lucio's rival for Genevora, responds to the latter's gender-change by exclaiming:

> There's anger in his eyes too:
> His gesture, voyce, behaviour, all new fashion'd;
> Wel, if it does endure in act the triall
> Of what in show it promises to make good,
> *Ulysses* Cyclops, *Io's* transformation,
> *Eurydice* fetcht from Hell, with all the rest
> Of *Ovids* Fables, ile put in my Creed;

And for proofe all incredible things may be,
Write down that *Lucio*, the coward *Lucio*,
The womanish *Lucio* fought. (V.i.19–28)

Considering Lucio's crossgendered upbringing, the obvious tale to mention would be "Iphis and Ianthe." But that tale includes same-sex desire. As does "Orpheus and Eurydice." So Lamorall mentions only Eurydice, and manages to make it sound as if her rescue had succeeded. Forgotten is Orpheus's failure and his conversion to boy-loving. Depending on love to set things straight, to set things in order (the reverse of its effect in Ovid), *Love's Cure* preemptively purges *amor* of any same-sex potential, far exceeding the homophobic unknowing undertaken by the *Metamorphoses*.

Deviant gender, not deviant sexuality, is the play's concern. Yet even that's too broad a statement. Notwithstanding the subtitle (*The Martial Maid*), female masculinity proves a good deal less problematic than it might at first appear. For Clara exemplifies the most highly valued masculine qualities: honor, bravery, filial obedience, loyalty. And thus, as Mitchell notes, "Clara receives some respect from her family and the enemies of her family" (iii). Indeed, the subtitle itself testifies to the attractiveness of female valor, its popularity with audiences raised in a patriarchal culture, one that reveres masculinity. Instead, if a form of female deviance troubles the play, it is aggressive female (hetero)sexuality. Like Salmacis's effect on Hermaphroditus—indeed, like countless women's supposed effect on men in history, literature, and myth—Malroda fairly bewitches Vitelli with her sexuality, costing him, for a time, his honor and thus his manhood. She's defeated by Clara, who may appear masculine, but who is always unswervingly feminine in the most important respect: chastity. Nature has to be taught to blush in this play; Clara does not.

But even more than aggressive female (hetero)sexuality, masculinity is what truly preoccupies *Love's Cure*. The problem the play confronts is that there are multiple potential masculinities, rather than a single inevitable one or a neatly opposed pair (as with femininity: chaste woman vs. whore). As in Ovid, effeminacy is one possibility, and for most of the play it seems to pose the greatest threat to the masculine characters, even to the entire sex/gender/sexuality system. And yet effeminacy is also the play's prime source of humor. Until his gender change, Lucio's effeminate ways provoke laughter, pure and simple, confirming the masculine values he so clearly fails to exemplify.

The *serious* threat to order, happiness, even life, proves to be unadulterated masculinity itself, in the twin forms of uncontrolled sexual desire and uncontrolled aggression and violence. The former, as we've seen, can be cured by chaste femininity: Clara rescues Vitelli from Malroda and recalls him to himself. But she does so specifically by a promise of submission. In response to his fear that, once married, she'll outman him ("should I offend you," he worries, "...You are of so great a spirit, that I must learn/ To weare your petticoat, for you wil have/ My breeches from me" [IV.ii.180–84]), Clara vows:

> Rather from this houre
> I here abjure all actions of a man,
> And wil esteem it happinesse from you
> To suffer like a woman: love, true love
> Hath made a search within me, and expel'd
> All but my naturall softnesse, and made perfect
> That which my parents care could not begin.
> I wil show strength in nothing, but my duty,
> And glad desire to please you, and in that
> Grow every day more able. (IV.ii.184–93)

Whereas Malroda unmans Vitelli, Clara promises him a future of manly dominance. He "naturally" chooses the latter.

Far more challenging, and troubling, is the problem of masculine violence. It's the first disturbance to which the play draws attention, the one from which all other problems flow: Don Alvarez killed Don Pedro; exiled as a result, he raised Clara as a boy; at home, to escape Vitelli's vengeance, Eugenia raised Lucio as a girl; and now, in the play's opening scene, Vitelli vows to avenge his uncle's murder and uphold his own honor by killing Alvarez and son, notwithstanding the king's decision to forgive the original crime:

> My deadly hate to *Alvarez*, and his house,
> Which as I grew in years, hath still encreas'd,
> As if it cal'd on time to make me man,
> Slept while it had no object for her fury
> But a weak woman, and her talk'd of Daughter:
> But now, since there are quarries, worth her flight
> Both in the father, and his hopefull son,
> I'le boldly cast her off, and gorge her full
> With both their hearts… (I.i.119–27)

Vitelli personifies his hate as a female bird of prey, yet the metaphor is deceptive. His concept of *manhood*'s requirements, of *masculine* honor, is what sets him on this bloody course. And while at first the vow appears admirable, if problematic (since Vitelli presumes to act as the king's proxy and make "[his] arme the Kings" [118]), by play's end, when both he and his antagonists are on the verge of mutual slaughter, proving their manhood with their swords (V.iii.173), such masculinity is revealed as a deadly mistake.

Ironically, as Jonathan Dollimore points out, the play's manly men, including post-metamorphosis Lucio, could learn a thing or two from pre-metamorphosis Lucio, for "[the latter's] effeminacy, construed by Bobadillo as an affront to 'heav'n, nature, and thy Parents' (II.ii.22)… actually embodies positive civilized virtues" (301; cf. Franceschina). Yet Dollimore is only partially correct. True, in contrast to Vitelli—who believes his honor forbids him emulating the king by pardoning Alvarez, and even justifies taking revenge on Alvarez's son—Lucio draws upon Christian teaching to urge forgiveness and oppose the punishment of children for the crimes of their parents (II.ii.45–54). But Lucio is a coward. The speech he delivers urging Christian forgiveness is meant to quiet Vitelli and save his own life (II.ii.54–55). Lucio does *not* provide the play's positive alternative to unbridled masculine aggression and inflexible masculine honor. Instead, it's Clara, Genevora, and Eugenia who prevent bloodshed at play's end by combining "feminine" qualities such as peacefulness, cooperation, forgiveness, and respect for life with the "masculine" quality of bravery. When all arguments and pleas fail to deter the men from dueling, the women threaten to stage a monstrously parodic duel of their own: the moment the men cross swords Clara and Genevora will do the same, each plunging her weapon into the breast of the other, while Eugenia will have Bobadilla shoot her dead. Faced with the women's impending deaths, and shamed by such self- rather than other-sacrificing bravery, the men agree to lay down their swords and make peace.

Of course, as Dollimore himself argues, the play's attempt to critique both gender deviation and dominant masculinity generates ideological contradictions. Or as Anne Duncan puts it, "Even in this most conservative of plays about cross-dressing, the possibility of gender transgression lurks" (397). Duncan goes even further, emphasizing the play's subversive implications:

> The cross-dressing and valorous masculine behavior of Clara, the 'martial maid,' constitute a kind of transgressive reinscription of masculinity as (only) performance. She is presented as the only 'real man' in the play. When she 'becomes' a woman, she performs equally well in that role, revealing that gender (and not just masculinity) is only a performance, and furthermore, in a reversal of English Renaissance stage practice, that a woman can perform a man best. (398; see also 407)

In applying Dollimore's concept of transgressive reinscription to *Love's Cure*, Duncan explicitly disagrees with his reading of the play. He sees its contradictions emerging unintentionally from its attempt to "contain… the transvestite challenge [of early modern drama].… It is as if containment, in reinstating nature over culture—that most fundamental and violent of binary oppositions—says too much about both" (300). Duncan, instead, interprets the play's presentation of masculinity—fundamentally performative, and perhaps best performed by a woman—as a form of transgression. Exciting as this reading is, though, I agree with Dollimore. Duncan's is a *resistant* reading, smart and revealing, but proceeding against the grain of the text.

As in previous chapters, what's at issue here is the question of intentionality. Duncan doesn't give the play enough credit for ideological self-consciousness. At the same time as *Love's Cure* asserts that gender is grounded in biology, that biological sex, gender, and sexual desire must all align perfectly along a male/female axis, it critiques masculinity, arguing that the noblest masculinity, the one that best lives up to its own highest ideal, its honor, is one tempered by an admixture of "feminine" traits—chastity, honesty, a preference for peacefulness over violence (although violence is necessary in self-defense or defense of others)—just as the noblest femininity was often widely believed to include an admixture of "masculine" virtues—particularly bravery, even heroism, in defense of one's chastity. Of course, this ideology is contradictory. And such topics are notoriously difficult to keep under authorial control. Thus, at play's end, the extremely conservative attempt to fix gender by affixing it firmly to the body (not to mention Clara's earlier pledge of wifely submission, even to the point of suffering) seems to defend against the threat posed by advocating a substantially womanish masculinity, a defense to which the erasure of same-sex sexuality is key. But the transgressive reinscription Duncan sees the play staging was not intended to be legible. Unlike *Gallathea*, which fairly flaunts its radical implications, or *The Maydes Metamorphosis*, which either winks knowingly at the audience or simply can't be bothered to conceal its forays into deviant sexuality, *Love's Cure* seems intent on disavowing its most radical implications.[14]

And regarding same-sex sexuality in particular, it helps to remember that, as Susan Zimmerman writes regarding the erotics of transvestite acting on the Jacobean comic stage, it was the *norm* for "[t]heir comedy [to] offer… a range of transgressive opportunities—hetero- and homoerotic fantasies to be customized by the individual spectator" and "[to] privilege… a kind of democratic eroticism, accessible to all, emanating from the *process* of creating sexual confusions, from the jumbling of overlapping sexual nuances" (55). *Love's Cure*'s refusal, in such a context, to seriously—or lightheartedly—entertain the possibility of homoerotic desire bespeaks a conscious exclusionary choice to which the modern term *homophobic* quite accurately applies.

"A male heart filled with a female spirit": *Iphis* goes to University

Like the three works just examined, loosely inspired by "Iphis and Ianthe" and related tales, stricter seventeenth-century dramatizations of "Iphis and Ianthe" vary in their ideological bent. Yet like *Gallathea*, *The Maydes Metamorphosis*, and *Love's Cure*, their explorations of sex, gender, and sexuality circle round the same set of provocative topics—lesbianism, male homosexuality, sex-change, crossdressing, effeminacy, aggressive female sexual desire, narcissistic desire, incest, twinning, misogyny, and patriarchal tyranny—revealing far more continuity with both Augustan Rome and the modern West than recent histories of sexuality have taught us to perceive.

---

[14] For competing notions of heroism, and their gendering, over the course of the seventeenth century, see Rose.

Ideologically speaking, of the three plays we've examined, Henry Bellamy's *Iphis* most closely resembles *Love's Cure*. Bellamy, a student at Oxford, most likely dramatized "Iphis and Ianthe" for performance at his college, St. John's, in the 1620s or early 1630s. He relies on Ovid's original story for basic plot, as well as for some language (his play, incidentally, is in Latin). But Bellamy introduces innovations. Some merely amplify the Ovidian material: Ianthe becomes a full character, as does her father, Telestes; both Iphis's nurse and Iphis and Ianthe's teacher become minor characters. But as recent editors of the play point out, "It is… in his creation of Nisus, would-be suitor to Ianthe and ultimate comic villain, that Bellamy makes his most profound departure from Ovid" (Freyman et al., 5). Nisus courts Ianthe, with the encouragement of Iphis's mother, Telethusa, but Ianthe rejects him. Telethusa then discloses Iphis's true sex in an attempt to persuade Nisus to transfer his love from Ianthe to Iphis. Her efforts backfire: he tries to stop the marriage by "outing" Iphis at the altar. But the metamorphosis has already taken place. The laugh is on Nisus, the marriage proceeds, the play ends.[15]

Bellamy's treatment of lesbianism sticks close to Ovid's. He suggests that Iphis and Ianthe are twin-like (e.g., 93; IV.iii.713–22). He repeats much of Iphis's lament, altering it mainly by giving a few of the lines to Iphis's mother:

Iphis: Harsh divinity! I live in misery, destined not to
         die a common death. A strange end awaits me, a
         strange fate. Never does a woman set passion a-
         flame in another woman, except in my case. Phoebus,
         although a prophet, has never known such a thing.
Telethusa: Illustrious Pasiphae, daughter of the knowing
         Sun, desired a bull, a female desiring a male. But,
         unhappy one, your love is more outrageous [*furiosus*]. She
         acquired what she sought; she obtained her wishes.
Iphis: Even if Daedalus should fly back on his wings,
         could he change me or delicate Ianthe by his arts? (97)

Because Bellamy assigns some of the lines to Telethusa, their presentation of lesbian desire as completely unprecedented, and impossible to fulfill, reads less clearly than in Ovid as a humorous comment on Iphis's ignorant innocence (although mother and daughter might both be naive). Regardless, in *Iphis*, even more so than in "Iphis and Ianthe," the lament's construction of lesbianism shouldn't be taken as evidence of the inconceivability of lesbian sex. In "Iphis and Ianthe" the lament's assertions were contradicted by numerous other texts of Ovid's time; in *Iphis* they're contradicted by evidence from within the text itself.

---

[15] See Bellamy (1986). According to Freyman et al., the play does not seem to have been translated or printed until recently. Regarding its dating, they argue (1–2) that 1622–24 is most likely, although 1622–26 or even 1628–32 are possible. See also Bellamy (1983).

In the final scene, Nisus condemns rather than unknows lesbianism, declaring, "Iphis is a woman! Does any god join tender women on the same marriage bed? You are deceived. The gods greatly fear this unspeakable evil" (109). Using the word *nefas*, a terrible crime or sin, something contrary to divine law, Bellamy makes forbiddenness rather than impossibility the key concept. (Unspeakability is the translators' not-inappropriate addition: although literally claiming impossibility—such and such *cannot* be named or put into words—in practice 'unspeakable' underlines forbiddenness—such and such *ought not* to be spoken.) The fact that the desperate, spurned comic villain utters these words doesn't invalidate them. They're humorous, but their humor derives from Nisus's ignorance of Iphis's sex-change. His declaration that Iphis is a woman is now untrue. However, his characterization of lesbianism, although irrelevant in the new circumstances, is accurate according to the play's ethos. He is clearly voicing its dominant ideology. Nothing in the play suggests that were Iphis revealed to be still female, other characters would react with anything but horror and condemnation.

Iphis also registers the ambiguity of Ovid's treatment of patriarchal tyranny by offering a deceptive critique of Lygdus. As Freyman et al. observe, Bellamy uses Ianthe's father Telestes "as a foil to Lygdus…[,] contrast[ing] the extreme reaction of Lygdus to the possible birth of a daughter to the loving response of Telestes to the actual birth of a daughter, and… counterpoint[ing] the insistence of Telestes that Ianthe must approve of her future husband with the demand of Lygdus that Iphis must marry whether or not he [Iphis] approves" (4). Yet despite this apparent critique, piety rather than paternal authority is the issue for Bellamy. Lygdus is "a pious man of modest means" (Freyman, et al., 4), tortured by the prospect of financial ruin and familial suffering should his child be female. His opening soliloquy invites compassion, as he struggles to figure out what to do: "But, behold, my mind swells; I am drawn this way and that. Burning pain orders that a female child be destroyed, although piety forbids this. Pain sets piety to flight and piety drives out pain. Thus I am borne upon a rising sea, and I, fool that I am, do not know what I shall do" (64). Once Lygdus has decided that his child, if female, must die, and once we see him persisting in this decision despite his wife's fervent supplications, we feel increasingly less sympathy for him. Yet the play soon lets him off the hook. As Freyman et al. point out, "the emergence of Nisus as comic villain… softens the unpleasant side of Lygdus' nature and gives the characters, and the audience, someone other than Lygdus to reject" (6). In the end, Nisus, not Lygdus, gets the comeuppance.

There is one moment, though, when Lygdus feels he's being punished, and it centers upon *Iphis*'s most important thematic deviation from "Iphis and Ianthe," although not from the *Metamorphoses* as a whole: Iphis's effeminacy. As Pintabone remarks regarding Ovid's tale, before Iphis's sex-change "Ovid makes no mention of anyone doubting she was male" (277). No one, apparently, questioned her masculinity, or at least her boyishness. In contrast, from the first moment Bellamy's Iphis appears onstage, "his" failure to behave like a man is emphasized. "[Y]ou know nothing manly, nothing strong," his teacher scolds. "The things which you can do are unbecoming to men. You should be running over rocks and coursing over the sea. Why are you amazed at the thought of these things?" (83). Yet the teacher is actually quite tolerant, defending Iphis against Lygdus's angry disapproval by characterizing the effeminate boy as a mistake of Nature, and hence beyond human power to change. As he explains to Lygdus, "[N]ature sins, not they themselves. Iphis, although not taught, sings. His spirit, although worked on, shudders at manly arts; and he pursues soft trifles although the arms of Achilles are given to him" (84). Such reasoning fails to reassure Lygdus, who bewails his misfortune:

> O just punishment from heaven! The evil answers the fault, and the punishment fits the crime in every way. My mind impudently wished for a male child, almost demanding it. It has what it wishes (o sorrow!), but it is a male heart filled with a female spirit. Will Crete, already known for such things, always bring forth new monstrosities? (85)

At this moment at least, Lygdus seems punished for his impiety. Even more importantly, his refusal to accept any deviation from normative masculinity seems implicitly criticized. The text, like the teacher, appears to defend effeminacy, using arguments that, interestingly, would come to be used as apologies for male homosexuality in the mid-nineteenth to mid-twentieth century: however strange, even freakish, the fact seems, and indeed is, Nature sometimes puts a female soul in a male body; when this is the case, we must let things be (after, of course, repeatedly attempting, and failing, to masculinize the boy.)

Yet this pathologizing tolerance for gender deviance is not, in fact, ultimately supported by the text. Bellamy makes the plot-resolving metamorphosis at play's end as much a change of gender as of sex. Iphis comments as much upon mental and emotional as upon physical transformation:

> What new strength wanders through my awestruck breast? What blood flows in my heart? Scarcely am I in possession of myself! A great seething boils within me. My strong feet are eager to trample troops slain by swords in warfare; my hand desires to brandish torches and fierce swords. My eyes dart fire; my hair flows loosely down....
>
> And I am changing totally. Does someone order unwilling hands to destroy the cowardly form of this face? Goodbye to the tricks of my former countenance. Put on virile wrinkles, a shaggy visage; be a Cretan man! What my former spirit shuddered at my bold spirit now encourages. Nothing does it fear, except fear. (106)

As evidenced by the passivity of Ovid's Iphis prior to her sex-change, gender in "Iphis and Ianthe" is assumed typically to follow sex. Consequently, Iphis's initial lack and then possession of a penis is the textual focus. Concern that a person with a penis might nonetheless *not* behave in properly masculine fashion (might, for instance, choose to use an orifice rather than the appendage) is repressed and displaced, expressed obliquely through "Narcissus," "Orpheus," the tales Orpheus tells, "Caenis/Caeneus," "Salmacis and Hermaphroditus." But in Bellamy's play such anxieties are made explicit. Not just the person, but his body must have the properly gendered emotions: "My strong feet are eager...; my hand desires...." Sex and gender must be indivisible. Like Beaumont and Fletcher's Lucio declaring, "in every part/ I suffer alteration," Bellamy's Iphis announces, "I am changing totally."

One might, perhaps, read this climactic speech as parodic or comic. And yet the work as a whole doesn't support such a reading. In contrast to Woodward's poem to Donne about "mistique tribadree" (discussed above, ch.1), or Donne's own "Sapho to Philenis," *Iphis* lacks the playfulness of other attempts by young, educated male writers of the late sixteenth and early seventeenth century to inhabit a lesbian textual consciousness.[16]

One might argue, alternately, that Bellamy's focus on mental and emotional metamorphosis is simply a practical dramatic expedient: a change in the character's internal state requires no change in the actor's costume or makeup, much less his actual physical body.[17] But up until this moment, the audience knew it was watching a male actor portray a female character. Why would such an audience demand realistic visual evidence of the character's physical sex-change? The metamorphosis passage addresses a problem in ideology, not stagecraft. It attempts to shore up a dominant sex/gender/sexuality construct, all the while refusing to admit the construct needs any support.[18]

I should be more precise, however, when I speak of a dominant sex/gender/sexuality construct, because *Iphis* isn't concerned with sex, gender, and sexuality in general, but rather masculinity in particular. Despite the supposedly monstrous possibility that one woman might love and desire, let alone have sex with, another, the attention Bellamy devotes to this frightening prospect derives wholly from Ovid and is perfunctory. In contrast, he lavishes creative energy on the subject of masculinity and effeminacy. Indeed, effeminacy effectively replaces lesbianism as the wrong to be righted during the course of the play, as when, in the passage quoted above, Lygdus rhetorically asks, "Will Crete, already known for such things, always bring forth new monstrosities?" [*Nova/ Semperne monstra nota iam Crete feret?*] The wording—the use of *monstra*, the focus on Cretan

---

[16] On Donne's poem, see Traub (2002), as well as the numerous critics she discusses and cites (463–64, n.26–30).

[17] Bellamy's possible beliefs about ancient Cretan hairstyles aside, the odd remark about Iphis's hair flowing loosely down—in Ovid's tale Iphis's hair grows *shorter*—makes more sense in this light: it makes possible a simple, easily manageable physical alteration—letting the actor's hair (or wig) down—that can stand in for more extensive bodily changes requiring greater ingenuity in the use of costume and makeup.

[18] On the Shakespearean stage as anti-mimetic (with particular reference to the use of boy actors), see Solomon (1997), as well as Parry. One might also wonder whether Iphis's final, bloodthirsty speech is parodic, yet there have been no suggestions of parody until that point.

tales—obviously recalls the opening lines of "Iphis and Ianthe"—"The story of this strange marvel would perhaps have filled the hundred/ Cretan cities, if Crete had not recently,/ with Iphis' transformation, borne miracles closer to home" (H.IX.666–68)—except with effeminacy as the wonder, the monstrosity, in question.

In another work, such substitution might reasonably suggest that, ideologically speaking, lesbianism is *more* threatening than effeminacy, the obvious fear of the latter masking a deeper, unacknowledgeable fear of the former, a thematic ruse James Creech neatly characterizes (in a discussion of male homosexuality, incest, and Melville's *Pierre*) when he writes, "we might do well to recall the warning that the French post next to the trickiest railroad crossings: 'One train can hide another'" (85). And yet, if this were the case in *Iphis*, how would we explain Nisus's explicit acknowledgement of lesbianism in the final scene, condemning such tenderness between women as forbidden? Rather than camouflaging a deeply panicked reaction to lesbianism with a more manageable concern about effeminacy, Bellamy's play does seem more genuinely worried about the latter than the former, more concerned about men's behavior than women's.

Which isn't really surprising. *Iphis* was written by an Oxford student to be performed by and for other members of his college. In such an all-male setting, devoted to the formation of ruling-class men, the question of the proper way to be a man finds its way to the center of a great many endeavors. And considering that in *The Metamorphoses* masculinity and effeminacy are implicitly linked, through related stories, to "Iphis and Ianthe," Bellamy's foregrounding it is as much an imitation of as departure from his Ovidian model.

"Whether I have reason to laugh, or to be distressed about it?": Benserade's *Iphis et Iante*

Not that Bellamy could prevent his play from affording unsanctioned meanings and pleasures to dissident performers, audience members, and readers. For instance, the onstage kiss between the actors playing Iphis and Ianthe during the concluding marriage ceremony (110; V.vi.1131) certainly offered the possibility of transgressive pleasure for them and for homoerotically inclined audience members, as did, for boys or men attracted to effeminacy, the spectacle of male actors portraying feminine characters throughout the play. Yet any such homoerotic or gender-transgressive pleasure is clearly marked as illicit. The play's insistence on the horrors of effeminacy and the glories of a decidedly bloodthirsty masculinity (again, think of Iphis's metamorphosis speech) may or may not read as a rather panicked defense against precisely such pleasures, pleasures well-nigh inseparable from all-male theatrics—I would read it this way. But panicked or not, the text is clearly defensive.[19]

In comparison, Isaac de Benserade's almost contemporaneous *Iphis et Iante* (perf. 1634; pub. 1637) is relaxed and playful. The text is far more willing to admit not only that an ideological faultline exists, but that exploring it can be pleasurable.[20]

Benserade supplements and alters Ovid's story more than Bellamy does. In addition to the expected characters from "Iphis and Ianthe"—here called Iphis, Ligde, Teletuze, Iante, Teleste—he adds Ergaste, in love with Iphis and (unbeknownst to her) privy to the secret of her true sex; Nise, a friend of Ergaste; Merinte, sister to Nise, in love with Ergaste; and a confidante for Teletuze, identified only as the sister of Ergaste. The timeframe of the story is narrowed: it begins the afternoon preceding the wedding evening and ends the following day. In the interim, Ergaste attempts to break off the match by revealing Iphis's true sex, Nise falls out violently with him because he won't marry Merinte, and Ergaste agrees to marry her if, after Iphis and Iante's wedding night, Iphis turns out actually to be a man, disproving Ergaste's accusation. The metamorphosis, of course, defeats him. In this case, unlike in Ovid and Bellamy, the transformation occurs in front of everyone, after Teletuze has recounted the story of Iphis's birth. But Benserade introduces a far more radical change: he places the metamorphosis *after* the wedding night instead of before.[21]

We'll return to the play's handling of that night of lesbian love. First, though, I'd like to examine its handling of men, masculinity, male power, and male sexuality. For like Ovid's *Metamorphoses* and Bellamy's *Iphis*, Benserade's *Iphis et Iante* links lesbianism to these equally fraught topics.

Once again, patriarchal tyranny rears its head, receiving the same treatment—seemingly critical yet ultimately lenient—that it's accorded in the other texts we've explored, with the exception of *Love's Cure*. Teletuze speaks of Ligde "using an absolute power" (7), and regrets having openly argued with him to postpone or cancel the wedding, since by doing so she succeeded only in hastening it: her husband brooks no opposition (I.iii; p.9). At the wedding itself, Ligde forces the

---

[19] I would, of course, make a similar argument about the potential homoeroticism of Lucio and Genevora's onstage kisses in *Love's Cure*—the text labors, through erasure, to rule out any awareness that two male actors are kissing. As for the sort of fears both plays were likely fending off, fears voiced in anti-theatrical writing of the time, see Levine, as well as Solomon (2002).

[20] I have used Benserade (1637). Since acts and scenes are numbered, but not lines, I have cited the page, following the act and scene, for every quotation. See Verdier's preface (7–33) to the recent edition for an excellent contextual and interpretive introduction, as well as Leibacher-Ouvrard's excellent essay (2003; discussed below), which has led me to revise my previous (2001c) assessment of the play.

[21] The nearly identical names of Bellamy's Nisus and Benserade's Nise suggest both authors drew from a common source—perhaps the lost play *Iphis and Ianthe* attributed to Shakespeare (Sibley, 79), perhaps another unknown work.

unwilling Teletuze to give her written consent (IV.ii; p.64). Eventually, when Iphis's true sex is revealed and Teletuze recounts the reason for their deception, Ligde repents his behavior, crying, "O Heaven! o just Gods! o blood! o piety!/ Are you the witnesses of my brutality!" (87). Almost immediately, Isis reappears in answer to Teletuze's prayer and calls Ligde "inhuman father" (*pere inhumain* [91; V.vi]).

Yet she barely allows this condemnation to register before relieving any discomfort Ligde might feel:

> And you inhuman father, instead of punishing you,
> Listen to the happiness that should warn you,
> I want to compose your family according to your liking,
> And you will no longer be the father of a girl,
> His/her sudden change will remove your doubt,
> Iphis was a girl, Iphis is a boy.... (91)

Teletuze has suffered years of anxiety and fear. Iphis has undergone the same, and reached the brink of suicide. Ligde suffers a few pangs of conscience, perhaps a moment's fear of retribution, but is then rewarded with the son he always wanted. Of course, the play is a comedy and Ligdus isn't a villain, so we expect him to share in the happy ending. But Benserade could have made him sweat a bit while learning his lesson—if condemning abuse of patriarchal authority were truly one of the play's aims. It isn't.

Not that *Iphis et Iante* is unconcerned with male misbehavior. Like Bellamy, Benserade touches upon effeminacy, and like Ovid, upon male homosexuality. He takes Ovid's approach, however, in treating these subjects. Both—especially male homosexuality—are handled in an ambiguous, even evasive manner.

Effeminacy is first mentioned by Ergaste, as he offers Nise reasons why he cannot return Merinte's love. He claims, for instance, to be averse to romantic love itself:

> To tell you the truth, to this day my heart
> Never abased itself in this dishonorable trade
> That makes one lose one's judgment to win a woman:
> I prize the beauties, but among their attractions
> They have humours that don't please me,
> I have an aversion for a flighty sex,
> The soft courting of which effeminizes a [manly] heart [*un courage*]. (25)

As Joseph Cady reminds us, 'effeminate' conveyed potentially contradictory meanings in the Renaissance. Then as now, it could be a homophobic slur: homosexual desire or activity makes a man like a woman. But as we've seen, it could also be used as a quasi-heterophobic insult: heterosexual desire or activity also makes a man like a woman, makes him soft, unfit for war, enslaves him to an inferior creature, subjugates his reason to his appetites, his mind to his body, and so on. Ergaste is using this second, now obsolete meaning of 'effeminate' (targeting what Craig Williams calls "the womanish womanizer" [145]), pretending to be so manly he has no interest in love.[22]

The play critiques this misogynist model of masculinity, but can't quite shake it. Since we know Ergaste is putting on an act, motivated solely by desire for Iphis, his claim not to be interested in women is literally laughable. Nise, moreover, responds to his objection by asking, "Is one less valiant for courting women? You well know that in earlier times/ [P]roud conquerors submitted to their laws" (25), instancing heroes such as Achilles, who "was quite the woman" (*fut bien femme*; i.e., when disguised as a girl, living at the court of King Lycomedes of Scyros, where he fathered a son by the king's daughter) and Hercules, "whose invincible strength purged the Universe [of monsters]" (25, 26). For the most part, this response seems persuasive: many a hero has been both fighter and lover.[23]

And yet Benserade is most likely having fun here, mocking Nise as well as Ergaste. For Achilles' crossdressing is more usually explained (as in *Metamorphoses* XIII) as an attempt by his mother to keep him out of war than as a way to seduce or rape a woman he desired, and Hercules' love for a woman (Deianira) leads to his death (as in Sophocles' *Trachiniae*). Audience members familiar with these stories might very well have wondered whether Nise could have chosen better examples, and thus whether the play's otherwise positive portrayal of heterosexual love is being tempered with gentle mockery.

This possible conflict between heterosexuality and masculinity is raised again at play's end. As part of the evidence for his metamorphosis, Iphis asserts that, all of a sudden, "Venus who all alone occupied my cares,/ Contracts in my eyes to make place for Mars" (92). The statement is unexpected, and probably perfunctory. Unlike in Bellamy's version, the metamorphosis here, as in Ovid's original, is described as primarily physical (although not genital), rather than mental or emotional. And that makes sense, since nowhere in the play has Iphis's masculinity been called into question (she's been portrayed as neither particularly masculine nor particularly feminine). And indeed, as soon as these lines are uttered they appear to be forgotten. Ergaste agrees to keep his word and marry Merinte, and Iphis looks forward to the "real" wedding night to come with Ianthe. The play even concludes with Iphis offering to remove any doubts of his new sex, not by making war, but by making love (and procreating): "And my dear [other] half in a good way/ Will prove in nine months that Iphis is a boy" (95). Venus, not Mars, occupies Iphis's, and the text's, attention. (But see below for more on these final lines.)

---

[22] See Cady (1996) 132–33 and (1993) 151–53, and Williams, ch.4.

[23] The Achilles episode is recounted in the *Achilleid*, Statius's unfinished, late first-century epic. Ovid includes it in his *Ars Amatoria* (*ll*.663–80); see Richlin (1992b) and Raval. It's interesting to note that both Achilles and Hercules were famously paired with males as well as females (Achilles with Patroclus, Hercules with Iolaus).

And yet Venus herself sometimes appears in the guise of Mars, if not to the audience, at least to some of the characters. Thus, when I wrote above that Ergaste, in the effeminacy passage, pretends to be so manly he has no interest in love, I told only half the story. Immediately before the lines I quoted, we hear the following:

ERGASTE.
...You see that I love Iphis as much as one can love
The most divine object that could charm us,
And that for the virtues with which his beautiful soul abounds,
I find him preferable to the most beautiful women of the world.

NISE.
You are speaking of friendship, but I am speaking of love. (25)

Ergaste pretends to be not only uninterested in women, but very interested—too interested—in men (one man in particular). As Bruce Smith explains, this was a recognizable Renaissance type: the aggressively manly man (often a soldier) whose "greater emotional loyalties lie... with other men [rather than] with women" (65). Such a man is dismissive of women, sometimes virulently so, while simultaneously combative and comradely with men, forming intense, undeniably erotic male bonds. In contrast to sodomitical relationships, fiercely denigrated in Renaissance England and France, these bonds are culturally approved, even celebrated—but uneasily so. For they're dangerous, always threatening to disclose the ideological faultline they pretend doesn't exist. Despite pronouncements such as Nise's "You are speaking of friendship, but I am speaking of love," friendship and love, friendship and sodomy, fierce love and fearsome love are *not* clearly distinguishable—as we saw in *The Maydes Metamorphosis*. As Alan Sinfield succinctly puts it, "Above all, perhaps, the situation was confused.... Sodomy was a continual threat around the edges of male bonding. It is not a matter of whether Coriolanus and Aufidius fucked, but of the text being unable, and perhaps unwilling, to dispel the ghost of such an inference."[24]

Benserade exploits the tense ambiguity of male homoeroticism for comic effect. As the play proceeds and Ergaste changes tactics—claiming Iphis is actually a woman—other characters become increasingly unsure what to make of his declarations of passionate love for what they believe to be another man. At first they think he's joking: when he tells Iante, "in the love of Iphis I [am] your rival.../ Know that Iphis is a girl, & that I am dying for her" (49), she exclaims, "Oh the amusing speech!/ ...Truly Ergaste's humour, & his beautiful madness/ Will make the company laugh a great deal." When she in turn tells Ligde, "He burns for Iphis with a disorderly fire" (53), Ligde replies, "The joke is not bad." Teleste thinks it's a drunken prank (54), while Nise and Merinte suspect it's a sly,

---

[24] Sinfield (1994) 18–19; the characters named are from Shakespeare's *Coriolanus*. Again, see Bruce Smith (1991, 1992) and DiGangi (1997).

strategic ploy to avoid marrying Merinte (54, 55). But Ergaste's persistence eventually make people wonder whether something else is going on. Teleste thus concludes the young man is crazy, possessed by a strange mania [*estrange manie*] (70; IV.iv), and anticipates having "the pleasure/ Of seeing in the vapors with which his soul is filled/ The point to which the excess of his madness will be carried" (70–72).

What's odd about all this analysis of Ergaste's behavior is that male homosexuality—often called in the Renaissance and early seventeenth century *socratic love, masculine love, amour viril, libido mascula,* and the like—is never directly mentioned. Ergaste's manly man passage surely suggests it, as does Iante's phrase "a disorderly fire" [*un feu desordonné*], wording with longstanding homoerotic connotations. Yet the text goes no further than such ambiguous, impossible-to-pin-down suggestions. More strangely still, while the audience can't help but think of male homosexuality, the characters seem unable to conceive of it.[25]

Even Iphis herself appears not to consider it, although Ergaste takes pains she should in the following exchange:

> ERGASTE.
> I say that my love would be more vehement
> For the kind (*gentil*) Iphis, as for the beautiful Iante.
>
> IPHIS.
> Well yes your friendship.
>
> ERGASTE.
>   I always get lost
> In these distinctions of friendships and loves.
> Whatever it is, my heart above all wishes
> That Heaven would make a metamorphosis in you,
> So that I could love you in another way,
> Too beautiful are you for a boy;
> Nature who pleased herself in making you adorable,
> Should have made you born either a girl, or less lovable,
> ...I would have burned for you with a more legitimate fire,
> And my heart would have been for you only a victim;
> ...But could you have loved me?
>
> IPHIS.
> How frivolous these attentions (*soins*) are,

---

[25] For *disorderly/désordonné*, see Cady (1992) 34, n.4, on "E.K.'s mention of 'paederastice' ('pederasty') in his gloss about the Colin-Hobbinol relationship in the 'January' eclogue of Spenser's *Shepherd's Calendar* (1579)."

And what a vain waste of time & words!
Let us talk more wholesomely (*sainement*).... (37–38)

Ergaste's all-but-explicit courting of Iphis, the implication that he burns with an "illegitimate" fire, and his declared inability to distinguish between friendship and love unavoidably suggest male homosexuality (particularly when taken together). Yet if the possibility occurs to Iphis, she shows it only ambiguously, for a single instant, in the connotations of unhealthiness suggested by the word *sainement*. The moment Ergaste leaves, she voices her suspicion that he knows her true sex, since his sister is Teletuze's confidante. Such suspicions are of course warranted, particularly given the double sense of one of Ergaste's parting remarks: "In making children [with Iante], you will make miracles" (38). But given that Iphis is a girl in love with another girl, it seems odd she doesn't also consider the possibility Ergaste is a boy in love with (what he supposedly thinks is) another boy, especially since he's gone to some trouble to suggest the idea. In other words, the play teases the audience with the possibility of male homosexuality, obliquely alluding to it for comic effect but refusing to be caught suggesting it explicitly. (The similarity with Ovid's handling of same-age male homosexuality in "Narcissus" is worth noting.)

The play's treatment of lesbianism provides a similar tease. Like "Iphis and Ianthe," *Iphis et Iante* admits, indeed hinges on, the representation and hence possibility of lesbian *desire*, the sexual desire of one woman for another, but ultimately figures lesbian *sex*, the fulfillment of that desire, as impossible. Until the play ends, however (and particularly once the wedding has taken place sans metamorphosis), the audience is made to wonder whether fulfillment might occur after all, and lesbian sex turn out to be possible, to be real, in this revision of Ovid's tale. More than that, they're repeatedly incited to imagine just what this (im)possibility might consist of. In essence, the audience is put in the same predicament as Ergaste when he ponders his beloved's passion for another woman:

Who wouldn't marvel at a love of this sort?
And who wouldn't admire a flame so strong?
I don't know anymore what to believe about it, & I cannot judge
Whether I have reason to laugh, or to be distressed about it? (18)

Benserade keeps his audience uncertain but titillated (or uncertain hence titillated), alternating between laughter and discomfort, thereby providing much of the suspense the play would otherwise lack (since the audience knows how the story ends). But this approach serves ideological purposes as well.

As in Ovid's version, Iphis's feelings for Iante are often described as strange, new, mysterious, unnatural. Thus when Teletuze asks if she really loves Iante, Iphis calls her feelings "strange" and a "mystery" (I.ii; p.7), and Ergaste refers to

Iphis's love as "a new flame" (18), speaks of "the novelty of the fire that consumes her" (19), and worries that its "monstrous effect...troubles nature" (19). In Ovid's story, as we saw, opposition to Nature was not an option; lesbianism was unnatural in the sense of being impossible, not forbidden. Benserade isn't so clear.[26]

Certainly, the impossibility of lesbian sex is asserted several times, as when Ergaste's sister states that, in the pairing of Iphis and Iante, "Their marriage lacks the better part" (10)—that part being a penis. In fact, Teletuze's confidante displays no anxiety lest the girls have sex, reassuring her friend with the following prediction:

> One will be ashamed, & the other will be vexed,
> Chastity will make her throne from their bed:
> If similar knots united everyone,
> There would be no point in nature's fecundity;
> Incense would no longer be offered to the immortals,
> And this great Universe would be a great desert.
> Lose with good reason the fear with which you are carried away,
> One just doesn't finish off a hymen in that way. (11)

The prospect of Iphis and Iante sharing a marriage bed doesn't perturb this woman, since she conflates sex in general with reproductive sex. She cannot even imagine the possibility of lesbian sex.

The play, however, hints at precisely such a possibility from the very first scene, when Teletuze stresses the forbiddenness of her daughter acting on desire for another girl. "Cease paying homage to [Iante's] divine charms,/ Nature and the Gods do not permit it," she warns (7). She treats the marriage as a great danger to be prevented, telling Ergaste, "It is no longer time to laugh about it, ...& I swear to you/ That one is braving the laws of nature today;/ If you love Iphis, as I believe,/ Turn aside this calamity" (15). As for Iphis herself, at times she gives voice to a resistant discourse, as when she claims to have "[a] heart that nature made contrary to others" (60), thus contesting the branding of her desires as unnatural. Even when she speaks of the impossibility of acting on these desires, her language seems to hint at unspoken possibilities, as in the following soliloquy:

> Ha lamentable Iphis! Unfortunate Iante!
> Which of us two will be able to consummate the marriage?
> What, that charming treasure would be in my arms,
> I would possess it, & would not enjoy it [*n'en jouïrois pas*]?
> What, I would hold the object with which my soul is in love,

---

[26] Note that in seventeenth-century French, 'new' [*nouveau/nouvelle*] could also mean 'unknown' [*inconnue*], and 'novelty' [*nouveauté*] could also mean 'strangeness' [*étrangeté*] (Dubois et al., 346). Note also that along with newness and strangeness, the subject of incest is raised here, although briefly (27).

And I would make such bad use of a favor acquired?
What, Heaven would make me[,] without extinguishing my fires,
From a happy Lover, an unhappy possessor?
What, I would go to sleep next to that beauty,
And I would not do the impossible for her?
I would be useless in a role so noble?
No, the good Goddess will have pity on me. (39–40)

Iphis imagines herself in bed, physically touching and holding the woman she loves, and cannot believe she'll be unable to make love to her. In particular, the line "I would possess it, & would not enjoy it?" brings the issue of sex right to the surface: the verb *jouir de* meant (and still means) both "to enjoy" and "to have sex with," giving the line the alternate meaning, "I would possess her and not have sex with her?" (Guiraud, 403–404). Throughout the passage, Iphis turns declarations of impossibility into questions, makes doubtful what people like Ergaste's sister treat as certain. And significantly, at the end, she doesn't specify in what way the Goddess will have pity on her. Rather than say, "No, the good Goddess will turn me into a man," she leaves the question open, allowing herself, and the audience, to imagine anything they like.[27]

That Benserade is enticing his audience to imagine two women having sex becomes undeniable when Iphis describes her wedding night. As she recounts the experience to her mother:

...although my ardor was so useless for us,
I forgot sometimes that I was a girl,
I never received so much contentment,
I gave in to my transports of joy,
With a kiss I assuaged my amorous fevers,
And my soul came up to the edge of my lips,
In the sweet feeling of these superfluous joys
I forgot the very one to which I aspired the most,
I embraced that beautiful body, of which the extreme whiteness

---

[27] Even when the play associates the marriage of Iphis and Iante with criminality, the connotations are usually ambiguous. After the wedding (but well before the sex-change), Iphis reassures Iante, "The marriage that converts crime into innocence/ To my young desires gives complete license" (62). The morning after the wedding, Ligde repeats the message (V.ii; p.74). The passages are humorous, but also ambiguous. Normally, the mystery of marriage converts crime to innocence, sin to sanctity, unlicensed lust to licensed love. But, by implication, this marriage, this love, this mystery (I.ii; p.8) converts connubial innocence, sanctity, and love to—to what? To crime, sin, lust? Perhaps, but perhaps not, depending on whether two women together can commit a sexual crime, sin, or act. Unlike in England, sex between women was criminal in France. Yet the situation was still ambiguous (cf. Wahl, 20–23).

Excited me to make room for it in myself,
I touched, I kissed, my heart was content. (81)

In bed with her beloved Iante, forgetting things she knows (she is a girl; she had wanted more than anything to "consummate her marriage," a phrase that in the French—*consommer l'hymenée*—makes the wished-for act clear: penetrating the woman's vagina and breaking her hymen), Iphis finds contentment in the "superfluous" pleasures of nonpenetrative, nonprocreative, non–climax-oriented sex. Iphis even perhaps intimates that she stopped being confined to the masculine, penetrator role, and was moved to try somehow to encompass Iante within herself (whether figuratively or literally). In any case, the audience is all but forced to picture what the women did together, and to imagine what else was possible.

The blissful moment does not last, however. As Iphis further recounts, once Iante realizes her husband is a girl, she withdraws inward, lies there sighing, as responsive to Iphis's kisses and touches as a block of wood. When dawn comes, the newlyweds rise and dress, Iante's tears falling nonstop (V.iv; p.82). Neither one speaks of their situation, neither expresses what she thinks or feels.

Iphis thinks she knows what goes through her beloved's mind: the girl is vexed and unhappy at having been deceived and not having found the object of her desires (82). And perhaps those were indeed Iante's initial sentiments. But we have already learned, from a soliloquy Iante delivers at the beginning of Act V, that she thinks and feels things of which Iphis has no inkling.

Not surprisingly, Iante has a hard time believing what has happened; it seems like a dream. Also not surprisingly, she fears she and Iphis will be punished somehow ("A girl, great Gods! to wed another,/ It's enough to draw down heavenly wrath,/ And to make us spoken of in the theaters,/ Such a circumstance is worthy of being acted,/ That fear distresses me, I must admit" [72–73]). But she expresses no anger or resentment toward Iphis. On the contrary, she voices altogether unexpected feelings and desires:

This marriage is sweet, and I find in it enough charms,
And if people didn't laugh at it, I wouldn't complain of it:
I wouldn't regret that we were joined together,
If one weren't profaning the knot that unites us,
And if our good parents weren't abusing as they pleased
That marriage [*hymen*] that is held so holy and sacred;
If a girl married a girl like her,
Without offending Heaven and natural law,
My heart assuredly would not be at all upset [*fasché*] about it,
I would content myself with not having sinned;
But since nature and heaven both decree
That the fidelity of a girl is given to men,
And that it is only a man who obtains it,
Iphis not being one, that is where the pain [*mal*] grips me.
But what an irksome war I am going to suffer

From those who are content with my sad fortune,
And who not judging anything but by the exterior,
Know very badly what I have in my heart. (73)

Startlingly, knowing Iphis is female, Iante still wants to stay married. Iante's unwanted conclusion clearly derives from what she has been taught about marriage, and possibly about lesbianism: heaven and natural law decree that girls must marry men. It is even hinted she accepts this teaching less from personal conviction than from social pressure, for it is immediately after having admitted she fears her situation with Iphis will be spoken of in the theaters that she avers, "if people didn't laugh at [this marriage], I would not complain of it." Those who judge only by exterior appearances may mock, but in her heart the marriage is sweet.

Simply by giving Iante a voice, this passage is remarkable. As Leibacher-Ouvrard (2003) points out, "Benserade innovates... in giving voice to the *other* lover in this pair of female lovers, she who is always forgotten, doubtless because one attributes nothing masculine to her (nothing 'butch'...)" (372; my trans.). Yet the content of the passage, what Benserade has her say when she is allowed to speak, makes it extraordinary. Indeed, it ought to make us wonder whether *Iphis et Iante* might not be, at least in part, a pro-lesbian text. For, upon a first reading, the passage seems not to utilize any of the anti-lesbian rhetorical strategies common at the time. Instead, it seems to treat Iante and her feelings quite sympathetically.

However, further consideration may suggest a less welcome conclusion. For one thing, Benserade is the author of a long poem, "On the Love of Uranie and Philis" ["Sur l'Amour d'Uranie et Philis"], in which the poetic speaker reacts to his mistress Uranie's falling in love with another woman by rehearsing a veritable litany of anti-lesbian and misogynist charges: it is doubly shameful for a man to lose to a female rival; lesbian sex is an impossibility, lacking as it does what is needed to satisfy a woman; thus lesbian desire is vain desire; indeed lesbian desire, like lesbian sex, is an impossibility, since only men desire (women are desired); lesbianism is an imitation of heterosexuality; lesbianism is childish; lesbianism is fraudulent; women are nothing apart from men; a woman's desire for a woman is an attack upon men.[28]

Of course, an author may take a certain position in one text and a contrary position in another. And one shouldn't automatically conflate the sentiments of poet and speaker—perhaps Benserade intends the speaker's misogyny and anti-lesbianism to read as the laughable attempts of a jilted lover to assuage his ego.[29] Yet the existence of this possibly lesbophobic poem ought to give us pause. At the

---

[28] Orig. date unknown; rpt. Benserade, *Poésies*, 165–73, and Benserade, *Iphis et Iante*, ed. Verdier, 142–48. For an excellent discussion of the poem, see Wahl; also Bonnet (1995) and Verdier.

[29] I thank Turner for offering this possibility.

very least, "Uranie et Philis" might suggest Benserade expects his audience to recognize, and perhaps be amused by, Iante's naiveté, her ignorance: in love with Iphis and never having known sex with a man, Iante is satisfied with lesbian love (never portrayed in this play as penetrative). If only she knew better—and she soon will, when Iphis becomes a man—she would change her mind.[30]

More importantly, evidence internal to the play suggests a similarly superior attitude. Consider, in particular, a moment quoted above, when just before Iante admits the marriage is sweet, she worries, "A girl, great Gods! to wed another,/ It's enough to draw down heavenly wrath,/ And to make us spoken of in the theaters,/ Such a circumstance is worthy of being acted." This sudden, unexpected moment of meta-theatricality—in which a character in a play worries about being turned into a character in a play—demands explanation. Why does it occur, precisely here, immediately prior to what could easily appear to be a pro-lesbian passage? The answer, I believe, is that it functions as a form of belittlement, undermining what follows.

First, it makes the audience more knowing than Iante—little does she realize what we know: her situation *is* being acted onstage. Her ignorance is thus foregrounded from the start.

Second, since part of what Iante fears is already happening (her situation is being acted onstage), perhaps the second part (its being ridiculed) is happening as well. For a couple of lines later, Iante makes clear that the reaction she anticipates is laughter ("And if people didn't laugh at [the marriage], I wouldn't complain of it"). Perhaps, then, Benserade uses this meta-theatrical moment to signal that the audience should indeed laugh at two naive girls who have mistaken lesbian superfluities for the real thing, foolish girls who don't know they're experiencing a mere illusion, a simulacrum, an inferior imitation of heterosexual love.

Third, this meta-theatrical gesture reminds the audience that Iphis and Iante's story is only the stuff of drama, not reality. It reassures us that the events are occurring in a space for fantasy, and that whatever is imagined there (especially something as potentially threatening as lesbianism, above all the idea that a woman would knowingly choose to be coupled for life with another woman) is indeed only imaginary. As such, Iante's secretly voiced desire to remain wedded to Iphis can be represented without being taken seriously. The text can tease its audience with the possibility of lesbian sex—even, momentarily, the possibility that lesbian sex might compete with heterosex—but in the end reassert lesbian sexual *im*possibility, reaffirming its own (deliberately constructed) ignorance of any alternative to transforming Iphis into a man in order to save her marriage.[31]

---

[30] Such a view—which Wahl espouses (64–67)—would accord with the superior, libertine attitude the speaker of "Sur l'Amour d'Uranie et Philis" shares in general with Brantôme, particularly in regard to lesbianism.

[31] Of course, the theater can stage pathos as well as farce. But, again, I think the meta-theatrical playfulness of watching a character in a play worry about being turned into a

The titillation factor has been high, however, including a prolonged pair of kisses between the actresses playing Iphis and Iante (II.iii-iv; p.33–34).[32] And certainly, despite the meta-theatrical moment, some audience members likely found Iante's sentiments more endearing than amusing. By the time Isis finally sets things straight, lesbianism, however imagined, may very well have seemed intriguing and attractive enough to make the metamorphosis unwelcome to some. Which might, perhaps, explain the aforementioned eruption of hypermasculinity at the end of this otherwise relaxed and playful text. By having the newly male Iphis suddenly assert, "Venus who all alone occupied my cares,/ Contracts in my eyes to make place for Mars," perhaps Benserade is overcompensating, momentarily invoking his culture's warlike ideal of masculinity in the hope that, joined to a gentle and obedient Iante in a marriage of opposites, a hypermanly Iphis will offset the lingering attraction that the androgynous, lesbian Iphis, paired to a freethinking and willing Iante in a union of likes, might otherwise exert.

Or then again, as Leibacher-Ouvrard argues, perhaps the play remains playful to the very end, undercutting Iphis's manly metamorphosis with a touch of farce: "It is, in effect, by a rather hackneyed boastfulness that Iphis starts out in the world of men; by the quite bourgeois promise of 'quite tangible effects' so that his 'dear half' might prove 'in nine months that Iphis is a boy'" (373; my trans.). Indeed, Leibacher-Ouvrard makes a strong case for reading Benserade as mocking the masculinism and heteronormativity of Ovid's tale and most of its adaptations. If the possibility of lesbianism is erased by play's end, as it surely is, nevertheless, contends Leibacher-Ouvrard, *Iphis et Iante* is most notable for refusing to naturalize that erasure, instead calling attention to, even parodying, the constraint, the ideological work, involved (375).

And yet, I can't help feeling Benserade would be heartily amused at such an earnest conclusion. For in keeping with his given name, Isaac—which, as both Leibacher-Ouvrard and Verdier point out, refers in Hebrew to laughter or laughing—he seems to laugh, and to invite laughter, at *everyone* (as in the exchange discussed above [224–25] between Ergaste and Nise). When it comes to love, everyone in the play looks foolish. If Iphis and Iante are more endearing than

---

character in a play tips the scene toward the latter, with the invocation of theatergoers' laughter serving almost as a stage direction to the audience. Moreover, the humorous treatment of male homosexuality, discussed earlier, encourages the audience to treat Iante's non-normative feelings as a joke, too. (On a similarly revealing, meta-theatrical moment in Shakespeare's *Antony and Cleopatra,* see Steve Brown, 243–44.) For a different reading of this moment, see Leibacher-Ouvrard (2003) 371–72. Verdier argues that Iphis and Ianthe are the only characters not mocked by the play (32).

[32] Since women acted on the French stage, and since Iphis doesn't become a man until the very end of the play, I think it most likely she was portrayed by an actress *en travestie*. Verdier leaves the question open, pointing out the implications of each possibility in terms of illusory versus non-illusory theater (22).

their fellow characters, it is because their naiveté is unmixed with arrogance, not because they aren't naive.

"Oh! whither would my Transport tend?": *Friendship Improv'd*, Sodomy Unknown

In the end, a final assessment of *Iphis et Iante*'s sexual politics comes down to a matter of emphasis or perspective. Not so for the final work I want to explore, Charles Hopkins's *Friendship Improv'd; Or, The Female Warriour. A Tragedy* (perf. 1699; pub. 1700). In this play, as in Benserade's, a man in love with a woman passing as a man wishes aloud that his beloved be transformed into a woman. But here the beloved responds, "Those Metamorphoses, alas! are past" (I.10). The line seems to explain the genesis of the play, as if Hopkins's reworking of Ovid's tale derives from the question, "If a metamorphosis, a sex-change, is no longer dramatically possible, how can the story of Iphis and Ianthe still be told?" The answer (at least for Hopkins) is to make Iphis fall in love with a man rather than a woman. The obstacle to their love will therefore be removed, rather than revealed, once her true sex is known. No physical transformation is needed. But as we shall see, if Hopkins all but banishes physical impossibility from his play (with the exception of a ghostly warning delivered long ago), he more than makes up for the loss by a marked increase in ideological impossibility.[33]

Hopkins alters "Iphis and Ianthe" far more drastically than either Bellamy or Benserade, recalling instead *Gallathea, The Maydes Metamorphosis,* and *Love's Cure*. Like Beaumont and Fletcher, he removes the story from its Ovidian pastoral setting; unlike them, he also transposes the story from comedy to heroic tragicomedy. The story is now set in Sicily. The father is called Zoilus, and he is the country's usurper, having killed its rightful ruler, Orontes, twenty years earlier. His wife is named Semanthe, and his daughter, secretly raised as a boy, Locris. Locris is in love with her father's general, Maherbal, who, unbeknownst to everyone, including himself, is Orontes's son Araxes. Maherbal clearly loves Locris, and wishes they could somehow be more than just friends (hence the play's title, *Friendship Improv'd*). At Zoilus's command, Locris is soon to be married to Orontes's daughter, Orythia, and Maherbal to Locris's older sister, Cyllene. Both Orythia and Cyllene love their husbands-to-be.[34]

---

[33] The play is divided into acts, but not scenes; lines are unnumbered. I cite the act number, followed by page number, for all quotations. Regarding the obsolescence of metamorphosis: John Dennis, in the preface to his translation of Ovid's *Byblis*, entitled "The Passion of Byblis, Made English" (1692), explains that he has changed the ending of the tale (Byblis goes mad and then dies, instead of being transformed into a fountain) for precisely this reason.

[34] On tragicomedy, see DiGangi (1997) ch.5, although, as DiGangi himself admits,

More than any of the texts we have examined—with the possible exception of *Love's Cure*—*Friendship Improv'd* focuses upon and condemns the abuse of patriarchal authority. The tyrant Zoilus is both a bad *pater familias* and a bad *pater patriae*. His vaunting ambition—refusal to accept the existing disposition of power in the world, refusal to accept his place in the divinely ordained hierarchy and submit to the patriarchal authority of his rightful king—is the ultimate cause of all the play's conflicts. It leads him to usurp the kingship of Sicily, thus disordering the political realm, and to value a male heir so highly he threatens to kill his own child if female, thus disordering the familial realm. (That Maherbal and Locris eventually fall in love only reinforces this complete blending of the political and familial.) His tyrannical behavior also precipitates the play's immediate action, as he attempts to force Locris and Maherbal to marry the women he has chosen.

And yet, like earlier versions, Hopkins's retelling reproduces rather than resists the ideology of the Ovidian original. As the play progresses, Zoilus is supplanted as chief villain by his daughter Cyllene, her villainy the direct outgrowth of aggressive female heterosexual desire. Rather than wait for Maherbal to speak first, she has already confessed her passionate feelings to him (II.18). Even worse, despite rejection, she proceeds to woo him ever more fiercely, her resolve neatly summed up in these words: "Down then the strugling Woman in my Breast,/ I'll forfeit Modesty to purchase Rest" (II.22). A woman without modesty is no longer a woman; she is a monster. Cyllene accordingly becomes monstrous. Turned down by Maherbal yet again, she resolves to make him fear "the Revenge of a rejected Maid" (III.31) and instigates his arrest.

Although she then balks at the prospect of his death and helps Locris engineer his escape, when she learns Locris is really a girl, and Maherbal and this girl are in love, Cyllene gives herself over entirely to hatred, imagining herself, and prompting us to imagine her, a veritable demon, as in the following soliloquy:

> Now leap my ravish'd Heart, now mount my Soul,
> And each extended Arm grasp either Pole.
> Reach yonder Starry roof, and Chrystal Spheres,
> And shew the Gods a Genius great as theirs.
> Then downwards drive, search the deep Plots of Hell,
> And learn if Women, or if Feinds excel.
> Make Fate with industry thy task pursue,
> For thou hast set it work enough to do.
> If half tir'd Furies at their toyl repine,
> Give them new Fury; Woman, give them thine. (V.50)

She is the living embodiment of the saying, "Hell hath no fury like a woman scorned." As in "Byblis," "Myrrha," and "Salmacis and Hermaphroditus," so here:

"'homoeroticism' and 'sodomy' make more tenuous appearances in [his] reading of tragicomedy than elsewhere in [his] study" (160).

sexual desire is the root of all female evil.[35]

The play's misogyny extends further, however. Not only does Cyllene replace Zoilus as chief villain, she is responsible for his worst crimes. When he becomes truly tyrannical toward Locris and Maherbal, Cyllene turns out to have stirred up "his Passion" against them (IV.34). When he later kills Semanthe, Cyllene drives him to it (V.49), after boasting of her matricidal (and sororicidal) intentions: "Fly all respect of Nature and her Laws,/ 'Tis Nature bids Revenge in such a Cause./ Mother, and Sister shall my Victims fall,/ And universal Ruine swallow all" (V.48; notice the echo of *Myrrha* [X.346–48], where a monstrous daughter's flouting of Nature's laws confounds all familial order, perhaps all order itself).

Moreover Zoilus, bad as he is, eventually feels remorse (V.48). Indeed, after killing his wife, he kills himself, unable to bear "the sting/ Of Conscience giv[ing] at last the secret Wound" (V.52). In contrast, Cyllene hasn't a shred of humanity left; she becomes entirely evil, and remains so to the extravagantly bitter end. After attempting, and failing, to stab Locris, she turns the dagger on herself, and dies cursing her sister:

> Gods! tho' on [Maherbal] your Blessings you conferr,
> Be Just by halves—heap Plagues—heap Hell on her.
> Soon may she Die—shall that poor Curse suffice?—
> Long may she Live, long slighted, e're she dies.
> May she most Vertuous be, most chastly good,
> But he believe her most abandon'd lewd!
> Then may this flourishing, yet happy she
> Die thus Desdain'd, thus in Dispair like me. [*Dies.*] (V.55)

The substance of the curse is significant. The worst thing a woman can be believed is "most abandon'd lewd," a fact of which Cyllene herself is dying proof: her uncontrollable desire for Maherbal makes her the text's arch-villain, eclipsing her murderous tyrant of a father.

As often happens, the play attempts to disavow its ideological nastiness. Hopkins would have us believe it *anti*-misogynist. He does so by first depicting both Zoilus and Maherbal as blatant misogynists, then condemning the former and reforming the latter. Thus Zoilus at one point philosophizes, "In vain with life-long Trouble we contend,/ Where women are concern'd, it cannot end./ On them we lavish our unhappy Life,/ The Mistress plagues us first, and then the Wife" (II.13). He later communicates his views on women more succinctly, calling Semanthe "Traytress, Viper, Monster, Woman, Wife!" (V.51; see also I.8). For his part, Maherbal focuses upon women's voracious and duplicitous sexuality, advising his "friend" Locris:

---

[35] The "Hell hath no fury" notion had recently been expressed in Cibber's *Love's Last Shift* ([1696] IV.i) and Congreve's *The Mourning Bride* ([1697] III.viii.42–43), as cited by Stevenson, ed., 2566–67.

> Believe me, Youth, who know what Women are,
> The Sex was never worth a Soldier's Care.
> Hard to be won, inconstant when obtain'd,
> Like new forc'd Towns, lost with more Ease than gain'd.
> The foolish Bridegroom makes the Nuptial Feast,
> But he that gives the Banquet shares the least.
> Safe in that State, to worst Extreams they fall,
> They wed but one, their Wishes are for all. (I.11)

Zoilus is a villain, and the woman he derides, Semanthe, a loving mother. His words thus serve as further evidence of evil-mindedness. Maherbal, however, is a hero. He must therefore be made to recant his misogyny. The eventual sight of Locris's bared breast, which reveals her true sex, elicits this recantation, in the form of an extravagant, fourteen-line paean to Woman, source of the soldier's courage, theme of the poets' words and prophets' dreams (V.47). The play, we are meant to conclude, opposes misogyny.[36]

Yet Maherbal's new sentiments prove the flip side of the same old sexist coin. Women—at least good ones—are mere objects in his enlightened view of the sexes: women inspire, men act (so active women, like Cyllene, are bad). As the play concludes, Maherbal, now identified as Araxes, proceeds to treat them accordingly. Although he had once declared, "He tyrannizes most o're human Life,/ Who would, against our Will, impose a Wife" (III.28), Araxes, at the end of the play, orders Orythia to marry a young man he wishes to reward, telling her, "On that brave Youth you must your Love bestow,/ For you can Rival me no longer now" (V.55). He doesn't give her the option of remaining single, now that her beloved Locris is unattainable. In fact, he doesn't allow her even to respond to the news that her husband-to-be is actually a woman and is about to be married to someone else. Orythia's wishes and feelings are irrelevant to Araxes. And to the play: she has no more lines. Araxes, meanwhile, appears to have forgotten his recent conversion to philogyny, for he sums up Cyllene's horrifying end by observing:

> What sad extreams make most of Women's Fate,
> Raging with love, relentless in their hate:
> Successive passions in their turns prevail,
> Less fair their Person's, than their tempers frail. (V.55)

Only a short while ago he had declared to Locris, "The gods for your Creation we adore/ But still we Worship you their Creatures more" (V.47). Now, in one of the

---

[36] On this scene, in the context of other Restoration scenes in which an actress's bared breast or two reveals her character's true sex, see Stallybrass, 66–68, and the rest of his article for such scenes in Renaissance drama, when the "actresses" proving their characters' true sex were male, not female.

oldest ideological oscillations known to man—Woman is Angel, Woman is Devil—he paints Cyllene as the rule rather than exception where females are concerned.

Araxes is not through oscillating, however. A few minutes later, his final reversal displays the literally stupefying ability of dominant ideology to unknow whatever might contradict it. When Locris momentarily swoons at the sight of her parents' dead bodies, Araxes comforts her with the assurance, "You shall not grieve alone, my Charming Fair,/ Give me your Sorrows, or at least my share;/ Too soon your Sex is with your woes opprest,/ Which would sit better in a manly Breast" (V.56). He and the text have somehow forgotten that throughout the play, up until the moment Locris revealed her true sex, she too was a soldier, a "fearless Hero in the Field," and "tho' a Maid, [had] a Manly Heart" (I.5). Nurture had triumphed over Nature (Locris was "bred up to wield/ The Shining Sword, to lift the pondrous Shield" [I.5]). The text seemed to approve of this gender reversal, to take pleasure in it and invite the audience to do the same. Indeed, the play's subtitle, *The Female Warriour*, advertises female manliness as a main attraction.

But everything changes when Locris bares her breast. As if magically—or rather, as if naturally—Maherbal converts from misogyny to philogyny, delivering his panegyric on womanhood. And as if with equal inevitability, as if hailed irresistibly by sexist ideology (but without the spontaneous, love-induced internal transformation Clara undergoes in *Love's Cure*), Locris accepts normative femininity. "Here all the Warfare of my life is o'er," she declares, "And I must play the Man's great part no more" (V.47). In addition to the double meaning of "the Man's great part" (both the masculine role and the anatomical equipment needed for playing it, both of which together equal the phallus), the ambiguity of "must" in this sentence—does Locris mean "I no longer have to" or "I no longer am allowed to"?—is fitting. Locris loved warfare and bids it a very fond, almost regretful, farewell (thirteen lines, with nine repetitions of "Farewel"). As she does so, the text itself renounces the pleasures of gender-transgression. From here on in, what was wrong will be made right, what was crooked will be made straight.

And lest the text's earlier enjoyment of female masculinity provoke guilt, now that such pleasures have been renounced, Cyllene will be scapegoated for this sin as well. Standing by the newly dead body of her father, she intones, "Farewel, great soul; and now farewel all Fear,/ I am thy Off-spring, and thy Spirit's heir" (V.53). The repetitions of "Farewel" draw attention to the substitution underway: Locris has just bid goodbye to gender-transgression; Cyllene now embraces it, usurping a son's place as heir. As a sexually aggressive woman, Cyllene was already masculinized. In case we didn't get the point, we now learn she's a woman with a man's spirit. She thus takes the rap for gender-transgression, as she took it for patriarchal tyranny.

By killing off Cyllene, turning "The Female Warriour" into a fainting woman, and silencing Orythia, Hopkins expunges any remaining trace of female masculinity from the play. My inclusion of Orythia may seem strange, but after all, she has been passionately in love with another woman. Unwittingly, it's true. Nor is there reason to believe she would have continued to love Locris once the latter's true sex had been revealed. Locris, at least, earlier reassures herself, and us, "[Orythia's Passion] will be cur'd as soon as I am known" (II.16). Unlike Benserade, who dared suggest (even if only jokingly, as a sign of Iante's naiveté) that a woman who has fallen in love with what she thinks is a man needn't stop loving him once she learns he's a she, Hopkins will not admit the merest whiff of such a possibility. In his play, as in *Love's Cure,* lesbian desire, let alone lesbian sex, does not exist. It's at most an illusion, and thus likened (in a soliloquy by Locris), not to Iphis's passion for Ianthe, but to Narcissus's self-love:

> What an odd fortune must I hourly prove,
> A Woman still prest with a Woman's Love;
> *Narcissus* like, the Love-sick Nymph betray'd,
> Pursues, and woes her own deceitful Shade;
> She Follows that in following of a Maid. (II.14)

A love so unknown—actively imagined as insubstantial—poses no risk to dominant practices or ideologies. And yet the play's final, bizarrely harsh treatment of Orythia betrays the very fear it seeks to deny: that love between women could rival love between women and men.

The play has not been concerned solely with transgressive sex/gender/sexuality in women, however. It devotes equal, and equally schizoid, attention to, flirts with and then recoils from, male homosexuality. But not just any old kind. The text constructs, and then cures, a hypermasculine, misogynist male homosexuality.

The issue arises in the first exchange between Maherbal and Locris, when their weddings have been indefinitely postponed due to the outbreak of war:

> *Ma.* ...The Clash and din of War your Soul delight,
> And you love Glory gain'd in open Fight,
> More than the secret Pleasures of the Night.
> By Heav'n, I swear, when *Hymen*'s sacred Tye
> Was broke abruptly off; a suddain Joy
> Sprung in my Soul, and yet I knew not why.
>   *Lo.* My Thoughts no other End but Fame pursue,
> To fight, to conquer, or to dye with you.
> Young as I am, I love a glorious Field,
> More than the Bliss my charming Bride could yeild.
> Thou art the Center where my Wishes joyn,
> My Fame, my Friendship, and my Soul is thine.
> Your very Sight transports me, for I see
> My Champion and my Genius move in thee.
>   *Ma.* I love you with a Fondness far above
> All that was ever known in Woman's love.
> My Friend—Oh! whither would my Transport tend?

Can I say more than what I say? my Friend!
Something there is beyond that very Name,
Something that sets my Spirits in a Flame,
I wish I were a Maid of Form divine,
To make your Soul and Body ever mine.
Rather I wish that you, dear Youth, could be
That charming Maid to be belov'd by me.
Friendship alone to wond'rous Heights may soar,
The change of one of us would make it more.
    Lo. Those Metamorphoses, alas! are past,
Could Wishes do, mine should not be the last.
But from our Theme our Thoughts are wander'd far,
We talk of Love, when we were bent for War.
And yet your Words such tender Passion move,
That I could ever talk with you of Love.
    Ma. Had not your Arms establish'd your Renown,
Were not your vast Exploits and Valour known,
By those sweet Looks, that charming Face betray'd,
My sight would all my other Sence invade,
And make me think you, what I wish, a Maid.
Oft have I entertain'd that pleasing Thought,
Till my Mistake your manly Actions taught,
And spight of them destroy'd the hopes I sought.
    Lo. Were I that Maid, already so intire,
My Love is grown, it never could aspire,
To a more Sacred or Cœlestial Fire.
My Friendship has attain'd to that Excess,
Fond as she is, my Sister loves you less.
But hark, ...Trumpets and Drums summon their Chiefs away,
Who want *Maherball* to begin the day.
    Ma. Then farewell Love, leave all those empty Joys,
To longing Maids, and to deluded Boys. (I.9–11)

Maherbal is, and Locris pretends to be, the sort of man Ergaste imitated in Benserade's play: the man of war, intensely bonded to other men, contemptuous of women (Maherbal's misogynist remarks, discussed earlier, conclude the exchange). Locris's feelings are perfectly acceptable—she knows she is a woman in love with a man. Maherbal's feelings are decidedly problematic—his feelings are identical to Locris's, yet he believes they are directed toward a man (or at least a youth). How does the text handle this danger?

Above all, by unknowing. Maherbal and the text stress his inability to articulate or even imagine the precise implications of his love. Joy sprang into his soul when the weddings were postponed, "yet [he] knew not why." He wonders "whither... [his] Transport[s] tend?" He senses that "Something there is beyond" friendship, but doesn't name that "Something." Or rather, he names it—"To make [Locris's]

Soul and Body ever [his]," to share sex as well as feelings with his friend—only when he imagines one of them transformed into a woman. "Friendship Improv'd" is friendship with sex, which the text would have us believe necessarily requires a man and a woman. What it steadfastly refuses even to consider is the possibility the same result could be achieved between men.

Sex between men, with or without friendship, would, at the turn of the eighteenth century, be sodomy. And sodomy, ever since the medieval Church "invented" the concept, had been conceived of as a malignancy requiring extirpation. Now, with the growing visibility of molly-house culture in late seventeenth-century northwestern Europe, sodomy was becoming inextricably associated with effeminacy. Benserade's Ergaste, at the end of the Renaissance, could feign passion for a pretty boy and not automatically be branded effeminate. Maherbal, at the turn of the eighteenth century, immediately runs that risk, even though he is a triumphantly heroic soldier whose masculinity ought to be beyond question.[37]

Not that all effeminacy was equally negative. In the Renaissance, the man considered effeminate because of homosexual activity was despised, even hated. But the man considered effeminate because of excessive *heterosexual* activity was as likely to be admired as criticized. Being a man's man may have been a cultural ideal, but being a ladies' man came in for its share of praise. This tolerance or admiration for heteroeffeminacy continued into the Restoration. Thus Maherbal can indulge in the startling fantasy of being a woman ("I wish I were a Maid of Form divine") in the service of hetero love and sex ("To make your Soul and Body ever mine"). His momentary, fantasmatic gender-transgression is excused by heterosexual desire, as is the equally fantasmatic gender-transgression of any men in the audience who identify with him.

The exculpatory powers of hetero desire extend even further here, for such desire is used to explain—to explain *away*—not only an imaginary sex-change, but also what would otherwise have to be recognized as sodomitical desire. Maherbal is not a sodomite, because we know, intuitively, he knows, intuitively, Locris is really a girl. We are sure he wouldn't feel these desires for an actual man, only for a woman disguised as a man. (Whether he would have felt them for a woman *not* disguised as a man is a question we'll consider in a moment). One might say he, or rather his heart or penis—his heart-on?—has X-ray powers, a special hetero ability to penetrate disguise to the true sex underneath. Even more precisely, perhaps this

---

[37] On the coining of "sodomy," both the word and the idea(s), see Jordan (for sodomy as "malignant," see 43). On the representation of sodomites and sodomy in the Restoration and eighteenth century, see Bray (1982, 1990), Norton, McFarlane, Netta Murray Goldsmith, and Hammond, as well as essays in Gerard and Hekma, eds. On changing conceptions of sexuality and gender in this period, see Trumbach's book (1998), and his earlier essays. But see also Haggerty's review (2000) of Trumbach (1998), and Robinson's critique (1993) of both Bray and Trumbach.

is not just a hetero power but a hetero*male* power, as my use of the word 'penetrate' suggests, since Orythia seems not to possess it. If she did, we would have to perceive her as a tribade, since we would know, intuitively, she knows, intuitively, her beloved is really a girl. Instead, whereas Locris's concealed sex excuses Maherbal's desire, Locris's displayed gender excuses Orythia's. Despite the latter's silencing at play's end, she is not portrayed as a tribade.[38]

To appreciate just how phobic this play really is, it helps to compare it to other depictions of male-male friendship and love on the Restoration stage. As Haggerty has demonstrated, Restoration theater-goers were regularly treated, when watching tragedy, to the spectacle of eroticized friendship between men. These idealized, heroic friendships—between such figures as Antony and Dolabella in Dryden's *All for Love* (1677), Alexander and Hephestion in Lee's *The Rival Queens* (1677), and Valentinian and Lycias in Rochester's *Valentinian* (1684)—were sometimes more explicitly, sometimes less explicitly sexual. Haggerty (1999) argues, for instance, that although Dryden "hints at a physical intimacy" between Antony and Dolabella, "[t]his is not to say that [they] are sodomitical partners, but rather that Dryden wants to make it clear that their love has a decidedly erotic power" (28). In contrast, Lee emphasizes his hero's "violation of social hierarchy," thereby "mark[ing] Alexander's love as sodomitical as clearly as any keyhole testimony of physical penetration would" (33), while Rochester goes even further, delivering "the most homoerotic expression in Restoration tragedy," one that deliberately exposes "[t]he very contradictions of Restoration culture," and "suggests that male friendship is more than platonic and that male-male love is more than sodomitical" (38). Yet, however different from one another, these and other heroic tragedies of the period treat male friendship as do the French romances on which some of them (such as *The Rival Queens*) are based: "seem[ing] to cross and recross the boundaries between male friendship and the eroticization of male bonds so often as to make any such distinction meaningless" (34). And as Haggerty so crucially stresses, such eroticized male friendship was a *normal* feature of the Restoration stage.[39]

Friendship Improv'd, however—performed on the early Augustan rather than Restoration stage—works hard to reestablish boundaries such previous texts blur (much as *Love's Cure*—revised most likely in the 1620s and published in 1647— worked to correct erotic transgressions of Renaissance transvestite theater). Whether because of a less permissive ideological climate under William and Mary; an increase in cultural anxiety about male-male sexuality specifically; Hopkins's

---

[38] An alternative hypothesis is that this special X-ray power operates only when ideologically convenient.

[39] See also Haggerty (2002), which somewhat revises his earlier work; and see Franceschina (ch.6) on the wide range of Restoration plays that portray one or more varieties of male or female homoeroticism, and (ch.7) the Augustan theater's targeting of effeminate "beaus."

own anxieties about sex, gender, and sexuality; the heterosexist pressures imposed by an ultimately comic rather than tragic plot (notwithstanding the title's self-identification as "A Tragedy"); or some combination of these and other factors, Hopkins's play is founded upon a deeply conservative sexual ideology. Whatever pleasure it may take, and offer, in the spectacle of a temporarily heroic woman (a *Female Warriour*), it makes sure everyone knows that manly Maherbal cannot even imagine "something" one might add to heroic male friendship to "improve" it to love. And although for much of the play Maherbal clearly senses he has fallen in love with someone he thinks is a man, the play makes sure we know his heart-on knows better than his head—Maherbal could only ever love a woman.

As for whether he would have fallen in love with a woman *not* disguised as a man, the passage we've been examining would have us believe so. Maherbal says he was attracted "By those sweet Looks, that charming Face," the sight of which "would make [him] think [her], what [he] wish[ed], a Maid." These fancies, these "hopes," are then habitually "destroy'd" by Locris's "manly Actions." Yet a later passage suggests otherwise. Maherbal, once again rejecting Cyllene's advances, describes the only relationship that attracts him: soldierly comradeship. With feigned regret he declares:

> [W]ould you were a Man to make a Friend....
> Then should we never part, but side by side,
> Thro' broken Ranks in batter'd Armour ride.
> Urge on our foaming Horses o're the slain,
> And pant with noble Toyl along the Plain.
> Our chief Concern should for each other be,
> I guarding you, and you defending me.
> Shielding from either's Head the falling Blow,
> So should we live,—*Locris* and I live so. (II.21)

Granted, Maherbal is playing up his manly-man-who-doesn't-like-women act in order to let Cyllene down gently, let her save face. But his description of battle seems unduly erotic, with its riding, panting, and foaming side by side, never to part. It recalls the opening of his exchange with Locris, his praising the latter's preference for soldiering over "the secret [hetero] Pleasures of the Night." I would thus argue that, his remarks about Locris's prettiness notwithstanding, Maherbal (by which I really mean the play itself) is attracted as well to Locris's valiant masculinity, displayed in wartime male friendship. Officially, of course, there is nothing wrong with men enjoying battle together; it's the most "natural" thing in the world. But in this ideologically conservative play, any homoeroticism is potentially perilous, likely to cause anxiety, and thus necessitate counterbalancing by further "proofs" of the characters' heteromasculinity.

Which is why, only a few pages later, we learn Maherbal was warned against marriage by his foster-father Archias, against the "Charms" of "Syren Women" in general and those of Cyllene in particular (III.24). His coldness, even antipathy, toward women is thus not innate. Indeed, although he doesn't know it, his sexual desires, blocked by paternal command from their normal target, have nevertheless located a woman he can love.

Yet even this reassuring information seems insufficient to guard against homophobic anxiety. So the text labors on, trying to banish the idea that Maherbal's desires for Locris are sodomitical. It does so by excessively proliferating obstacles to the confession (let alone fulfillment) of the couple's love.

Already, from the start, Hopkins has overdone things, as in Locris's lament:

I love a Man, from whom I hide my Fires,
And with my Sex conceal my fond Desires.
A Man, a Stranger, whom no Kindred claim,
Of Parentage obscure, tho' known to Fame. (II.16–17)

In most plays, the heroine's need to conceal her sex would suffice as the requisite obstacle in True Love's path. Here, though, an additional impediment, inequality of birth, is immediately added. Although Locris resolves never to let this second obstacle stand in her way (since by marrying Maherbal she can raise him to her level, or indeed above it, making him "[her]... and [her] Empire's Lord" [17]), it eventually becomes a non-issue when Maherbal's royal parentage is revealed. Locris's sex-disguise ought then to be the sole barrier to love's fulfillment.

It is not: the revelation that Maherbal is Araxes turns Locris and her beloved into mortal enemies, since she is heir to the usurper who murdered his father. "Is he I Love *Araxes*?—" Locris cries. "Ah! since he is, he never can be mine" (V.42). Yet, in the space of a single soliloquy, Locris overcomes this obstacle as well, vowing to resign her crown and empire to Maherbal, as she has already resigned her heart. Once again, we are back to a single, easily removable impediment. And once again, the text introduces another.

Or rather, the text reintroduces the impediment just banished: the hatred between the houses of Orontes and Zoilus. For although Locris is willing to sacrifice family loyalty to love, Maherbal is not. His honor, he believes, demands he henceforth treat his dearest friend as bitterest foe. The protagonists' love remains doubly impeded.

This time, however, the implausibility—worse, the injustice—of Maherbal's attitude makes the obstacle's superfluity glaring. At worst, he ought to be struggling between conflicting claims on his honor: family versus friendly loyalty. But despite protestations that Locris has "wrong'd [his] Honour" (V.43), Maherbal's implacable determination to cast off his beloved companion in arms (who, moreover, has just betrayed her own father by rescuing their "Houses mortal Foe" from prison [V.42]) seems motivated by something else. Even when, in response to Maherbal's objection that "[a] Crown divides us," Locris asserts, "Here our diff'rence ends,/ Divide the Crown; that should not sep'rate Friends," Maherbal refuses to make peace: "Crowns will admit no Rivals," he retorts, "I'll resign/ Not the least Jewel that enriches mine" (V.45). We must agree with Locris when she accuses the "Poor man" of being "with Frenzy, and Ambition lost" (45). He seems almost eager to cross swords in a battle to the death.

Taking the obstruction of Locris and Maherbal's love to new, almost fatal lengths—the two actually draw swords—this last obstacle, so unnecessary, so unbelievable, seems to cry out for ideological analysis. The text's production of impediments seems hysterical, as if serving some purpose other than the ostensible, ordinary one of keeping hero and heroine apart til story's end. The primary purpose, I would argue, is to defend against the horror the play has come too close to staging: sodomitical love. An overabundance of obstacles, of forbiddenness factors, substitutes for this unmentioned, unknown one—itself a substitution for the female homosexuality at the center of "Iphis and Ianthe," which Hopkins has rewritten.[40]

In the end, the long-delayed moment when all obstacles to love are removed, combined with the additional contradictions and incoherencies this moment produces, furthers the sense of unacknowledged ideological strain. Letting his "Rage... have its course," Maherbal is ready to battle Locris. Until, that is, she offers him her "bare Breast" to strike with his sword. In an instant, rage is replaced by love, repentance, and forgiveness. Prepared to kill Locris for being Zoilus's son, Maherbal now not only absolves the daughter of responsibility for the father's crimes, but even feels capable of forgiving the father for the daughter's sake (V.46). For her part, rather than reproach Maherbal for not having chosen love over vengeance when he thought her male, Locris actually takes responsibility for his murderous fury, claiming, "I wrought your rage, high as I could to see/ That if (when known) I might forgiven be,/ And then concluded you could Love like me" (46). Even worse, although Maherbal earlier made clear that his "friendship" for Locris was actually romantic love, identical to her feelings for him, Locris—and through her the text—rewrites their earlier exchanges by declaring, "*Maherbal* was my Friend, *Araxes* loves" (47).

It is tempting to try to smooth out these contradictions. One might thus recall or imagine that even when Maherbal and Locris were companions in arms, their relationship was unequal: his having been older, the commanding officer, and (if he's to be believed) having "more oft preserv'd [Locris's] Life.../ And Sheilded [him/her] in a more dang'rous strife" (44), might explain his inability to continue their friendship after she rescues him from Zoilus's dungeon. Before, what must have felt to him (consciously or unconsciously) like sodomitical desire, was nonetheless tolerable (if uneasily so), since it was directed, in time-honored, semi-approved fashion, toward a pretty, androgynous, subordinate youth; now, when this youth becomes his equal, Maherbal has no choice but to fight his former comrade. Indeed, given his sudden eagerness to cross swords with Locris, he seems

---

[40] The text's repetition of the word "unnatural," albeit regarding Zoilus as a father (III.23; V.48, 51) reinforces this impression.

more than ever a repressed *erastes*, suddenly directing against his *eromenos*, now that the latter has challenged his superiority, the aggression through which he has always channeled his desire. As for Locris, one could say that, like the properly feminine woman she really is, she fell in love with and subordinated herself to a properly masculine man. Justified in upsetting this hierarchy in order to save his life, she of course wishes to restore the former, natural power differential as quickly as possible. Hence the extravagance of her submission once she reveals her true sex, as when she tells Maherbal, "Our [hers and her father's] Fates to thee, as to a God we trust,/ Mild amidst Wrongs, more Merciful than Just" (46).

And yet, such attempts to make the text ideologically coherent and psychologically plausible are decidedly forced. Having eliminated Iphis's physically impossible sex-change, Hopkins feels no further need to attend to questions of plausibility. One might even say his elimination of the physically unbelievable is designed to distract attention from the psychologically and ideologically unbelievable. The play is riddled with ideological holes so big one could drive a deus ex machina through them. These culminate, as we have seen, in the replacement of Iphis's spontaneous sex-change with a spontaneous gender-change (Locris gives up warfare to become a conventional, submissive woman), in addition to a spontaneous sexuality-change (Maherbal, once attracted to a sword-wielding pretty-boy buddy—whom he sometimes fantasized was a woman—is now attracted to a fainting *femme* female).

Indeed, the text also pretends to subject Maherbal to a gender-change, to turn him effeminate (in the ladies' man sense): he responds to Locris's "Farewell to Warfare" speech with a matching, although shorter, renunciation of soldiering ("Hear me, My *Locris*, take my Farewel too,/ Ye sevenfold Sheilds, and shiv'ring Spears adieu,/ Farewel to War— to all the World— but you" [V.47]). However, he never follows through on these words. The next we hear—"Romans and Rebels ravage all the Town,/ *Araxes* marches on to Snatch the Crown./ *Archias* Proclaims him at his Army's head,/ And the War done, he and... *Locris* wed" (53) — Maherbal/Araxes has assumed the normative masculine role: aggressively manly and exclusively heterosexual. All that remains is to complete the scapegoating and purging of Cyllene for her father's tyranny, for the play's misogyny, and for its gender-transgression, and then to silence and punish the unwittingly woman-loving Orythia for having rivaled, however ridiculously, the now hetero hero—leaving us, at play's end, exactly as do Ovid, the author of *The Maydes Metamorphosis*, Beaumont and Fletcher, Bellamy, and even Benserade (but *not* Lyly): with a sex/gender/sexuality–conforming male-female couple.

Conclusion

Ever since Foucault's *History of Sexuality* revolutionized the writing of LGBT history and the history of sexuality more generally, most of the field's historians, critics, and theorists have treated contemporary constructions of sex, gender, and sexuality (both normative and deviant) as relatively new—"inventions" of the modern or early modern age. To some extent, they may be correct. The waning of the active/passive divide and waxing of the homo/hetero binary; the disappearance of the "ladies' man" sense of effeminacy; the exaltation of hetero marriage bonds over same-sex (especially male) friendship—these are just a few of the changes to which one could point in asserting difference, and indeed they merit continued investigation and consideration. By no means do I wish to suggest that Ovid's Rome is identical to Lyly's, Beaumont and Fletcher's, Bellamy's, or Massinger's England, or that any of these places and times are identical to Benserade's France, Hopkins's England, or my (or your) early twenty-first-century West.

Still, I offer my readings of Ovid's *Metamorphoses* and half-a-dozen sixteenth- and seventeenth-century dramatizations of "Iphis and Ianthe" and related tales, as evidence that there are also strong continuities and similarities between these different places and times. More specifically, I have tried to demonstrate that, despite significant and often striking change over the past 2,000 years, dominant Western conceptions of sex, gender, and sexuality have remained remarkably consistent in some key respects: demonizing female sexual desire; stigmatizing effeminacy; rejecting or unknowing female homosexuality; rejecting or unknowing most forms of male homosexuality; exalting hierarchical hetero bonds between sharply gender-differentiated men and women; simultaneously criticizing and excusing patriarchal authority, especially tyranny; and associating these topics with sex-change, narcissism, incest, twinning, and the potential breakdown of fundamental societal distinctions and divisions more generally. By recognizing and exploring such continuities and similarities across place and over time, without ignoring or denying discontinuities and differences, we gain a better understanding not only of the past, but also of the present, and have a better chance of denaturalizing, and thereby loosening the grip of, these highly resilient, highly destructive ways of thinking, many of which remain at the center of battles over sex, gender, and sexuality today.

Postscript

I have been working on this book—or the project it culminates—off and on for the past twenty years, ever since writing an essay on homosexuality in *Roderick Random*, for a life-changing undergraduate course taught by Margaret Anne Doody. Since the early 1990s, one of my two principal aims has been firmly in place: to demonstrate, against the overwhelming consensus in the History of Sexuality, Lesbian and Gay Studies, and queer theory, that there are important continuities in the history of male and female same-sex love and lust, spanning the periods before, during, and after the modern "invention" of homosexuality.

I opened this book by alluding to "recent demonstrations of greater theoretical openness by leaders in the field." One of the most important such leaders—given his widespread influence, and the welcome contrast between his past and present response to continuist scholarship—is David Halperin. Although his recent collection of essays (2002a) still insists on hierarchy as the sine qua non of past same-sex models and arrangements (cf. Dalton, 221–23), it explicitly promotes a Foucauldian resistance to dogmatism.[1]

But for a sense of the current state of the field, it's perhaps best to turn to recent multi-author anthologies. Not coincidentally, three of the finest focus on the Middle Ages: Burger and Kruger (2001), Sautman and Sheingorn (2001), and Farmer and Pasternack (2003). I realize, of course, the irony of recommending medievalist scholarship at the end of a book that, however unconventional in other respects, replicates the field's larger pattern regarding the Middle Ages: all but ignoring it. In part, this neglect stems from my sources themselves: the texts I've been exploring allude repeatedly to classical works, rarely to medieval ones. Yet my inattention to medieval material reflects the limits of my expertise—indeed, of my even passing familiarity.

And yet, although I've studied few medieval texts, I've read a fair amount of LGBT and queer medievalist scholarship, especially since the sudden flowering of such work in the mid- to late 1990s. And to my gratification, I've found abundant confirmation of my arguments there (especially in the anthologies just mentioned). Perhaps because, at a formative period, differentist history, criticism, and theory

---

[1] The evolution in Traub's own work, from wholehearted discontinuism (1992b) to a blend of discontinuism and continuism (2002), is another heartening sign of the field's development.

was so often defined in opposition to the work of a medievalist—John Boswell—yet displayed so little knowledge of the Middle Ages, subsequent gay and queer medievalists, even if critical of Boswell's work, have tended not to accept differentist assumptions and assertions as uncritically as non-medievalists.[2]

As for getting a sense of the field's recent early modern and eighteenth-century scholarship, it would be difficult to surpass O'Donnell and O'Rourke's *Love, Sex, Intimacy, and Friendship between Men, 1550–1800* (2003), which contains, in addition to an introduction by Halperin, essays by pioneering gay historians George Rousseau, Randolph Trumbach, and the late Alan Bray; well-established scholars George Haggerty, Mario DiGangi, and Alan Stewart; and emerging critics Nicholas Radel and Jody Greene. The essays, taken together, are cause for celebration, suggesting we may have finally reached the point where the premature consensus regarding difference and discontinuity in the history of sexuality can no longer be assumed, where questions declared closed or hopelessly old-fashioned can now be reopened by the field as a whole, instead of being left to its gadflies, dissidents, throwbacks, and small fry (myself included). Similarities and continuities in the history of homosexuality—or histories of homosexualities—are once again up for consideration.

But if I've been harping this continuist tune for many years, I've recognized my other major theme only since finishing this book. My dissatisfaction with scholarship asserting overwhelming difference between here-and-now and there-and-then has itself been motivated by *a belief in homosexual difference*. By that phrase I mean two interrelated things, one political, one historical. Speaking politically: unlike many fans of anti-identitarian theory, queer or otherwise, I believe in the positive value of concepts, categories, labels, and even identities—*especially* identities—such as 'gay,' 'lesbian,' and 'homosexual.' Speaking historically: I believe that in many places and at many times prior to the modern "invention" of homosexuality, same-sex sexual desire and activity have been perceived, at least by some people, to make a significant difference in life—sometimes positive, sometimes negative, but significant.

Not that I don't value the often groundbreaking, even paradigm-shifting work of scholars who have emphasized *love* between women and *love* between men, both those to whom Halperin alludes in his introduction to O'Donnell and O'Rourke's anthology (Smith-Rosenberg, Faderman, Bennett, Haggerty, Bray), and others such as Rich (1980), Bonnet (1981/1985), and—last but *never* least—Kopelson (1994; especially noteworthy for exploring lesbian and gay love together). Indeed, the first large-scale incarnation of my project (Robinson [1986]), anticipated, in its own rudimentary way, Haggerty's crucial insight in *Men in Love* (1999): that the history of sex and sexual desire between men in eighteenth-century

---

[2] For supporting examples from medievalist work, see the online coda, omitted here for lack of space, but included with the online appendix (www.davidmrobinson.net).

England (and the history of male and female homosexuality more generally) mustn't be divorced from the history of love.[3]

Nevertheless, in this book I've been most interested in exploring ways in which the specifically *sexual* aspect of same-sex love has been historically significant. Hence my focus on both closeted homosexual and closeted homophobic writing. Authors of the former believed homosexuality made an important and dangerous enough difference to communicate clandestinely. Authors of the latter believed homosexuality ought *not* to make a difference, at least to sophisticates, but it disturbed them nonetheless. While I thus wholeheartedly encourage the expansion of lesbian and gay historical inquiry into realms beyond, above, below, around, and athwart the sexual, I believe there's a great deal more to learn about how sex and sexual desire between women and between men have been discussed, depicted, understood, and experienced in the past.

Moreover, despite the encouragement I derive from O'Donnell and O'Rourke's volume, it confirms my belief that continuist approaches to our field will require advocates for the foreseeable future, particularly where friendship and homosexuality are concerned. I'm thinking specifically of an exchange between Haggerty and Halperin. Haggerty takes issue with Halperin's much-celebrated essay "How to Do the History of Male Homosexuality" (2000), which pluralizes the roots of modern homosexuality by specifying four distinct, if related, "pre-homosexual" categories: effeminacy; pederasty or active sodomy; friendship or male love; and passivity or inversion. Haggerty finds Halperin's distinctions "fairly rigid" (76) and, at least for the English eighteenth century, "counter-productive" (73). Having reached similar conclusions about the essay in question, I was relieved when, in Halperin's introduction to O'Donnell and O'Rourke's collection, he clarified his intentions:

> In addition to indicating that my hypothesis was tentative, provisional, and heuristic, I emphasized at the outset of my argument that the different traditions or figures of pre-homosexual discourse I had identified were both separate and interrelated. I wanted those models to be flexible, not rigid; I tried to avoid reifying them. ([2003] 9).

Yet I was troubled by what followed:

> In the case of the tradition of male love or friendship, my thinking was based in no small part on the superb essay by Alan Bray and Michel Rey... [1999] [which] persuaded me that it would be wrong to sexualize what might look to us like expressions of physical love among friends before the eighteenth century and that it was during the eighteenth century that the English in particular became very uncomfortable with any physical expression of friendly feeling between males.... Haggerty's quarrel, if he really wants to have one, ought properly to be with Rey and Bray, not with me. (9)

---

[3] Nor, indeed, of other emotions (cf. Halperin [2003] 2, and especially Rousseau [2003]).

I agree that contesting the notion "that it would be wrong to sexualize what might look to us like expressions of physical love among friends before the eighteenth century" means contesting Bray's work (I'll do so in a moment). But at the risk of seeming to hanker for a quarrel, too, I must respectfully disagree with Halperin's overall assessment of Haggerty's critique: that he misunderstands Halperin's argument (9, 10–11).[4]

For in the very next paragraph, Halperin makes precisely the kind of distinction between friendship and sex to which Haggerty objects:

> Furthermore, although Haggerty convincingly argues that *some* relations between men in the eighteenth century actually combined sex, friendship, and love, Alan Bray's contribution to this volume presents irrefutable evidence that the discursive traditions of friendship and sodomy still managed to remain hermetically separate even in eighteenth-century England.... The fact that same-sex pairs of friends, whether male or female, had been buried together and memorialized together in English churches... from the fourteenth century right up through to the nineteenth indicates the perennial ease with which their contemporaries were able to draw the distinction between love or friendship, on the one hand, and sodomy, on the other. For if the funerary monuments Bray describes had conveyed even the faintest suggestion that the *connubium* of friends celebrated in them had consisted in a sodomitical union, we would not find those monuments enshrined in Christian churches.... [T]he *rhetoric* of friendship or love employed in those monuments succeeded in sealing off the relationships represented in them from any suggestion of being sodomitical. And that was precisely my reason for wishing to foreground the multiplicity of different discursive traditions, or models, or figures of sex and gender practices that are now subsumed by the modern paradigm of homosexuality and that now appear as among its manifold aspects. (9–10)

I see two major problems here, both of which have long characterized differentist work. The first involves the logic behind the assertion that "if the funerary monuments Bray describes had conveyed even the faintest suggestion that the *connubium* of friends celebrated in them had consisted in a sodomitical union, we would not find those monuments enshrined in Christian churches." Yet as Sedgwick, Miller, and others have taught us, and as I write near the start of this book, there are various constructed ignorances—conscious, unconscious, and semi-conscious—achieved through suppression and repression; avoidance, denial, disavowal; open secrets; taboos; censorship and self-censorship; and more. Any of these mechanisms might have enabled the construction of funerary monuments honoring friendships that some individuals might nevertheless have suspected (or even known) to be sodomitical. One may safely conclude that those involved in proposing, creating, and approving the monuments must have felt reasonably sure they wouldn't provoke anti-sodomitical public comment or action. But that's a far

---

[4] On Rey's contribution to Bray's work, see Bray and Rey (1999), Bray (2003), and Freccero (2004).

cry from concluding they mustn't have "conveyed even the faintest suggestion... [of] a sodomitical union."

Lesbian and feminist historians' debates in the 1980s and early 1990s over "romantic friendship" covered this very ground. As Liz Stanley wrote regarding Faderman's understanding of such friendships in *Surpassing the Love of Men*, the idea that "these passionate friendships were neither seen as 'unnatural' nor as sexual, even though their romantic character was widely recognized and accepted" is incorrect. It "romanticizes the past by constructing a lost age of innocence, a time before... sexologists invented 'lesbianism.'" Moreover, it's based on insufficient historical research:

> A paradigmatic example of Faderman's approach concerns the 'Ladies of Llangollen', Sarah Ponsonby and Eleanor Butler..., who ran away from Ireland in 1778 and then lived together in Llangollen a life of 'sweet contentment' in rural retreat from the corruptions of urban social life. Faderman argues that everybody knew they were romantic friends, everybody approved, nobody thought it was a sexual relationship, nobody shunned them because they thought the relationship was 'unnatural'. (196)

To support this argument, Faderman relied on the published diaries and letters of Hester Thrale Piozzi. For although Piozzi had a great many caustic things to say about sapphists and sodomites, she "was a close friend and neighbor to the Ladies, visited them frequently, and wrote them cordial letters. In her correspondence with others, she refers to them as 'fair and noble recluses' and 'charming cottagers.'" Faderman's conclusion: "Mrs. Thrale must have believed that," communing with nature, reading, tending garden, and otherwise "follow[ing] to the letter the prescriptions for romantic friendship," the Ladies "could not possibly desire what would give 'Offence towards God and Reason and Religion and Nature.'"[5] But Stanley's research disproved that argument: in Piozzi's unpublished diaries, she "refers to the ladies and their friends as 'damned sapphists' and writes that this is why various literary women will not visit them overnight unless accompanied by men" (196). As Emma Donoghue then wrote, building on Stanley's work, "Hester Thrale is a fascinating example of doublethink that made it possible to be aware of lesbian possibilities, yet defend romantic friendship as the epitome of moral purity. Mostly she hid away in the back of her mind the suspicion that some of her best friends were Sapphists" (150). Halperin is thus right to remind us of Smith-Rosenberg and Faderman's pioneering work on female friendship. But historians of male friendship must assimilate, as well, the subsequent lesbian and feminist work that challenged and refined those early efforts.

The other major problem with Halperin's argument—one that, again, has long

---

[5] Faderman, 124–25, quoting *The Intimate Letters of Hester Piozzi and Penelope Pennington*, ed. Knapp (1914), and *Thraliana: The Diary of Mrs. Hester Lynch Thrale (Later Mrs. Piozzi): 1776–1809*, 2 vols, ed. Balderston (1942), Vol. II, 949.

characterized discontinuist work—is that, while "wishing to foreground... multiplicity," he nevertheless reinforces dualism. To write that "the discursive traditions of friendship and sodomy still managed to remain hermetically separate" is to write as if there are only two such discursive traditions, one regarding friendship and one regarding sodomy. And yet, as I've argued in this book, and as others have argued before me, what is and isn't said about same-sex love and sex varies considerably, even drastically, depending on context, especially genre. Law codes, medical treatises, confession manuals, sermons, tragic plays, comic plays, lyric poetry, satiric poetry, scandal texts, criminal biographies, pornography, respectable fiction—these and many other textual genres (not to mention other historical artifacts, including funerary monuments) often present markedly different conceptions of same-sex love and sex.

Even within relatively coherent traditions, the relation between friendship and sexual love is often a bone of contention. Indeed, within a single work, a clear distinction between friendly and sexual love (the former understood as nonsexual, the latter sexual) may at one moment be assumed and at another erased (think of *The Maydes Metamorphosis*, discussed in chapter seven). And as we saw while exploring Manley's *New Atalantis*, satirists and celebrants of same-sex love have for centuries drawn repeatedly on one another's texts, arguments, ideas, and even language to either distinguish between or render indistinguishable spiritual and physical relations between men and between women, creating a sophisticated textual tradition stretching from ancient Greece and Rome to early modern and eighteenth-century Europe. Based on that tradition alone, it's clear that same-sex friendship has been open to suspicions of concealing homosexuality since *long* before the late nineteenth century.

Halperin himself knows this, as he subsequently explains:

> In the revised version of "How to Do the History of Male Homosexuality," which appears in my book [2002a], I qualify even further the already tentative hypotheses that Haggerty objects to, and I do so partly in order to meet some of his objections.... In particular, I allow for the possibility that the *rhetoric* of the friendship tradition could be used by dramatic characters as a cover for what the dramatists and their audiences alike might well have understood as a sexual relationship.... Of course, if I am now correct in supposing (following Haggerty) that [certain characters'] language would have been interpreted to function as a transparent cover for a sexual relationship, it would still be necessary to posit in the first place that there was a certain separation between the rhetoric of friendship and the rhetoric of sodomy, since otherwise the former could not be used to protect and dignify the latter. (10)

In the preceding paragraph Halperin had declared, "Alan Bray's contribution to this volume presents irrefutable evidence that the discursive traditions of friendship and sodomy still managed to remain hermetically separate even in eighteenth-century England"; here he posits only "a certain separation between the rhetoric of friendship and the rhetoric of sodomy." The change is significant, and welcome.

Yet still I'm troubled by a recourse to dualism ("the rhetoric of friendship and the rhetoric of sodomy"). A clearly nonsexual rhetoric of friendship and a clearly sexual rhetoric of sodomy were only two of many possibilities upon which to draw when discussing same-sex friendship, love, or sex. Better to study individuals' various motives and methods for drawing upon and mingling certain traditions and not others—including the choice made by some to reduce the possibilities to two self-evidently distinct extremes—than to repeat the reductive move ourselves. In many cases (as with Ovid's *Metamorphoses*) an apparently simple, schematic, binary system, starkly divergent from present-day sexuality, conceals traces of laborious construction, including signs that other erotic and emotional possibilities have been excluded.

I want to re-emphasize that I dwell here on Halperin's most recent formulations because his work has had and continues to have widespread influence, and because of the welcome contrast between his past and present response to continuist scholarship. Indeed, there's no better example of that latter development than the conclusion of his response to Haggerty:

> In short, I'm happy to admit that the hypotheses in that article of mine are wrong: in fact, they're so general, and so historically ungrounded, that they're bound to be wrong, or at least misleading and imprecise, within the context of many different historical periods and geographic locations. And I would be delighted if others would refine my approach and apply it more concretely and more intelligently than I do. (10)

That I've taken the time (and used precious word count!) to argue that his hypothesis regarding same-sex friendship, love, and sex is indeed misleading will not, I hope, be interpreted as an attempt to "trash" him. If our field is entering a new stage, it is thanks in part to Halperin's reassessment and revision of his extremely influential, earlier work.

As for Bray, in some respects I enthusiastically applaud his posthumously published book, *The Friend* (2003). As a continuist, how could I not? In truly radical fashion, he traces a socially central, publicly recognized, religiously sanctioned tradition of same-sex friendship over nearly a millenium, from the year 1000 to the turn of the nineteenth century—thus challenging the medieval/early-modern divide accepted unquestioningly by so many scholars. Yet despite its manifest strengths (eloquently captured by Freccero [2004] and Davidson [2005]), the book is weakest in registering the eroticism of many of these relationships, and the anxieties it arouses.[6]

As in his previous work, concern over sex between friends seems visible to Bray almost solely as a deflection of political anxieties. He argues that before the

---

[6] Readers interested in how my readings of particular texts would differ from Bray's might compare our discussions of Jeremy Taylor's treatment of friendship and marriage in *Discourse of Friendship* (1657): see Bray (2003) 142–43; Robinson (1998) ch.2, 64–67.

late seventeenth or even eighteenth century, male friendship was suspected of sodomy only when associated with treachery or similarly terrifying threats to the social, religious, and political order, associations that began to be publicly voiced, he claims, only in the mid-sixteenth century (yet see Kuefler for examples from the *twelfth* century). Although more nuanced than the book's unsigned, inside-front-cover copy would suggest ("He debunks the now-familiar readings of friendship by historians of sexuality who project homoerotic desires onto their subjects when there were none"), Bray overcompensates in countering what he felt was the narrow sexualization of male friendship by historians of homosexuality (most notably Boswell, but also Boswell's constructionist opponents).

Not that I don't appreciate the subversiveness and daring of Bray's achievement, as expressed by Davidson (2005):

> *The Friend* politely ravages the territory of the history of homosexuality, pillaging many of its materials and handing them over to the history of same-sex loving coupledom, which comes to seem like an alternative and more coherent field of research. For in *The Friend* the probably sodomitical and the probably non-sodomitical but (nevertheless) devoted pairs sit very happily side by side, looking for all the world as if they are part of one story.

Bray's book, like Faderman's before it, reveals fundamental distortions and limitations in most histories of Western love, histories centered myopically on marriage and kinship. And yet Bray's achievement, like Faderman's, comes at a steep price: reinforcing the devaluation and erasure of same-sex sexuality. In their work, homosex and homolust don't really matter, only homolove.

Of course, it's both true and important to remember that same-sex sexual desire and activity per se, let alone same-sex love, have not been everywhere and always non-normative. Both work like Bray's, focused on same-sex love, and non-homo queer work remain essential to contesting the heteronormative fantasy that masquerades as historical truth in most popular and many scholarly accounts of the past. At the same time, even as we strike out in new directions, reinventing ourselves and our field, it's both true and important to remember that same-sex lust and sex *have* mattered to many people, in many ways, at many times and in many places. The history of homo*sex*uality has only begun to be told.

Bibliography

Note: In the interest of conserving space while preserving citations, I've compressed bibliographic entries, most noticeably by providing the year but not the publisher for each work, except where the latter might be difficult to locate. For chapters in anthologies, I've included the anthology title only when the chapter in question is the only one here cited; for anthologies from which I have cited two or more chapters, the anthology title can be found in the entry for the anthology itself (listed by editors' names).

Abelove, Henry; Barale, Michèle Aina; and Halperin, David M., eds. (1993). *The Lesbian and Gay Studies Reader*.
Adams, Stephen (1997). *Poetic Designs: An Introduction to Meters, Verse Forms, and Figures of Speech*.
Adelman, Janet (1999). "Making Defect Perfection: Shakespeare and the One-Sex Model," Comensoli and Russell, eds., *Enacting Gender on the English Renaissance Stage*, 23–52.
Aers, David (1992). "A Whisper in the Ear of Early Modernists; or, Reflections on Literary Critics Writing the 'History of the Subject,'" Aers, ed., *Culture and History 1350–1600*, 177–202.
Anderson, William S. (1982). "The Orpheus of Virgil and Ovid: *flebile nescio quid*," Warden, ed., *Orpheus: The Metamorphoses of a Myth*, 25–50.
_____, ed. 1972. *Ovid's* Metamorphoses *Books 6-10*.
Andreadis, Harriette (2001). *Sappho in Early Modern England: Female Same-Sex Literary Erotics 1550–1714*.
Ballaster, Rosalind (1992). *Seductive Forms: Women's Amatory Fiction, 1684-1740*.
_____ (1995). "'The Vices Of Old Rome Revived': Representations of Female Same-Sex Desire in Seventeenth and Eighteenth Century England," Raitt, ed., *Volcanoes and Pearl Divers*, 13–36.
Barash, Carol (1996). *English Women's Poetry, 1649–1714: Politics, Community and Linguistic Authority*.
Barbour, Richmond (1995). "'When I Acted Young Antinous': Boy Actors and the Erotics of Jonsonian Theater," *PMLA* 110 (5) 1006–1022.
Barkan, Leonard (1991). *Transuming Passion: Ganymede and the Erotics of Humanism*.

Barrin, Jean [attrib.] (1968). *Vénus dans le cloître, ou la religieuse en chemise...* (Tchou); reimpression of 1719 Cologne edition.
Baruth, Philip E., ed. (1998). *Introducing Charlotte Charke: Actress, Author, Enigma.*
Bate, Jonathan (1993). *Shakespeare and Ovid.*
Beaumont, Francis and Fletcher, John (1976). *Love's Cure or, The Martial Maid*, Williams, ed., *The Dramatic Works in the Beaumont and Fletcher Canon*, v.3, 1–111.
_____ (1992). *Love's Cure or, The Martial Maid*, Mitchell, ed. (Nottingham Drama Texts).
Behn, Aphra (1994). "To The Fair Clarinda Who Made Love To Me, Imagin'd More Than Woman. By Mrs. B.," Faderman, ed., *Chloe Plus Olivia*, 27.
Bellamy, Henry (1983). *Iphis*, Nugel, ed., *Iphis; Cephalus et Procris* (Olms).
_____ (1986). *Iphis*, Freyman et al., *Iphis: Text, Translation, Notes* (Salzburg).
Bennett, Judith (2000). "'Lesbian-Like' and the Social History of Lesbianisms," *Journal of the History of Sexuality* 9 (1–2) 1–24.
Benserade, Isaac de (1637). *Iphis et Iante. Comedie* (Paris).
_____ (1875). *Poésies* (O. Uzanne).
_____ (2000). *Iphis et Iante, comédie*, Verdier, with Biet, Leibacher-Ouvrard (Lampsaque).
Berger, Harry, Jr. (1983). "Orpheus, Pan, and the Poetics of Misogyny: Spenser's Critique of Pastoral Love and Art," *ELH* 50 (1) 27–60.
Berland, K.J.H. (1999). "William Byrd's Sexual Lexicography," *Eighteenth-Century Life* 23 (1) 1–11.
Betteridge, Tom, ed. (2002). *Sodomy in Early Modern Europe.*
Beynon, John (2001). *Men of Mode: Taste, Effeminacy and Male Sexuality in Eighteenth-Century England*, Ph.D. diss. (UC Riverside).
_____ (2003). "'Traffic in More Precious Commodities': Sapphic Erotics and Economics in *Memoirs of a Woman of Pleasure*," Fowler and Jackson, eds., 3–26.
Blumenfeld-Kosinski, Renate (1996). "The Scandal of Pasiphae: Narration and Interpretation in the *Ovide moralisé*," *Modern Philology* 93 (3) 307–26.
Bly, Mary (2000). *Queer Virgins and Virgin Queans on the Early Modern Stage.*
Boehringer, Sandra (2000). "L'homosexualité feminine dans le discours antique," Tin and Pastre, *Homosexualités* (Stock) 38–48.
Bonnet, Marie-Jo (1995). *Les relations amoureuses entre les femmes du XVIe au XXe siècle* (Odile Jacob); orig. version (1981).
_____ (1997). "Sappho, or the Importance of Culture in the Language of Love: Tribade, Lesbienne, Homosexuelle," Livia and Hall, eds., *Queerly Phrased: Language, Gender, and Sexuality*, 147–66.
Borris, Kenneth (2001). "R[ichard] B[arnfield]'s Homosocial Engineering in *Orpheus His Journey to Hell*," Borris and Klawitter, eds., 332–60.
_____ (2004). "General Introduction," Borris, ed., 1–21.

_____, ed. (2004). *Same-Sex Desire in the English Renaissance: A Sourcebook of Texts, 1470–1650.*

_____ and Klawitter, George, eds. (2001). *The Affectionate Shepherd: Celebrating Richard Barnfield.*

Boswell, John (1980). *Christianity, Social Tolerance, and Homosexuality: Gay People in Western Europe from the Beginning of the Christian Era to the Fourteenth Century.*

_____ (1989a). "Jews, Bicycle Riders, and Gay People: The Determination of Social Consensus and Its Impact on Minorities," *Yale Journal of Law and the Humanities* 1 (2) 205–28.

_____ (1989b). "Revolutions, Universals, and Sexual Categories," Duberman et al., eds., 17–36.

_____ (1990a). "Categories, Experience and Sexuality," Stein, ed., *Forms of Desire: Sexual Orientation and the Social Constructionist Controversy* (Garland [rpt. Routledge, 1992]) 133–73.

_____ (1990b). "Sexual Categories, Sexual Universals: A Conversation with John Boswell," Mass, ed., *Homosexuality as Behavior and Identity: Dialogues of the Sexual Revolution, Volume 2,* 202–33.

Boucé, Paul-Gabriel (1976). *The Novels of Tobias Smollett.*

Brantôme, Pierre de Bourdeille, Seigneur (1972). *Vies des dames galantes,* rpt. *Les Dames galantes,* Haumont, ed. (Jean de Bonnot).

Braunschneider, Theresa (1999). "The Macroclitoride, the Tribade and the Woman: Configuring Gender and Sexuality in English Anatomical Discourse," *Textual Practice* 13 (3) 509–32.

Bray, Alan (1982). *Homosexuality in Renaissance England* (Gay Men's Press); rpt. w/ afterword (Columbia, 1995).

_____ (1990). "Homosexuality and the Signs of Male Friendship in Elizabethan England," *History Workshop Journal* 29: 1–19; rpt. Goldberg, ed., *Queering the Renaissance* (1994) 40–61.

_____ (2003). *The Friend.*

_____ and Rey, Michel (1999). "The Body of the Friend: Continuity and Change in Masculine Friendship in the Seventeenth Century," Hitchcock and Cohen, eds., *English Masculinities 1660–1800,* 65–84.

Bredbeck, Gregory W (1991). *Sodomy and Interpretation: Marlowe to Milton.*

Brewer, William (1941). *Ovid's Metamorphoses in European Culture (Books VI-VII-VIII-IX-X),* pub. with More, *Ovid's Metamorphoses (Books VI-VII-VIII-IX-X) In English Blank Verse* (Marshall Jones).

Brisson, Luc (2002). *Sexual Ambivalence: Androgyny and Hermaphroditism in Graeco-Roman Antiquity,* tr. Lloyd.

Brooten, Bernadette J. (1996). *Love Between Women: Early Christian Responses to Female Homoeroticism.*

Brown, Steve (1990). "The Boyhood of Shakespeare's Heroines: Notes on Gender Ambiguity in the Sixteenth Century," *SEL* 30: 243–63.

Bruce, Donald (1964). *Radical Doctor Smollett.*
Bruhm, Steven (1993). "Roderick Random's Closet," *English Studies in Canada* 19 (4) 401–16.
_____ (2001). *Reflecting Narcissus: A Queer Aesthetic.*
Burger, Glenn and Kruger, Steven F., eds. (2001). *Queering the Middle Ages.*
Burrow, Colin (2002). "Re-Embodying Ovid: Renaissance Afterlives," Hardie, ed., 301–19.
Burton, Gideon O. (1996–2003). "Silva Rhetoricae" <rhetoric.byu.edu>.
Butler, Shane (1998). "Notes on a *Membrum Disiectum*," Joshel and Murnaghan, eds., *Women and Slaves in Greco-Roman Culture: Differential Equations*, 236–55.
Byrd, William, II (1941). *The Secret Diary of William Byrd of Westover, 1709–1712,* Wright and Tinling, eds.
Cady, Joseph (1992). "'Masculine Love,' Renaissance Writing, and the 'New Invention' of Homosexuality," Summers, ed., 9–40.
_____ (1993). "Renaissance Awareness and Language for Heterosexuality: 'Love' and 'Feminine Love,'" Summers and Pebworth, eds., 143–58.
_____ (1996). "The 'Masculine Love' of the 'Princes of Sodom' 'Practicing the Art of Ganymede' at Henri III's Court: The Homosexuality of Henri III and His *Mignons* in Pierre de L'Estoile's *Mémoires-Journaux*," Murray and Eisenbichler, 123–54.
Callaghan, Dympna (2000). *Shakespeare Without Women: Representing Gender and Race on the Renaissance Stage.*
Cantarella, Eve (1992). *Bisexuality in the Ancient World.*
Cardon, Patrick, ed. (1989). *Cahiers GKC* 4.
Carnes, Jeffrey S. (1998). "This Myth Which Is Not One: Construction of Discourse in Plato's *Symposium*," Larmour et al., eds., 104–21.
Carvajal, F. Garza (2000). "Silk Laced Ruffs and Cuffs: An Inherent Link between 'Sodomie' and Notions of Effeminacy in Andalucía and Mexico 1561–1699," *Thamyris* 7 (1–2) 7–39.
Castle, Terry (1982). "'Matters Not Fit to be Mentioned': Fielding's *The Female Husband*," *ELH* 49: 602–22.
_____ (1993). *The Apparitional Lesbian: Female Homosexuality and Modern Culture.*
_____ (2003). "Introduction," Castle, ed., *The Literature of Lesbianism: A Historical Anthology from Ariosto to Stonewall,* 1–56.
Cavendish, Margaret, Duchess of Newcastle (1666/1668). *The Description of a New World Called the Blazing World* (London).
Charke, Charlotte (1756). *The History of Henry Dumont, Esq; and Miss Charlotte Evelyn* (London).
Chauncey, George (1994). *Gay New York: Gender, Urban Culture, and the Making of the Gay Male World, 1890–1940.*

Chorier, Nicolas (1680). *L'Academie des dames, divisée en sept entretiens satiriques* (Ville-Franche); tr. and adapt. Jean Nicolas?

_____ (1910). *L'Œuvre de Nicolas Chorier: Satyre Sotadique de Luisa Sigea sur les Arcanes de l'Amour et de Vénus[,] en Sept Dialogues...* intro. and notes, *Villeneuve* (Paris: Bibliothèque des Curieux).

Chudleigh, Mary, Lady (1993). *The Poems and Prose of Mary, Lady Chudleigh,* Ezell, ed.

Clark, Robert L.A. and Sponsler, Claire (1997). "Queer Play: The Cultural Work of Crossdressing in Medieval Drama," *New Literary History* 28 (2) 319–44.

Clarke, John R. (1998). *Looking at Lovemaking: Constructions of Sexuality in Roman Art 100 B.C.–A.D. 250.*

Cleland, John (1985). *Fanny Hill: or Memoirs of a Woman of Pleasure,* Wagner, ed.

_____ (1985). *Memoirs of a Woman of Pleasure,* Sabor, ed.

Conner, Randy (1997). "Les Molles et les chausses: Mapping the Isle of Hermaphrodites in Premodern France," Livia and Hall, eds., 127–46.

Connery, Brian A. and Combe, Kirk (1995). "Theorizing Satire: A Retrospective and Introduction," Connery and Combe, eds., *Theorizing Satire,* 1–15.

Cottin, Paul, ed. (1891). *Rapports inédits du Lieutenant de Police René D'Argenson....*

Courouve, Claude (1985). *Vocabulaire de l'homosexualité masculine.*

Creech, James (1993). *Closet Writing/Gay Reading: The Case of Melville's* Pierre.

Cressy, David (1991). "Foucault, Stone, Shakespeare and Social History," *ELR* 21 (2) 121–33.

Crompton, Louis (1985). *Byron and Greek Love: Homophobia in 19th-Century England.*

Culham, Phyllis (1997). "Did Roman Women Have an Empire?" Golden and Toohey, eds., 192–204.

Daileader, Celia R. (2002). "Back Door Sex: Renaissance Gynosodomy, Aretino, and the Exotic," *ELH* 69: 303–34.

Dall'Orto, Giovanni (1983). "Antonio Rocco and the Background of His *L'Alcibiade fanciullo a scola* (1652)," Duyves et al., *Among Men, Among Women* (Sociologisch Instituut) 224–32.

_____ (1989). "'Socratic Love' as a Disguise for Same-Sex Love in the Italian Renaissance," Gerard and Hekma, eds., 33–65.

Dalton, Andrew (2004). "Review essay" (on Halperin [2002a]), *Sexualities, Evolution & Gender* 6 (2–3) 217–24.

Davidson, James (2001). "Dover, Foucault and Greek Homosexuality: Penetration and the Truth of Sex," *Past and Present* 170: 3–51.

_____ (2005). "Mr and Mr and Mrs and Mrs" (review of Bray [2003]), *London Review of Books* 27:11 (2 June).

Davidson, N.S. (1982). "Sodomy in Early Modern Venice," Betteridge, ed., 65–81.

Day, Robert Adams (1982). "Sex, scatology, Smollett," Boucé, *Sexuality in Eighteenth-Century Britain*, 225–43.
DeJean, Joan (1991). *Tender Geographies: Women and the Origins of the Novel in France.*
_____ (1993). "The Politics of Pornography: *L'Ecole des Filles,*" Hunt, ed., 109–23.
_____ (2002). *The Reinvention of Obscenity: Sex, Lies, and Tabloids in Early Modern France.*
Delcourt, Marie (1958). *Hermaphrodite, mythes et rites de la bisexualité dans l'Antiquité classique.*
DiGangi, Mario (1997). *The Homoerotics of Early Modern Drama.*
_____ (2001). "'Male deformities': Narcissus and the Reformation of Courtly Manners in *Cynthia's Revels,*" Stanivukovic, ed., 94–110.
Dinshaw, Carolyn (1999). *Getting Medieval: Sexualities and Communities: Pre- and Postmodern.*
Dollimore, Jonathan (1991). *Sexual Dissidence: Augustine to Wilde, Freud to Foucault.*
Donne, John (1967). *The Satires, Epigrams and Verse Letters,* Milgate, ed.
Donoghue, Emma (1993). *Passions Between Women: British Lesbian Culture 1668–1801.*
Doody, Margaret Anne (1996). *The True Story of the Novel.*
Dooley, Mark (2001). "Inversion, Metamorphosis, and Sexual Difference: Female Same-Sex Desire in Ovid and Lyly," Stanivukovic, ed., 59–76.
Dryden, John (1974). *The Works of John Dryden, Vol. IV: Poems 1693–1696,* Swedenberg et al., eds.
Duberman, Martin Bauml; Vicinus, Martha; and Chauncey, George, Jr., eds. (1989). *Hidden from History: Reclaiming the Gay and Lesbian Past.*
Dubois, Jean; Lagane, René; and Lerond, Alain, eds. (1992). *Dictionnaire du français classique: le xviie siècle.*
duBois, Page (1995). *Sappho is Burning.*
Duncan, Anne (2000). "It Takes a Woman to Play a Real Man: Clara as Hero(ine) of Beaumont and Fletcher's *Love's Cure,*" *ELR* 30 (3) 396–407.
Easton, Celia A. (1990). "Excusing the Breach of Nature's Laws: The Discourse of Denial and Disguise in Katherine Philips' Friendship Poetry," *Restoration* 14 (1) 1–14.
Edelman, Lee (1990). "The Sodomite's Tongue and the Bourgeois Body in Eighteenth-Century England," rev. Edelman (1994) 121–28.
_____ (1991). "Seeing Things: Representation, The Scene of Surveillance, and the Spectacle of Gay Male Sex," Edelman (1994) 173–91.
_____ (1994). *Homographesis: Essays in Gay Literary and Cultural Theory.*
Eisenbichler, Konrad (2001). "Laodomia Forteguerri Loves Margaret of Austria," Sautman and Sheingorn, eds., 277–304.

Elfenbein, Andrew (2001). "Lesbian Aestheticism on the Eighteenth-Century Stage," *Eighteenth-Century Life* 25: 1–16.
Ellis, James Richard (2003). *Sexuality and Citizenship: Metamorphosis in Elizabethan Erotic Verse.*
Elsner, John (1991). "Visual Mimesis and the Myth of the Real: Ovid's Pygmalion as Viewer," *Ramus* 20 (2) 149–68.
Epstein, Julia (1989). "Fanny's Fanny: Epistolarity, Eroticism, and the Transsexual Text," Goldsmith, ed., *Writing the Female Voice*, 135–53.
Epstein, William H. (1974). *John Cleland: Images of a Life.*
Eribon, Didier (2001). "Michel Foucault's Histories of Sexuality," *GLQ* 7 (1) 31–86.
L'Escole Des Filles ou La Philosophie Des Dames, Divisée en deux dialogues... (1988); rpt. Dubost, gen. ed., *Œuvres érotiques du XVIIe siècle, L'Enfer de la Bibliothèque Nationale*, v. 7 (1988) 167–288.
Faderman, Lillian (1981). *Surpassing the Love of Men: Romantic Friendship and Love between Women from the Renaissance to the Present.*
Fahrner, Robert (1993). "A Reassessment of Garrick's *The Male-Coquette; or, Seventeen-Hundred Fifty-Seven* as Veiled Discourse," *Eighteenth-Century Life* 17: 1–13.
Farmer, Sharon and Pasternack, Carol Braun, eds. (2003). *Gender and Difference in the Middle Ages.*
Fielding, Henry (1983). *Amelia,* Battestin, ed.
Firenzuola, Agnolo (1992). *On the Beauty of Women,* tr. and ed. Eisenbichler and Murray.
Fletcher, R[obert] (1970). *The Poems and Translations of Robert Fletcher,* Woodward, ed.
Florio, John (1598). *World of Wordes* (London).
Folkerth, Wes (2001). "The Metamorphosis of Daphnis: The Case for Richard Barnfield's *Orpheus,*" Borris and Klawitter, eds., 305–31.
Fone, Byrne (1995). *A Road to Stonewall: Male Homosexuality and Homophobia in English and American Literature, 1750–1969.*
―――― (2000). *Homophobia: A History.*
Forker, Charles (1990). "Sexuality and Eroticism on the Renaissance Stage," *South Central Review* 7 (4) 1–22.
Foucault, Michel (1976/1978). *The History of Sexuality,* v.1: *An Introduction,* tr. Hurley; rpt. 1990.
―――― (1984/1986). *The Use of Pleasure: The History of Sexuality, Vol. Two,* tr. Hurley (1986).
Fowler, Patsy S. (2003). "'This Tail-Piece of Morality': Phallocentric Reinforcements of Patriarchy in *Memoirs of a Woman of Pleasure,*" Fowler and Jackson, eds., 49–80.
―――― and Jackson, Alan, eds. (2003). *Launching Fanny Hill: Essays on the Novel and Its Influences.*

Foxon, David (1965). *Libertine Literature in England 1660–1745.*
Fradenburg, Louise and Freccero, Carla (1996). "Introduction: Caxton, Foucault, and the Pleasures of History," Fradenburg and Freccero, eds., xiii–xxiv.
_____, eds. (1996). *Premodern Sexualities.*
La France devenue italienne avec les autres déréglements de la cour, excerpted & tr. Merrick and Ragan (2001) 119–24.
Franceschina, John (1997). *Homosexualities in the English Theatre: From Lyly to Wilde.*
Freccero, Carla (2004). "Passionate Friendship" (review of Bray [2003]), *GLQ* 10 (3) 503–507.
Frier, Bruce W. (1999). Review of Williams, *Roman Homosexuality,* in *Bryn Mawr Classical Review* (05.11.1999).
Fyge Egerton, Sarah (1703). "The Emulation," from *Poems on Several Occasions* (London); rpt. Literature Online (lion.chadwyck.com).
Gaca, Kathy L. (2003). *The Making of Fornication: Eros, Ethics, and Political Reform in Greek Philosophy and Early Christianity.*
Gallagher, Catherine (1994). *Nobody's Story: The Vanishing Acts of Women Writers in the Marketplace 1670–1820.*
Garber, Marjorie (1992). *Vested Interests: Cross-Dressing and Cultural Anxiety.*
Garrick, David (1747). *Miss in Her Teens; or, The Medley of Lovers* (London).
Gerard, Kent and Hekma, Gert, eds. (1989). *Male Homosexuality in Renaissance and Enlightenment Europe.*
Gervaise de Latouche, Jacques Charles (1969). *Histoire de Dom B... Portier Des Chartreux* (l'Or du Temps).
Gilbert, Arthur N. (1974). "The *Africaine* Courts-Martial: A Study of Buggery and the Royal Navy," *Journal of Homosexuality* 1 (1) 111–22.
_____ (1976). "Buggery and the British Navy, 1700–1861," *Journal of Social History* 10 (1) 72–98.
Gleason, Maud W. (1990). "The Semiotics of Gender: Physiognomy and Self-Fashioning in the Second Century C.E.," Halperin, Winkler, and Zeitlin, eds., *Before Sexuality: The Construction of Erotic Experience in the Ancient Greek World,* 389–415.
Goldberg, Jonathan (1992). *Sodometries: Renaissance Texts, Modern Sexualities.*
Golden, Mark and Toohey, Peter, eds. (1997). *Inventing Ancient Culture: Historicism, Periodization, and the Ancient World.*
Goldhill, Simon (1995). *Foucault's Virginity: Ancient Erotic Fiction and the History of Sexuality.*
Goldsmith, Netta Murray (1998). *The Worst of Crimes: Homosexuality and the Law in Eighteenth-Century London.*
Goode, Okey (1990). "Finding a Character's Voice in Smollett's *Roderick Random,*" *Style* 24 (3) 469–83.
Goulemot, Jean Marie (1994). *Forbidden Texts: Erotic Literature and its Readers in Eighteenth-Century France,* tr. Simpson.

Grahn, Judy (1984). *Another Mother Tongue: Gay Words, Gay Worlds.*
Grant, Damian (1977). *Tobias Smollett: A Study in Style.*
Greenberg, David (1988). *The Construction of Homosexuality.*
Greenblatt, Stephen (1988). "Fiction and Friction," *Shakespearean Negotiations: The Circulation of Social Energy in Renaissance England*, 66–93.
Greene, Ellen, ed. (1996). *Reading Sappho: Contemporary Approaches.*
Greene, Jody (2003). "Arbitrary Tastes and Commonsense Pleasures: Accounting for Taste in Cleland, Hume, and Burke," Fowler and Jackson, eds., 221–65.
Griffin, Dustin H. (1994). *Satire: A Critical Reintroduction.*
Guiraud, Pierre (1993). *Dictionnaire érotique.*
Gunn, Daniel P. (2004). "Free Indirect Discourse and Narrative Authority in *Emma*," *Narrative* 12 (1) 35–54.
Guy-Bray, Stephen (2002). *Homoerotic Space: The Poetics of Loss in Renaissance Literature.*
Haggerty, George E. (1999). *Men in Love: Masculinity and Sexuality in the Eighteenth Century.*
⎯⎯⎯ (2000). "Heteromachia," *GLQ* 6 (3) 435–50.
⎯⎯⎯ (2002). "'The Man I Love': The Erotics of Friendship in Restoration Theater," Solomon and Minwalla, eds., 106–23.
⎯⎯⎯ (2003a). "Keyhole Testimony: Witnessing Sodomy in the Eighteenth Century," *ECTI* 44 (2–3) 167–82.
⎯⎯⎯ (2003b). "Male Love and Friendship in the Eighteenth Century," O'Donnell and O'Rourke, eds., 70–81.
Hallett, Judith P. (1978). "Morigerari: Suetonius, Tiberius, 44," *L'Antiquité Classique* 47: 196–200.
⎯⎯⎯ (1997). "Female Homoeroticism and the Denial of Roman Reality in Latin Literature," Hallett and Skinner, eds., 255–73.
⎯⎯⎯ and Skinner, Marilyn B., eds. (1997). *Roman Sexualities.*
Halley, Janet E. (1989). "Textual Intercourse: Anne Donne, John Donne, and the Sexual Politics of Textual Exchange," Fisher and Halley, eds., *Seeking the Woman in Late Medieval and Renaissance Writings*, 187–206.
Halperin, David M. (1990). *One Hundred Years of Homosexuality and Other Essays on Greek Love.*
⎯⎯⎯ (1992a). "Historicizing the Sexual Body: Sexual Preferences and Erotic Identities in the Pseudo-Lucianic *Erôtes*," Stanton, ed., *Discourses of Sexuality: From Aristotle to AIDS*, 236–61.
⎯⎯⎯ (1992b). "Plato and the Erotics of Narrativity," Hexter and Selden, eds., *Innovations of Antiquity*, 95–126.
⎯⎯⎯ (1995). *Saint Foucault: Towards a Gay Hagiography.*
⎯⎯⎯ (1998). "Forgetting Foucault: Acts, Identities, and the History of Sexuality," *Representations* 63: 93–120; rev. and rpt. Halperin (2002a) 24–47.
⎯⎯⎯ (2000). "How to Do the History of Male Homosexuality," *GLQ* 6: 87–123; rev. and rpt. Halperin (2002a) 104–37.

_____ (2002a). *How to Do the History of Homosexuality.*
_____ (2002b). "Introduction: In Defense of Historicism," Halperin (2002a), 1–23.
_____ (2003). "Introduction: Among Men—History, Sexuality, and the Return of Affect," O'Donnell and O'Rourke, eds., 1–11.
Hamilton, Anthony (1713). *Mémoires de la Vie du Comte de Grammont; Contenant Particuliérement L'Histoire Amoureuse de la Cour d'Angletterre, sous le Regne de Charles II* (Cologne).
_____ (1714). *Memoirs of the Life of Count de Grammont: Containing, in Particular, the Amorous Intrigues of the Court of England in the Reign of King Charles II. Translated from the French by Mr. Boyer* (London).
_____ (1994). *Mémoires du comte de Gramont* (l'école des loisirs/Le Seuil).
Hammond, Paul (1996). *Love between Men in English Literature.*
_____ (2002). *Figuring Sex between Men from Shakespeare to Rochester.*
Hardie, Philip (2002). *Ovid's Poetics of Illusion.*
_____, ed. (2002). *The Cambridge Companion to Ovid.*
Harley, Marta Powell (1986). "Narcissus, Hermaphroditus, and Attis: Ovidian Lovers at the Fontaine d'Amors in Guillaume de Lorris's *Roman de la rose*," *PMLA* 101 (3) 324–37.
Hekma, Gert (1989). "Sodomites, Platonic Lovers, Contrary Lovers: The Backgrounds of the Modern Homosexual," Gerard and Hekma, eds., 433–55.
Hell Upon Earth: Or, the Town in an Uproar... (1985), ed. Trumbach, *Hell upon Earth* and *Satan's Harvest Home.*
Heller, Wendy Beth (2003). *Emblems of Eloquence: Opera and Women's Voice in Seventeenth-Century Venice.*
Hexter, Ralph (1991). "Scholars and Their Pals," *Helios* 18: 147–59.
Hirschfeld, Heather (2003). "What Do Women Know?: *The Roaring Girl* and the Wisdom of Tiresias," *Renaissance Drama* New Series 32: 123–46.
Hobby, Elaine (1991). "Katherine Philips: Seventeenth-Century Lesbian Poet," Hobby and White, eds., *What Lesbians do in Books*, 183–204.
Holderness, Julia Simms (2004). "Feminism and the Fall: Boccaccio, Christine de Pizan, and Louise Labé," *Essays in Medieval Studies* 21 (2004) 97–108.
Holiday, Barten, tr. (1673). *Deciums Junius Juvenalis, and Aulus Persius Flaccus...* (Oxford).
Holsinger, Bruce W. (2001). *Music, Body, and Desire in Medieval Culture: Hildegard of Bingen to Chaucer.*
Hopkins, David (1985). "Nature's Laws and Man's: The Story of Cinyras and Myrrha in Ovid and Dryden," *Modern Language Review* 80 (4) 786–801.
Hopkins, Charles (1700). *Friendship Improv'd; Or, The Female Warriour. A Tragedy* (London).
Howard, Jean E. (1992). "Sex and Social Conflict: The Erotics of *The Roaring Girl*," Zimmerman, ed., 170–90.

_____ (1993). "Cross-Dressing, The Theater, and Gender Struggle in Early Modern England," Ferris, ed., *Crossing the Stage: Controversies on Cross-Dressing,* 20–46.

_____ (1994). "Power and Eros: Crossdressing in Dramatic Representation and Theatrical Practice," *The Stage and Social Struggle in Early Modern England,* 93–128.

Hubbard, Thomas K., ed. (2003). *Homosexuality in Greece and Rome: A Sourcebook of Basic Documents.*

Hunt, Lynn (1993). "Introduction: Obscenity and the Origins of Modernity, 1500–1800," Hunt, ed., 9–45.

_____, ed. (1993). *The Invention of Pornography: Obscenity and the Origins of Modernity, 1500–1800.*

Hutcheson, Gregory S. (2001a). "Leonor López de Córdoba and the Configuration of Female-Female Desire," Sautman and Sheingorn, eds., 251–75.

_____ (2001b). "The Sodomitic Moor: Queerness in the Narrative of *Reconquista,*" Burger and Kruger, eds., 99–122.

Hutson, Lorna (1996). "On Not Being Deceived: Rhetoric and the Body in *Twelfth Night,*" *Texas Studies in Literature and Language* 38 (2) 140–74.

Jacob, Margaret C. (1993). "The Materialist World of Pornography," Hunt, ed., 157–202.

Jankowski, Theodora (2000). *Pure Resistance: Queer Virginity in Early Modern English Drama.*

Jardine, Lisa (1983). "'As boys and women are for the most part cattle of this colour': Female Roles and Elizabethan Eroticism," *Still Harping On Daughters,* 9–36.

_____ (1992). "Twins and Travesties: Gender, Dependency and Sexual Availability," Zimmerman, ed., 27–38.

Johnson, W.R. (1996). "The Rapes of Callisto," *The Classical Journal* 92: 9–24.

Jonson, Ben (1963). *The Complete Poetry of Ben Jonson,* Hunter, ed.

_____ (1982). *The Complete Poems,* Parfitt, ed.

Jordan, Mark D. (1997). *The Invention of Sodomy in Christian Theology.*

Joshel, Sandra R. (1997). "Female Desire and the Discourse of Empire: Tacitus's Messalina," Hallett and Skinner, eds., 221–54.

Juvenal (1684). *D. Junii Juvenalis & Auli Persii Flacci Satyræ Cum Veteris Scholiastæ & variorum Commentariis. Editio nova* (Amstelædami).

_____ (1967). *The Sixteen Satires,* tr. Green.

Keach, William (1977). *Elizabethan Erotic Narratives: Irony and Pathos in the Ovidian Poetry of Shakespeare, Marlowe, and Their Contemporaries.*

Keiser, Elizabeth B. (1997). *Courtly Desire and Medieval Homophobia: The Legitimation of Sexual Pleasure in* Cleanness *and Its Contexts.*

Kennedy, Hubert (1988). *Ulrichs: The Life and Work of Karl Heinrich Ulrichs, Pioneer of the Modern Gay Movement.*

Kernan, Alvin (1959). *The Cankered Muse: Satire of the English Renaissance.*

Kilmer, Martin (1997). "Painters and Pederasts: Ancient Art, Sexuality, and Social History," Golden and Toohey, eds., 36–49.

Kimmel, Michael S. (1990). "'Greedy Kisses' and 'Melting Extasy': Notes on the Homosexual World and Early 18th Century England as Found in *Love Letters Between a certain late Nobleman and the famous Mr. Wilson*," *Love-Letters…*, 1–9.

Kinkead-Weekes, Mark (1973). *Samuel Richardson: Dramatic Novelist*.

Klawitter, George (1992). "Verse Letters to T.W. from John Donne: 'By You My Love Is Sent,'" Summers, ed., 85–102.

Koertge, Noretta (1990). "Constructing Concepts of Sexuality: A Philosophical Commentary," McWhirter et al., eds., *Homosexuality/Heterosexuality: Concepts of Sexual Orientation*, 387–97.

Kolve, V.A. (1998). "*Ganymede/Son of Getron:* Medieval Monasticism and the Drama of Same-Sex Desire," *Speculum* 73: 1014–1067.

Konstan, David (1994). *Sexual Symmetry: Love in the Ancient Novel and Related Genres*.

_____ (1997). "Philosophy, Friendship, and Cultural History," Golden and Toohey, eds., 66–78.

Kopelson, Kevin (1992). "Seeing Sodomy: *Fanny Hill*'s Blinding Vision," Summers, ed., 173–83.

_____ (1994). *Love's Litany: The Writing of Modern Homoerotics*.

Krouse, Tonya (2003). "'Truth! Stark naked truth': Performing Authority in the Pornography of *Memoirs of a Woman of Pleasure* and Jong's *Fanny*," Fowler and Jackson, eds., 289–314.

Kubek, Elizabeth (2003). "The Man Machine: Horror and The Phallus in *Memoirs of a Woman of Pleasure*," Fowler and Jackson, eds., 173–97.

Kuefler, Mathew S. (2003). "Male Friendship and the Suspicion of Sodomy in Twelfth-Century France," Farmer and Pasternack, eds., 145–81.

Lancaster, Nathaniel (1747). *The Pretty Gentleman: Or, Softness of Manners Vindicated From the false Ridicule exhibited under the Character of William Fribble, Esq*. (London).

Lange, Jennifer (1995). "'Hearts Thus Intermixed Speak': Erotic 'Friendship' in the Poems of Katherine Philips," Ph.D. diss. (Bowling Green).

Lanser, Susan S. (1998–99). "Befriending the Body: Female Intimacies as Class Acts," *Eighteenth-Century Studies* 32 (2) 179–98.

_____ (1999). "Singular Politics: The Rise of the British Nation and the Production of the Old Maid," Bennett and Froide, eds., *Singlewomen in the European Past, 1250–1800*, 297–323.

_____ (2001a). "'*Au sein de vos pareilles*': Sapphic separatism in Late Eighteenth-Century France," Merrick and Sibalis, eds., 105–16.

_____ (2001b). "Sapphic Picaresque: Sexual Difference and the Challenges of Homoadventuring," *Textual Practice* 15 (2) 1–18.

_____ (2002). "Bluestocking Sapphism and the Economies of Desire," *Huntington Library Quarterly* 65 (1–2) 257–75; rpt. Pohl and Schellenberg, eds., *Reconsidering the Bluestockings* (Huntington Library) 257–75.

_____ (2003a). "The Author's Queer Clothes: Anonymity, Sex(uality), and The Travels and Adventures of Mademoiselle de Richelieu," Griffin, ed., *The Faces of Anonymity: Anonymous and Pseudonymous Publications from the Sixteenth to the Twentieth Century*, 81–102.

_____ (2003b). "'Queer to Queer': The Sapphic Body as Transgressive Text," Kittredge, ed., *Lewd & Notorious: Female Transgression in the Eighteenth Century*, 21–46.

Laqueur, Thomas (1990). *Making Sex: Body and Gender from the Greeks to Freud*.

Larmour, David H.J.; Miller, Paul Allen; and Platter, Charles, eds. (1998). *Rethinking Sexuality: Foucault and Classical Antiquity*.

Leach, Eleanor Winsor (1974). "Ekphrasis and the Theme of Artistic Failure in Ovid's *Metamorphoses*," *Ramus* 3 (2) 102–42.

Leibacher-Ouvrard, Lise (1992a). "Pseudo-féminocentrisme et ordre (dis)simulé: La *Satyra sotadica* (1658–1678) et l'*Académie des dames* (1680)," Duchêne and Ronzeaud, *Ordre et contestation au temps des classiques* (Biblio 17) 193–202.

_____ (1992b). "Sexe, simulacre et 'libertinage honnête': La Satyre sotadique (1658/1678) de Nicolas Chorier," *Romanic Review* 83 (3) 267–80.

_____ (1995). "Transtextualité et construction de la sexualité: La *Satyra Sotadica* de Chorier," *L'Esprit créateur* 35 (2) 51–66.

_____ (2000). "Decadent Dandies and Dystopian Gender-Bending: Artus Thomas's *L'Isle des hermaphrodites* (1605)," *Utopian Studies* 11 (1) 124–31.

_____ (2003). "Speculum de l'Autre Femme: Les avatars d'*Iphis et Iante* (Ovide) au XVIIe Siècle," *Papers on French Seventeenth-Century Literature* 30 (59) 363–77.

Lentricchia, Frank and DuBois, Andrew (2003). "Introduction," Lentricchia and DuBois, eds., *Close Reading: The Reader*, 1–40.

Levine, Laura (1994). *Men in Women's Clothing: Anti-theatricality and Effeminization, 1579–1642*.

Lilley, Kate (2001). "'Dear Object': Katherine Philips's Love Elegies and Their Readers," Wallwork and Salzman, eds., *Women Writing 1550–1750*, special book issue of *Meridian, The La Trobe University English Review* 18 (1) 163–78.

Livia, Anna and Hall, Kira, eds. (1997). *Queerly Phrased: Language, Gender, and Sexuality*.

Lloyd, G.E.R. (1990). *Demystifying Mentalities*.

Lochrie, Karma (1996). "Don't Ask, Don't Tell: Murderous Plots and Medieval Secrets," Fradenburg and Freccero, eds., 137–52.

Lonsdale, Roger, ed. (1989). *Eighteenth-Century Women Poets: An Oxford Anthology*.

Loscocco, Paula (2003). "Inventing the English Sappho: Katherine Philips's Donnean Poetry," *Journal of English and Germanic Philology* (2003) 59–87.

Love, Harold (1995). "Hamilton's *Mémoires de la vie du comte de Grammont* and the reading of Rochester," *Restoration* 19: 95–102.

Love-Letters Between a certain late Nobleman And the famous Mr. Wilson... (1990), Kimmel, ed.

Lucian (1684). *Erôtes* [tr. as "The Loves"], *Lucian's Works, Translated From the Greek. By Ferrand Spence. The Third Volume* (London).

Lyly, John (1998). *Gallathea* 1592, Scragg, ed., Malone Society Reprints, v.161.

Maccubbin, Robert Purks, ed. (1987). *'Tis Nature's Fault: Unauthorized Sexuality during the Enlightenment*.

Machin, Lewes (1607). *Apollo and Hyacinth*, in Machin, *Three Eglogs*, appended to William Barksted, *Mirrha The Mother of Adonis: Or, Lustes Prodegies* (London); rpt. *ESTC* microfilm collection, reel 575.

Mack, Sarah (1988). *Ovid*.

Mackie, Erin (1991). "Desperate Measures: The Narratives of the Life of Mrs. Charlotte Charke," *ELH* 58 (4) 841–65.

MacMullen, Ramsey (1982). "Roman Attitudes to Greek Love," *Historia* 31: 484–502.

Makowski, John F. (1996). "Bisexual Orpheus: Pederasty and Parody in Ovid," *Classical Journal* 92 (1) 25–38.

Manley, Delarivier (1709/1972). *Secret Memoirs and Manners of several Persons of Quality, of Both Sexes. From the New Atalantis, an Island in the Mediterranean...* (London); rpt. Mary de la Rivière Manley, *Secret Memoirs from the New Atalantis*, (Garland).

Martin, Roberta C. (1998). "'Beauteous Wonder of a Different Kind': Aphra Behn's Destabilization of Sexual Categories," *College English* 61 (2) 192–210.

Masten, Jeffrey (1997). *Textual Intercourse: Collaboration, Authorship, and Sexualities in Renaissance Drama*.

The Maydes Metamorphosis (London, 1600).

McCormick, Ian, ed. (1997). *Secret Sexualities: A Sourcebook of 17th and 18th Century Writing*.

McFarlane, Cameron (1997). *The Sodomite in Fiction and Satire 1660–1750*.

McIntosh, Mary (1968). "The Homosexual Role," *Social Problems* 16 (2) 182–92; rpt. Plummer, 30–44, w/ "Postscript: 'The Homosexual Role' Revisited," 44–49.

Mengay, Donald H. (1992). "The Sodomitical Muse: *Fanny Hill* and the Rhetoric of Crossdressing," Summers, ed., 185–98.

Mermin, Dorothy (1990). "Women Becoming Poets: Katherine Philips, Aphra Behn, Anne Finch," *ELH* 57: 335–55.

Merrick, Jeffrey (1996). "The Marquis de Villette and Mademoiselle de Raucourt: Representations of Male and Female Sexual Deviance in Late Eighteenth-Century France," Merrick and Ragan, eds., *Homosexuality in Modern France*, 30–53.
_____ (1997). "Sodomitical Inclinations in Early Eighteenth-Century Paris," *Eighteenth-Century Studies* 30 (3) 289–95.
_____ (1999). "Sodomitical Scandals and Subcultures in the 1720s," *Men and Masculinities* 1 (4) 365–84.
_____ and Ragan, Bryant T., Jr., eds. (2001). *Homosexuality in Early Modern France: A Documentary Collection.*
_____ and Sibalis, Michael, eds. (2001). *Homosexuality in French History and Culture.*
Merritt, Henry (1981). "A Biographical Note on John Cleland," *Notes and Queries* 28:226:4 (08.1981) 305–306.
Miller, D.A. (1989). "Sontag's Urbanity," *October* 49: 91–101; rpt. Abelove, Barale, and Halperin, 212–20.
_____ (1991). "Anal *Rope*," Fuss, ed., *inside/out: Lesbian Theories, Gay Theories,* 118–41.
Miller, Jo E. (1997). "'And All This Passion for a Boy?': Cross-Dressing and the Sexual Economy of Beaumont & Fletcher's *Philaster*," *English Literary Renaissance* 27 (1) 129–50.
Miller, Nancy K. (1981). "'I's' in Drag: The Sex of Recollection," *The Eighteenth Century* 22 (1) 47–57.
Montaigne, Michel de (1613). *Essayes Written in French by Michael Lord of Montaigne,... Done into English, according to the last French edition, by John Florio.*
Moore, Lisa L. (1997). *Dangerous Intimacies: Toward a Sapphic History of the British Novel.*
Moulton, Ian Frederick (2000). *Before Pornography: Erotic Writing in Early Modern England.*
Mudge, Bradford K. (2000). *The Whore's Story: Women, Pornography, and the British Novel, 1684–1830.*
Mueller, Janel (1993). "Troping Utopia: Donne's Brief for Lesbianism," Turner, ed., *Sexuality and Gender in Early Modern Europe: Institutions, Texts, Images*, 182–207.
Murat, Henriette de Castelnau, Comtesse de (1697). *Les Memoires De Madame La Comtesse De M***. Avant Sa Retraite. ou La Defence Des Dames...* (Lyon).
Murray, Jacqueline and Eisenbichler, Konrad, eds. (1996). *Desire and Discipline: Sex and Sexuality in the Premodern West.*
Norton, Rictor (1992). *Mother Clap's Molly House: The Gay Subculture in England 1700–1830* (GMP).
_____ (1997). *The Myth of the Modern Homosexual: Queer History and the Search for Cultural Unity* (Cassell).

_____, ed. (2000–2004). *Homosexuality in Eighteenth-Century England: A Sourcebook,* <http:// www.infopt.demon.co.uk/eighteen.htm>.

_____, ed. (2002). *Eighteenth-Century British Erotica,* v.5: *Sex Doctors and Sex Crimes* (Pickering and Chatto).

Nugent, Georgia (1990). "This Sex Which Is Not One: De-Constructing Ovid's Hermaphrodite," *differences* 2 (1) 160–85.

Nussbaum, Felicity A. (1984). *The Brink of All We Hate: English Satires on Women, 1660–1750.*

_____ (1995). "One Part of Womankind: Prostitution and Sexual Geography in *Memoirs of a Woman of Pleasure,*" *differences* 7 (2) 16–40; rpt. from *Torrid Zones: Maternity, Sexuality, and Empire in Eighteenth-Century English Narratives.*

_____ (1998). "Afterword: Charke's 'Variety of Wretchedness,'" Baruth, ed., 227–43.

Nussbaum, Martha (1979). "The Speech of Alcibiades: A Reading of Plato's *Symposium,*" *Philosophy and Literature* 3 (2) 131–72.

O'Donnell, Katherine and O'Rourke, Michael, eds. (2003). *Love, Sex, Intimacy, and Friendship between Men, 1550–1800.*

Orgel, Stephen (1996a). "Gendering the Crown," de Grazia, Quilligan, and Stallybrass, eds., *Subject and Object in Renaissance Culture,* 133–65.

_____ (1996b). *Impersonations: The Performance of Gender in Shakespeare's England.*

Ovid. *Metamorphoses* I–IV (1985), V–VIII (1992), IX–XII (1999), XIII–XV (2000), Hill, ed.

_____ (1970). *Ovid's Metamorphosis englished, Mythologized, and Represented in Figures by George Sandys,* Hulley and Vandersall, eds.

_____ *The XV Bookes of P. Ovidus Naso, entytuled Metamorphosis, translated oute of Latin into Englysh meeter, by Arthur Golding Gentleman* [1567], B.F., ed. (http://www.elizabethanauthors.com/ovid00.htm).

Pappas, Nick (2002). "Was Plato Antigay?" *Gay & Lesbian Review* 9 (5) 23–25.

Park, Katharine (1997). "The Rediscovery of the Clitoris: French Medicine and the Tribade, 1570–1620," Mazzio and Hillman, eds., *The Body in Parts: Fantasies of Corporeality in Early Modern Europe,* 171–93.

_____ and Nye, Robert A. (1991). "Destiny Is Anatomy" [review of Laqueur], *New Republic* 204 (02.18.1991).

Parker, Holt N. (1997). "The Teratogenic Grid," Hallett and Skinner, eds., 47–65.

Parker, Patricia (1993a). "Gender Ideology, Gender Change: The Case of Marie Germain," *Critical Inquiry* 19: 337–64.

_____ (1993b). "Preposterous Reversals: *Love's Labor's Lost,*" *Modern Language Quarterly* 54 (4) 435–82.

Parker, Todd C. (2000). *Sexing the Text: The Rhetoric of Sexual Difference in British Literature, 1700–1750.*

Parry, P.H. (1990). "The Boyhood of Shakespeare's Heroines," *Shakespeare Survey* 42: 99–109.

Patterson, Steven J. (1997). "Pleasure's Likeness: The Politics of Homosexual Friendship in Early Modern England," Ph.D. diss. (Temple U).

Peakman, Julie (2003). *Mighty Lewd Books: The Development of Pornography in Eighteenth-Century England*.

Pebworth, Ted-Larry and Summers, Claude J. (1984). "'Thus Friends Absent Speake': The Exchange of Verse Letters between John Donne and Henry Wotton," *Modern Philology* 81: 361–77.

Philips, Katherine (1669). *Poems. By the most deservedly Admired Mrs Katherine Philips, The Matchless Orinda...* (London); rpt. of 1667 edition.

_____ (1990). *The Collected Works of Katherine Philips, The Matchless Orinda*, Thomas, ed. (Stump Cross).

Pintabone, Diane T. (2002). "Ovid's Iphis and Ianthe: When Girls Won't Be Girls," Rabinowitz and Auanger, eds., 256–85.

Plain Reasons for the Growth of Sodomy, in England... (1985). Trumbach, ed., *Hell upon Earth* and *Satan's Harvest Home*.

Plato (n.d). *The Republic*, tr. Jowett <www.gutenberg.org> EText-No.1497.

_____ (1993). *The Symposium and The Phaedrus: Plato's Erotic Dialogues*, tr. Cobb.

Poirier, Guy (1993). "French Renaissance Travel Accounts: Images of Sin, Visions of the New World," Mendès-Leite and de Busscher, eds., *Gay Studies from the French Cultures: Voices from France, Belgium, Brazil, Canada and the Netherlands*, 215–29.

_____ (1996a). *L'homosexualité dans l'imaginaire de la Renaissance* (Honoré Champion).

_____ (1996b). "Masculinities and Homosexualities in French Renaissance Accounts of Travel to the Middle East and North Africa," Murray and Eisenbichler, eds., 155–67.

Price, Bronwen (2001). "A Rhetoric of Innocence: The Poetry of Katherine Philips, 'The Matchless Orinda,'" Smith and Appelt, eds., *Write or Be Written: Early Modern Women Poets and Cultural Constraints*, 223–45.

Rabinowitz, Nancy Sorkin and Auanger, Lisa, eds. (2002). *Among Women: From the Homosocial to the Homoerotic in the Ancient World*.

Radel, Nicholas F. (1995). "Fletcherian Tragicomedy, Cross-dressing, and the Construction of Homoerotic Desire in Early Modern England," *Renaissance Drama* New Series 26: 53–82.

Rambuss, Richard (1998). *Closet Devotions*.

Raval, Shilpa (2002). "Cross-Dressing and 'Gender Trouble' in the Ovidian Corpus," *Helios* 29 (2) 149–72.

Rey, Michel (1987). "Parisian Homosexuals Create a Lifestyle, 1700–1750: The Police Archives," Maccubbin, ed., 179–91.

Richlin, Amy (1983). *The Garden of Priapus: Sexuality and Aggression in Roman Humor* (Yale); rev. edition (Oxford, 1992).

_____ (1991). "Zeus and Metis: Foucault, Feminism, Classics," *Helios* 18: 160–80.

_____ (1992). "Reading Ovid's Rapes," Richlin, ed., *Pornography and Representation in Greece and Rome,* 158–79.

_____ (1993a). "The Ethnographer's Dilemma and the Dream of a Lost Golden Age," Rabinowitz and Richlin, eds., *Feminist Theory and the Classics,* 272–303.

_____ (1993b). "Not Before Homosexuality: The Materiality of the *Cinaedus* and the Roman Law against Love between Men," *Journal of the History of Sexuality* 3: 523–73.

_____ (1997). "Towards a History of Body History," Golden and Toohey, eds., 16–35.

_____ (1998). "Foucault's *History of Sexuality*: A Useful Theory for Women?" Larmour et al., eds., 138–70.

Rivers, Christopher (1995). "Safe Sex: The Prophylactic Walls of the Cloister in the French Libertine Convent Novel of the Eighteenth Century," *Journal of the History of Sexuality* 5 (3) 381–402.

Robinson, David M. (1986). "Male Friendship in the Eighteenth-Century British Novel," Undergraduate Senior Thesis (Princeton).

_____ (1989). "Unravelling the 'cord which ties good men to good men': Male Friendship in Richardson's Novels," Doody and Sabor, eds., *Samuel Richardson: Tercentenary Essays,* 167–87.

_____ (1993). "Mollies Are Not The Only Fruit: being comprised of an Exploration of Male Homosexuality in some Eighteenth-Century British and French Fiction with a Testy and Querulous Analysis of Recent Gay Historiography," MA Thesis (UC Berkeley).

_____ (1998). "To Boldly Go Where No Man Has Gone Before: The Representation of Lesbianism in Mid-Seventeenth- and Early Eighteenth-Century British and French Literature," Ph.D. Diss. (UC Berkeley).

_____ (2001a). "The Abominable Madame de Murat," Merrick and Sibalis, eds., 53–67.

_____ (2001b). "'For How Can They Be Guilty?': Lesbian and Bisexual Women in Manley's *New Atalantis,*" *Nineteenth-Century Contexts* special issue ("Women's Friendships and Lesbian Sexuality") 23 (2) 187–220.

_____ (2001c). "The Metamorphosis of Sex(uality): Ovid's 'Iphis and Ianthe' in the Seventeenth and Eighteenth Centuries," Mounsey, ed., *Presenting Gender: Changing Sex in Early-Modern Culture,* 171–201.

_____ (2004). "Pleasant Conversation in the Seraglio: Lesbianism, Platonic Love, and Cavendish's *Blazing World,*" *The Eighteenth Century: Theory and Interpretation* (Summer–Fall 2003 [actually 2004]) 133–66.

Robinson, M. (1999). "Salmacis and Hermaphroditus: When Two Become One (Ovid, *Met.* 4.285–388)," *Classical Quarterly* 49 (1) 212–23.

Rocco, Antonio (1998). *L'Alcibiade fanciullo a scola*, Coci, ed. (Salerno Editrice) Omikron series 27.

―――― (1995). *Alcibiade enfant à l'école*, Godbout, ed. (Éditions Balzac).

―――― (2000). *Alcibiades the Schoolboy*, Mader, ed. (Entimos).

Rocke, Michael (1996). *Forbidden Friendships: Homosexuality and Male Culture in Renaissance Florence.*

Rose, Mary Beth (2002). *Gender and Heroism in Early Modern English Literature.*

Rousseau, G.S. (1987). "The Pursuit of Homosexuality in the Eighteenth Century: 'Utterly Confused Category' and/or Rich Repository?" Maccubbin, ed., 132–68; rpt. Rousseau (1991) 2–43.

―――― (1991). *Perilous Enlightenment: Pre- and Post-Modern Discourses.*

―――― (2003). "'Homoplatonic, Homodepressed, Homomorbid': Some Further Genealogies of Same-Sex Attraction in Western Civilization," O'Donnell and O'Rourke, eds., 12–52.

Roussel, Roy (1986). *The Conversation of the Sexes: Seduction and Equality in Selected Seventeenth- and Eighteenth-Century Texts.*

Rowland, Jon Thomas (1998). *"Swords in Myrtle Dress'd": Toward a Rhetoric of Sodom: Gay Readings of Homosexual Politics and Poetics in the Eighteenth Century.*

Rubin, Gayle (1975). "The Traffic in Women: Notes on the 'Political Economy' of Sex," Reiter, ed., *Toward an Anthropology of Women,* 157–210.

―――― (1984). "Thinking Sex: Notes for a Radical Theory of the Politics of Sexuality," Vance, ed., *Pleasure and Danger: Exploring Female Sexuality*; rpt. Abelove et al., eds., 3–44.

Sabor, Peter (1985). "Introduction," "Note on the Text," "Explanatory Notes," Cleland, ed. Sabor, vii–xxvii, 189–204.

―――― (2000). "From Sexual Liberation to Gender Trouble: Reading *Memoirs of a Woman of Pleasure* from the 1960s to the 1990s," *Eighteenth-Century Studies* 33 (4) 561–78.

Salih, Sarah (2002). "Sexual Identities: A Medieval Perspective," Betteridge, ed., 112–30.

Santesso, Aaron (2000). "The New Atalantis and Varronian Satire," *Philological Quarterly* 79 (2) 177–204.

Saslow, James M. (1986). *Ganymede in the Renaissance: Homosexuality in Art and Society.*

―――― (1988). "'A Veil of Ice between My Heart and the Fire': Michelangelo's Sexual Identity and Early Modern Constructs of Homosexuality," *Genders* 2: 77–90.

―――― (1989). "Homosexuality in the Renaissance: Behavior, Identity, and Artistic Expression," Duberman et al., eds., 90–105.

Sautman, Francesca Canadé and Sheingorn, Pamela, eds. (2001). *Same Sex Love and Desire Among Women in the Middle Ages.*

Schachter, Marc (1997). "Orpheus Dismembered: Metamorphoses, De planctu naturae, Le Roman de la rose," MLA Special Session #578, "Orpheus and the Poetics of Loss" (Toronto).

_____ (2001). "'That Friendship Which Possesses the Soul': Montaigne Loves La Boétie," Merrick and Sibalis, eds., 5–21.

Schibanoff, Susan (2001). "Sodomy's Mark: Alan of Lille, Jean de Meun, and the Medieval Theory of Authorship," Burger and Kruger, eds., 28–56.

Schleiner, Winfried (1988). "Male Cross-Dressing and Transvestism in Renaissance Romances," *Sixteenth Century Journal* 19 (4) 605–19.

_____ (1992). "Le feu caché: Homosocial Bonds Between Women in a Renaissance Romance," *Renaissance Quarterly* 45 (2) 293–311.

_____ (1993). "Burton's Use of *praeteritio* in Discussing Same-Sex Relationships," Summers and Pebworth, eds., 159–78.

_____ (1994). "'That Matter Which Ought Not To Be Heard Of': Homophobic Slurs in Renaissance Cultural Politics," *Journal of Homosexuality* 26 (4) 41–75.

Scott, Tom (1982). "The Note of Protest in Smollett's Novels," Bold, ed., *Smollett: Author of the First Distinction*, 106–25.

Sedinger, Tracey (1997). "'If Sight and Shape be True': The Epistemology of Crossdressing on the London Stage," *Shakespeare Quarterly* 48 (1) 63–79.

Sedgwick, Eve Kosofsky (1985). *Between Men: English Literature and Male Homosocial Desire*; rpt. with new preface (1992).

_____ (1988). "Privilege of Unknowing: Diderot's *The Nun*," *Genders* 1: 102–24; rpt. Sedgwick (1993) 23–51.

_____ (1990). *Epistemology of the Closet.*

_____ (1991). "Jane Austen and the Masturbating Girl," *Critical Inquiry* 17 (4) 818–37; rpt. Sedgwick (1993) 109–29.

_____ (1993). *Tendencies.*

_____ (1997). "Paranoid Reading and Reparative Reading; or, You're So Paranoid, You Probably Think This Introduction Is about You," Sedgwick, ed., *Novel Gazing: Queer Readings in Fiction*, 1–37.

Segal, Charles P. (1989). *Orpheus: The Myth of the Poet.*

Select Trials for Murders, Robberies, Rapes, Sodomy, Coining, Frauds, and Other Offences... From the year 1720, to this Time (London, 1742).

Senelick, Laurence (1990). "Mollies or Men of Mode?: Sodomy and the Eighteenth-Century London Stage," *Journal of the History of Sexuality* 1 (1) 33–67.

Shannon, Laurie (2000). "Nature's Bias: Renaissance Homonormativity and Elizabethan Comic Likeness," *Modern Philology* 98 (2) 183–210.

_____ (2002). *Sovereign Amity: Figures of Friendship in Shakespearean Contexts.*

Shapiro, Michael (1994). *Gender in Play on the Shakespearean Stage: Boy Heroines and Female Pages.*

Shapiro, Stephen (2002). "Of Mollies: Class and Same-Sex Sexualities in the Eighteenth Century," Chedgzoy, Francis, and Pratt, eds., *In a Queer Place: Sexuality and Belonging in British and European Contexts,* 155–76.

Sharrock, Alison (1991). "The Love of Creation," *Ramus* 20 (2) 149–53, 169–82.

―――― (2002). "Gender and Sexuality," Hardie, ed., 95–107.

Sibley, Gertrude Marion (1933). *The Lost Plays and Masques 1500–1642.*

Silberman, Lauren (1988). "Mythographic Transformations of Ovid's Hermaphrodite," *The Sixteenth Century Journal* 19 (4) 643–52.

Simmons, Philip E. (1990). "John Cleland's *Memoirs of a Woman of Pleasure*: Literary Voyeurism and the Techniques of Novelistic Transgression," *Eighteenth-Century Fiction* 3 (1) 43–63.

Simons, Patricia (1994). "Lesbian (In)Visibility in Italian Renaissance Culture: Diana and Other Cases of *donna con donna*," Davis, ed., *Gay and Lesbian Studies in Art History,* 81–122.

Sinfield, Alan (1992). *Faultlines: Cultural Materialism and the Politics of Dissident Reading.*

―――― (1994). *Cultural Politics—Queer Reading.*

Sissa, Giulia (1999). "Sexual Bodybuilding: Aeschines against Timarchus," James Porter, ed., *Constructions of the Classical Body,* 147–68.

Skinner, Marilyn B. (1996). "Zeus and Leda: The Sexuality Wars in Contemporary Classical Scholarship," *Thamyris* 3 (1) 103–23.

―――― (1997). "*Ego Mulier:* The Construction of Male Sexuality in Catullus," Hallett and Skinner, eds., 129–50.

Smith, Bruce R. (1991). *Homosexual Desire in Shakespeare's England: A Cultural Poetics.*

―――― (1992). "Making a Difference: Male/Male Desire in Tragedy, Comedy, and Tragi-Comedy," Zimmerman, ed., 127–49.

―――― "Rape, Rap, Rupture, Rapture: R-rated Futures on the Global Market," *Textual Practice* 9 (3) 421–43.

Smith, Jad (2003). "How Fanny Comes to Know: Sensation, Sexuality, and the Epistemology of the Closet in Cleland's *Memoirs,*" *ECTI* 44 (2–3) 183–202.

Smith, Peter J. (1995). "Playing with Boys: Homoeroticism and All-Male Companies in Shakespearean Drama," *Social Shakespeare: Aspects of Renaissance Dramaturgy and Contemporary Society,* 182–215.

Smith-Rosenberg, Carroll (1975/1976). "The Female World of Love and Ritual: Relations between Women in Nineteenth-Century America," *Signs* 1: 1–29.

Smollett, Tobias (1964). *The Adventures of Peregrine Pickle,* Clifford, ed.

―――― (1979). *The Adventures of Roderick Random,* Boucé, ed.

Snyder, Jane McIntosh (1997). *Lesbian Desire in the Lyrics of Sappho.*

Solomon, Alisa (1997). "Much Virtue in If: Shakespeare's Cross-Dressed Boy-Actresses and the Non-Illusory Stage," *Re-Dressing the Canon: Essays on Theater and Gender*, 21–45.

_____ (2002). "Great Sparkles of Lust: Homophobia and the Antitheatrical Tradition," Solomon and Minwalla, eds., 9–20.

_____ and Minwalla, Framji, eds. (2002). *The Queerest Art: Essays on Lesbian and Gay Theater*.

Spencer, Jane (1986). *The Rise of the Woman Novelist: from Aphra Behn to Jane Austen*.

Spencer, Richard A. (1997). *Contrast as Narrative Technique in Ovid's Metamorphoses, Studies in Classics*, v.6 (Edwin Mellen).

Stallybrass, Peter (1992). "Transvestism and the 'Body Beneath': Speculating on the Boy Actor," Zimmerman, ed., 64–83.

Stanivukovic, Goran V. (2003). "'Knights in Armes': The Homoerotics of the English Renaissance Prose Romances," Relihan and Stanivukovic, eds., *Prose Fiction and Early Modern Sexualities in England, 1570–1640*, 171–92.

_____, ed. (2001). *Ovid and the Renaissance Body*.

Stanley, Liz (1992). "Epistemological Issues in Researching Lesbian History: The Case of Romantic Friendship," Hinds et al., eds., *Working Out: New Directions for Women's Studies*, 161–72.

Stanton, Domna C. (1981). "The Fiction of Préciosité and the Fear of Women," *Yale French Studies* 62: 107–34.

Stapylton, Robert, tr. *Mores Hominum. The Manners of Men, Described in sixteen Satyrs, by Juvenal...* (London, 1660; rev. of 1644).

Stevenson, Burton, ed. (1948). *The Macmillan Book of Proverbs, Maxims, and Famous Phrases*.

Stewart, Alan (1997). *Close Readers: Humanism and Sodomy in Early Modern England*.

_____ (2002). "Queer Renaissance Bodies? Sex, Violence, and the Constraints of Periodisation," Chedgzoy, Francis, and Pratt, eds., *In a Queer Place: Sexuality and Belonging in British and European Contexts*, 137–54.

Stiebel, Arlene (1993). "Subversive Sexuality: Masking the Erotic in Poems by Katherine Philips and Aphra Behn," Summers and Pebworth, eds., 223–36.

Stone, Lawrence (1977). *The Family, Sex and Marriage in England, 1500–1800*.

Straub, Kristina (1987). "Indecent Liberties with a Poet: Audience and the Metaphor of Rape in Killigrew's 'Upon the Saying That My Verses' and Pope's *Arbuthnot*," *Tulsa Studies in Women's Literature* 6 (1) 27–45.

_____ (1992). *Sexual Suspects: Eighteenth-Century Players and Sexual Ideology*.

Summers, Claude J. (1992). "Homosexuality and Renaissance Literature, or the Anxieties of Anachronism," *South Central Review* 9: 2–23.

_____, ed. (1992). *Homosexuality in Renaissance and Enlightenment England: Literary Representations in Historical Context*.

_____ and Pebworth, Ted-Larry, eds. (1993). *Renaissance Discourses of Desire.*

Tarán, Sonya Lida (1985). *"ΕΙΣΙ ΤΡΙΧΕΣ*: An Erotic Motif in the *Greek Anthology,*" *Journal of Hellenic Studies* CV, 90–107; rpt. Dynes and Donaldson, eds., *Homosexuality in the Ancient World,* v. 1 (1992) 434–51.

Taylor, Rabun (1997). "Two Pathic Subcultures in Ancient Rome," *Journal of the History of Sexuality* 7: 319–71.

Teague, Frances (1995). "Early Modern Women and 'the muses ffemall,'" Evans and Little, eds., *"The Muses Females Are": Martha Moulsworth and Other Women Writers of the English Renaissance* (Locust Hill) 173–79.

Todd, Janet (1980). *Women's Friendship in Literature.*

_____ (1989). *The Sign of Angellica: Women, Writing and Fiction 1660–1800.*

Toulalan, Sarah (2003). "Extraordinary Satisfactions: Lesbian Visibility in Seventeenth-Century Pornography in England," *Gender & History* 15 (1) 50–68.

Traub, Valerie (1992a). *Desire and Anxiety: Circulations of Sexuality in Shakespearean Drama.*

_____ (1992b). "The (In)Significance of 'Lesbian' Desire in Early Modern England," Zimmerman, ed., 150–69.

_____ (1996). "The Perversion of 'Lesbian' Desire," *History Workshop Journal* 41: 23–49.

_____ (2002). *The Renaissance of Lesbianism in Early Modern England.*

Trumbach, Randolph (1987a). "Modern Prostitution and Gender in *Fanny Hill*: Libertine and Domesticated Fantasy," Rousseau and Porter, eds., *Sexual Underworlds of the Enlightenment,* 69–85.

_____ (1987b). "Sodomitical Subcultures, Sodomitical Roles, and the Gender Revolution of the Eighteenth Century: The Recent Historiography," Maccubbin, ed., 109–21.

_____ (1989). "The Birth of the Queen: Sodomy and the Emergence of Gender Equality in Modern Culture, 1660–1750," Duberman et al., eds., 129–40.

_____ (1993). "Erotic Fantasy and Male Libertinism in Enlightenment England," Hunt, ed., 253–82.

_____ (1998). *Sex and the Gender Revolution,* v.1, *Heterosexuality and the Third Gender in Enlightenment London.*

Turner, James Grantham (2002). *Libertines and Radicals in Early Modern London: Sexuality, Politics and Literary Culture, 1630–1685.*

_____ (2003). *Schooling Sex: Libertine Literature and Erotic Education in Italy, France, and England 1534–1685.*

Tvordi, Jessica (2002). "'Queering' Elizabeth: National Boundaries, Heterosexual Desire, and Deviant Bodies in Lyly and Spenser," in "Deviant Bodies and the Reordering of Desire: Heterosexuality and Nation-Building in Early Modern England," Ph.D. diss. (U Arizona).

Vanita, Ruth (1996). *Sappho and the Virgin Mary: Same-Sex Love and the English Literary Imagination.*

Velasco, Sherry M. (2000). "Early Modern Lesbianism on Center Stage: Cubillo de Aragón's *Añasco El De Talaver,*" Delgado and Saint-Saëns, eds., *Lesbianism and Homosexuality in Early Modern Spain: Literature and Theater in Context,* 305–21.

Vélez-Quiñonez, Harry (2000). "Concealing Pleasures: Cross-dressers, Tribades, and Sodomites in Lope de Vega's *El rufián Castrucho,*" Chávez-Silverman and Hernández, eds., *Reading and Writing the Ambiente: Queer Sexualities in Latino, Latin American, and Spanish Culture,* 43–61.

Viarre, Simone (1985). "L'Androgynie dans les *Métamorphoses* d'Ovide," *Journées Ovidiennes de Parménie: Actes du Colloque sur Ovide* (Latomus) 229–43.

Villedieu, Madame de (Marie-Catherine Desjardins) (1977). *Mémoires de la vie de Henriette-Sylvie de Molière,* Cuénin, ed. (l'Université François Rabelais).

Vinge, Louise (1967). *The Narcissus Theme in Western European Literature Up to the Early 19th Century* (Skanska Centraltryckeriet).

Wagner, Peter (1988). *Eros Revived: Erotica of the Enlightenment in England and America.*

Wahl, Elizabeth (1999). *Invisible Relations: Representations of Female Intimacy in the Age of Enlightenment.*

Walters, Jonathan (1997). "Invading the Roman Body: Manliness and Impenetrability in Roman Thought," Hallett and Skinner, eds., 29–43.

Ward, Roy Bowen (1997). "Why Unnatural? The Tradition Behind Romans 1:26–27," *Harvard Theological Review* 90: 263–84.

Watt, Diane (1997). "Read My Lips: Clippyng and Kyssyng in the Early Sixteenth Century," Livia and Hall, eds., 167–77.

_____ (2003). *Amoral Gower: Language, Sex, and Politics.*

Weber, Harold (1995). "Carolinean Sexuality and the Restoration Stage: Reconstructing the Royal Phallus in *Sodom,*" Canfield and Payne, eds., *Cultural Readings of Restoration and Eighteenth-Century Theater,* 67–88.

Weed, David (1997). "Fitting Fanny: Cleland's *Memoirs* and the Politics of Male Pleasure," *Novel: A Forum on Fiction* 31 (1) 7–20.

Weigert, Laura (1995). "Autonomy as Deviance: Sixteenth-Century Images of Witches and Prostitutes," Bennett and Rosario, eds., *Solitary Pleasures: The Historical, Literary, and Artistic Discourses of Autoeroticism,* 19–47.

Wheeler, Stephen M. (1997). "Changing Names: The Miracle of Iphis in Ovid Metamorphoses 9," *Phoenix* 51 (2) 190–202.

Williams, Craig A. (1999). *Roman Homosexuality: Ideologies of Masculinity in Classical Antiquity.*

Williams, Walter L. (1986). *The Spirit and the Flesh: Sexual Diversity in American Indian Culture.*

Wimsatt, W.K., Jr. and Beardsley, Monroe C. (1946). "The Intentional Fallacy," *Sewanee Review* 54; rpt. Wimsatt, *The Verbal Icon: Studies in the Meaning of Poetry* (1954) 3–18.

Winkler, John J. (1990). "Unnatural Acts: Erotic Protocols in Artemidoros' *Dream Analysis*," *The Constraints of Desire: The Anthropology of Sex and Gender in Ancient Greece*, 17–44.

Wixson, Christopher (2001). "Cross-Dressing and John Lyly's *Gallathea*," *SEL* 41 (2) 241–56.

Young, Michael B. (2000). *King James and the History of Homosexuality*.

Zimmerman, Susan (1992). "Disruptive Desire: Artifice and Indeterminacy in Jacobean Comedy," Zimmerman, ed., 39–63.

———, ed. (1992). *Erotic Politics: Desire on the Renaissance Stage*.

Index

Adams, Stephen 135–36, 205n
Adelman, Janet 4n
Aers, David vi, 4n
Akenside, Mark 54n
al-Tîfâshî, Ahmad
    The Delight of Hearts 120n
Anderson, William S. 170, 175, 181n, 186–87, 192–95
Andreadis, Harriette viii (n), xiv, 5–6, 11n, 17, 19n, 20n, 26, 29n, 30n, 103, 119, 120n, 131, 135
Astell, Mary 146
Auanger, Lisa, *see* Nancy Sorkin Rabinowitz
Auden, W.H. 3n
Austen, Jane 133n

Bacon, Francis 83
Baker, Thomas, *Tunbridge-Walks* 60n, 61
Ballaster, Rosalind 30n, 119, 120n, 122n, 134n, 143–44
Barash, Carol 20n, 22n
Barbour, Richmond 202n
Barkan, Leonard 15n, 172n, 185n
Barksted, William, "Mirrha The Mother of Adonis; Or, Lustes Prodegies" 209
Barney, Natalie Clifford 151
Barrin, Jean, *Vénus dans le cloître* 13n, 30–31, 33n, 99n
Barthes, Roland iv, 25, 40, 80, 82
Baruth, Philip E. 58n
Bataille, Georges 42

Bate, Jonathan 180n, 181n, 193n, 200n
Beardsley, Monroe C., *see* W.K. Wimsatt
Beaumont, Francis, and John Fletcher (and Philip Massinger?)
    Love's Cure 199, 212–19, 220, 223, 225, 237–38, 241–42, 245, 249–50
Behn, Aphra 33, 146–48, 150
    "To The Fair Clarinda Who Made Love To Me, Imagin'd More Than Woman" 29–31, 102, 143, 148, 153
Bellamy, Henry, *Iphis* 197, 219–27, 237, 249–50
Bennett, Alexanda G. 252
Benserade, Isaac de
    Iphis et Iante 199, 224–37, 242–44, 249–50
    "On the Love of Uranie and Philis" ["Sur l'Amour d'Uranie et Philis"] 234–35
Bentham, Jeremy 63
Berger, Harry, Jr. 179–181, 189
Berland, Kevin 153
Beynon, John 38n, 65–67, 68n, 73n, 74n
Bickerstaff, Isaac 158
Blumenfeld-Kosinski, Renate 195n, 200n
Bly, Mary 9n, 200n, 209–11
Boccaccio, Giovanni, *Decameron* 13

Boehringer, Sandra 170, 197
Bonnet, Marie-Jo 20n, 27n, 234n, 252
Borris, Kenneth x, xv–xvi, 8, 9n, 15–16n, 17n, 20n, 35, 131, 133n, 164n, 200n
Boswell, John 4, 5n, 87n, 185n, 187n, 251–52, 258
Boucé, Paul-Gabriel 62, 65n, 68n, 74n
Brantôme, Pierre de Bourdeille, Seigneur de
   Vies des dames galantes 14–17, 92n, 100, 108, 131–32, 143, 164n, 170, 235n
Braunschneider, Theresa 18n
Bray, Alan 4, 164n, 244n, 252–54, 256–58
Bredbeck, Gregory W. 200n
Brewer, William 174–76
Brisson, Luc 15n, 174n, 183, 190n, 192n, 194
Brooten, Bernadette J. xiii (n), 4, 20n, 141n, 170, 196–97
Brown, Steve 202n, 236n
Bruce, Donald 65n
Bruhm, Steven 65n, 67–69, 74n, 176n, 200n
Bulstrode, Cecilia 19
Burger, Glenn, and Steven F. Kruger 251
Burrow, Colin 182, 200n
Burton, Gideon O. 136
Butler, Judith vi, 4, 197n
Butler, Shane 185n, 192n
Byrd, William, II
   The Secret Diary of William Byrd of Westover, 1709–1712 152–53

Cady, Joseph xiii (n), xv (n), 4n, 164n, 226–27, 229n
Callaghan, Dympna 202n
Cannon, Thomas 38–39
Cantarella, Eve 179n
Cardon, Patrick 130n
Carnes, Jeffrey S. 15n, 123
Carpenter, Edward viii (n)
Carrier, Benjamin
   PURITANISME The Mother, SINNE THE DAUGHTER 130–31n
Carvajal, F. Garza 131n, 164n
Castle, Terry x, xiii (n), xiv, 4, 115, 119n, 136n, 137n, 151
Cavalli, Pietro Francesco, *La Calisto* 17n
Cavendish, Margaret, Duchess of Newcastle 83
   The Blazing World iv (n), ix, 35, 45n, 89, 164n
   The Convent of Pleasure 33n
   The Lady Contemplation 19n
Chappuzeau, Samuel
   L'Académie des femmes 106
Chauncey, George 168n
Charke, Charlotte
   The History of Henry Dumont, Esq; and Miss Charlotte Evelyn 37, 55–58, 60, 155
   A Narrative of the Life of Mrs. Charlotte Charke, Written By Herself 57–58
Chorier, Nicolas
   Satyra sotadica 13n, 30, 88–90, 92–93, 95–96, 98, 106–108, 164n
Chorier-Nicolas (Nicolas Chorier and Jean Nicolas)
   L'Academie des dames v, 12–13, 30, 87–115, 135, 155, 163, 164n
Chudleigh, Mary, Lady, "To the Ladies" 151–53, 154
Cibber, Colley, *Love's Last Shift* 239n

Clark, Robert L.A., and Claire Sponsler 200n
Clarke, John R. 173n
Cleland, John 37–47, 49–51, 53–54, 58, 61, 77–80, 83, 163
  Memoirs of a Woman of Pleasure (Fanny Hill) iv, 37–47, 49–51, 53–55, 58, 61, 77–80, 83, 88, 94, 99n
Clifford, James 54n
"Cloe to Artimesia" 150–54, 155, 159
Cobb, William S. 122n, 124
Combe, Kirk, and Brian A. Connery 145n
Congreve, William, *The Mourning Bride* 239n
Conner, Randy xv
Connery, Brian A., *see* Kirk Combe
Conon 177n
Courouve, Claude 27–28
Creech, James iv, 4n, 9, 82–83, 224
Cressy, David 4n
Crompton, Louis 63n
Crowne, John, *Calisto: or, The Chaste Nimph* 164n
Cuénin, Micheline 27n, 28
Culham, Phyllis 173n

d'Aragona, Tullia 132
d'Argenson, René 26–28, 32–33
Dall'Orto, Giovanni xv (n), 133n
Dalton, Andrew 251
Davidson, James 172, 257–58
Davidson, N.S. 74n, 133n
Day, Robert Adams 55n, 65n, 67–69
DeJean, Joan 31–32, 106n, 164
Dekker, Thomas, *see* Thomas Middleton
Delcourt, Marie 183, 192n
Dennis, John 237n
Derrida, Jacques iv, vi, 25, 40, 81
Devereux, George 172n

DiGangi, Mario 179n, 185n, 200n, 202n, 210, 213n, 228n, 237n, 252
Dinshaw, Carolyn 4n
Dollimore, Jonathan 40–41, 202n, 217–18
Donne, John 11, 19, 223
  "To Mr. B.B." 19n
  "Sapho to Philenis" 223
Donoghue, Emma xiii (n), 4n, 33n, 40n, 58n, 119, 121n, 141n, 170, 255
Doody, Margaret Anne 169, 251
Dooley, Mark 200
Dover, K.J. 172n
Dryden, John
  All for Love 245
  translation of Juvenal's *Satires* 139–41
DuBois, Andrew, *see* Frank Lentricchia
Dubois, Jean, et al. 17n, 90n, 93, 102, 231n
duBois, Page 172n
Duncan, Anne 199n, 218–19

Easton, Celia A. 20n
Edelman, Lee 40–42, 49n, 54n, 66n, 79
Egerton, Sarah Fyge, "The Emulation" 151–53
Eisenbichler, Konrad 15n
Elfenbein, Andrew ix (n)
Elizabeth I 202n
Ellis, Edith viii (n)
Ellis, Havelock viii (n)
Ellis, James Richard 200n
Elsner, John 176n
Epstein, Julia 39, 51n
Epstein, William H. 39n, 42
Eribon, Didier viii (n), 4n
EROTOPOLIS. The Present State of Betty-Land 33n

L'Escole Des Filles 30, 90, 106–107
Estienne, Henri, *Apologie pour Hérodote* 20n

Faderman, Lillian 30n, 252, 255, 258
Fahrner, Robert 60n
Farmer, Sharon, and Carol Braun Pasternack 251
Fielding, Henry, *Amelia* 58n, 69n
Firenzuola, Agnolo
    On the Beauty of Women (Dialogo delle bellezze delle donne) 15–17, 131
Fletcher, John, *see* Francis Beaumont
Fletcher, Robert 10–11
Florio, John 12,
    World of Wordes 14n
Folkerth, Wes 200n
Fone, Byrne 65
Foote, Samuel 158
Forker, Charles 202n
Forteguerra, Laodomia 15–16n, 164n, 131–32
Foucault, Michel iii, vi, viii, xiv, 4, 9, 34, 41, 80, 82, 169n, 171, 179, 184–85n, 250, 251
Fowler, Patsy S. 40n, 46n; and Alan Jackson 40n
Foxon, David 30n, 39n, 79, 89
Fradenburg, Louise, and Carla Freccero iii–iv (n), vi (n), xiii (n), 4n, 5–6, 8n, 166n
France devenue italienne, La 61, 129–31, 138, 153, 159
France galante, ou Histoires amoureuses de la cour, La 130
Franceschina, John 58, 61, 66n, 158n, 202n, 211n, 218, 245n
Freccero, Carla 254n, 257; *see also* Louise Fradenburg

Freud, Sigmund 194n
Freyman, et al. 220–21
Frier, Bruce W. 168n, 172n

Gaca, Kathy L. vi (n), xiv, 123–24n
Gallagher, Catherine 119n, 120n, 146–50,
Garber, Marjorie 202n
Garrick, David
    The Male-Coquette; or, Seventeen-Hundred Fifty-Seven 60n
    Miss in Her Teens; or, The Medley of Lovers 37, 58–61, 154, 157–59
Genuine Narrative of All the Street Robberies Committed since October last..., A 41n
Gerard, Kent, and Gert Hekma x, 4n, 244n
Gervaise de Latouche, Jacques Charles (or Jean Charles or Jean-Charles)
    L'histoire de Dom B***, Portier Des Chartreux 45, 47–48, 94–95, 99n
Gilbert, Arthur N. 51n
Gleason, Maud W. 172n, 184n
Goldberg, Jonathan 164n
Golden, Mark 169n
Goldhill, Simon 10, 11–12, 23, 173n
Golding, Arthur 178n, 210
Goldsmith, Netta Murray 51n, 244n
Goode, Okey 65n
Goulemot, Jean Marie 94n, 97
Grahn, Judy 68n
Grant, Damian 74n
Greenberg, David 8
Greenblatt, Stephen 202n
Greene, Ellen 173n
Greene, Jody 77n, 252
Griffin, Dustin H. 138n, 145n
Guiraud, Pierre 14n, 232

Gunn, Daniel P. 133n
Guy-Bray, Stephen 121n

Haggerty, George E. 40n, 46n, 47n, 53n, 54n, 65n, 66n, 72, 83n, 244n, 245, 252–54, 256
Hallett, Judith P. 165, 170, 180n, 196, 197; and Marilyn B. Skinner 172n
Halley, Janet E. 11n, 19n
Halperin, David M. iv (n), viii (n), xiv, xv, 4, 5n, 9n, 13–14, 16n, 40n, 123, 126n, 127n, 166–67, 169n, 171n, 172n, 184n, 251, 252–57
Hamilton, Anthony, Count *Mémoires de la Vie du Comte de Grammont* 28, 136–38, 153, 154, 155, 159
Hamilton, Antoine, *see* Count Anthony Hamilton
Hammond, A. (ed.), *A New Miscellany* 150, 153; *see also* "Cloe to Artimesia"
Hammond, Paul vi, viii–ix (n), 12n, 35n, 46n, 65, 72, 80–82, 157, 244n
Hardie, Philip 179n
Harley, Marta Powell 200n
Head, Richard, *The English Rogue* 66n
Hekma, Gert, *see* Kent Gerard
Hell Upon Earth 138n
Heller, Wendy Beth 191n
Hill, D.E. 165n
Hirschfeld, Heather 190n
Hitchcock, Alfred *Rope* 137
Hobbes, Thomas 12n
Hobby, Elaine 20–22
Holderness, Julia Simms 23n
Holiday, Barten 140, 141n
Holsinger, Bruce W. 200n

Hopkins, Charles, *Friendship Improv'd; Or, The Female Warriour* 199, 237–49
Hopkins, David 188n
Howard, Jean E. 202n, 211
Hubbard, Thomas K. 11–12, 123, 126n, 164n, 172n, 173n, 177
Hulley, Karl K., and Stanley T. Vandersall 165n
Hunt, Lynn xv (n)
Hutcheson, Gregory S. 82, 120n
Hutson, Lorna 4n

Incorvati, Rick 118n, 151n
The Intriguing Courtiers; or, The Modish Gallants 61

Jackson, Alan, *see* Patsy S. Fowler
Jacob, Margaret C. 89n, 106n
James, Henry, "The Beast in the Jungle" 82
Jankowski, Theodora A. 200n, 202n
Jardine, Lisa 202n
Johnson, W.R. 191n
Jonson, Ben, "Epigram on the Court Pucell" 19–20
Jordan, Mark D. 244n
Joshel, Sandra R. 190n
Juvenal 141, 182
   Satire 2 12, 156–58, 184n
   Satire 6 139–41

Keach, William 200n
Keats, John iv
Keiser, Elizabeth B. 164n
Kennedy, Hubert viii (n), 4n
Kernan, Alvin 149
Killigrew, Anne, "Upon the saying that my Verses were made by Another" 22n
Kilmer, Martin 173n
Kimmel, Michael S. 120n, 181n
Kinkead-Weekes, Mark 71

Klawitter, George 11n
Knapp, Oswald 255n
Koertge, Noretta 87n
Konstan, David 173n, 185n
Kopelson, Kevin 40–42, 79, 252
Krouse, Tonya 40n, 46n
Kruger, Steven F., *see* Glenn Burger
Kubek, Elizabeth 40n, 46n
Kuefler, Mathew S. 164n, 258

La Boétie, Etiènne de 13n
Lacan, Jacques 81
Laclos, Choderlos de, *Liasons dangereuses, Les* 133–34
Lagane, René, *see* Jean Dubois
Lancaster, Nathaniel, *The Pretty Gentleman* 61, 154–59
Lange, Jennifer 20n, 22n, 30n, 119n
Lanser, Susan S. xii, 20n, 40n, 150–51, 163–64
Laqueur, Thomas 4
Leach, Eleanor Winsor 180
Lee, Nathaniel, *The Rival Queens* 245
Leibacher-Ouvrard, Lisa 89n, 164n, 199n, 225n, 234, 236
Lentricchia, Frank, and Andrew DuBois v (n)
Lerond, Alain, *see* Jean Dubois
Levine, Laura 202n, 225n
Lilley, Kate 20n
Liseux, Isidore 89n
Lloyd, G.E.R. 168
Lochrie, Karma 10
Lonsdale, Roger 151n
Loscocco, Paula 5–6, 20n
Love, Harold 137n
Love-Letters Between a certain late Nobleman and the famous Mr. Wilson 120n, 181n

Lucian 122n, 126n, 128, 171 *see also* pseudo-Lucian
Lyly, John, *Gallathea* 199–202, 208–09, 211–13, 219, 237, 249–50

McCormick, Ian 77n, 138n, 158n
McFarlane, Cameron 40–42, 47n, 55n, 65–67, 69–70, 73n, 75, 79–80, 244n
McIntosh, Mary 164n
Machin, Lewes, "Apollo and Hyacinth" 209–211
Mack, Sarah 191n
Mackie, Erin 57–58
MacMullen, Ramsey 185n
Makowski, John F. 165, 179, 185n
Manley, Delarivier 35, 163
    New Atalantis, The v, 28, 33n, 88, 117–60, 256
Margaret (Marguérite) of Austria 16n, 131–32, 143
Martial, "Ad Bassam tribadem" 10–11, 104
Martin, Roberta C. 30n
Marvell, Andrew, "Upon Appleton House" 33n
Massinger, Philip, *see* Francis Beaumont
Masten, Jeffrey 6–7
Maydes Metamorphosis, The 199, 202–14, 219, 228, 237, 249, 256
Melville, Herman, *Pierre* 224
Mengay, Donald H. 39–42
Mermin, Dorothy 22n
Merrick, Jeffrey 27n, 28n, 33n, 53n, 129n; and Bryant T. Ragan, Jr. 14n, 27n, 129n, 130n; and Michael Sibalis 27n
Merritt, Henry 38, 42

Middleton, Thomas, and Thomas Dekker, *The Roaring Girl* 190n
Miller, D.A. 28, 49n, 115, 136n, 137, 254
Miller, Jo E. 202n
Miller, Nancy K. 38–39
Mitchell, Marea 215–16
Montaigne, Michel de 12–13, 195n
Montesquieu, Charles-Louis de Secondat Baron de 132
Moore, Lisa L. 40, 41n, 43, 47n, 66n
Moulton, Ian Frederick xv (n)
Mounsey, Chris 165n
Mudge, Bradford K. 106n
Mueller, Janel 19n
Murat, Madame de (Henriette de Castelnau, comtesse de Murat) 26–27, 31–35, 147, 163
   Les Memoires De Madame La Comtesse De M*** iv, 19, 26, 31–35, 88, 147

Nicander, *On Changes of Shape* (*Heteroioumena*) 194
Nicolas, Jean, 12, 88–89; *see also* Chorier-Nicolas
Norton, Rictor 41, 49n, 53n, 63n, 73n, 77n, 134–35, 158n, 244n
Nugent, Georgia 193n, 194n
Nussbaum, Felicity A. 42–44, 58n, 80, 83, 139, 141
Nussbaum, Martha 123, 124n
Nye, Robert A., see Katherine Park

O'Donnell, Katherine, and Michael O'Rourke 252–53
Orgel, Stephen 11n, 202n
O'Rourke, Michael, *see* Katherine O'Donnell
Ovid

Ars Amatoria 95–96, 177–78, 227n
Fasti 185n
Metamorphoses iii, vi, ix, xvi, 34, 92n, 163–251, 257
  "Apollo and Cyparissus" 177, 185
  "Apollo and Daphne" 20–22, 210
  "Apollo and Hyacinthus" 177, 185, 204, 208, 210
  "Atalanta and Hippomenes" 179, 180n, 192n
  "The Birth of Bacchus" 188–90, 194
  "Byblis and Caunus" 165, 174–76, 182, 192, 196, 197, 237n, 238
  "Caenis/Caenus" 165, 182–84, 192, 203–04, 211, 223
  "Callisto" 190–91n
  "Daedalus" 178n, 197
  "Diana and Actaeon" 189n, 190n
  "Iphis and Ianthe" vi, 22–25, 98, 121, 163–65, 168–97, 199–250
  "Jupiter and Ganymede" 177, 179n, 183n, 204, 208, 210
  "Myrrha" 175–76, 180–82, 187, 192, 196, 197, 238–39
  "Narcissus and Echo" 165, 176–77, 178n, 179, 182, 186–89, 192–93n, 195, 202, 210, 222, 230
  "Orpheus" 92n, 170n, 177–82, 184–86, 195, 202, 216, 222–23
  "Pentheus" 188–89
  "Pygmalion" 175, 179–82, 189
  "Salmacis and Hermaphroditus" xvi, 165,

191–93, 196, 216, 223, 238–39
"Tiresias" 176, 182, 189–90, 193, 208
"Venus and Adonis" 179–80, 182, 188

Pappas, Nick 126n
Park, Katharine 20n; and Robert A. Nye 4n

Parker, Holt 167
Parker, Patricia 4n, 49n
Parker, Todd C. 41n, 46n
Parry, P.H. 223n
Pasternack, Carol Braun, *see* Sharon Farmer
Patterson, Steven J. 9n
Peakman, Julie 47
Pebworth, Ted-Larry 11n
Petronius, *Satyricon* 12n, 89
Philips, Katherine (aka "Orinda") 19–22, 24–26, 31, 34, 83, 164n
  Poems iv, xiv, 5, 19–20, 22, 24–25, 34
Philo-Philippa 19–26, 163, 164n, 210
  "To the Excellent *Orinda*" 20–26, 34, 35
Pintabone, Diane T. 165, 170–71, 195n, 196–97, 199, 221
Piozzi, Hester Thrale 255
Plain Reasons for the Growth of Sodomy, in England 65–66, 73; *see also Satan's Harvest Home*
Plato xvi, 10, 92, 94, 119, 130
  Laws 125n
  The Republic 159
  The Symposium 12, 15–16, 100, 120, 122–29, 131–32, 152, 153, 156, 158, 186n

Pliny the Elder, *Natural History* 174n
Plumb, J.H. 39
Plutarch 156
Poirier, Guy 164n
Price, Bronwen 20n
Proceedings on the King's Commisions of the Peace..., The 51–53
pseudo-Lucian, *Erôtes* 93, 120, 126–33, 152, 153, 157, 159, 189, 210
Puttana errante, La 99

Rabinowitz, Nancy Sorkin, and Lisa Auanger 173n
Rabutin, Roger de, comte de Bussy 129n
Radel, Nicholas F. 202n, 252
Ragan, Bryant T., Jr., *see* Jeffrey Merrick
Rambuss, Richard x
Raval, Shilpa 172, 191n, 195n, 197n, 227n
Rey, Michel 14, 253, 254n
Rich, Adrienne 252
Richardson, Samuel, *Sir Charles Grandison* 69n
Richlin, Amy 4, 5n, 111n, 124, 141n, 156–57, 164n, 166n, 169n, 172n, 182, 184n, 185n, 187n, 188n, 191n, 192, 227n
Rivers, Christopher 32–33
Robinson, David Michael iv (n), 20n, 27, 30n, 35, 40n, 45n, 48n, 55n, 65n, 69n, 71n, 75n, 83, 89, 92n, 97n, 118n, 120n, 121n, 164n, 165n, 191n, 225n, 244n, 252, 257n
Robinson, M. 192n
Rocco, Antonio 12n, *L'Alcibiade fanciullo a scola* 90, 94, 132–33

Rocke, Michael 8, 73–74n
Rose, Mary Beth 219n
Ross, Andrew xvi
Rousseau, G.S. 41, 65n, 67, 68, 252, 253n
Roussel, Roy 47n
Rowland, Jon Thomas 54n
Rubin, Gayle 174n

Sabor, Peter 37–39, 45n, 46n, 47n, 49n
Salih, Sarah vi, ix (n), 9n
Sandras, Gatien de Courtilz de 129n
Sandys, George xvi, 21, 165n, 169, 176–77, 178n, 181, 210
Santesso, Aaron 119n, 122n, 138
Sappho xvi, 14–15, 104n, 108, 111, 131, 170, 172–73n, 182
Saslow, James M. 164n, 185n
Satan's Harvest Home 37, 39, 65–66, 88, 104n; *see also Plain Reasons for the Growth of Sodomy, in England*
Sautman, Francesca Canadé, and Pamela Sheingorn 251
Schachter, Marc 12n, 13n, 111–12n, 112n, 178n, 180–82, 185
Schibanoff, Susan 136n, 178n, 181n
Schleiner, Winfried 4n, 136n
Scott, Sarah 83
Scott, Tom 68
Sedgwick, Eve Kosofsky v–vii, xiv–xv, 3–4, 7, 9, 28, 34, 42, 44, 67, 81–83, 87–88, 94–95n, 168, 169n, 254
Sedinger, Tracey 202n
Segal, Charles P. 178n, 179n
Select Trials... From the year 1720, to this Time 53n, 77
Senelick, Laurence 60n, 61, 158n
Shakespeare, William 83, 122n, 178n, 223n, 225n
 Antony and Cleopatra 236n

 Coriolanus 228n
 The Merchant of Venice 204
Shannon, Laurie 201–202
Shapiro, Michael 202n
Shapiro, Stephen 58n
Sharrock, Alison 173, 175n, 179–81, 184n, 188–89, 190n
Sheingorn, Pamela, *see* Francesca Canadé Sautman
Sibalis, Michael, *see* Jeffrey Merrick
Sibley, Gertrude Marion 225n
Silberman, Lauren xvi, 200n
Simmons, Philip E. 42, 80
Simons, Patricia 21n, 33n, 191n
Sinfield, Alan xv, 3, 4n, 228
Sissa, Giulia 172n
Skinner, Marilyn B. 184, 185n; *see* Judith P. Hallett
Smith, Bruce R. 4, 122n, 164n, 185n, 200n, 202n, 213n, 228
Smith, Jad 40n, 46n, 47n, 77n, 78
Smith, Peter J. 202n
Smith-Rosenberg, Carroll 252, 255
Smollett, Tobias 37, 68, 153
 The Adventures of Ferdinand Count Fathom 75
 The Adventures of Peregrine Pickle 37, 48n, 51, 53–54, 57–58, 60, 63, 67, 75
 The Adventures of Roderick Random 37, 61–77, 251
 The Adventures of Sir Launcelot Greaves 75
 Advice 67, 72
 The History and Adventures of an Atom 67
Snyder, Jane McIntosh 172n
"Sodom and Onan, A Satire" 63n
Solomon, Alisa 202n, 223n, 225n
Sophocles, *Trachiniae* 227
Spence, Ferrand 126–29
Spencer, Jane 147n

Spencer, Richard A. 176n, 177–78n, 179n, 187n
Spenser, Edmund, *Shepherd's Calendar* 229n
Sponsler, Claire, *see* Robert L.A. Clark
Stallybrass, Peter 200n, 240n; and Allon White 40
Stanivukovic, Goran V. 130–31n, 204n
Stanley, Liz viii (n), 4n, 255
Stanton, Donna C. 138
Stapylton, Robert 140, 141n
Statius, *Achilliad* 227n
Stern, Simon 151n
Stevenson, Burton 239n
Stewart, Alan x, xv, 252
Stiebel, Arlene 30n
Stone, Lawrence 4
Straub, Kristina 22n, 58n, 158–59
Suleri, Sara iii (n)
Summers, Claude J. xiii (n), 4n, 5n; and Pebworth 11n
Swift, Jonathan 145n

Tarán, Sonya Lida 123
Tatius, Achilles, *Kleitophon and Leucippe* 11–12, 93
Taylor, Jeremy, *Discourse of Friendship* 257n
Taylor, Rabun 172n, 184n
Teague, Frances 19n, 22n
Thomson, James 83
"Those Glorious Platonicks" 134–35, 144
Todd, Janet 40n, 78n, 119, 143–44
Tomkins, Silvan 34
Toohey, Peter, *see* Mark Golden
Toulalan, Sarah 89n, 106n
Traub, Valerie xv–xvi, 5–8, 11n, 17n, 19n, 20n, 29n, 30n, 33n, 103, 131, 136n, 164n, 173–74, 191n, 200n, 202n, 223n, 252n
Trumbach, Randolph 4, 8, 41, 47n, 48, 94, 164, 244n, 252
Turner, James Grantham x, xv (n), 20n, 30n, 33n, 88–90, 92–94, 96n, 98n, 106–109, 111–12n, 114–15, 132, 133, 141n, 144n, 145n, 152, 164n, 234n
Tvordi, Jessica 200n, 202n
Tylney, Earl 63

Ulrichs, Karl Heinrich viii

Vandersall, Stanley T. *see* Karl K. Hulley
Vanita, Ruth 100n
Velasco, Sherry M. 35n
Vélez-Quiñonez, Harry 202n
Verdier, Anne 225n, 234n, 236
Viarre, Simone 184n, 193n
Vignali, Antonio, *La Cazzaria* 133n
Villedieu, Madame de (Marie-Catherine Desjardins)
    Mémoires de la vie de Henriette-Sylvie de Molière 28–30
Vinge, Louise 176n
Virgil 93
    Aeneid 185n
    "Second Eclogue" 94
Vivien, Renée 151

Wagner, Peter 38, 47
Wahl, Elizabeth 5, 11n, 19n, 20n, 25n, 27n, 29, 30n, 33n, 103, 106–107, 119, 121n, 131, 137n, 142–44, 164n, 232n, 234n, 235n
Walters, Jonathan 166, 183–84
Ward, Roy Bowen 126n
Watt, Diane 200n
Weber, Harold 120n, 181n
Weed, David 47n

Weekly Journal or Sunday Post, "Those Glorious Platonicks" 134–35, *144*
Weigert, Laura 33n
Wheeler, Stephen M. 165n
White, Allon, *see* Peter Stallybrass
Williams, Craig 166–67, 168n, 172–73n, 177, 179n, 183–85n, 187n, 227
Wilmot, John, Lord Rochester 94, 136–37
   Sodom 120n, 181n

Valentinian 245
Wimsatt, W.K., and Monroe C. Beardsley iv, 25
Winkler, John 166, 172
Wixson, Christopher 200n
Wolfe, Maxine 9n
Woodward, Thomas, "Have mercy on me and my sinfull Muse" 11, 19–20
Young, Michael B. xiii (n), 164n

Zimmerman, Susan 202n, 211n, 219